# GROWING UP FEELING GOOD

Ellen Rosenberg's

# GROWING UP FEELING GOOD

Illustrations by Ellen Gold

**BEAUFORT BOOKS, INC.**
*New York / Toronto*

Library of Congress Cataloging in Publication Data
Rosenberg, Ellen.
Growing up feeling good.

Summary: Examines the physical and psychological
changes that come with maturity and explores the
choices and responsibilities that each person faces
as he or she grows up.
1. Child development—Juvenile literature.
2. Sex instruction for youth—Juvenile literature.
3. Adolescent psychology—Juvenile literature.
[1. Behavior. 2. Conduct of life. 3. Psychology.
4. Sex instruction for youth] I. Title.
HQ767.9.R65 1983 305.2'3 83-7238
ISBN 0-8253-0163-7

Published in the United States by Beaufort Books, Inc.,
New York. Published simultaneously in Canada by
General Publishing Co. Limited

Printed in the U.S.A. First Edition

10 9 8 7 6 5 4 3 2 1

# Thanks

To George Greenfield, my agent and manager, who has been like a brother to
   me:
   Thank you for your wonderfully creative energy, your supportive, "just
   wanted to see how you're doing" phone calls in the middle of the night,
   and for never being too tired to listen to a passage or two.
   I feel like we have shared a "birth" experience since you and I have worked
   together on this concept from the very start. Through your efforts,
   GROWING UP FEELING GOOD has become a reality. I will forever be
   grateful.

To Valerie Pinhas, Ph.D:
   Thank you for your invaluable reviewing and consulation throughout, for
   sharing your expertise especially in the chapter relating to Growing Up
   Drugged Up, Drinking and Smoking, and for your friendship, which I
   treasure.

To Professor Helene Sloan, my mentor and dear friend:
   Our relationship has meant so much to me, personally and professionally. It
   was you who "planted the seed" which lead to my concentration on
   programs for and relating to children and ultimately, this book.
   Thank you for your wisdom, sensitivity, and encouragement. Knowing you
   has enriched my life and has so positively influenced my growth.

To the children and parents who participated in my RAP sessions:
   Special thanks for your trust and all that you taught me. The more we
   shared, the more I realized that such sharing (talking about feelings) is so
   tremendously needed. My Growing Up Feel Good Programs and book
   are an outgrowth of our beginning experiences together.

To all who shared their professional knowledge and experience:
   Thank you for your time, resources and information, as well as your en-
   thusiastic response to what this book represents.

To all the wonderful people who let me into their personal lives and spent hours
   talking with me about their feelings, I am deeply touched and thankful for
   all you shared. GROWING UP FEELING GOOD is that much richer
   because of you.

Special, special thanks to my parents: For all you have given, for all you are, for always caring enough to listen, and for all you continue to teach me about expressing and sharing love. Largely because of you, I have wonderful memories of "growing up feeling good"!

To my relatives and friends:
Thanks for understanding that my isolation and "no's" during those months of writing had nothing to do with my love for you. Your encouragement and support was most appreciated.

To Emma:
Without your assistance I could never have had the freedom to complete my book.
Love, hugs and gratitude.

To Tony, my computer:
I can't imagine ever having written this book without you!

To Susan Suffes, my editor:
Working with you has been such a pleasure!
Thank you for your openness, for being so accessible, for your time, sound advice, and commitment to GROWING UP FEELING GOOD.

To Tom Woll and everyone at Beaufort Books, Inc.:
Thank you for believing in GROWING UP FEELING GOOD!

# Dedication

To Roger, my husband and best friend:

    Thank you for understanding and respecting my commitment to writing this book, for surprising me with those ice cream treats which were so inspirational, and for all you did to keep our family life balanced even though I was in hibernation.

    Most of all, thank you for your love, for the trust that has always been between us, and for continuing to share your life with me in such an incredible way.

To my children, Andy and Hillary:

    Thanks for understanding, even though sometimes it was hard, that I had to write instead of spending time with you for all those months.

    Special thanks for never running the other way when you knew once again I was coming to ask you if you would "just read these few pages and tell me what you think. . . ." Your comments and suggestions were a tremendous help!

    Thanks for the happy notes, the phone calls (from upstairs to downstairs in my little writing room) asking how I was progressing, and all the terrific extra hugs. The love we have for each other is something I will treasure all my life.

To all Children:

    May you be blessed with a lifetime of love, good health, and inner peace.

    May you have the wisdom and sensitivity to be able to respect not only yourself, but those around you.

    May you have the strength and confidence to be who you are and the courage to become all that you dream to be.

# Table of Contents

# A Special Note
# to All Readers

After speaking with thousands of boys and girls at my Growing Up Feeling Good Programs, I decided that there were too many unanswered questions and too many unsure feelings about growth, development, friends, family, school, etc.

Every time I ended a program, I felt sad and frustrated that there were still so many concerns that we didn't have time to talk about. So I decided to write a book that would answer all those questions plus the ones that kids didn't think to ask.

I wrote *Growing Up Feeling Good* for YOU—with love—so you would have a special chance to learn more about yourself, your feelings, what you can expect to happen as you mature, and what you can do to be ready for the changes and choices that will be part of your life as you grow.

Growing up can be very exciting, almost magical. But it also can be scary because it's something that never happened to you before. It's hard and kind of strange to imagine what you'll look like and how you'll feel as you develop and mature.

I hope that *Growing Up Feeling Good* will bring you smiles, relief, and understanding. All those questions that you whispered about on the playground or in the locker rooms at school will finally be answered with straight facts and loads of feelings to think about. You might even want to have a notebook nearby so you can write down your own feelings.[1]

You may decide to gulp this book down all at once or take little munchy bites and read several chapters at different times. You can share *Growing Up Feeling Good* with a friend, your family, discuss it in school, or curl up in a private place and read it all to yourself.

---

[1] Keep a record of any questions you still want answered in order to discuss them with your parents, teachers, older brother or sister, or any other person you trust.

# GROWING
# UP
# FEELING
# GOOD
# ABOUT
# YOUR BODY

**B**efore I explain *what* the changes are, it's very important for you to understand *why* they happen in the first place.

You may have been told about the *pituitary* (pi-too-i-terry) *gland* that is located below your brain and is in charge of when and how your body will grow. Development will begin when the pituitary gland signals the release of hormones or chemicals which travel around your body in your bloodstream.

*Estrogen* (es-tro-jen) in girls and *testosterone* (tes-tos-ter-own) in boys are the main hormones that are responsible for causing the changes in you that take place during *puberty* (pew-ber-tee: the period of growth when you develop and mature). Both boys and girls have boys' and girls' hormones in their bodies. Boys have more boys' (male) hormones and girls have more girls' (female) hormones.

Perhaps it would be easier to imagine that inside each person is a "growth clock" with an alarm set to go off when his or her body is ready to begin to mature. Some time, it may be as early as age nine or not until age sixteen or seventeen, your body will start to change. If you start later, you may not finish developing until you are in your early twenties.

The signal from your pituitary gland is set at a special time for *you*. It has nothing to do with when your friends start to develop. And you cannot change the timing of the clock.

This means that boys and girls who are the same age will be at different stages of development throughout the "growing years." Though there will be many in-between, some of your friends will be first to mature and some will be last. There's no telling exactly where you will fit in.

Danny, who's fourteen, admits changing his sheets at summer camp even when he didn't need to "just so the other kids would think I had wet dreams like they did." Laurie, now twelve, told me, "I lied about not having my period except to my best friends, because I got mine when I was ten and that was earlier than most kids that I knew. I didn't want to be the only one."

Both Danny and Laurie said they didn't like lying, but it helped them feel more like they belonged. How do you think you would feel if you developed first? Last? In the middle? Maybe some of the feelings you think you would have will help you understand how other kids feel if that's what happened to them.

15

Physical development doesn't always match feelings or maturity. Some kids who feel very grown up and mature inside might find that they will have to wait years for their bodies to develop and catch-up to those feelings. Others might be physically developed at an early age but not yet mature inside.

If children thought aloud, you might hear someone say, "I'm thirteen, and I'm *supposed* to have started to develop by now. Why do I have to be the one to wait? I hope there's nothing wrong with me." Lots of kids wonder whether they are growing as they should. I asked myself these same questions.

If you're very concerned about waiting too long to start developing, speak with your parents and together with them you can check with your doctor. Chances are it's your old friend, the pituitary gland, that's taking its time with your "signal." Hang in there. Just keep telling yourself that your time will come too!

Hard as it may seem, it's important to try to accept your own time schedule for development. Try to be patient. Though you can't do anything about your size or how quickly you will grow, you can be concerned with your emotions and try very hard to feel good about yourself no matter what size you are.

How does your size compare to that of your friends right now? If you are more or less developed, does it add or take away from how good you feel about yourself? Maybe this is the first time you've thought about this.

Important note: I purposely wrote Chapters 1, 2, and 3 to girl readers and 4, 5, 6, and 7 to boy readers. It seemed more personal to write it that way. But I want you to know that even though I write *you*, all chapters are for both boys and girls. I feel it's not only important to understand your own development but also what happens to the other sex.

If you became aware of the many feelings and concerns that might relate to each other's growth, perhaps there will be greater understanding, respect, and less teasing.

Well, let's begin—we've got a lot to talk about!

# Growing Up
# FEMALE
# Feeling Good

# 1
# Breasts

## What Are Breasts?

When a girl's body begins to change and mature, she will notice two bumps in her chest area. These bumps will grow into soft, sensitive, round organs known as breasts. People also call them mammaries, bosoms, and boobs. Lots of kids refer to them as tits.

You may be interested to know that it is also normal for some boys to experience breast swelling during puberty. This is caused by hormones and has nothing to do with being like a girl. In time this swelling will go away. Both girls and boys may feel some tenderness in their breasts as development takes place.

Breasts are composed mainly of soft tissue (not Kleenex!) and mammary glands. These glands produce milk when a woman gives birth to a baby.

The openings of the mammary glands are in the nipples. A nipple can be found in the center of the darkened area, called *areola* (air-ee-o-la), in the middle of each breast. Nipples may stand out a lot or a little. Sometimes they may even point inward (called inverted nipples).

You may find that hairs will grow around your nipples and breasts. Many girls and women have such hairs. It is important not to pull them out as you might cause an infection.

Both boys and girls breasts can be sensitive when touched. The nipple is usually the most sensitive part of the breast and may become erect (stiffened and pointy) from time to time, such as when brushed over by a bed sheet, if the temperature is cold, or when touched directly.

Breasts help to round out a girl's shape and add nicely to her appearance. The shape and size of the breasts is mostly due to the amount of soft tissue that is present around the mammary glands. Though the amount of soft tissue may vary from woman to woman, all women have about the same supply of mammary glands. So, whether larger or smaller, no matter how different breasts appear on the outside, they all work the same on the inside. (Yes, even if you're flat!)

## What Size Will You Be?

If you just look around your classroom, in department stores, on street corners, especially at the beach, or anywhere, you will notice that breasts develop in many shapes and sizes (check this out if you haven't noticed already).

When I was younger, we used to call smaller sized breasts lemons, oranges, or even tangerines. Medium sized breasts were called grapefruits, cantaloupes, or just plain melons, and big boobs were called watermelons. We were sure that women with "watermelons" didn't need a life preserver when swimming because "the bigger they were, the better they would float!" We would say things like, "Oh, can you believe how big Debby got this summer? Hers are almost like watermelons! It's amazing she doesn't fall over when she walks!"

Even though we laughed and giggled and whispered about her breasts (which appeared "humongous" compared to our flat chests!), Debby seemed to be very proud of her development. She never toppled over and even played soccer as well as she did before she grew. We soon stopped whispering and got used to Debby's new shape. I think we were secretly jealous because most of us didn't have even a hint of a bump on our chests and were beginning to worry that we would be flat-chested forever.

Girls today continue to wonder about what size they will be. The fact is, you may be as large, larger, or smaller than your mother, sister, or grandmother. Breast size can be very different in the same family (my sister is larger than I am and she's younger!).

When your breasts start to grow, usually it will take several years for them to reach their full size. Only then will you have an exact answer. I'd have to be a wizard to be able to figure it out for you ahead of time. You may develop like other women in your family. Or you may not!

It's also important to know that like feet, breasts can be different in size even on the same body. Though some girls worry that they will be lopsided, especially when one breast begins to develop earlier than the other, this difference is quite normal (and won't make you lopsided!). In time they usually grow to be about the same size.

Some people think large breasts are terrific. Others prefer smaller breasts. Ten-year-old Amy said, "I don't want those big things hanging on my body." Jennifer, age eleven, told me she wears three sweatshirts just to make it seem like she is very developed.

There are girls who want to make themselves appear larger and those who are so glad their body has not yet begun to change. Still others are very happy just the way they are, developed or not.

How do you feel about breast size? Have you already started to develop? It really is so hard to imagine how it will feel to have breasts. It might help to realize that it is not better or worse to be larger or smaller. Everyone is different.

Karen's breasts were small when she was growing up. She remembers comparing herself with friends who were very developed and thinking that maybe the boys would be more interested in them because they were bigger. Girls still compare and wonder about this. Boys still look! But there's a difference between liking to look at breasts and liking a person because they have breasts.

I think you'll find, as Karen did, that people will like you because you're you, not because of how developed you are. If someone cares more about your size than about you as a peson, they're not much of a friend anyway.

The size of your breasts has nothing to do with the kind of person you are, or whether people will think you are more womanly. That depends upon how you feel and who you are inside.

## When Will Your Breasts Develop?

Another concern about breast development is when? How quickly will breasts appear and when can you expect them?

Just as you cannot know for sure what size you will be, you also won't know exactly when your body will start to change . . . until it does.

Maybe that's very frustrating to you. I know it was to me. I was impatient. I was tired of looking like a child, especially when many of my friends were beginning to look more and more like women. I wanted to know when and no one could tell me. Have you had any of these feelings?

The plain truth is that your breasts will grow when they're ready to. It all depends upon when your pituitary gland gives the signal to start the release of your hormones. It's up to your body not you! No amount of watering will make your breasts develop faster or sooner. Praying won't even help. Neither will exercises.

Well at least you don't have to study for breasts! They will simply start to swell, possibly when you least expect them to grow. You do not have to worry about going to sleep flat and waking up with breasts. (I can remember getting out of bed in the middle of the night just to check if my breasts had appeared!)

Since growth is a process that takes place over a period of time, your body will have time to get used to having breasts.

## Feeling Good About Breast Development Is Not Always Easy

Some girls do not seem to be able to feel good about their breast development. They may curve their shoulders forward in order to make their breasts seem smaller or less noticeable. They may also curve their shoulders to try to hide breasts that seem too tiny.

Judy, now thirty-two, remembers carrying her school books in front to try to hide her growing chest. I, of course, carried my books in front to try to hide the fact that I didn't have a growing chest!

Susan, a thirteen-year-old with large breasts, shared, "Every time the teacher is ready to call on someone to come up to the blackboard, I wish I could hide under my desk. I'm afraid to walk up to the front of the room because people tease and make fun of me when I'm up there. The teacher can't hear them, but I know they do it."

It may not always be easy to be more developed than most other girls, just as it can be hard to be much less developed. Being right in the middle seems the easiest. But, as I mentioned before, certain girls will be larger and others will be smaller. That's just the way things are, and it can't be helped!

I suppose there will always be children who like to tease. Breasts seem to be a great target for teasing. Some children tease because they are embarrassed about their own lack of development. If they call attention to others, then maybe less attention will be on them. Still others might need to tease because development is so new and a bit strange. They may be jealous or uncomfortable about the changing bodies all around them.

Accepting these changes may take time. I wonder what would happen if Susan stood tall, walked proudly to the front of the room, completed her work at the blackboard, and walked proudly back to her desk—smiling at everyone as she moved!

Do you think Susan's classmates would still feel like teasing if she seemed so confident and ignored any remarks? What else do you think she could do?

Dawn, age fourteen, shared the same kinds of feelings that Susan had. But Dawn was embarrassed about going up to the front of the classroom because she didn't yet start to develop breasts!

I wonder if anyone really grows to the exact size they hope to be, when they hope to be. Dawn and Susan might feel better about themselves if they could accept where they are in their development. It would also help if others would realize that development cannot be controlled.

**It would really help if people would try to be strong and happy about who they are and worry less about what size they are.**

### Wearing a Bra

A friend of mine told me she came home the third day of junior high school and told her mother she had to have a bra. The boys snapped the girls' bra straps while on the lunch line in the cafeteria, and she would have "died" if they tried to snap her bra and didn't find one to snap!

Jodi, an eighth-grader now, so clearly remembers coming home one day in the sixth grade and saying to her mother, "I must have a bra today! I can't wait until tomorrow."

Said Jodi, "If size was considered, I probably could have waited a few years. But Mom took me for a bra that afternoon." Jodi's Mom must have understood that the bra was more important because of Jodi's friends (many of them wore bras) than her tiny breasts. Jodi told me she got a training bra and felt terrific, like she really belonged.

Did you ever wonder why it's called a training bra? It really doesn't do any training. I can't imagine what breasts could be taught to do!

Marge, now in her forties, remembers, "I was so excited to get a bra before my close friend. But I never grew out of that first bra into a bigger size! The bra that I wear now is the same as when I was twelve." (Not the same bra—new bra, same size!) "When my friend finally did get her bra, she bulged out of it really soon, then kept bulging and bulging and needing new sizes. I was so jealous!"

It might be fun to ask your mom, grandma, aunt, or older sister about their first bras. Though it may have been many years ago, you might be surprised to find they will smile and talk about special, often funny experiences that will be wonderful to remember and even better to share with you!

Girls often ask me, "What if I don't want to wear a bra? Do I have to?" Wearing a bra is a matter of your own choice and comfort, even if you are playing a sport. Whether you are larger or smaller breasted, you may prefer to wear a bra for support if you run and jump for long periods of time. Or, you may not.

Many doctors feel you will not harm or stretch the breast tissue if you do not wear a bra during exercise or at all. You may wish to wear a bra, but you don't have to.

Lisa, age eleven, said she plans to wait until her best friend wears a bra so they can start wearing them together. Lisa is very developed and her friend has not yet begun (Lisa could be waiting for years!).

Jessica, age twelve, said she refused to wear a bra at home but made sure to take one away with her when she went to summer camp in case the other girls in her cabin wore bras. Sure enough they did and she was glad she brought one. Much to the surprise of her parents she even sent home for more bras!

Debra, age ten, said, "I think I would feel uncomfortable about wearing a bra because if I wear light colored shirts, boys might see my bra and make fun of me." Jill, age eleven, said, "It makes me feel very grown-up to wear a bra. Sometimes I wear shirts that you can see through a little just so other people can know I'm wearing one!"

Lisa did not want to be the only one wearing a bra. Jessica did not want to be the only girl without a bra. Debra thought she would feel funny and be teased if anyone noticed she was wearing one. Jill sometimes wore clothes that would make sure other people knew she was wearing a bra. As you can see, there are so many different ways girls may feel about wearing a bra. How about you? What are your feelings?

As far as I know, "Bra Laws" just do not exist! I have never seen a sign anywhere that states, "Girls with breasts will not be allowed in without wearing a bra." The choice is up to you.

Take a good look in the mirror. If you can say to yourself "I feel really great about the way I look," then you'll be able to feel more confident and proud about your appearance, bra or no bra (no matter what anyone else is doing!).

## Talking About Bras

Many girls have told me they find it hard to share their feelings about such things as wearing a bra or not. They feel kind of funny or embarrassed. They're not sure what to say and are sometimes worried about what parents or friends will say back.

If you have ever had those funny feelings, at least you know you are not alone. Lots of girls have them (grown-ups too!). Since parents or friends can't know exactly how you feel unless you tell them your feelings, it would be important to get your courage up to try!

Once you begin, you'll probably be surprised and relieved to find it will be easier and easier to talk. And it usually feels a lot better if you get your feelings out rather than keep them inside of you.

The first words are often the hardest to get out. Here are some ideas about how you might begin to talk about your feelings (you can add your own ideas to this list):

*What you might say to your parents if you want a bra*
"Mom, Dad . . . I really want to wear a bra!"

"Most of my friends are wearing bras. I'd feel better if I could wear one too."

"This is kind of funny to talk about, but I want to get a bra (or go shopping for a bra)."

"I don't know if you've noticed or not, but I think I'm ready to wear a bra."

"I want to talk with you about wearing a bra."

"Mom, what age were you when you started to wear a bra?"

*What you might say to your parents if they insist*
*on getting you a bra and you don't want to wear one*
"Mom, Dad . . . I really don't want to wear a bra!"

"Please don't make me wear a bra. I don't want to wear one."

"I want to talk with you about not wearing a bra."

"Most of my friends don't wear bras and I think I'd feel better if I waited a little longer before I got one."

"It's hard for me to say this to you, but I hate bras! Please don't make me wear one!"

*What you might say to your friend if you think she needs a bra*

"Did you ever think about how great you might look if you wore a bra?"

"This is not easy for me to say, but I really think you need a bra."

"Wouldn't it be fun to go shopping for a bra?"

"——, you need a bra!"

"I really think you would look great (or even better) if you wore a bra."

Many girls feel it would be better to say such things when you're alone with that friend. If you consider the other person's feelings and try to be nice, you'll find it easier to be honest.

## How To Figure Your Bra Size

In case you are thinking about getting a bra, you might be interested in knowing how to figure out what size bra you can wear or if you are ready to wear one.

If you place a tape measure around your body just below your rib cage (right under your breasts) and add five inches to that number, you will determine your bra size. For example, if right under your breasts measures 29, you would add 5 inches to 29 inches. This equals 34 inches, so your bra size would be 34.

Cup size can be measured by placing the tape around your body at the fullest part of the bust (at the nipples). The difference between this measurement and your bra size gives you the cup size. If the numbers are equal, the cup size would be AA. If the difference is one inch, the cup size equals A, two inches would equal a B cup, and so on up to D and DD.

A first bra usually has no cup and can start at size 28. During the years when your body is growing and changing, it's a good idea to check your measurements every six months.

There are many different styles of bras from which to choose. Most stores carry bras up to size 42 or 44. Larger sizes can be bought at specialty stores.

Just like there are salespeople who are trained to fit your shoe size properly there are women who are trained to fit bras. My sister and I called these women "bra ladies." It is their job to help you find a bra that is comfortable and the right size.

You may be thinking, "Oh gross! I'm not going to let anyone measure me!" Well, it might help to realize that these women fit bras all day long for girls and women of all ages, shapes, and sizes. They are used to seeing lots of breasts. They'll probably understand that this experience is new for you and will be sensitive to your feelings.

If you do not feel comfortable, it may help if you tell your feelings to the saleswoman (or at least to the person who might be shopping with you). You might say, "This is the first time I'm being fitted for a bra. I feel funny (or embarrassed or uncomfortable)."

These feelings are very natural. And if you really object to having someone you don't know measure you, you can do what my Mom and I did when I got my first bra. We had the "bra lady" explain to us what we needed to do and then did all the figuring ourselves. The saleswoman was able to check if we were right once I tried on the bra. After a while I didn't mind letting her help me. I just had to get used to the idea; so will you.

It's nice to know there are several ways to feel even better about shopping for a bra.

## Bra Giggles

My friends and I used to call bras "over-the-shoulder-boulder-holders" and laughed at bras and underwear in store windows and magazines.

We laughed even harder when we tried on our mothers' bras and stuffed them with socks and stockings. How amazing it was to imagine that we would fill our own bras some day. We were excited, scared, and impatient at the same time.

Once while playing volleyball in gym class in the eighth grade, I was positioned in the back row and noticed something fall onto the floor right in front of the net. It was round and white.

I remember thinking it was a strange looking volleyball. Did the ball lose all its air? When we realized what had happened, we dropped to the floor and doubled up with laughter.

The one girl who remained standing in the front row (who was definitely not laughing) appeared very red—no, purple in the face. She

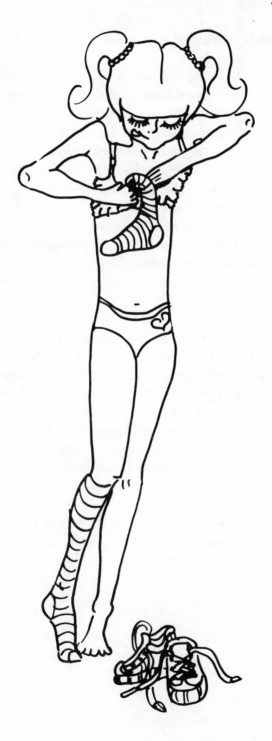

had stuffed her bra with a good-sized piece of cotton and it flew out while she was jumping for the ball.

If it were me, I think I would have run into the locker room, crawled into the nearest locker, and thrown away the combination, never again to appear on the gym floor! But she really took it very well. After a few minutes, she just started laughing with the rest of us.

Funny and embarrassing things just seem to happen while a person is growing up. In fact they never stop happening. It's wonderful to have a good sense of humor and be able to laugh at yourself!

When the laughter quieted down, we all continued the volleyball game (I still smile when I see balls of cotton).

We would have liked her—and did—even without what appeared to be breasts. All she had to be was herself.

### I Hope by Now You Realize . . .

Though there may not be anything you can do about how and when you develop, I hope by now you realize there are many things you can do to try to feel as good about yourself as possible. You can understand what is happening to your body and why. You can wear clothes that are flattering to your size, whatever it may be.

You can let yourself be the special person you are inside and accept yourself, whether you have "watermelons," "grapefruits," "lemons," or have not yet begun to grow. You may be very happily surprised that your friends will respect you as you respect yourself.

Remember: People do not make friends with breasts;
they make friends with people!

# 2
# Private Parts

Did you ever wonder what is inside the different parts of your body? Though each part is important, I think the sex organs, also called *genitals*, (jen-i-tulls) are especially interesting because they are involved with *reproduction*, being able to create babies.

There are lots of slang names for these organs, probably because kids and even some adults might feel embarrassed or don't know their real names.

No matter what you call them, it's important to at least know the correct names and learn as much as you can about how these organs work. The more you understand about your body and yourself, the more confident and comfortable you will be.

First, let's take a look at the inside (internal) parts.

If you make a paper circle that measures four inches from side to side, then put the top of the circle about one inch below your belly button, you'll have a better idea of about how much room your internal reproductive organs take up. Such a small area for such important organs!

**Uterus** (you-ter-us), also called the womb (rhymes with room), is shaped like an upside-down pear. This is the special place where an unborn baby grows when a woman is pregnant. (The unborn baby is called an *embryo* [em-bree-yo] in the first two months of development and after that called a *fetus* [fee-tus] in the later stages of development.) It's almost like magic that the uterine walls are able to stretch and stretch as the unborn baby gets larger and larger (sort of like a balloon that slowly gets filled with more air).

The uterus gives the unborn baby protection. Since the lining of the uterus has many blood vessels, it helps the baby develop by supplying nourishment (food) and oxygen. The uterus also has strong muscles that help move the baby out when it is ready to be born.

**Cervix** (sir-vicks) is the "neck" of the uterus. Since the uterus sticks its "neck" out into the back of the vagina, the cervix is between the back of the vagina and the uterus. The glands in the lining of the cervix secrete a sticky fluid, mucous (mew-kuss). When a woman is pregnant, the cervix is usually closed by a plug of mucous which prevents bacteria from entering the uterus.

**Ovaries** (o-va-reez) are about the size of a walnut and can be found on either side of the uterus. When a girl is born, her ovaries contain from tens to hundreds of thousands of follicles. Each follicle is a small sac that contains an immature or unripe egg cell (not the kind of egg you find in the supermarket!).

The ovaries are responsible for releasing female hormones or chemicals that help to make a girl's body develop and mature. They also have the important job of releasing one ripened egg cell each month usually beginning when a girl gets her period.

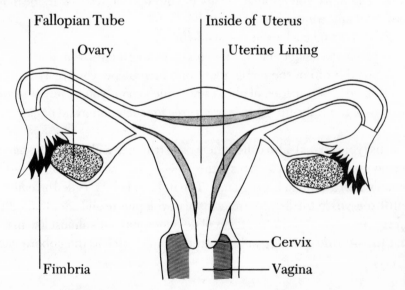

Fallopian Tube

Ovary

Inside of Uterus

Uterine Lining

Cervix

Vagina

Fimbria

JUDY GOLDEN

A single egg cell is called an *ovum;* many eggs are called *ova.* These are the egg cells that can be *fertilized* (fer-ti-lized) by a male's sperm cells in order to develop into a baby. Because the ovum is so tiny (much smaller than the head of a straight pin), the only way you can see it is under a microscope.

More about egg cells and what happens when they ripen will be included in the next chapter on menstruation.

You can get an idea of what your **Fallopian Tubes** (fa-lo-pee-an) look like if you put your arms out at your sides, shoulder height, and point your fingers to the floor. (Try it! It's really fun to imitate fallopian tubes!) Each tube is about four inches long, and each extends down from either the left or right side of the uterus toward the ovary.

Each fallopian tube is like a roadway that transports the ovum from an ovary to the uterus. If fertilization (sperm meets egg) is going to take place, it will happen in one of the tubes (lucky tubes!).

The outside ends of the tubes look like fingers and are called *fimbria* (fim-bree-a). They flare toward each ovary but do not *connect* with the ovaries. That's why when an egg ripens in an ovary, it has to burst through the surface of the ovary in order to get out and be drawn into the fallopian tube to start its journey toward the uterus.

So now you know it's the fallopian tubes that receive the egg cell that is released by the ovary. The tubes have tiny, wavy hairs called *cilia* (silly-a) that help move the egg along since it can't move by itself.

**Vagina** (va-jie-na). The *vagina,* if you spread your legs apart, is the second opening between your legs. (The *urethra* [you-ree-thra] through which liquid waste or urine passes, is the first; and the *anus,* the passageway for solid wastes, is third.) Since solid waste passed through the anus contains bacteria (back-teer-ee-a) that can cause infections if spread to your vaginal and urethral opening, it's healthier for you to wipe yourself from front to rear after having a bowel movement.

Since the vagina connects the uterus with the outside genitals, it's not surprising that it is the birth canal. It's fantastic how the vaginal walls are able to stretch and allow a baby to pass through. If a girl uses tampons, this is the place where they are inserted.

Most of the time the walls of the vagina are close together, though they are able to expand when necessary. They form a tube that measures about three to five inches long. The opening of the vagina can be seen if the *labia* (lay-be-a) or lips, are parted. Sometimes the walls of the vagina will feel moist, as if they were sweating.

There are vaginal muscles that you can tighten, relax, and even exercise. You can locate them when you go to the bathroom by trying to stop your urination in the middle. The outer part of the vagina (including the opening) is sensitive to touch. The innermost part is not.

The *hymen* (hi-men) is a flexible fold of tissue that surrounds and partly covers the opening of the vagina. It looks slightly different on each girl. Some girls are born without one (they can get along fine without it).

The appearance of the hymen changes when it becomes pushed back or stretched. Some parents are concerned that using tampons (inserted through the opening of the vagina) will cause the hymen to be pushed back, but it's flexible enough to prevent this from happening.

The usual way for the hymen to become pushed back is when a woman has *sexual intercourse* (sex-you-al in-ter-corse) with a man. (See special note.)

Special Note: Even though I'm going to talk about sexual intercourse later, here's an explanation (just so I'm sure we're both talking about the same thing). When a man and woman have sexual intercourse, they hug and get very close, then they move together in a special way that allows the man's penis (Chapter 4) to be placed inside the opening of the woman's vagina. They just fit snugly together! Remember, the walls of the vagina are able to stretch to allow this to happen in a comfortable way.

There are lots of feelings that go along with having sexual intercourse. The penis and vagina are only parts of people. Penises and vaginas don't love each other; people do! More about intercourse, feelings, and the responsibilities that go with it, later.

P.S. Since people don't usually talk openly about these kinds of things, it may surprise you to learn what sexual intercourse really is. You might find it hard to imagine being so close to someone and might even be saying to yourself, "Yich!" That's very natural. But, as you continue to read about how each sexual organ works and learn more about the feelings that can go along with such closeness, you'll have a better understanding of what intercourse means, and why a man and a woman fit together this way.

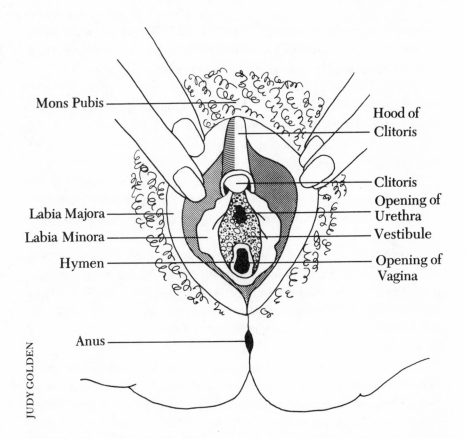

Mons Pubis

Hood of Clitoris

Clitoris

Labia Majora

Opening of Urethra

Labia Minora

Vestibule

Hymen

Opening of Vagina

Anus

JUDY GOLDEN

Now for a look at the outside (external) genitals.

The **vulva** (vull-va) refers to the entire outside genital area of a girl or woman. Lots of people mistakenly call the outside, vagina.

Many girls find it confusing to look at their vulva. There are so many overlapping folds of pink skin, that it is often hard to know which part is which. After reading about these parts it might be very interesting to see if you can identify them on yourself!

If you look in a mirror, I think you'll agree that the many soft folds look a lot like the petals of a flower. Each girl's vulva has a slightly different pattern or design, even though all the parts are the same.

The **mons pubis** (monz pew-bis) is the area of soft tissue that forms the shape of a triangle pointing down between your legs. This soft moundlike area is the place that becomes covered with *pubic* (pew-bick) hair when your body develops.

The **major lips** or **labia majora** (lay-be-a) are two folds of skin that run up and back from the mons pubis. They usually appear close together and don't have hair on the outer part until a girl reaches puberty.

The **minor lips** or **labia minora** are the two pink, hairless folds of skin found inside the major lips. Sometimes these lips are very small and sometimes they're large and flappy. Girls and women can have different sizes just like with breasts.

The space between the minor lips is called the *vestibule* (ves-ti-bewl). It is rich in nerve endings and blood vessels. Located inside this vestibule are the urethra (first opening) and the vaginal opening (second).

The **clitoris** (clit-or-iss) is located where the top folds of the minor lips come together, and it looks like a little button peeking out from under a "hood" that gives it protection. It's very important to wash regularly under this hood. Be sure to wash your entire vulva often as it is a nice cozy area for bacteria, germs that cause infections, to grow if you don't keep yourself clean.

The clitoris has so many nerve endings that make it very sensitive and sometimes tingly when touched. (More about these tingly when touched feelings later.) Some people say the clitoris looks like a tear drop. What do you think yours looks like?

There are a few different glands in the genital area which give off small amounts of fluid at certain times.

I can still hear the voice of twelve-year-old, Ruthie, when I identified the clitoris on a diagram of the female genitals at a program I conducted several years ago. With eyes wide open and a big grin on her face, she said, "So that's what that thing is!" Maybe you've been wondering too.

I hope this chapter was able to clear up any questions that you might have had about which part is which and does what. I also hope you have a greater appreciation of how magical some of these organs are.

Let's go on to Chapter 3. I think you'll find menstruation to be fascinating and much easier to understand now that you know so much more about how the organs of reproduction work.

# 3
# Getting Your Period

**Menstruation** (men-stroo-ay-shun), or the time of a girl's period, is a special event in her life. It means that she is officially on her way toward becoming a woman. The start of a girl's first period is called *menarche* (men-ar-kee).

If you've already got your period, congratulations! You can review this information so you're sure you understand exactly what's happening inside. You can also check out any concerns you still might have about getting it.

If you haven't got yours yet, you may be waiting another month, a few years, or just a few more days (tomorrow at 2 o'clock?). Once again there's no way to predict *exactly* when it will arrive, except to tell you some time between ages nine and sixteen or seventeen, when your body is ready.

Whether you want it or not, your period will be a regular part of your life. I hope this chapter will help you feel as good as possible about getting it. Most important is that you get your facts straight, understand how you feel, and have a real good idea about what you need to do when you get it.

## What's a Period and Why Do You Get It?

Your body will begin to get ready to menstruate when your ovaries get a chemical signal from your pituitary gland. This signal will tell the ovaries, "Hey, give this kid a break. She's been waiting for her period long

37

enough! It's time to pick one of those thousands of unripened eggs so it can begin to mature. Don't forget to release that special female hormone called estrogen so that development of her body and genital organs can take place. And make sure the uterus knows its lining must get thicker, kind of spongy and real cozy, in case the egg is fertilized!"

Since there's a right and a left ovary, it's only fair that they usually take turns getting an egg ready.

Let's turn the scene to the ovaries.

Though many eggs start to ripen, one lucky egg gets to fully develop with the help of those hormones from the pituitary gland. It takes about two weeks for the unripe egg to mature. Then it's ready to leave the ovary. You know from Chapter 2 that the egg has to break through the surface of the ovary since there is no tube or passageway leading out of it.

Let's say it's "break-out" time. The ripened egg is ready to go, and it's out! When the egg is released, we say that *ovulation* (ov-you-lay-shun) has taken place. Or a girl has ovulated.

With the help of the fingerlike ends of the fallopian tube (fimbria) and the wavy hairs called cilia, the egg can now be drawn into the tube where it might be fertilized (entered by a sperm from a male so that it will grow into a baby).

If a woman's egg is fertilized, she has become pregnant. In fact the reason why a girl is born with eggs in the first place is so she can choose if she would like to have a baby when she becomes an adult.

The egg will only live about forty-eight hours, so it has to be fertilized during that time. If not it will simply disintegrate or break down.

Meanwhile in the uterus.

After ovulation another special female hormone called *progesterone* (pro-jes-ter-own) joins with estrogen to help the uterus build up its lining. It will continue to become thicker and richer with blood and nutrients.

The lining will be thickest about one week after ovulation. If an egg is fertilized, a chemical signal will let the uterus know that the lining is needed to supply food and oxygen and should stay.

If no signal is sent, the uterus will know that no egg was fertilized and the lining will not be used. Blood vessels and tissues from the lining along with the discarded egg mix together and then pass from the uterus, through the cervix, into the vagina to the outside. It takes several days for the lining or "special blood" to completely pass out of a girl's (or woman's) body.

The passing out of this lining or "special blood" is called menstruation or getting your period. The same thing happens all over again about every four weeks.

Whew! Are you still with me? I hope so. How about a quick review.

Each month, an ovary will develop and release an egg. The lining of the uterus becomes thick and snugly in case the egg is fertilized. If it is, the lining stays to nourish and supply oxygen to the growing fetus. If the egg is not fertilized, the lining is not needed and passes out of the body slowly through the opening of the vagina. After the lining flows out, another egg is developed and the whole cycle starts all over again.

It's very important for you to know that it's possible for a girl to get her first period before beginning to ovulate or release an egg. That may come a bit later. It's also possible for a girl to start ovulation before she begins her first period.

## Sometimes Periods "Skip"—Keeping a Calendar

In the first years when you get your period, you might find it will skip a month or more until your body gets used to menstruating. Things like a change of climate, very heavy physical activity (like training for a marathon, running many hours a day), losing a lot of weight, emotional changes like those brought on by a divorce or moving to a new town, might have an affect on your hormones and may alter the schedule of your period.

Stephanie, age fourteen, shared, "When I was thirteen, I spent the summer at a camp which was in another state from where I lived. Even though I seemed to be on a regular schedule, I remember not getting my period for the whole summer. I was really nervous that something was wrong with me and wrote my mother about it. She told me it was normal and not to worry (I worried anyway). Sure enough, about a month after I got home again, my period came back."

It's a great idea to keep a record of when you get your period. You can put a big dot or circle on your calendar around the day your period starts. You can also make marks for when it finishes. That way you'll have a pretty good idea of when you can expect it to come again and can be prepared.(For example, if you think your period might be starting soon, you can wear jeans or other dark colored clothing instead of light colors. You can also be sure to have some form of sanitary protection with you.)

Keeping a record also lets you check how often your period comes. Remember not to be surprised if it's not on a regular schedule, at least in the beginning months.

If you count getting your period as day 1 of the month, you'll probably find it will start again a few days before or after day 30. Each person's schedule will be slightly different. Even your own schedule will change from time to time. For example you might get your period on day 29 one month and not until day 32 another month. Once they start, periods can last 3 to 7 days or maybe more.

*Days* means days and nights. Periods don't stop at night and start again in the morning. Once they begin, they'll keep going until they end.

## Is It Scary to Get Your Period?

Jill, age eleven, said, "I have a cousin who didn't know what was happening when she got her period. She was scared stiff that something was wrong with her when it started."

My mother told me she first heard about periods from her older sister who said, "All of a sudden you just bleed." My mother answered, "What do you *mean* you bleed? I never heard of anything so stupid!"

I suppose it really can be scary to get your period if you don't know anything about it. But it also can be scary if you don't know enough about it. Periods aren't scary! In fact it's very exciting to get your period. It means you're developing and on your way to being a woman. Kids only think periods are scary because nothing like that ever happened to them before and they can't imagine what it is like. Also the word "blood" makes some people squirm and think that they're going to be hurt.

Now you know that when you get your period and it seems like you are "bleeding," it's only the cozy old lining of the uterus that wasn't needed. Because it includes blood, mucous, and tissue, it will appear reddish, like you know blood to be. The color can be slightly different each time you get your period. It might be bright red, darker red, or even brownish.

Though most of the time the fluid or flow will be smooth, it will sometimes appear "clumpy" because of thickened, tiny blobs or clots of blood, tissue, and mucous.

Since you know what to expect, I hope you will not be scared when you notice reddish stains on your clothing. It will simply mean that your period has begun. And that's great!

Another reason why some kids are scared is because they think all of a sudden blood is going to gush down their legs for all to see. Not so! Periods don't gush, they trickle!

The lining drips out bit by bit over several days. (Remember, that means nights too!) It's not like turning on a faucet! It's more like when you don't completely shut off a faucet and it drips out steadily but only a tiny bit at a time.

You can take a measuring spoon and put four to six tablespoons of water in a cup, that's about how much fluid will slowly flow out during your period. Not so much, eh? It seems like much more than it really is.

Ten year old, Jennifer, said, "I don't want it. Do I have to get it? Please." Well, Jen, periods are just a part of life for us women folk. Want it or not, your period will come. Wouldn't it be terrific if you could look forward to getting it and know that whenever it begins, you'll be ready!

## How Will You Know When You Have It?

Periods don't seem to care about tests, bus trips, baby-sitting jobs, summer vacations, soccer games, swimming, white pants, or anything. They just begin when your body is ready, no matter where you are or what you are doing or what you're wearing. Time of day doesn't matter. You don't even have to be awake.

Periods often start about a year or two after your breasts begin to develop or a year or so after those cute, curly pubic hairs start to appear. But even if you have breasts and lots of pubic hair, there's no guarantee that your period will start right away. You may still have some waiting to do. Menarche (the onset of your period, remember?) may also have to do with when your growth spurt starts.

If you are awake and get your period, you might notice a dampness on your underpants or between your legs. Sort of like if you have urinated and haven't quite wiped yourself completely.

You might also feel damp if you have a discharge. This is a clear, odorless fluid that also passes out of the vagina. It is not a period and doesn't mean for sure that your period is about to arrive. Rather it means that your hormones are working. Although discharges are usually normal, if they cause itching, change color, increase in amount, have an unpleasant odor, or seem to have changed in any way, this can mean that you might have a type of infection in your vaginal area. It is important to speak with your parents about the changes so that you can be properly treated, by your doctor if necessary. Lots of girls have talked with me about having discharges and have been relieved to know thay aren't the only ones to have them. Be sure to let your parents know if you have any concerns at all about your discharge.

You might not even feel any dampness. In fact you might not feel anything different. You might simply go to the bathroom one day and notice that you have started your period. You'll know because your underpants may have reddish or brownish "stains." (My children didn't want me to use the word *stains*. They thought it sounded "yucky." But it's a good way to describe what will probably happen. Don't worry about the stains. They'll wash out with a little soap and cold water.)

Another signal could be if you feel cramps in your lower abdomen or belly. Since the uterus has to get rid of the lining it doesn't need, the uterine walls contract (draw together, squeeze) so that the lining can be passed out. This contraction is sometimes felt as a cramp.

Because hormones can effect feelings and moods, some girls and women can sense their periods will soon begin because of the change in their emotions. You might find this to be true for you.

## What If Anyone Sees?

Still another way you'd know is if someone else told you they think they noticed a stain on your clothing. You're probably thinking that you'd "die" of embarrassment if anyone ever told you that. Or that you could never imagine saying to someone that you think they might have got their period. This has happened to me a few times. I guess I was a little (maybe a lot!) embarrassed, but I was more thankful that the person was nice enough to realize I would want to know. And the times I've told other people that they had better go to the bathroom to "check," they've really appreciated my telling them.

Maybe the more boys and girls understand about periods, the easier it will be to try to help each other. For example if you let someone else know that they might have gotten their period, you could also ask if there is anything you can do to help . . . like going to their locker to get an extra change of clothes for them or going to the nurse's office and getting them a sanitary pad.

What would you do? Would you tell someone else or keep quiet? Would you want someone else to tell you?

## Parents and First Periods

A first period means different things to parents as well as to the girl that gets it.

My mom was so excited! She gave me a long, hard hug that I'll always remember. I think we both couldn't believe it! Only later did I understand why there were tears in her eyes.

Stacey, age fourteen, was so surprised when her parents told her to pick her favorite restaurant so they could take her out for dinner to celebrate getting her period.

Martha, age seventy-two, remembers getting her period when she was "ten years and ten months." She had never even thought about periods because she believed they were for when you were older. Her sister helped her get set and then they went to tell their mother. Her mother smiled, turned around, and gave her a real hard slap in the face. She has never forgotten that slap!

If a mother slaps her daughter today, you can probably guess that her mother slapped her, and she's carrying on the tradition. Consider it for good luck. The old reason was to knock the devil or evil spirit out of you because people didn't understand periods and thought the blood meant something evil.

If you're wondering if your mom is planning to do that to you, why not talk with her about it.

Seanne, age twelve, said her mom invited her whenever she wants to join her women friends when they have coffee or tea in the afternoons because now she's "one of them." It made her feel so grown up!

Bernice, now in her fifties, also remembers getting her period when she was ten years old. She said, "her mother did a terrible thing when she took away her dolls and carriage because she was now a woman." She was very upset because she loved playing with her dolls and she "really didn't feel like a woman yet, anyway." Even though her father and mother argued about this, her mother wouldn't give in. Bernice had to sneak to her older sister's house to play with her niece's dolls. Her father felt so badly that he secretly made her a carriage out of old bicycle wheels.

Dean, now in her forties, remembers having sad feelings and crying when she got her period at the age of thirteen. Said Dean, "On top of this [her sadness], my mother gave me a lecture! She never had much discussion with me about sex or reproduction, but now that I had my period, I guess she felt it was time. She told me, Now you can get pregnant! Rules about boys became stricter and I had the feeling from my mother that bad things could happen now that I had it.

"Because I had such a sad beginning to my period, I wanted to make sure my daughters felt very good about theirs when the time came. My oldest daughter got hers a few months ago and our family celebrated by having a special toast with some punch."

When Kelly got her period at age twelve, she and her mom went to tell her dad. (Yes, dads know about periods too!) He gave her a huge hug, told her he was proud to have such a grown-up daughter, and handed her a cigar!

While different parents have different reactions to a daughter's first period, most daughters seem to feel relieved. They no longer have to wonder about when and where it will happen. They no longer have to go to the bathroom all day long to keep "checking" if they "got it." And now they can say, "Me too," to their friends who have already started to menstruate.

## Will Getting Your Period Hurt? What About Cramps?

You may have heard your mom or sister complain about being uncomfortable during her period. That doesn't mean you will be uncomfortable. Once again, each body is different.

Yes, you could get cramps in your lower belly or even in your lower back. This is normal. You could also get headaches, feel depressed (those mood changes I spoke about), feel kind of "swollen" or bloated (because your body might keep in fluids), and find that a few pimples might appear.

Remember the uterus is working very hard to contract so the lining will flow out. The contractions, along with changes in hormones, may cause any one or many of these reactions. Most cramps are mild, some are pretty strong.

It might sound like periods are a real bother to have. I admit that I have felt that way many times. But menstruation is just one of those things that you're going to have to try to accept as part of you.

Not everyone gets cramps. And if you do, there are things you can do to help you feel better. You can use a heating pad, rub your lower belly, lie down and take it easy, curl up with your knees to your chest. Getting exercise can really be helpful too.

If you are still uncomfortable, it's important to let your parents know so they can help you. If necessary, you can speak with your family doctor. He or she may recommend one of the medications that are specially made to relieve cramps or aches from periods. Remember never to take any medication before speaking to your parents.

You see, you've got lots of choices to help you feel good!

It would be impossible for me to tell you if your own period will be more or less comfortable. There were times when I had my period when I actually forgot that I had it. Every once in a while I had slight cramps. But they were often a signal that my period was coming. Once I had it and the first day or so was over, the cramps seemed to go away and I wasn't uncomfortable at all.

I suppose the best thing is to realize that there may be some cramps to deal with. They probably won't last too long. And, if they bother you, you can do some of the things I've suggested as well as get advice from your parents and doctor. You can also ask your friends who have their period what they do.

## What About Baths and Showers

Yes, yes, yes. Go right ahead and wash! (You know, the thing you do with soap and water?)

The water won't bother your period. Your period won't even bother the water! But body odor will bother your friends, family, and make it unpleasant to even be with yourself. So, do yourself and everyone a favor and keep clean! Not only during your period but all the time.

## Can You Still Play Sports?

Yes, yes, yes. You can do everything you usually do. Just because you have your period doesn't mean "stop everything." Exercise is great, with or without your period.

If you have cramps and don't feel like playing, do what you feel is most comfortable. But remember that exercise is one of the things that can help cramps. So you might push yourself a little and try to play.

## What About Swimming?

So many girls have asked me, "What if you get your period in the pool?" "If you get your period when you're in the pool, what should you do?" or "If you're in the pool, would you know it or feel it?"

It will be harder to tell if you get your period while swimming because you'll already be damp between your legs (and all over!). So probably you'd notice it if you got out of the pool and went to the bathroom. Or if someone you're swimming with notices a slight "spot" on your bathing suit and tells you about it so you can go to the nearest bathroom and check.

Though I'll talk about sanitary pads and tampons later, if you are swimming and have your period, you need to wear a tampon. A sanitary pad will not be able to work in the water. The fibers will break down and probably come apart.

I learned about not wearing pads in the water from an experience that still makes me smile. When I was younger, I tried swimming in a lake with a pad on. All of a sudden I felt it float away from me (horrors!) and I swam as fast as I could to shore. I prayed that it would sink before anyone noticed and never stayed around to find out!

It's also not very sanitary to wear a pad instead of a tampon in the water.

## What If You Get Your Period in School?

If you haven't got your period yet, or even if you have, this seems to be one of the biggest concerns about periods. After reading this section I hope you'll feel more comfortable about getting your period in school as you realize there are many different ways you can take care of your needs. You have more choices than you probably think you have.

Let's imagine you are in math class, in the middle of taking a test. And you're not quite sure, but you think you've got your period. What would you do?

Would you tell your teacher? Would you ask to be excused so you could go to the bathroom? Would you wait until you finished your test before doing anything? Would you do nothing and pray that it's really not your period? Think about this before reading further.

Well, do you have an answer? Maybe you'd tell your English or social studies teacher but not your math teacher. Maybe you'd feel differently if you weren't taking a test. Maybe if your math teacher was a woman instead of a man, you'd ask for help. If you are fourteen, you might give one answer, eleven, another.

It's so hard to know exactly what you would do and how you would feel if this happened to you. Since you're going to have your period many times, chances are you'll at least have a few periods that start in school.

Perhaps the most helpful thing is to realize that you do have several choices. Whether you're in English, gym, lunch, math, library, or any class, only you will be able to decide what choice will make you feel the most comfortable and which will be easiest for you at the time.

There are many things that might make a difference in what you choose to do. You might talk about your period with a teacher with whom you feel close and probably won't go near one that you don't like. You may really want to talk to your teacher about this, but may be too embarrassed or just not know what words to use.

While I was writing this, my own daughter, Hillary, age eleven, said to me, "No way would I go up to any one of my teachers. Come on, Mom, you know kids won't do that!"

Well, maybe they wouldn't. Maybe you wouldn't. And since there are several choices, you certainly don't have to, unless you want to. But if you realize you can, you might take a chance and be happily surprised at how helpful some of your teachers really can be.

Here are some questions that have been asked over and over again. I think you'll find that my answers and suggestions will help you think about which choices seem right for you.

*"What if I have a man teacher?"* or *"What if the nurse is a man?"*
Though men don't get a period, you can be sure that they know about periods. Knowing that a man teacher as well as a woman teacher will be able to understand may make it easier for you to talk about getting your period with them.

Both men and women teachers also know that it's not so easy for you to just come up to them and blurt out, "Hi, I think I got my period. . . . " They'll probably try to be as helpful to you as possible. But they can't help you unless you let them know you need help.

Many teachers have told me they keep a box of sanitary pads in their back closet or in a special drawer so that anyone who needs one can just take it. If your teacher hasn't mentioned a "pad supply," it's a good thing to suggest even if you haven't got your period yet. (Are you thinking that you'll have to sneak over to the pads so your classmates don't see? Keep reminding yourself that periods are natural—expected. If anyone makes fun of you, they probably don't really understand what periods are all about. They might even be jealous!)

You may have to get up your courage to speak with your teacher and ask for help. Sometimes the thing that can help you the most won't always be the most comfortable thing to do. It's okay to realize you're not comfortable, then go ahead and do what you have to do anyway.

I'm not saying you must speak with your teacher, just that you can if you want to.

*"What should I tell my teacher?"*
What you say will depend upon whether or not you've decided to tell your teacher about your period.

If you want to talk with your teacher about it, you might say: "Mr., Miss, or Mrs. so-and-so, I think I got my period. May I please go to the nurse's office or to the main office to make a phone call?" Or simply, "May I go to the bathroom?"

If you don't want to tell your teacher about your period, you might

say: "Mr., Miss, or Mrs. so-and-so, may I please go to the bathroom or the nurse's office?" If need be, you can even say, "I don't feel well and would like to go down to the nurse."

Sometimes teachers won't let you go to the nurse unless you say you don't feel well. It's usually best to tell the truth. But if you must say that you don't feel well in order to get out of the classroom, do so.

Some teachers have told me that they have a special signal in case a girl needs to leave the room because of her period. She can just leave, no questions asked. Perhaps the best thing would be for your class, or at least the girls in your class, to get together and speak with your teacher about being able to leave the classroom, even if it's in the middle of a test!

### "What if your teacher won't let you leave the classroom?"

While most teachers are understanding, I suppose there will always be a few that will make it really tough to leave the room. They may have certain times that you're allowed to go to the bathroom during the day, and that's it!

You may have to say, "It's an emergency." If that doesn't work and they still won't let you leave, *don't stay*! Just say something like, "I'm very sorry, but it really is an emergency, and I have to go." Then keep walking out. Just remember to be respectful. Don't talk back or be fresh.

If your teacher follows you into the hall, you can explain privately. If not, you can explain later. The worst thing would be to stay in your class worrying about your period. It's not fair for you to have to do that. It's your right to leave the classroom to take care of your own needs. No teacher should make it embarrassing or difficult to leave so that you're forced to stay.

I know this is easier for me to say and much harder for you to do, but imagine how you would feel if you couldn't go to the bathroom when you thought you had your period, and you'll understand why I feel so strongly about this. (You can tell your parents what made you walk out without permission and they can talk to your teacher with you, if need be.)

### "What if you're too embarrassed to tell the nurse?"

Here again, you have a choice. A nurse knows a lot about periods and is a good person to go to, especially since nurses usually have sanitary pads. They won't laugh or tease and will be happy to help you.

But if you're much too embarrassed and just can't push yourself to talk with the nurse about your period, then you don't have to. The choice is up to you. (Sometimes it helps to say things quickly, so you'll be less embarrassed.)

While many girls have a nice relationship with their school nurse and can talk easily with her (usually the nurse is a woman), some girls don't wish to speak with the nurse because they don't like her. Just a reminder—you don't have to like someone to let them help you. You don't need to be the nurse's friend, you just need her pads and her advice! (It's one of the reasons why she's there.)

If you decide not to tell her, then you'd better have another choice so that you can take care of yourself. The first thing you might do, if you don't want to talk with the nurse or your teacher, is go to the bathroom. The bathroom is a good *first* stop, no matter what you choose to do. You can put some toilet paper or tissues in your underpants, so you know you're protected until you get a pad!

If you don't have any sanitary pads in your classroom, locker, or pocketbook, most girls' bathrooms have sanitary napkin dispensers. If you put in a nickel, or whatever the sign on the machine says, you will be able to buy a pad, put it in place, and then go back to your classroom.

### *"What if the nurse isn't there?"*

Even if you want to talk with the nurse, she could be out for lunch, or just not in your school on that day. What to do?

Many nurses have told me they keep a supply of sanitary napkins in a certain place so that even if they are not there, any girl can come in and get what they need.

If you do not know where your school nurse keeps the supply, it would be a good idea to talk with her now, even if you haven't got your period yet (so you'll be prepared!).

If the nurse's door is locked or she doesn't keep an open supply, you can also go to the main office. The secretaries often keep sanitary pads in the office closet just in case someone like you comes in for help. They, too, will understand your needs.

If you don't want to talk with the office secretaries about your period, you can ask to use the telephone (with a first period, you might want to call home, share the good news, and get any help from your mom, dad, or someone close).

Or you can keep your own supply of sanitary pads so you can always count on yourself to be prepared! You can put one in a glasses case, a pencil case (one that's not see through), your pocketbook, locker, or in the special mini pad case that some of the companies make.

If you don't want to keep a mini pad around, there's no excuse for not keeping a supply of tissues in your desk, zippered pencil case, pocketbook, locker, or jacket pocket.

From this minute on you know that you can always be prepared (by putting tissues in your underpants to absorb the menstrual flow until you get a pad). Remember it's not a gush, so with tissues in place, you'll have time to figure out what to do next. You may walk a little funny so the tissues won't fall out, but you'll be protected, at least for a while!

### *"What if you get your period in school and you have white pants on?" or "What if the blood gets on your clothes?"*

If you've already got your period, you can keep that calendar and know to wear jeans or something dark around the time you expect your period. You can even wear a panty liner or mini pad so your clothes won't get stained. But if you've never had it before, you can't know when it will begin.

Even a calendar can't always exactly predict when it will start. So getting the special blood on your clothes is not only possible—but almost guaranteed. Not guaranteed all the time, but often enough for you to be prepared to know what to do.

If your clothes are stained, you can do one of several things. You can call home and ask someone to bring you a change. In case no one is home, it would be smart to have a key. Then someone in the office or even a teacher, an aide, the nurse, or anyone who is free can drive you to your home so you can change. If no one is home, schools usually require that you put several names on an Emergency Information form. Perhaps a relative or one of your parents' friends can pick you up and take you home.

It's a better idea to keep an extra pair of sweat pants or jeans plus a plastic bag or two in your locker or in the back closet of your classroom, just in case. You can go to the girls' bathroom, nurse's office, or even gym locker room, rinse your clothing in cold water (the blood stains usually come out easily), place anything damp in the plastic bag, and keep it in your locker or back closet until it's time to go home.

*"What if I think my clothes are stained and
I'm afraid to get up from my desk chair?"*
If you're pretty sure that your dress, pants, or skirt might be stained in a
way that could be noticed if you stand up from your desk—here again
you've got another choice!

Call your teacher over to your desk and either write a note so they can
read it as if looking at your work or whisper that you need their help. Ask
your teacher to stand behind you as you get up and to keep on walking
closely behind you as you walk out of the room.

That way, no one will see and you can get to the bathroom quickly.
Have the teacher send a friend in to help you. If you're right about the
stains, your friend can go to your locker, closet, or wherever you keep
your extra change of clothes. She can try to get a sanitary pad for you
from the bathroom dispenser, your locker, the teacher, nurse, or school
office. She or he can also make a phone call for you if necessary.

You see, school can be a real friendly place to get your period. You've
got lots of choices. All of them will help you take care of yourself. Think
about what might feel best to you and know that you can always try
something else the next time. Maybe you can even add to my list of
choices!

*"What if you get your period on the bus, on vacation, at camp, at
your grandparents' house, while baby-sitting, on a date, when
you're sleeping at a friend's house, on a plane, in the back seat
of your family's car with your brother sitting next to you, or
anywhere?"*
Okay, imagine yourself in any one of those situations. Go down the list.
Do you have an answer for each? Which one(s) would be the hardest for
you to deal with? Do you know why?

Believe it or not, you are already prepared for most of these areas,
possibly all. After I share a few more thoughts with you, I think you'll be
able to feel more confident about getting your period, no matter where.

There's really no magic. All you have to do is be *prepared*. Not so
much with sanitary napkins as with an understanding of what your
choices might be.

For example if you're on a bus, simply wait until you get off in order
to go to the nearest bathroom, put the tissues in place, and arrange to get
a sanitary pad. If you're on a bus trip with school and you're not

scheduled to stop anywhere, you can speak with the teacher or parent in charge and they will instruct the bus driver to pull into the nearest gas station so you can go to the bathroom.

Always have your own supply of tissues. Put them in the glove compartment of your family car, bring them with you when you baby-sit, go on a date, etc. You can also keep one or two pads in the car and bring them on vacation or to camp with you, just in case.

If you anticipate (think ahead about what your needs might be), then you can prepare yourself for most situations.

Even a plane has a bathroom. Even if you have to wait until you land before getting a sanitary pad, you can keep putting new tissues in your underpants to continue to absorb the flow.

If you go away to summer camp or go on a vacation, you can always pack away a small box of sanitary pads. (Keep them in a drawer, your cubby or shelf, or your suitcase in case you need them, but always have tissues with you!)

If you're on a date and think you have your period, find the nearest bathroom. If you do have it, your clothes are okay, and you happen to have a pad with you, then fine. Put the pad in place and go back to your date (just as you would if you had gone to the bathroom for regular reasons).

If your clothes are stained and you need to change, or if you need to get a pad, ask to stop back home or ask a parent to meet you with whatever you need. (It may seem awkward to you, but probably the easiest thing would be to straight out tell your date that you got your period and have to take care of things. Probably, you're not the first girl he knows who has got her period. If your date doesn't know about periods, it's time he learned!)

If you're in the backseat of your car, with your good old brother right next to you, you can ask your parent to pull over or drive to the nearest bathroom. If that's too far away for you to wait, ask your brother to turn around and close his eyes (no cheating!) until you tell him you're ready. Then you can easily slip some tissues (or even a pad that you've kept in the glove compartment) into your underpants and know that you'll be fine.

If you're baby-sitting, at your grandparents', at your friend's house, or anywhere, you can follow these same ideas. Bathroom first. If there's none around, use the tissues that you now know to have with you. If you don't have a sanitary pad or tissues, you can also use napkins, paper towels, or anything like that which will absorb the flow. Then take it from there. Change if you need to change; get a pad as soon as possible, and try to realize that you're not alone . . . there are lots of people who care and will help you.

### "How should you act if you're having your period, and it's all around school that you have it?"

If it's all around your school that you've got your period, you've got a few things you can do. You can ignore anyone who bothers you or tell the person(s) it's none of their business. Or, you can give them an answer they'll never expect. If someone says something to you about your period, you can just say, "Yes, it's true! Isn't that great? I feel so good that I got it!" The main thing is to be calm. Don't let anyone rattle you. (If they do, don't let them know it!)

They may be expecting you to be really embarrassed. Instead, if you act proud, smile, thank them for mentioning it, and tell them how much you wanted it, what more can they say? You'll have taken all the joy out of it for them if you don't react as they hoped.

### "What if you don't have your period and people are saying you do?"

You've got some more choices! You can go along with it as if you really got it and say, "Thanks, it's true." Though this answer isn't really honest, it would take people by surprise and maybe stop their talk.

Some girls feel the need to say they have their period when they really don't, or that they don't have it when they really do (like Laurie in the beginning of the book). The more girls (and boys) understand and accept that each person is different and that's okay, the less they will have to lie just to feel like they belong.

You can also say, "It's a rumor. If you want to go on talking about it, be my guest. But it's a little silly because I haven't even got it yet. I wish I did already, but I didn't. Maybe if you keep talking, I'll get it and we'll all be happy!"

If you give them the idea that they're not driving you crazy with their teases and talk, they'll probably stop and go on to someone else.

The message that needs to come through for either situation is that periods are really okay, you're happy to have it or wish you did. If their talking about your period doesn't seem to bother you, my guess is it won't be much fun to talk about it any more. Just try to keep your cool and outwit them.

## Sanitary Pads and Tampons

It's time to take a good look at just what those pads and tampons are made of, how and why they work, when you need to wear them, and how often they should be changed. . . .

First, let's talk about sanitary pads.

Sanitary pads are made up of soft fibers that can absorb the menstrual flow. They are worn on your underpants. When the lining trickles out the vaginal opening, it will be absorbed by the pad waiting for it on the outside.

Pads are very easy to use. Most pads have a long sticker on the back that is protected by a strip. Once you peel that strip off, you can stick the pad onto your underpants and wear it until you need to change it again. They're very comfortable. Unless you're wearing super-super-super tight pants, they're hardly noticeable.

When I was growing up, we only had sanitary pads that you had to hook onto elastic sanitary belts (for sanitary napkins). My friends and I called them Mickey Mouse Pads. Even though most of us used them, we thought it was more mature to use tampons. I now know that it's simply a matter of choice. Anyone can use either pads or tampons, depending upon how they and their parents feel. These "hook-on pads" are still around, but it's much easier to use the ones that stick right to your underpants. Whoever invented the stick on pad sure was a clever person.

It's a great idea to get some pads even before you have your period. Put one on just to feel what it's like and learn how to use it. If you've never worn one before, it's likely you'll be relieved to realize that they really don't make you look like you are walking with a volleyball between your legs. As I've said before, they're soft, comfortable, and no one need know you have one on.

Pads (and tampons) absorb the flow much like a sponge takes in water. They can take in just so much and then can't take in any more. When a pad or tampon is "full" (has taken in all the flow it can), instead of squeezing it out so that it can be used again (like you do to a sponge), you simply wrap it up, throw it out, and put a new one in place. No big deal, eh?

A word about "wrapping it up": Sometimes bathrooms have a special little bag for throwing away sanitary pads, etc. Most of the time, they don't. So you can easily put layers of toilet paper or tissues around your pad and then throw it *in the garbage—not the toilet!* (You can't imagine how many people don't think about the poor old plumbing and clog up the toilet by tossing in their pad and trying to flush.)

All wrapped up, you don't have to be concerned about anyone ever bothering with it. I used to wrap mine many times, just to make sure no one would know what was underneath. One of the first few times I got my period, I wrapped my pad up real well (with tons of layers of toilet paper!) and tried to bury it in the garbage basket in the bathroom at school. I remember being so surprised to find there were five or six other "wrapped treasures" already buried.

Whether you've seen advertisements on television, packages in a pharmacy (drug store), or your mom's or sister's pads in the bathroom, you may have noticed that there are different types of sanitary pads and tampons. (Don't some of those ads make you giggle?)

Mini, maxi, junior, slender-regular, regular, super, and super-plus are all words to describe different types and sizes of sanitary pads and tampons. The supers, super-pluses, and maxis can absorb more, while the regulars absorb slightly less, and the mini's, slender regulars, and juniors, even less.

If you are at the beginning of your period when the flow is usually heavier, you would want a pad or tampon that is more absorbent. At the end of your period, when the flow is lighter, whatever you use can be less absorbent.

It also might depend upon how old you are. For example a young girl who is just starting to use tampons would probably begin using the slender regular or junior size. I'll save the question of whether to choose a tampon or a pad until after I discuss tampons.

Okay, let's think about tampons.

You already know what they're made of (soft, absorbent fibers). But how are they different from sanitary pads? For those of you who aren't sure, tampons offer protection by absorbing from the inside while sanitary napkins and pads protect you by absorbing from the outside.

Since the lining of the uterus leaves the body through the vagina, tampons are inserted (gently guided in) through the opening of the vagina so that the lining trickles right onto the tampon fibers and never reaches the outside. You can find your vaginal opening by parting your inner lips (minor lips or labia). Remember, the vagina is the second opening as you move down from your belly button!

Some girls have asked what would happen if they accidently placed the tampon in the wrong opening. Ouch! They'd feel it was wrong because you wouldn't be able to get it in without being pretty uncomfortable.

When a tampon is in place correctly, you shouldn't even feel that it is inside. In fact you just might have to remind yourself that you're wearing one so you can take it out before putting another in. It's so comfortable, you could forget all about your period! Pay attention to the time you put it in. If for some reason it doesn't feel right, you can just take it out and insert a new one.

Placing a tampon in your vagina may seem a little strange at first. But it comes easier with each try. (It helps to know which is the right opening!) The tampon comes in an applicator that makes it simple to insert. A removal cord (like a string) is attached to the end of the tampon, so you can take it out when you wish.

Are you ready? Wash your hands before opening the tampon wrapper. They all come wrapped like little presents so they remain sanitary. Hands clean? Now open and take off the wrapping and you're ready to insert (or at least to learn about how).

Notice that the applicator is made up of an outer tube and an inner tube. The soft, rounded top of the tampon peeks out of the outer tube while the removal cord hangs down behind it through the inner tube.

To insert it part the soft folds of skin at the opening of your vagina with one hand. (It's easier if you do this in a sitting or squatting position with your knees apart.) With your other hand place the outer tube end (with the peeking tampon) into the opening and tilt it toward your back as you move it just inside (yes, inside the vagina! How else will the tampon catch those trickles unless it's right there waiting for them?).

Hold onto the string with your finger and gently guide the tampon inside. Push it back and slightly upward until your finger reaches your body. Keep holding on to the removal string and the outer tube you just put in.

The next step is to push the inner tube all the way into the outer tube. Then, let go of the removal cord and take both the outer and inner tubes out. The tampon is now left snugly in place in your vagina! Remember, the walls of the vagina are amazing the way they can stretch. They'll just know how to make your tampon feel right at home.

If you are having difficulty inserting the tampon, it may be due to a tightening of the muscles around the opening of your vagina (like when you make a fist if you're a little nervous or concerned about something). It might help to use some lubricating (loo-bri-kay-ting) jelly on the tip of the tampon (it can be bought at most drug stores) so that it slides in easier—not Vaseline, since it's not healthy for the vaginal canal. It can also help to keep telling yourself, "Relax, relax . . . ," so that the muscles at the vaginal opening loosen up and make it easier to insert the tampon. (Can you just hear a chorus of "Relax, relax" coming from each stall of the girls' bathrooms at school?)

To take the tampon out just pull gently on the removal cord in a slightly downward but forward angle (don't yank!). Since the tampon is now moist, it will slip out easily through the entrance of your vagina.

Even though tampon and sanitary pad companies might suggest that you flush a used tampon in the toilet, it would be safest not to. My old "wrap method" is still a good one!

If you choose to use tampons, you'll be happy to know that tampon manufacturers include inserting instructions along with diagrams (pictures that show you how to insert) in just about every new package. It's a good idea to keep these with the package in case you need an extra review of the steps I've just described.

A reminder about the hymen (the tissue or "membrane" that surrounds the opening of your vagina): It's very flexible and won't be pushed back if you use tampons according to proper directions.

Remember in Chapter 2 when I explained that the usual way to push the hymen back is by having sexual intercourse? Now you can understand that parents who are concerned about the hymen and tampons really are much less concerned about the hymen, itself, and much more concerned about what pushing the hymen back can *mean*.

If your mom or dad has questions about this, ask her or him to read this information with you!

Important note: Wearing a tampon will not prevent you from urinating, since the tampon is placed in the vaginal opening and urine passes through your urethra (first opening).

## It's Very Important to Change Your Pads
## and Tampons Regularly...

You need to change pads or napkins often so that harmful *bacteria* does not build up. Such bacteria can lead to infections, and who wants that? Certainly not you!

A good guide is to change whatever you use every few hours during the heavier flow days in the beginning of your period. Toward the end, you can make less changes because the flow is less and less and your pad won't "fill up" as quickly. But even if the pad is not filled, don't leave it on more than those few hours. Put a new one in its place.

While it's easy to tell whether a sanitary pad is ready to be changed (all you have to do is look!), you might be wondering how you'll know when to change your tampon. Well, you really don't know for sure. Unless, of course, you discover a few spots on your underpants. That's one way to find out that your tampon can't absorb any more fluid!

A helpful idea with tampons is just to remember when you last put one in. As you learn more about how your body gets its period, you'll get to know how heavily you will trickle out that menstrual blood. That will help you decide how often you need to change.

Start by changing every couple of hours and see if that's often enough. If you find your tampons are just about full after two hours, you may want to change them after one and one half hours. Experiment. It's really the only way to find out. If you guess wrong about when to change, the worst that could happen is that you'll leave the tampon in even after it has absorbed all it can and you might get a few spots on your clothing that can easily be washed out with soap and water.

Even when you know what to expect during your period (how heavy or light your usual flow is, how often you usually need to change your sanitary protection), it's possible for you to forget or just not figure your changing schedule right.

Another thought about spots: If your pad is ready to be changed while you're still asleep, you might notice period stains on your pajamas, nightshirt or nightgown, and sheets. This, too, is *normal*. You can't help it unless you feel like setting your alarm every few hours so you can change. If it concerns you, change your own sheets. If not, at least know that whoever changes them will probably know about periods too.

## What About Toxic Shock Syndrome?

Well, for one thing, Toxic Shock Syndrome, or TSS, is an illness that is quite rare. Doctors feel that it is caused by a certain kind of bacteria that some women seem to have. It's *not* caused by tampons, but it's interesting that most cases have been among women who had their period and were wearing tampons at the time.

TSS has also been found in lesser numbers in men, children, and women who no longer get their periods (yes, periods do end. You can read about Menopause in the last section of this chapter).

Some of the symptoms (signs that you might have it) for TSS are violent, sudden vomiting and/or diarrhea along with fever that may be expected to reach 102 degrees or higher; a rash (like a sunburn); feeling like you're going to faint; and dizziness.

Since TSS can be serious (it can even cause death), it's very important for anyone who has one or more of these signs to contact her doctor. If at that time a tampon is in, the person should take it out until the doctor checks what the symptoms mean. (Since these symptoms could also signal other illnesses, you don't need to panic if you have them. Just know to check them out right away.)

## Are Tampons Safe?

Yes and no.

Yes, if you are able to remember to change your tampon every few hours. If it is left in too long, that's when the bacteria might have a chance to develop. A good rule is not to leave your tampon in for more than four to six hours at the most. You'll probably need to change it sooner than that, anyway. Another good rule is to wear junior or regular—not super tampons. This will force you to have to change them sooner than later.

It's a smart idea not to wear tampons when you go to sleep at night. Wear a sanitary pad instead. That way the tampon won't be left in place for too many hours. You might also want to take turns using tampons and sanitary pads once in a while during daily use.

Tampons may not be safe if you often forget about your tampon and leave it in for too many hours at a time. Wearing it too long is unhealthy.

To be totally safe, I suppose I have to say use sanitary pads. But I've spoken with enough doctors who believe that tampons are probably fine, as long as you have healthy changing habits and know what symptoms need a doctor's attention.

## Which Should You Use?

This is a very personal decision. It wouldn't even be fair if I tried to tell you what would be better for you. You've got to decide that for yourself.

It depends upon how you feel. You may think that one is easier or more comfortable to use than the other. You may just like one more than the other. It may also depend upon what your friends are using (or not using).

Your parents may have definite feelings about which to use, so be sure to talk with them about this. If they feel one way and you feel another, make sure you understand their feelings. And let them know how you feel, even if you don't agree. They can't know or act on your feelings unless you tell them.

I think by now you have enough information to make your decision. The nice thing is that you can always change your mind!

## Buying Sanitary Pads and Tampons

Sharon, age twelve, asked, "What happens if you go to the store and ask for sanitary pads? I would be ashamed." Jeannie, age thirteen, said, "Everyone will know!" There are so many girls who have told me they feel kind of funny about buying sanitary pads and tampons. Others have thought it was no big deal.

A fifty-year-old friend recalls feeling so shy when she had to buy her pads. After walking around the store for almost twenty minutes, she finally went over to the person behind the counter. She had such trouble getting the words out. She managed only to ask for "Ko——" and finished with "——dak" instead of saying the brand of pads that she really wanted. After all that time she walked out with film instead of her pads.

Most drug stores place their stock of sanitary pads or tampons right out on shelves where they're easy to see (and easy to reach). So, most of the time, you won't even need to ask for help. You can just take what you want, bring it up to the cash register, pay, and leave. (Don't forget to smile and say "thanks.")

Just in case you still feel really funny about buying pads or tampons yourself or if you can't find them on the shelves, here are some choices to think about.

You can ask your parents, sister, brother, or friend to do it for you. You can also walk up to the counter and say, "I'm buying this for a friend!" (No, not honest, but if you must, you must).

You can practice saying, "I'd like to buy these, thanks very much." The less you stand around the store waiting to be helped, the quicker you'll make your purchase.

Another choice is to very calmly approach the salesperson and ask, "Where do you keep the tampons or sanitary napkins?" Then bring one to the counter, say "thank you", smile, and walk slowly out the door. (Try it! You might be very surprised.).

If you're concerned or shy about buying pads or tampons, it might help to remember that the first time you buy them may be a bit awkward. The second time will probably be easier, and so on, until you feel you can order anything you want!


## Menopause (men-o-paws)

Just as your period has a beginning, it will have an end. The ending of menstruation is called *menopause*. Some people also refer to this as the "change of life." Perhaps that's because when your period finally stops, your ovaries will no longer release eggs, and you won't be able to become pregnant.

It's impossible to predict when you will reach menopause (like you can't tell exactly when menstruation will start!), but you can figure somewhere around age fifty (it could be a few years earlier or later). When this happens, hormone amounts get lower and your period gradually lessens until it stops completely.

Besides changing your period schedule the lowered amount of hormones may also cause a woman to have symptoms such as headaches and hot flashes (sounds like it could be a new rock group but it really means short, sudden feelings or rushes of heat). Your grandma or mom might have talked about them. Each woman will get symptoms in her own special way. They're signals that menopause is taking place, although not all women get such symptoms.

Just like a girl can start releasing eggs before she actually has her period, a woman can continue releasing eggs after her period seems to have stopped. It's not a case of stopping your period one month and that's it. Even after your period has changed, you still could be ovulating (ov-you-lay-ting: releasing an egg). Ovulation will stop when menopause is complete, a year or two after it started.

It's important to remember that menopause takes place over time.

## A Few More Thoughts

Lots of girls are confused about periods and getting pregnant. Just because you have your period doesn't mean you're going to be pregnant. Sperm from a man's body must be introduced in or around a woman's vagina so they can move through the vagina toward the fallopian tubes where they might find an egg. Only if a man's sperm fertilizes or enters an egg will a woman become pregnant.

So sperm do *not* live in your closet, under your bed sheets, hide in swimming pools, hang out in book bags. You don't have to be concerned about sperm or becoming pregnant until much later in your life at a time when you feel you're ready to have a baby.

One more time: Having your period allows you the choice to try to become pregnant. Even though your *body* might be ready to make that choice as a young girl (in my opinion), *you* are not ready! That decision is best saved until you are much older (more about this later on).

# Growing Up
# MALE
# Feeling Good

# 4
# Private Parts

A four-year-old boy came up to my son in a store several weeks ago and said, "I'll bet if I said *penis* real loud, people would laugh!"

Talk about boys' or girls' sex organs often brings with it giggles and red faces. I hear those giggles in the beginning of many of my programs. But as I talk about these organs and tell kids things about them that they have always wondered, they forget about their blushes and want to know as much as they can.

Just like for girl's sex or reproductive organs, there are many slang names that people use in place of the real names for boys' sex organs. You can probably make a list of them. While some of them might make you laugh, others are strong. These are sometimes used in a way that has little or nothing to do with the genitals and much more to do with being angry and trying to get at someone.

Even if you have a favorite slang name that you use, it's a good idea to at least know what the real names are. So let's use the real names to help you learn them.

Boys, too, have outside (external) and inside (internal) genitals. They mature during puberty because of the release and influence of the male hormones (the old "growth clock" does it again!).

We'll start with the outside (external) genitals.

A boy's outside sex organs include his penis and *scrotum* (skro-tum), the sac that has two pouches that is located behind the penis.

The **penis** (pee-nis) is a boy's main sex organ. The longer part is called the shaft and its smooth, round head is called the *glans* (glanz). The glans is very sensitive to touch because it has lots of nerve endings. The underside of the penis just below the glans is also sensitive, and the rest is much less.

At the very tip of the penis is the tiny opening of the *urethra* (you-ree-thra). In a boy the urethra carries urine from the bladder through the penis to the outside. It also carries a special fluid called *semen* (see-men), which I'll talk about later. Urine and semen are never carried at the same time so they can't get mixed together. (In a girl the urethra only carries urine from the bladder to the outside.)

You'll find that the skin of your penis is hairless and "loose." Imagine that the skin fits over the shaft as if it's a glove that's a slightly larger size. When the penis is soft, the skin seems like it's kind of wrinkled because it's a bit "roomy."

So many boys have asked me, "What's inside my penis?" Have you ever wondered about that? Just in case you're not sure, let's take a good look together.

Inside the penis are nerves, blood vessels, and different kinds of tissues. Some are "spongy" tissues because when blood flows into the penis, these tissues fill up like a sponge fills up with water. When the tissues are filled, the penis expands and gets stiffer or hard. This is called having an *erection* (ee-reck-shun).

During an erection the "loose" skin fills in and allows the penis to have enough stretching space to become longer and slightly wider. It stays this way for a short while because the blood vessels tighten and keep the blood in the spongy tissues. Very soon, the blood vessels slowly let the blood flow out of the spongy tissues and the penis returns to being soft.

I'll talk more about erections (how often, when, feelings about having them) in the next chapter.

## What Does *Circumcised* Mean?

A boy is born with a flap of skin attached to and covering the glans of his penis. Many parents decide to have this flap, or foreskin (4-skin), removed shortly after birth. Depending upon your religion, removing the foreskin might be done at a special ceremony.

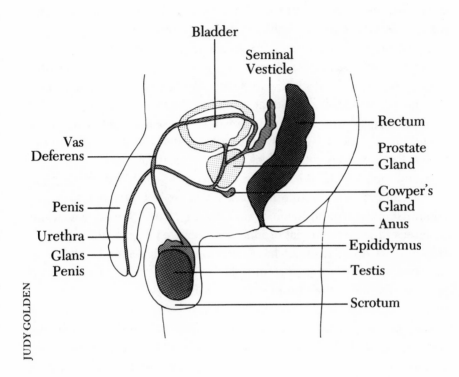

If your foreskin is removed, it's called being *circumcised* (sir-come-sized), or having a *circumcision* (sir-come-sizz-jun). If it is not removed, you're said to be *uncircumcised*. Most boys in the United States are circumcised. (This means not everybody is!) It's a decision that parents make.

One twelve-year-old boy asked, "If I'm not circumcised, does that mean that my penis won't grow normally?" No! Circumcision will not affect how your penis grows, how sensitive it is, or how it works. Your penis will grow because the male hormone, *testosterone* (tess-tos-ter-own), is released inside your body. The foreskin is on the outside and has nothing to do with growth.

On a circumcised penis the glans is showing all the time because there's no flap of skin covering it. Not being circumcised simply means that there will be a flap of skin at the tip of the penis that you will have to gently pull (or roll) back to see the glans.

Rich, age thirteen, shared, "I feel really embarrassed when I change in the locker room because I seem to be the only one who's not circumcised. No one has ever said anything to me. But mine looks different. Also my penis seems larger than that of a lot of other kids."

It would have saved Rich a lot of uncomfortable feelings if he realized earlier that it's natural for his penis to look different as well as slightly larger when soft. That's because of the extra flap of skin (foreskin). Rich also didn't know that if he and the other boys had erections, the size of his penis and theirs would probably even out. And, when erect, his foreskin would move back all by itself, making his penis look almost exactly like theirs. Each penis is going to look a little different anyway. Just like with faces, all the parts are the same, but each one is a little different!

An important thing to remember if you are not circumcised, is that you must clean around the foreskin regularly. There are small glands in the area of the foreskin that produce a substance which could store up or collect. If it does, it might have an unpleasant smell and could cause infection. So it's very important to keep the area clean. Most boys and men have to move the foreskin back in order to wash, but not to urinate (pee).

If you wash your penis often, especially in and around the foreskin, then things should be fine. Of course you also have to wash your penis and the rest of your body, even if you are circumcised!

If you're uncircumcised and find (at any time as you're growing up) that your foreskin is feeling a bit tight, and this makes you uncomfortable around the head of your penis, or if you're having trouble moving back your foreskin, be sure to tell your parents and have them take you to your doctor.

## What About Penis Size?

If you really wanted to measure your penis, you'd need to take two different measurements: one when your penis is soft or nonerect, and one when it's hard or erect. Your penis is larger when erect, smaller when nonerect.

More important is that size just doesn't matter, at least not to the penis and how it works. Those boys and men who are concerned about penis size seem to believe that a larger penis means you're more manly, a smaller one means less. Not so! Once again, being a man has much less to do with size and much more to do with how you feel about yourself inside.

If you looked up at your dad when you were little, you might have wondered if your penis would ever be like his. Maybe. Maybe not. Your penis might grow to be smaller than your dad's—or larger. All you can do is guess. Since it's all up to your hormones (and I've never heard a hormone speak), there's no way to predict.

You can't look at someone and guess how large their penis is. Just because someone is huge, plays football, and likes girls, doesn't mean that his penis is probably bigger than that of the smallest boy in your grade. It might even be smaller!

Though other books will tell you an average penis size in centimeters or inches, I refuse! There's no point sitting around waiting with a ruler, hoping you'll be a certain size. Nothing you do can change the size your body will be. Your size will be your size. Whatever it happens to be, you'll still be the special person that you are.

> Remember if you can:
> Penis size is not the measure of a man!

The **scrotum** (skro-tum) is a pouch that hangs behind and slightly below the penis. It's a bit darker in color than the rest of the body and becomes slightly covered with hair when a boy reaches puberty.

It has the very important job of holding and protecting the two *testicles* (tes-tic-kulls) that are inside. Most of you probably know the testicles as "balls" or "nuts"!

Sometimes, one or both testicles do not "drop" or move down into their section in the scrotal sac as they are expected to do shortly before birth. Instead they remain in the abdomen where the temperature would be too high for sperm to live. This condition is known as having *undescended* (un-dee-sen-ded) or *undropped* testicles and can be discovered by your doctor during a regular check-up (if you haven't already realized it yourself).

Doctors have several methods that they use to try to bring them into place. If you have this condition (or think you do), be sure to talk with your parents about any question or concern. Also make sure that your doctor fully explains anything he or she needs to do.

Temperature in the scrotal sac is important because sperm (male sex cells) are produced in the testicles when a boy reaches puberty. Females have egg cells and males have sperm cells. While a girl's ovaries develop so that they can release egg cells that can be fertilized, a boy's *testes* (tes-teez) develop so they can produce sperm cells. It's the sperm cells that can fertilize the egg cells.

The only place sperm cells are produced is in the testicles. In order for them to stay healthy, they have to be kept at a temperature that is about three degrees lower than the regular body temperature. That's why the scrotum is outside of a male's body.

The muscles of the scrotum respond to heat and cold so that the temperature inside can be right. For example if the weather is freezing and you're standing outside waiting for your school bus, the muscles will contract (squeeze together) so that the testicles will be pulled closer to your body and can be warmer. If you're sitting in a hot bath, the muscles will expand (relax) so that your testicles will be farther away from your body and will not get too warm.

Let's look at the inside (internal) organs.

**Testes** (tes-teez) or **testicles** (tes-tic-kulls). You've got two. They're delicate and very important. That's why many boys and men wear "jock straps" (a supporter or pouch that holds the genitals in place) when they exercise or play sports. Even though some boys wear it to be macho, cool or seem more grown-up, this strap is important because it helps support the scrotum and prevents the genitals from flopping around. Football players, baseball catchers, and other athletes even wear protection cups inside special jock straps, called cup supporters, to be extra safe. Your testicles need protection even when you're not playing sports, so don't let anyone kick or hurt you there!

If you looked inside the testicles, you'd see hundreds of tubes and compartments. Each testicle is suspended by a spermatic cord (sort of like a puppet on a strong string) in its own section on the right and left side of the scrotal sac.

Most boys and men find that their left testicle hangs slightly lower than their right one. Go ahead and check this out in a mirror. I promise to wait right here! There. Do you see what I'm talking about?

Don't be concerned if one testicle is a little lower; I mainly wanted you to understand that if it is, it's supposed to be that way! I've had many boys come up to me after my programs to tell me they were very relieved to learn that it's "okay to be lopsided" and nothing is wrong with them. Even dads have told me they didn't realize this is true. You may want to make sure your older brother and dad know this is normal.

In Chapter 2 you learned that girls have two ovaries that produce female hormones and release egg cells. The testes have the same kind of responsibilities in boys and men. They release the male hormones (most important is testosterone) and produce sperm.

A word about **testosterone:** A boy's testicles may start to release testosterone as early as age eleven or not until later. Only when this happens will his body begin to develop and change. Testosterone controls growth of hair on the body and face, genital growth, voice deepening, muscle and body development, and sexual interest. (Let's hear it for testosterone!)

**Sperm** are the male sex cells. They're made in the *seminiferous tubules* (sem-i-niff-er-us too-bewls) of the testicles. This is the only place in the body where sperm are made. Sperm have a head, neck, and a tail and look like teeny, cute tadpoles. The only way you can see them is under a microscope.

Though girls are born with all the immature eggs in their ovaries that they will ever need, boys do not begin to develop immature sperm until they reach puberty. Once sperm start to develop, it takes a few years for them to mature. Once matured they are capable of fertilizing a female egg cell. (Reminder: Just because your body is ready to fertilize a female egg, it doesn't mean that *you* are ready. That's something very special that you are better off saving for when you're an adult. More about that later on.)

Both testicles are able to produce millions of sperm each day. Once a boy begins to produce sperm, he continues for the rest of his life. Several things can lessen sperm production. Some examples are wearing very tight pants or underwear, sitting in the same position every day for long hours at a time (like truck drivers or bomber pilots), altitude, or being sick for a while. Sperm production usually goes back to normal when the conditions change (for example, if you're feeling better).

The inside organs work together so that the sperm can be produced, transported, and passed to the outside of a boy's or man's body. Join me as I follow the path that sperm take once they're produced in the testicles.

You already know that the sperm are produced in the seminiferous tubules in the testicles!

**Epididymis** (e-pi-di-di-miss—looks harder to say than it is!) is like a storage and ripening chamber that is attached to each testicle. After the sperm are produced, they are moved into the epididymus where they receive nourishment and stay for several weeks until they fully ripen or mature.

The epididymis also helps to weed out the stronger, healthier sperm so that they're the ones to move on. Many of the weaker or damaged ones simply get absorbed by the tubes in the epididymis and are passed out of the body as waste.

The mature sperm move from the epididymis into the **Vas Deferens** (vas deaf-er-enz) by contractions and the sweeping motion of cilia. They won't be able to swim by themselves (they have cute little tails!) until they mix with fluids from other internal (inside) organs. We're almost up to that part.

The vas deferens is like a long, thin roadway that transports sperm and also helps store them at its wider, upper end. Once in the vas deferens the sperm are moved up and away from the testicles, around the back of the bladder, and are passed on to mix with the fluid in the seminal vesicles (sem-i-nal ves-i-kulls).

Yup, you guessed! They're the next stop on our journey.

The two **seminal vesicles** (sem-i-nal ves-i-kulls) are small saclike glands that contribute an important part of the special fluid called semen. Once the sperm mix with this fluid, they can whip their tails and move along by themselves.

Besides giving the sperm the first chance to become active, this seminal fluid provides them with nourishment (seminal fluid from seminal vesicles, get it?).

From here the fluid that now contains sperm flows into the two

*Ejaculatory ducts* (ee-jack-u-la-tory). These two ducts connect the seminal vesicles with the opening of the urethra in the prostate gland (hang in there, we're almost through!).

There is only one **prostate gland!** It's found at the base of the bladder and is about the size of a walnut. The prostate gland contributes a thin, milky fluid that makes up the largest part of the semen. It also gives off fluid, which passes out with the urine.

Even though semen and urine pass through the urethra at different times, the urine leaves an acidy trail as it passes through. The prostate gland knows this and makes sure that its fluid is *alkaline* (al-ka-lin) or *basic.* That means that it offsets or balances out the acid so the sperm can pass through more quickly and easily. (Your science teacher will be proud if you know that when bases and acids are mixed together, they balance or neutralize each other.) It might also interest you to know that the vagina is acidy too.

The prostate gland is supposed to shrink when a man gets older. But sometimes it doesn't. You dad, uncle, or grandpa might have complained about an enlarged prostate gland. Because it's so close to the bladder, you can imagine that a larger prostate would cause pressure on the bladder and have an uncomfortable effect on urination.

**The Cowper's glands** are two tiny pealike glands that are found on either side of the urethra at the base of the penis just under the prostate gland.

Just before semen is about to be released through the urethra, these glands give off an alkaline fluid that helps the semen pass through more easily and safely. The fluid moistens the path of the urethra and offsets the acid path of the urine that passed before it. The fluid released from the cowper's glands contains a small amount of sperm.

A word about semen: As you now know, semen is made up of fluid from the seminal vesicles, prostate gland, and a smaller amount from the cowper's glands. It also contains millions of sperm that make up a very small part of the fluid.

The amount of fluid (usually about one teaspoon) can be slightly different from man to man and even different for the same man from time to time. It has to do with such things as a man's health, when he last released semen, or his age. Semen can be thick and almost like gelatin one time and be thin and more watery another.

Semen is passed out of a boy's or man's body through the opening at the tip of the penis. When this happens, it is called an *ejaculation* (ee-jack-cue-lay-shun). Or we can say that a boy has ejaculated.

A boy's first ejaculation is very exciting for him. It means he is officially on his way to manhood. I'll talk more about this in the chapter on ejaculation and wet dreams (that's when a boy ejaculates in his sleep).

Now that you've read this chapter, I think you'll find that the rest of the changes that boys go through in puberty will be much easier to understand.

# 5
# Erections

## How Often Do Boys Have Erections?
## When Might They Happen?

Boys can start having erections as soon as they're born. As I explained in Chapter 4, when a boy has an erection, his penis becomes stiffened, slightly longer and wider.

Erections can happen on and off throughout the day and night. Even though there's no special schedule for erections during the day (you'll probably get one but you may not), there seems to be an erection pattern that's connected with when you dream during sleep. If you wake up close to when you've just had a dream, you might wake up with an erection. An erection from dreams or pressure on the bladder is common for boys and men when they wake up. Erections during sleep can also relate to what you dream.

It wouldn't work for a boy to think to himself, "I want to have an erection now," wait three seconds, and expect to magically become erect. It's interesting that erections happen because of a reflex. That means that a message from a boy's brain or his body lets the nerves in charge of erection know that "it's time for another one!"

These erection nerves are located in the lower part of the spinal cord. After getting an "erection message," they then send signals that cause an extra supply of blood to flow into the spongy tissues of the penis. More blood flows in than is able to flow out. The penis gets larger bit by bit as the blood fills up and stays in these tissues. While this is happening, the color of the penis becomes slightly deeper, as if it's blushing.

The erection lasts as long as the messages continue sending in the extra blood supply. This keeps the spongy tissues filled. When the "erection messages" stop, blood flow gradually returns to normal and the penis once again becomes soft.

Lots of different things can cause an "erection message" to be sent: Seeing or talking with someone you like; touching the sensitive parts of your penis, scrotum, or other areas around the penis; certain sounds; smells; dreams; sexual feelings; physical activity.

A boy could get an erection while standing up in front of the class giving a book report, playing a sport, when he's talking with the new girl in his class, or while looking at pictures in certain magazines.

Because erection is a reflex, a boy can have an erection when he doesn't even expect it or want it. Once he has it, he just has to wait until it becomes soft again. He can't prevent it from happening, and he can't force his penis to bulge if it's not in the mood! Erections are just a natural part of being a boy.

Kids sometimes call an erection a boner. But the penis doesn't have a bone in it! A dog's penis does. So does the penis of a male fox (just in case you were wondering about foxes!). And those of other animals too—but not humans. "Boner" probably started because of how hard the penis can get.

Some erections end in ejaculation. That's when that milky whitish fluid called semen spurts out of the tip of the penis. You can read more about ejaculation and wet dreams in the next chapter.

## Erection Feelings, Concerns, and Confusions

Susan, age twelve, wanted to know what would happen if a boy has an erection when he's swimming. Asked Susan, "Would he have to get out of the water?"

If anything, Susan, a boy would probably keep right on swimming. (It might even help him float better! Ha-ha, only kidding.) Seriously, no matter what sport a boy is playing, erections won't prevent him from continuing. They usually don't last that long anyway.

Sometimes boys have erections in the water because the pressure and wetness can send a message to the erection control center. Just like

the fact that nipples often become erect when it's cold or when they're brushed lightly by clothing, so can the penis become erect in response to friction or pressure.

Another thought has to do with what a boy is wearing while he swims. Depending upon how tight and what style a boy's bathing suit is, he might purposely stay under water until his erection becomes soft. Or, his erection may be just the reason to come out of the water—boys have many different feelings about when and where they have erections.

Kevin, age twelve, told me, "I started wearing looser bathing suits so it wouldn't be so easy to notice when I get an erection. I used to be really embarrassed cause I thought everyone would know."

Jeff, age eleven, said his older brother likes to wear "bikini, skinny, tight bathing suits and just kind of parades around, showing off, when he gets hard."

While an erection may seem gigantic to you because it's on your body and you can tell a big difference from when you were soft, it doesn't mean that everyone else sees it too! (Unless, of course, you're the one wearing that "tight, skinny bikini"!)

Thirteen-year-old Josh described how he "takes care of" his erections when he's in school and doesn't really want people to notice. "I just fix it so it's flat against my stomach. I stick my hand in my pocket and adjust myself. If anyone sees me with my hand there, I make like I'm looking for something and then put my hands in my back pockets and search around. I can usually come up with a piece of paper or pen or something. It only takes a second to move my penis against my body. Then I don't think about it."

Kenny, age twelve, said, "I used to worry about blushing when I got an erection. They never bothered me when I was by myself, but I always thought other people would know. I don't know why, but it doesn't bother me any more. I guess I just got used to having them."

It's usually a relief to learn that you're not the only person in the whole world to feel a certain way or have a particular concern. So much of what these boys said was similar. Maybe you have felt the same way.

Now that you know more about your sex organs, semen, and how you get an erection, it's time to talk about wet dreams and ejaculation.

# 6
# Ejaculation
# and Wet Dreams

## What Is an Ejaculation?

Ejaculation is a special part of growing up for a boy. It means he's officially on his way to becoming a man. You now know that when ejaculation takes place, semen spurts out through the opening at the tip of a boy's penis. (You can read about semen on page 74 in Chapter 4.)

Ejaculation is the only way that semen can get outside a boy's or a man's body. Since semen is the fluid that transports sperm, this means that ejaculation is the way for sperm to move from the inside to the outside of the body, so that sperm might fertilize a female egg cell (when a man and woman decide they're ready to try to have that happen—more about this later).

Reminder: Sperm contained in the drops of fluid released from the Cowper's glands before ejaculation can also cause a female egg to be fertilized. This is often called pre-ejaculatory fluid.

Sperm may not be part of a boy's beginning ejaculations (just like ovulation may not occur when a girl first gets her period). In time each ejaculation will contain millions of sperm. Since sperm are very, very tiny, you can't just look at your semen and tell if sperm are present. They can only be seen under a microscope.

Many kids confuse a boy's ejaculations with a girl's periods. Ejaculation is *not* a period, but both signal the surest sign of puberty for boys and girls. That's probably the only thing they have in common. An ejaculation is nothing like a period except for the fact that a special fluid is passed out of the body through the genitals.

A girl can't control when she gets her period. It could start anytime, anywhere. An ejaculation is different. It doesn't spurt without advanced notice when a boy is awake. A boy will be able to feel an ejaculation coming on.

So, a boy doesn't have to be concerned that an ejaculation will take him by surprise, at least not while he's awake. It's a different story when he's asleep. His thoughts and dreams might excite the nerves that signal ejaculation, without him even realizing it. If a boy has an ejaculation when he's sleeping, it's called having a *wet dream*. (I'll talk more about this in a little while.) If he has an ejaculation when he's awake, it's just called an ejaculation.

Boys don't need pads for ejaculations like girls do for periods. The little spurt of semen simply comes out (some people call semen *come*) and will soon dry up. Periods are reddish in color; semen is whitish. While periods occur about every four weeks and flow out over several days, it takes only a few seconds for semen to be passed out during ejaculations. These may happen a few times a day—one, two, or more days in a row—or not for several days or weeks. There're no schedules for ejaculations like there are for periods.

Finally, a period is the specially built up lining of the uterus that is no longer needed. Semen is the important fluid that contains living sperm. Girls can't "get" semen and boys can't "get" a period. Amen!

## How Does a Boy's Body Know When to Ejaculate?

Like erections, ejaculations happen because of a reflex. Once again signals are sent to the lower spinal cord. This time the message is in two parts.

First an "ejaculation alert" message is signalled to the internal organs that help to make semen. This tells them to contract and force their fluids along with sperm into the passageway that will lead them into the urethra and out of the penis—sort of like getting ready in the "starting gate."

While the fluids are gathering together, other contractions shut off the bladder from the urethra so that urine does not mix with semen. (All you kids that were concerned about this can breathe a big sigh of relief!)

Now all is ready for the second message that will signal certain muscles in the penis to contract and squeeze the semen through the urethra so it can spurt out of the penis. The contractions usually have a rhythm to them and last for several seconds. How strong these contractions are can be different from man to man and can also vary in the same man from time to time.

Many people make a mistake and call semen, sperm. Sperm is found in semen. The fluid is called semen!

How about a review? A reflex causes a signal to be sent to the "ejaculation control area" in the lower part of the spinal cord. Two messages are sent. The first message tells the inside organs "ejaculatory alert, get your fluids together, be sure to shut off the bladder so that no urine mixes with semen, and get ready to go." The second message says, "Fire away...."

An interesting thing is that once that first message is sent, ejaculation can't be interrupted. That's because the reflex has already set everything in motion and it's too late to stop it. A boy will be able to feel that ejaculation is coming, but he can't prevent it from happening once it's started.

An erection is usually the first step leading to ejaculation, though *not all* erections end in ejaculation! At certain times a boy may wish to allow the sensations that caused an erection reflex (Chapter 5, p. 77) to continue so that stronger feelings of pleasure are felt in and around the area of the penis. These are usually sexual feelings.

If these feelings build up high enough—usually when a boy is touching his penis—the ejaculation reflex will be touched off, messages sent, and you know what happens from there. At the point where these pleasurable feelings are the strongest, a boy may or may not have what's known as an *orgasm* (or-ga-zum) along with his ejaculation. An ejaculation is often accompanied by an orgasm but doesn't have to be.

An orgasm can be felt as nice, kind of tingly feelings of warmth as well as several short contractions—or flutterings—in the genital area. This is a very personal experience and may be slightly different for each person. Both the orgasm and the ejaculation represent a release from the strong pleasurable feelings that were built up.

After erection and ejaculation the penis returns to being soft again. Girls as well as boys can experience orgasms. Even though girls don't have ejaculations as they are described for boys, similar feelings of warmth and pleasure can build up in their clitoris and around their vaginal opening, reach a high point, and can then be released through orgasm. This can happen to girls when they touch their vulva. More will be said about "tingly-when-touched" feelings in Chapter 9.

## When Can You Expect to Start Ejaculating?

Your first ejaculation will usually come after your genitals have begun to grow and after you have grown some pubic hair. But, once again, there aren't any rules. You could start ejaculating as early as age eleven or not until later in your teens. It's up to your hormone schedule.

I can't tell you that you'll ejaculate only when you have a hundred new pubic hairs or more. . . . I can't promise that you'll have started to ejaculate by the time you're fifteen.

All I can hope to do is let you know what to expect, so that if you wake up one morning and find that your sheets have a "funny" spot on them, you shouldn't worry that you've lost control and need diapers again!

Just pat yourself on the back, pinch your cheek in the mirror, and say, "Congratulations, you old thing, you!" And then go on about your day with a special smile because you know that something important has changed in you that will never be the same again. With this change comes new responsibilities, new feelings. . . . You now have the gift of being able to create a new life when and if the time is right for you.

## What About Wet Dreams?

As I told you, a boy is said to have a wet dream if he ejaculates semen while he's sleeping. Another name for wet dream is *nocturnal emission* (nock-ter-nal ee-mish-un). Nocturnal refers to night—you might have learned about nocturnal animals such as the owl or bat. Emission refers to a discharge or flow of fluid.

A boy's first ejaculation most often happens as a wet dream and goes along with pleasurable thoughts. Michael, age seventeen, said that he remembers that his first wet dream happened when he was twelve years old. He was dreaming of kissing his favorite female movie star while they were together on a far, far away private beach. When he woke up, his dream lady had vanished, and only the semen remained to remind him she was there. He said to me, "She was so real. I was disappointed that she went away."

Other boys' dreams are not as "real" and they only have slight memories of what went on. Still others who have wet dreams don't remember dreaming at all. All of these boys are normal.

If you've already had a wet dream, do you remember how you felt the first time you realized you did? If you haven't had one yet, think about what feelings you have about wet dreams. What questions would you like answered? What are your concerns? (You might want to write these down to make sure that you get all the information you need.)

Joel, age fourteen, learned about wet dreams before having them so he wasn't surprised when he discovered a wetness on his sheets. He told me, "When I had my first wet dream, it just proved to me what I thought all along . . . that I was normal!"

Hoorah for Joel! Hoorah for whomever it was who made sure Joel knew that wet dreams are normal and expected. Too many boys who didn't know about wet dreams before having them say they thought they peed in their bed or felt guilty for doing something they thought was wrong, even though they didn't have any idea what it was. They would have been so relieved to understand what was happening to them and to know there's nothing a boy can do to control them while he's asleep. Wet dreams can't be prevented, just accepted and understood as a natural thing for a boy's or man's body to do.

There are some boys and men who have told me they haven't noticed ever having a wet dream. It's possible that they still may have had one but not realized it. It's also possible that they haven't had one. I know of no rules that say you *must* have a wet dream as opposed to ejaculating when you're awake. But since a boy might not have realized his body is ready to ejaculate, the first time it might happen is when he's sleeping and not controlling his thoughts, dreams, and actions.

## How Will You Know If You've Had a Wet Dream?

You may or may not wake up after having a wet dream. If you wake up, you might feel that your pajamas or sheets are slightly damp or even a little sticky. That's how semen might be right after you ejaculate. Then it becomes more liquidy and just dries up.

Many boys are very concerned about being able to tell the difference between urine and semen. Remember I told you if you've been toilet trained for years and suddenly you find your sheets, pajamas, or under-wear (or pillow, sleeping bag, etc.) damp, you can bet it's not urine? Well just so you can make sure for yourself, check the color of the fluid and see how it feels. Semen can be a little bit sticky and has a milky whitish coloring. Urine looks like yellow water and is not sticky.

If you don't wake up, you might feel a slight dampness in the morning, depending upon how much time has passed since your wet dream. Or you may be able to find a spot or two on your sheets or whatever you're wearing, that seems to be slightly off-white where the semen might have dried up.

The amount of semen is usually around one teaspoon of fluid. If you check out how much this is in a measuring spoon, I think you'll agree that it's not very much fluid. So you might not even notice anything!

Just like it doesn't hurt to urinate (pee), it doesn't hurt to pass semen out of your body.

### Is It Scary to Have a Wet Dream?

Perhaps by now you realize that wet dreams are like all the other changes that I've mentioned so far. They're a natural, important part of growing up. Changes become scary when we don't understand what's happening or why.

A good example of how scary the unknown can be is the story told to me by Ralph, who is now nineteen years old. He has a twin brother who was sick on and off when they were younger. Ralph had already had a wet dream and never really discussed it with his twin brother.

One day Ralph walked into his brother's room and saw him hurrying to smear tomato sauce all over his sheets. Ralph said, "Are you crazy? What are you doing that for?" His brother answered in a whisper, "A terrible thing happened and I don't want to have to go to the doctor again. I'll just tell mom that I was eating in bed and accidentally dropped my spaghetti on my sheets. You better not tell!"

Ralph asked, "Well, what happened that was so terrible?" His brother replied, "This stuff came out of my penis and it never happened to me before, it must mean I'm sick again." Ralph said, "That happens to everybody; it's supposed to happen." And then he went on to explain what it was.

Those of you who are still laughing because of the tomato sauce, stop for a moment and think about how scared Ralph's brother must have felt even before he decided that tomato sauce would be a great "cover-up." He had been sick for too long—too many doctors, too much time in bed—and he didn't want to be sick anymore. If only someone had told him that ejaculations were just a natural part of growing up. Wet dreams are expected and can't be prevented.

> Wet dreams don't mean you're sickly,
> Just cause they're a little sticky.
> So be cool if you wake up one morning to see
> A "funny" spot that you know is not pee!
> (*I think these are getting worse?* . . . )

## What Can You Do With Your Sheets?

Well you've got a few choices. Only you can decide which one you feel is best. (I'm sure you can even add your own ideas to my list!)

The first choice is to simply do nothing! Since having a wet dream is so natural—and most boys have them, even dads, since wet dreams don't stop just because you get older—just let the semen dry, leave your sheets on your bed, and forget about it.

If you're embarrassed or concerned that anyone should see, then change your own sheets! Some boys think they need an excuse to have to change them. So they spill milk, chocolate milk, just something wet (yes, tomato sauce too), and that seems to make it okay to have to put them in

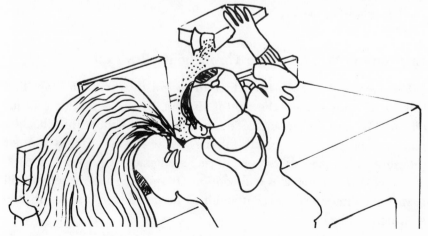

the hamper or wherever. That's really not truthful, but if you need to do that, that's up to you! (I'll never tell.)

## Who Should You Tell If You Have a Wet Dream?

Again the choice is up to you! Boys have asked, "Should I tell my parents? Or my friends?"

This is such a private, personal experience. I imagine if you told your parents about having a wet dream, they'd be really happy that you're developing as you should. It's not the kind of experience where you need help in making a decision—the decision has already been made for you! So it's more a matter of choosing to share because you want to, not because you need to.

One mother told me that she realized she hadn't discussed wet dreams with her thirteen-year-old son. So she went through a whole explanation, and when she was through, her son said, "Gee, thanks mom, I've been having them for two years!"

Ron, age twelve, said, "None of my friends ever discuss wet dreams." Bill, now in his fifties shared, "If we said anything at all about wet dreams it was just because we were trying to act like part of the crowd—and no one would ask questions, since we really didn't know what we were saying, anyway."

I suppose there will be some kids who'll want to discuss them and many others who won't. Use your judgment. It's your experience, so you decide. It might be fun to ask your dad, grandfather, older brother or uncles about when and how they learned about wet dreams. Maybe they used spaghetti sauce too.

## Ejaculations Will Continue Throughout a Boy's Life

When a man gets older—it's so hard to say exactly when, some men find this to be true around the age of sixty or beyond—the force of his ejaculations and the amount of semen may lessen slightly. But a healthy man will be able to ejaculate for the rest of his life. This is another difference from periods that end during menopause (Chapter 3, p. 63).

Since a man's testicles will continue to produce sperm, semen will always contain sperm, even though as he gets older, the number of sperm might be less.

# 7
# Voice Change

## What Does It Mean For Your Voice to Change?

This is one change that you don't have to check out at the beach. All you have to do is listen! Pay attention to the voices of your father, older brother, uncle, grandpa, male teachers, or men on TV and in the movies. Like with everything else you'll see that each person's voice sounds a little different. Some voices are higher, some lower, others soft, still others are deep and booming.

If you sing with your school or religious choir, you might have already noticed that every once in a while, another boy or two will need to move from the higher note to the lower note section. You, too, may have found that the notes you used to sing easily are beginning to be too high. When you strain to reach them, you might even sound squeaky. Yup, you guessed it! A change in the sound of your voice is another natural part of growing up.

When a boy's voice changes, his voice gradually becomes deeper, fuller, and richer.

## When Will Your Voice Start to Change?

Voice change usually takes place around the middle of puberty, after your pubic and body hairs have started to grow and often after genital growth and your first ejaculation.

89

I guess by now you may be tired of having to thank testosterone for your development, but I think it's only fair. After all it's amazing how your hormones keep track of all the changes they have to make! Imagine if your hormones didn't remember to change your voice or if a girl's hormones just plain forgot to give her breasts! (I know, you're probably thinking that you know some girls with forgetful hormones. Give them time, give them time!)

Deepening of your voice will start to happen when testosterone causes your vocal cords and voice box or *larynx* (lar-inks) to grow larger. Some people also call the voice box, the Adam's Apple. You can find it if you move your hand down along your neck from the tip of your chin. At about the middle of the front of your neck, you'll be able to feel a slight bump or ridge. That's it! Some people's bumps are easier to notice than others. That's normal.

Voice change is a good example that testosterone really is responsible for important development all over the body not just in your genital area.

### How Will Your Voice Sound?

Matt, age twelve, said, "I love it when I answer the telephone and people think I'm my father!" Jason, age twelve, said, "I *don't* love it when I answer the phone and people think I'm my mother!"

Though some boys may end up sounding like their parents or other relatives, there's no way to predict that you will too. The best thing is to wait and see. Let your larynx surprise you!

Matt's voice doesn't make him any more manly, and Jason's voice doesn't make him any less manly. There are plenty of grown men with softer, higher voices. It's not what a person sounds like, it's what and who he is.

### How Long Will It Take For Your Voice to Change and What Might It Be Like?

As with many changes in puberty, voice change often takes place over a period of time. While it's changing you might not be able to trust your voice not to crack when you're talking or singing.

Billy, now fourteen, told me, "It took about two years for my voice to finish changing. It really didn't bother me that much. There were a few embarrassing times when I was reading aloud in class and my voice cracked. Otherwise, it was no big thing."

John, age thirteen, said, "I really didn't notice it was happening to me. Other people started saying how different I sounded and then I heard it too. Some of my friend's voices have been cracking a lot, but mine never did."

Bruce, age seventeen, said, "I got used to my mother's friends calling me Lisa (my younger sister) when I answered the telephone. I just politely told them it was me. What I couldn't get used to was when my friends at school cracked up when my voice squeaked. My squeaky voice and their laughter went on for about a year. I stopped talking a lot in public. It was and sometimes still is very embarrassing to talk around girls."

As you can see, each person will grow and change in his own way. Since some boys feel a bit embarrassed that they can't stop their voice from cracking, it would probably be helpful if you wouldn't laugh or make fun when this happens. They're trying very hard to accept and deal with their own changes, just like you're trying to accept yours.

## A Word About Girls' Voices

Though voice change is not considered an official puberty change for girls, their voices also become richer, fuller, and more mature.

Hal, age ten, wanted to know if girls voices cracked like boys' voices do. Not that I know of, Hal. They may crack because a girl is hoarse from a sore throat or screaming but not because of her development.

Listening to the sounds of men's and women's voices around you can be an interesting way to prove that each person is unique. That's very special!

> Remember: Don't judge or make fun of anyone's voice,
> Since voice boxes never give kids a choice.

# Growing Up
# MALE AND FEMALE
# Feeling Good

# 8
# Pubic and Other
# Body Hair

Remember the growth clock idea? That's when your body signals the release of your hormones so you'll begin to experience the changes of puberty. Growing new hair is one of those changes. You can thank your hormones for causing them to appear.

## Pubic Hairs: Where Can You Find Them, Why Do They Grow, What Are They Like?

*Pubic hairs* (pew-bick) are those cute, little curly hairs that grow a few inches below the belly button. For a girl they cover the mons pubis (Chapter 2, p. 35) and continue down between her legs. For boys they grow around the base of the penis.

As with all the changes of puberty, pubic hairs will appear when your own body is ready. Your genitals can thank your pubic hairs for the extra protection. A girl's pubic hair usually starts growing after her breasts swell and before her period. A boy's pubic hair often appears after his penis and testicles show signs of growth, and before his first ejaculation. These are only guidelines—not rules—as sometimes pubic hair growth doesn't work out exactly that way.

You can start looking for them when you're about ten or eleven. But don't be surprised if they don't show up until later.

Since pubic hairs sprout a few at a time, you don't have to be concerned about going to sleep without them and waking up with hundreds. You'll start with two or three (my son, Andy, named his first three, "Harry, Sam, and Fred"!) then grow more and more until your pubic area appears "filled in."

Your body is very clever and knows just how much hair your pubic area should grow. I have never heard of anybody tripping over their pubic hair because it was too long.

Pubic hairs feel and are different than the hairs on your head. They're not as soft to touch. People with dark hair on top usually have dark pubic hair. Light haired people often have light pubic hair. The pubic hairs probably won't match exactly and will usually be a bit darker than on your head.

It's normal to find funny little pubic hairs in your bathtub, on your underwear, and on bathing suits or sheets, just like it's common to find head hairs on your coats, jackets, and sweaters. All you have to do is look at your hairbrush to know that hairs often come out. New hairs grow in to take their place. The same thing happens with pubic and other body hairs.

## When Pubic Hair First Grows In

Jodi, age thirteen, wishes that they would all grow in at once. Said Jodi, "It's really funny looking to just have half."

Bobby, age thirteen, said he was the first one of his friends to really have a lot of pubic hair. He loved to show it off in gym class by taking an extra long time to get out of the shower.

Thirteen-year-old David told me, "When I was at camp last summer, I was more developed than any other kid in my group. No one else had pubic hair and I had a ton. I was very self-conscious cause I remembered what they did to the guy that had them last year—they teased him to death. So I changed in the bathroom most of the time."

Fourteen-year-old Michael changed in the bathroom because he was the only one without pubic hair. The feelings work both ways.

Since pubic hairs are controlled by your hormones, they can't be forced to appear before their own schedule. They also can't be pushed back in once they come out. So the best thing you can do is try to accept yourself for who you are and trust that your body will develop when it's ready.

Repeat three times:   With or without pubic hair
I am a very special person!

## Underarm Hair

Hair will also begin to grow under your arms. It will probably grow some time after your pubic hairs and will be softer. Once again you'll notice a few hairs at first, then more and more. And your body will know how much hair to grow.

An eleven-year-old boy at one of my programs asked, "Does pubic hair grow under your arms?" Underarm hair is *not* pubic hair. Pubic hair is pubic hair. Also underarm hair is softer than pubic hair.

Shaving the hair under your arms seems to depend upon the customs or habits of the people where you live. In the United States most girls and women shave under their arms. They usually wait a few years until they have enough hairs to bother to shave. Shaving can sometimes irritate the tender skin, such as under your arms or on your face. So, if you feel you want to start shaving, it's important to talk about this with your mom or dad so they can help choose the best type of shaver for you and also show you how. In other countries it's common for women not to shave under their arms. Boys and men usually do not shave their underarms in any country. It's a very personal decision.

I often get the question, "If you don't have hair under your arms, should you use deodorant?" The answer is *yes*. Using deodorant doesn't depend on the amount of hair you have. It has to do with how much you sweat! Whether or not you have underarm hair, it's important to use deodorant if you find you're sweating a lot. (More about taking care of your body in Chapter 10.)

Peter, age ten, said, "My big brother wanted hair under his arms so badly. When he finally got it, he stretched out the arm holes of his short sleeved shirts so people could see his hair through the sleeve when he raised his hand in class." Peter went on to tell me that this was really important to his brother because he was shorter than many of his friends. Growing hair made him feel bigger.

Diane, age twenty-three, remembers developing very early. She had a lot of pubic and underarm hair by the time she was eleven and most of her friends had very little or none. She shared, "Whenever I had to change in front of them, I tried to keep my arms in close to my body so no one would notice how much hair I had. My mother thought eleven was too young to shave."

As with other hair that starts to grow during puberty, there can be many feelings that go along with getting underarm hair. So often these feelings are tied up with whether you're first or last among your friends to develop. There are usually less feelings about being different or the only one if you seem to be developing when most of your friends are developing too.

## Hair on Your Chest

Before I talk about hair on a boy's or a man's chest, I want to remind you that girls might also grow a few hairs. As I told you in Chapter 1, these hairs might be around the nipples or the breasts. This is very normal.

A friend of mine told me when he was growing up, his fathers always used to tease that he had a "basketball team of hair on his chest . . . five on each side" (that was supposed to make you smile). The interesting thing is, now that he's all grown up, there aren't that many more "players"!

Some men will be very hairy, with hairs all over their upper and lower chest, shoulders, and even upper back. Others, like my friend with the "basketball team," have only a few. Still others have medium amounts. The amount of hair a boy or man has might also depend upon what part of the world he is from. People from certain races have less body hair than others.

Chest hair usually appears later in puberty. If puberty starts late for you, chest hairs may not show up until you're twenty or older. The important thing to remember is that each boy is going to develop in his own way and the way of his race or ethnic group.

You may grow a lot of hairs on your chest or just a few. The amount of hair has nothing to do with being manly. That depends upon how you are on the inside.

## Mustaches and Other Facial Hair—Shaving

Both boys and girls grow new hairs on their face during puberty. One of the first things to show up is a darkening of the hair around the side burn area and over the upper lip. Depending upon how dark the hair is over the lip it may seem like a mustache. (And sometimes it is!)

I was in the supermarket a few weeks ago and on the check-out line saw a boy who used to be in one of my programs. When I went over to say hi, the first thing his mother said to me was "Look at him! Can you believe his mustache?" He turned right away from me and never looked back. (I was so upset with his mother for making him so embarrassed.)

Some kids are proud of this new growth of hair. Others wish it wasn't there. If anyone (including moms, dads, and kids who tease) talks about this or any other part of your development in a way that makes you feel funny, embarrassed, or angry—tell them how you feel. I hope that boy told his mother what he was feeling when he turned away. That's the only way she'll understand and learn not to do it again.

If the hairs over your lip seem very dark and you have strong feelings about not wanting them there, at least you know you're not the only one who's got those hairs! And you do have a few choices as to what you might do about them.

## If You're a Boy

Try speaking with your parents about shaving. Most parents that I've spoken with want their sons to wait as long as possible before starting to shave. As one parent said, "You shave because the hairs are dark and you don't want them there. But once you shave, they come in even darker and are sort of prickly. The longer you wait to shave again, the more prickly they get. So once you start to shave, you have to keep shaving. I want my son to start as late as possible cause he's going to be shaving for a long time!"

Boys usually do not need to shave until their middle or late teens. As that father said, once you start, that's it. You'll be shaving forever. Some boys will grow hair early, others later. Again you can be manly with or without hairs on your face. If you don't feel very manly, probably you won't be. If you do, then whether or not you have hairs won't matter as much.

When I was in high school, there was one boy in my class who had very dark hair on his face. We called him Shadow. Even if he shaved in the morning, he looked like he had "shadows" on his face before school was over. Though lots of boys were jealous because he needed to shave,

Shadow told me secretly (he was a good friend of mine) that he wished he didn't always have to shave so often.

I guess the best thing is not to compare. What may seem really terrific on someone else might not even be terrific for them and might not work out the best for you.

Do you remember watching and imitating your father shaving when you were a little boy? (I even imitated my father, and I was a little girl! I guess shaving seemed like it would be a lot of fun.) Did you look up and wonder, "When will it be my turn?" Well, your turn will come. If not this year, maybe next. But once you start, you'll do it forever, so think about whether or not you really want to rush it.

Each parent will probably feel a bit differently about shaving. If you're not sure how your parents feel, ask them! If you feel you're ready to shave, make sure you speak with your mom or dad to make sure you know what steps to follow.

### Very Important About Shaving (for both boys and girls)
Whether you use an electric shaver or one with a blade (there are many types to choose from, including disposables—ones you can throw away after using), make sure you clean your shaver properly after each use. You can run the blade shaver under hot water; electric razors are usually cleaned with a special kit. Ask your parents to help you if you're not sure what to do.

Be careful how you shave, since even the shavers that are considered to have safety blades can cut you if you don't know what you're doing (and sometimes even when you do). So remember to get your parents (or someone you trust) to teach you about shaving before doing it yourself.

### If You're a Girl
I strongly suggest you speak with your parents about any of these methods before using them. You would be wise not to use them without permission and proper adult guidance.

Here are a few things you might want to know about if you have unwanted hair on your face or other parts of your body (boys and men might also choose some of these methods).

Tweezing is fine for eyebrows (and even chin hairs) but it's a good idea not to tweeze your mustache. This method can be a bit uncomfortable and has to be done fairly often. Tweezing is not permanent. So if you tweeze just expect the hairs to grow in again and plan to keep on tweezing them out.

Waxing is another way to take care of unwanted hair (this can be used for eyebrows, legs, mustaches, and other areas). Wax is spread over the unwanted hair in the direction of the hair growth. A special cloth is used to remove the wax and with it comes the unwanted hairs. Properly done, waxing usually lasts several weeks and is best handled by someone who is trained to do this.

Bleaching unwanted hairs is another choice. Instead of removing hair, it's like using a cover up to lighten the hair that is still there. Bleaches that are prepared for facial (fay-shul) hair (hair on the face) can be bought in a drugstore. Sometimes bleaches will result in a difference in color, causing the area above the lip to look yellowish or orangy. Be sure to watch out for redness or irritation if you have sensitive skin.

You also might want to know about a procedure called *electrolysis* (ee-leck-tro-li-siss). This is a way to permanently remove unwanted hair from the face, legs, or other areas of the body. After several treatments (some people need many, others less) this method can remove hair permanently. It must be done by a trained electrolysist.

Be careful of you use any of the cremes for removing unwanted hair (often called superficial hairs) that can be bought in a drug store. The chemicals in them might cause irritation if your skin is sensitive. Along with the unwanted hair, it's also possible for fine, baby hair to be removed that would probably disappear by itself.

Even more desirable would be not to do anything. It may not make you feel completely better—but perhaps at least a bit better—to know that lots of kids have those same hairs to deal with, just like you! If you think you can live with them until the more permanent hairs take form, then just leave the hairs alone and wait.

## Important Message for Boys and Girls

If you tamper with your "shadows" in a way that harms your hair, it might never lighten up! Every time you tamper with your hair, you cause something to happen to it. Be careful not to take advice from someone who doesn't know the facts. Never use a chemical, creme, or anything on your hair that you have not first discussed with your parents, doctor, or at least a trusted and informed adult.

If you are concerned about mustaches or other hairs on your face, let your parents know how you feel. They may not be in favor of any correction method. I'm not suggesting any one in particular but hope it will be helpful for you to know what choices you have to consider. What you do is up to you and your parents to decide!

## Hair on Your Legs—Shaving

Shaving legs seems to be done mostly by girls and women. As with underarm hair, whether you shave your legs may depend upon the customs and habits of the people in your culture. It's another personal decision.

Cathy, now thirty-two, told me, "I used to be very embarrassed about having so much hair on my legs, even though it was very light. I used to hide my legs under my desk in school, putting them as far under as they could go. My mother finally gave me permission to shave them during the summer when I was sixteen. I was going to be in a talent show at camp and I begged for permission to shave because I was planning to wear shorts and didn't want all the hair on my legs to show up on stage. My mom figured it was time and let me do it. I was so relieved and have been shaving my legs every since."

Robin, now age twenty-eight, told me her "hairy-legs story." Picture this. Robin couldn't stand having such dark, hairy legs when she was growing up. At fourteen she refused to go to her aunt's wedding unless her mother let her shave. She claims that her stockings would have looked awful with tiny black hairs showing through the nylon stockings. Even though she pouted and sulked for a week before the wedding, her mother wouldn't give in. So Robin started a big fight and never went.

As with everything else, each parent will probably feel differently about if and when you should start shaving your legs. Once you start, you need to continue, because the hairs get prickly and slightly darker. But if you decided to stop shaving and let your hairs grow long again, they would eventually get softer.

A few weeks ago my daughter brushed up against my legs and I hadn't shaved that day. All she said was, "yuck!" Those little hairs become prickly if you wait too long to shave. If your hair is light, you probably can wait a few days or more in between shaves. Each girl has to decide for herself how often she needs to shave in order to feel good.

Talk with your parents if the hair on your legs concerns you. It might help to remember that what you feel is *so* noticeable, may only be noticeable to *you*. I don't know if anyone really paid attention to Cathy's legs before she hid them under her desk. She was the one who felt so self-conscious. (She told me no one ever said anything to her.) But she had to deal with her feelings and try to make herself feel as comfortable as possible. You owe it to yourself to be honest with yourself and your parents. (They can help!)

### Very Important About Shaving Your Legs

When you're ready to shave, don't shave above your knees. By the time you're in your twenties, this hair will not be very noticeable. If you shave or bleach it, the hair will change texture (become more coarse or rough feeling) and will not be as soft as it was.

> Remember: Hairs may be fuzzy, straight, prickly, fluffy, curly.
> You may want them, or may not—
> But what you get is what you've got!
>
> Hairs are hair.
> People are people.
> People can be special with or without hair!

Also remember: Even if your parents are set against your shaving or doing anything about hair that is bothering you, let them know how upset you are. They may not realize how strongly you feel.

# 9
# Tingly When Touched Feelings

## What Kind of Feelings Are They and Where Can They Be Felt?

Gently stroking your fingertips will probably make them feel nice and tingly. This is because there are lots of nerve endings at the tips of your fingers that make them extra sensitive to touch. The more nerve endings, the more tingly you can feel.

If you read Chapters 2 and 4 on girls' and boys' Private Parts, you'll probably remember that I spoke about certain areas in and around your genitals that also have many nerve endings. Like your fingertips, they can be sensitive or "tingly when touched."

Because your genitals are special, very personal, private areas of your body, the "tingly when touched" feelings that can be felt in the genitals are also thought of as personal, private feelings.

Sometimes these tingly feelings are felt when you're not even expecting them, like when tight clothing rubs against your genitals when you're bicycle riding, taking a shower or a bath, soaping your genitals, sleeping on your stomach, or pressing your thighs together.

Other times these "tinglies" can be felt because a person decides to make them happen. Girls or boys (adults too) may purposely touch the sensitive areas of their genitals just so they can feel those feelings. This kind of touching can result in having an orgasm (Chapter 6, page 83).

When this is done on purpose, it is said that the person is *masturbating* (mass-ter-bay-ting). Masturbating or *masturbation* (mass-ter-bay-shun) is a word that really perks up people's ears because it is private behavior and few people openly talk about it. So when someone takes the chance and decides to bring up this hush-hush topic, people's faces often get pink and red and they may giggle out of embarrassment.

## Why People Can't Talk About Masturbation

Feelings about masturbation have a very interesting history. False beliefs were passed down from generation to generation that made people think something bad would happen if they masturbated. For years and years people really believed masturbation would cause hair to grow out of the palms of their hands; make their genitals dry up and fall off; make them have a swaggering walk; make them have cold, clammy hands; give them shifty eyes, weak shoulders, hunch backs, and warts. The list goes on and on.

While I can promise you these are myths and won't happen, I know there are still many people who aren't sure. Somewhere in the back of your mind, even you may be wondering if masturbation is really okay.

When most little kids begin to discover their genitals, they usually touch them because they're curious and probably have no idea what their parents think about what they're doing. They often continue to touch because it makes them feel good and hardly ever know this is called masturbation.

As girls and boys reach puberty, they may or may not start to masturbate if they haven't already. Either way is fine! Those who do often seem to sense that this should be done alone and not talked about. A remark, look, or scowl made by someone either now or years ago may have given them the message to keep masturbation private or not do it at all.

Some kids who touch themselves privately would never say so in public because they'd expect the other kids would laugh or spread the word around (chances are, they would!).

If kids learn that genital touching is to remain private, and no one knows what anyone else is doing, then they never seem to be able to get the straight truth about it without someone joking, laughing, rolling his or her eyes around in their heads, or walking away. As a result kids can feel awfully guilty and surely won't talk about it. Kids who masturbate may feel they are doing something that no one else in the world is doing or has done. Now you know that's not true.

## There Are Lots of Different Feelings About Such "Tinglies"

Though many boys and girls masturbate, the amount of boys who do is greater than the amount of girls. Perhaps this has something to do with the fact that a boy's penis is "out there" and a girl has to explore the many folds of her vulva in order to find her clitoris and other sensitive parts.

Of the boys and girls who do not masturbate, some don't realize they can touch themselves in order to get tingly feelings. Others know they can if they wish but have made a decision not to. That's okay!

Kevin, age eleven, said, "Sometimes when I touch myself, I feel guilty because it feels so good and I don't think I'm supposed to have such feelings."

Lori, age twelve, said, "I don't think I'd ever want to do that!"

Thirteen-year-old JoAnn told me, "Yes, I do it. It feels really good. But I've never talked about it with anyone. I think if my parents found out, they'd kill me."

Sharon, age forty-five, shared, "My mother caught me touching myself when I was about eleven. She walked into my bedroom and asked me what I was doing. I was so glad the lights were dark because I was blushing horribly. I was so embarrassed and didn't know what to say. I didn't even know there was a name for what I was doing! She told me that she hoped never to catch me doing something like that again. Girls don't do that sort of thing!" (You know that touching is not for boys only!)

Ten-year-old Bobby said, "My Sunday school teacher told me it's a sin. Now I don't know what to do because how could something that feels so good be a sin?"

Fourteen-year-old Sari shared, "Masturbating is the last thing I'd think of doing. I don't understand why anyone would want to touch their genitals on purpose. It just seems strange."

Tom, age eighteen, shared that when he was in the seventh grade, he tried to talk about masturbation with a friend, just to see if his friend would say that he did it too. Instead his friend said, "Only weirdos do that." Tom didn't discuss it with his friends again until he was much older.

Twelve-year-old Todd told me, "I talked about this with my parents and they think it's a real healthy thing to do. They're glad it feels so good."

As you can see, there are so many different kinds of feelings about "tinglies." Some kids feel guilty and confused about having such feelings, especially if they're caught. Others feel "tinglies" are great; still others don't feel they're right for them at all. Lots of times these feelings come from how we are raised and what our parents, teachers, friends, brothers, sisters, and religious leaders tell us.

## How Parents Feel About "Tingly When Touched" Feelings

Most kids have told me they have not talked about this kind of touching with their parents. Most parents never discussed it with their parents either! Some parents would probably think it's great if their child felt good about these feelings. Many other parents, often due to religious teachings and values, feel masturbation is wrong and would probably be upset if they learned their child enjoyed such feelings.

So many parents still feel uncomfortable and confused about masturbation. They want the best for their children as they grow up but are still not sure whether such touching is healthy or not. And it's hard for them to talk about it.

Often times when parents don't have positive feelings toward masturbation and are concerned that their children might masturbate too much, they will give them a mean stare and ask them in their most parental tone of voice, "What are you doing?" Or they will try to discourage their children from touching themselves. This especially happens when children are young and don't realize that they should touch themselves privately. Do you remember any stares from your parents for something like this? Did they bring a new toy over to you in the middle of when you were touching just to take your attention away? Think back. . . .

Other parents feel that masturbation is a healthy, normal part of their child(ren)'s development. They want their child(ren) to understand that touching themselves can be a very pleasurable and joyful experience. But they also want their child(ren) to understand that certain behaviors are private and are to be done in one's bedroom not in public.

Learning about your body and especially your genitals starts very young. It might give you a better understanding of how you feel today if you try to think back to when you were little. What messages about your body and touching did your parents give you? Did they make you feel good, bad, or guilty about interest in your own body? Did you feel you could ask them anything about yourself and your development? What do you wish you could have asked them but never did? Can you ask them now?

## Touching Yourself Is a Choice

Touching yourself is a *choice*.

If you choose to touch, it's healthy. Lots of people of all ages do (yes, even senior citizens!). You won't grow warts or hair on your palms, or need special glasses if touching makes you "tingle" and feel good. Touching doesn't have anything to do with who you like or what type of person you are.

If you don't choose to touch, that's healthy too. Lots of people of all ages don't.

Wanting to touch your genitals is a natural part of growing up and developing sexual feelings. (In fact your hormones even help to bring out these new feelings.) What you do about these feelings has to do with what you feel and what you've been taught. If you've never discussed this or haven't been taught anything one way or another, then do what makes you feel comfortable and good.

If you find that touching your genitals feels good, but you know your parents or religious teachings say it's not right, then you'll have to try to balance your own feelings with respect for your parents and your religion. This is a very personal decision. If your feelings confuse you, I encourage you to talk about them with your parents or religious leaders.

Also many kids feel less confused when they discuss masturbation with their older sister(s) or brother(s). They can really help you to make up your mind about what's right for you. Sometimes a special friend (one you know would never laugh at you or make you feel foolish for bringing up the subject) can help clear up the mystery. Often times your friend can be relieved to know that you have the same feelings as he or she does.

Sometimes it's difficult to know how your friend, sister(s), or brother(s) might react to the topic of masturbation. But if you feel close to them, it's worth taking the risk.

# 10
# Taking Care of Your Body and Appearance

## Keeping Your Body Clean

Along with all the other physical changes of puberty, your sweat glands will cause you to perspire (sweat!) more and your oil glands will cause your skin to become more oily. All the more reason to shower or bathe regularly.

Even if you don't sweat a lot, make yourself a bathing or shower schedule. If you're old enough to be reading this book, you're old enough to really try to stick to that schedule.

If you take a shower in the morning, then play hard at a sport during the day, take an extra shower at night or at least take one the next morning. That way you'll keep your body fresh, feeling good, and clean. You'll also prevent unpleasant odors (phew!) from building up.

Regular washing habits are also important because your skin is constantly replacing old cells with new ones. It's healthy to wash the old ones from your skin surface. You can't really see the teeny cells sliding off your body, so don't bother to look for them. Just wash!

All parts of your body need washing . . . every little crack and fold.

## What Can You Do If Someone You Know Smells Awful

One of the harder things to tell someone is that they smell. Did you ever sit next to someone in class who had body odor (B.O.)?

There was a girl who sat next to me in my seventh grade math class who I remember smelled awful! I was too embarrassed to tell her. I thought of leaving a note on her desk or in her locker saying, please wash. I think I also thought of wearing noseclips! Or possibly leaving a bar of soap on her desk with a note saying, hint, hint. Finally I spoke with my teacher and asked to change my seat. I also asked the teacher to speak to that person about her washing habits and to tell her that maybe people would like her more if they could stand being close to her.

I guess if I were the one who smelled, it would be a bit (a lot?) embarrassing for someone to just come up and tell me that. But it would be more embarrassing if I just went on smelling with everyone gasping and whispering about it behind my back, trying to stay as far away as possible.

I feel the kindest thing that you can do if you're bothered by a person's smell, is speak with them in private. If it's hard for you to talk with them about this, you can start with, "This is not easy for me to say. . . ." You might go on saying, "I think you probably would want to know that kids are being bothered by your smell. They're beginning not to want to get close. Maybe if you washed more, people would be friendlier." Or, "You're really a nice person. But it's hard to be near you because of the way you smell."

Of course I suppose you could just go right up to someone and say, "You smell gross," but that wouldn't be very sensitive. Honest, yes. Kind, no! Just keep in mind that it will help to make them understand that you are saying whatever you say because you care about them. And you'd rather tell them straight out than whisper about it to other kids behind someone's back.

Sometimes it's the teacher who smells! That can be tougher to deal with. At least if you tell a classmate he or she smells, they won't give you a bad grade! (Only kidding that a teacher would change your grade if you told them.) I would like to think that teachers, too, would appreciate knowing that something about them is unpleasant to other people, especially when they can easily do something about it.

Jessica, age ten, told me, "I liked my piano lessons but my teacher's perfume was horrible. She was a very good teacher but I hated being near her because her perfume smelled too much." Jess asked her Mom to ask the teacher if she would mind not wearing perfume on lesson days. The teacher was happy to know about Jess's feelings and Jess liked her lessons much better without her teacher's smell.

Unless someone is told about body odor, he or she may not be able to guess. It's a real caring thing to do to let them know. Just imagine how you would feel if someone didn't tell you.

## Keeping Your Clothes Clean

Even if you shower very often, you can blow it by wearing dirty or unfresh clothing over your clean body.

Kids and adults need to change their underwear daily and change their jeans, shirts, or anything else every few days at the most. Kids notice when teachers wear the same thing every day. Kids also notice when other kids don't change their clothes.

Some people don't have much money to spend on clothes and may only have a few changes. But no matter how many clothes you own, there's no excuse for those clothes to be smelly and unclean. Even if they have a few holes in them, your holes can be clean too!

## Deodorants and Antiperspirants

If you find you're beginning to perspire a lot, it's time to use a *deodorant* (dee-o-dor-ant) or *antiperspirant* (an-tee-per-sper-ant). A deodorant helps to control the odor that can result from sweating while an antiperspirant helps to reduce wetness and control how much you perspire. (I'm beginning to feel like a commercial!)

Most brands give you a choice of sprays, roll-ons, sticks, and powders. You put them on under your arms (on your armpits) before putting on clothing. Some feel dry when you first apply them, others feel sort of wet. (It's a good idea to let your armpits dry before getting dressed.) Some are just deodorants, some are antiperspirants, and others are both in one.

You may have to test out a few until you find one that works for you. You can also choose if you want them scented, with a smell, or unscented, without a smell. You might want to try one that your parent is using, ask your friends what they use, or just make a decision on your own.

Be careful not to apply a deodorant or antiperspirant on broken skin or if you have a rash under your arms. If you have a rash that takes a long time to clear up, speak to your parents and they may need to check with your doctor.

*Reminder:* Even if you don't have hair under your arms, use deodorant or antiperspirant if you are perspiring more and more.

## Keeping Your Face Clean

Keeping your face clean goes deeper than just washing chocolate off the corner of your mouth after finishing an ice cream cone.

Here again you need to develop healthy washing habits. Your skin will probably look and feel better if you do.

Washing your face daily with good mild soap and water will help open up the pores of your skin and keep them clean.

If your skin is sensitive or allergic and breaks out in a rash or pimples from your regular soap, let your parents know there are soaps that your druggist or doctor can suggest that are specially made for allergic skin.

If you're wearing any kind of makeup—I'll talk about this soon—it's very important to wash it off each day. *Don't* leave it on for the next morning.

## Keeping Your Teeth and Breath Clean

I don't need to say much more than brush regularly—in the morning, after meals, if possible, and before going to bed—but you know that already. I used to say that people who didn't brush in the morning had flannel mouth. Yuck!

It's also important that you learn how to floss your teeth with dental floss. You can ask your dentist or dental *hygienist* (hi-gee-en-ist) to instruct you in moving the thin string through your teeth to prevent decay and the buildup of dental *plaqué* (plack).*

You can use a mouthwash after you brush to make your breath feel that much more fresh. (Some kids don't need to take anything to have a fresh mouth!)

Even nice people can have bad breath. Keep in mind the kind of things you eat. They can give you a clue as to times your breath might be stronger than others. For example if you eat onion rings for lunch and don't get a chance to brush, you might want to stay a little farther away from your friends when you talk with them. Onions can be yummy but can really affect your breath. Or you can simply say, "Watch out, don't come too close. I have onion breath!" And then it won't matter as much because they'll know that you know.

Since we eat different things all the time, some stronger than others, it's hard to completely keep unpleasant odors away. Besides cleaning your teeth and trying to prevent cavities, regular brushing (along with

---

*Dental plaqué is made up of germs and food bits and is held onto the teeth by the sticky substance in *saliva* (sa-lie-va), the fluid given off by the mouth, like when your mouth waters. Right after it forms, it is soft enough to be removed by brushing your teeth and flossing. If you leave it on the surface of your teeth for too long, it can harden and become difficult to get rid of. The hardened dental plaqué has to be removed by a dentist or dental hygienist.

It's important to keep in mind that dental plaqué forms about every twenty-four hours and therefore should be removed each day.

mouthwash, if you wish) will help to cover up the old smells and make way for the new ones.

If someone has bad breath most of the time, the same things I suggested for body odor apply here. Telling someone about his or her bad breath is a caring thing to do. As uncomfortable as it might be for you to say it and for them to hear it, usually people would rather know than not know. Only then will they realize they've got to do something about it.

Once again a teacher with bad breath can be a bit tougher to deal with than a friend. Steve, now twenty, told me, "When I was in high school, my friends and I left a gift-wrapped bottle of mouthwash on one of our teachers' desk. We were thankful he took the hint. I guess we just didn't realize we could have spoken to him about it."

## Braces

If you're one of the thousands of kids that must wear braces, just keep telling yourself, "I'm going to look great when the braces come off!"

You may feel they're a big pain and probably wish you never had to deal with them, but this is one of those times when a few years of "bother" can be worth the happiness and good feelings about how you look when you don't have to wear them anymore.

Be sure to get lots of information from your dentist (who takes regular care of your teeth) and orthodontist (who puts on braces and cares for your teeth when they are not lined up properly) about what kinds of food are right for you to eat with your braces. Gooey, gummy, hard, chewy food is usually a "no-no"; fresh vegetables and fruit are easier to manage when cut into smaller pieces.

It's very important to clean your braces after meals (so you don't walk around with your lunch stuck in between the wires—gross!). Make sure to ask your orthodontist or dentist how to do that properly.

## Keeping Your Hair Clean

More washing habits—shampoo your hair regularly. If you don't it can start to smell and will probably look like spaghetti that should have been thrown out last week! Washing it daily or every other day would be terrific. Try not to wait more than a few days, unless, of course, you're sick. It's important not to use a shampoo that will dry out your hair. If your shampoo label says acid balanced or low pH, you'll know it will nourish your hair properly.

If your hair is very dry and that's bothering you, speak with your parents about your concerns. It may be that you need to change shampoos. Or you may need to use a *conditioner* (con-dish-un-er) along with your shampoo.

Some conditioners, like creme rinses, work on the top layer of your hair to help to reduce tangles so you can comb it more easily and not break the hair strands (that's when you get split ends).

Other conditioners work on the deeper layers in your hair and add ingredients that help prevent hair damage. They help to give hair the ability to stretch and return to normal (so it won't break), add moisture (moisturizers do this), and make it softer to touch.

Some day you might find little flaky, white flecks appearing around your shoulder. They especially show up on dark sweaters, shirts, or coats. Not to worry! This simply means that your scalp is dry and it's a helpful signal for you to try to do something about it by using moisturizers. Also check the shampoo you're using. It may be irritating your scalp and causing this problem. You may want to try a different shampoo.

If you can't clear your dandruff up by using a quality shampoo with a conditioner, speak to your parents. Advice from your doctor may be necessary.

## Hairstyles

I guess one of the most important things about your hairstyle is whether you can look in the mirror, pinch your cheeks, and say, "You delicious looking thing." Your hairstyle should be attractive for you and make you feel good about yourself!

This means that even if fifteen of your friends have decided to wear their hair a certain way, you can decide for yourself if you even want to think about that style for you. Their hairstyle may not make you feel good. Each person has a right to his or her own style.

If the only way you'll be accepted is to wear your hair like everyone else, then I suggest you may need to start finding other friends who realize that hairstyles don't make the person. People can have beautiful hair and be awful people inside—or they can be wonderful. (Beautiful hair people can even smell from body odor!) People without the latest hairstyle can really be nice—or not. Being nice usually has nothing to do with hairstyles.

Tammy, age fourteen, told me, "I got a new haircut and really liked it. Then I went to school and the kids teased me and made me feel awful." Rachel, age twelve, said, "It took me three weeks before I tried wearing my hair in a ponytail to school. I loved it at home but was afraid people wouldn't like it because it was different than my other style."

Billy, now age forty, had lots of hair until his famous very very short haircut in the seventh grade. He refused to take his hat off in school for three weeks until some new hair grew in. Says Billy, "I felt like a freak. Everyone would have made more fun of me if I took off my hat. It was bad enough with it on because everyone knew why I was wearing it!"

It's real natural for kids to care what other people say. Adults do the same. But it's one thing to let other people tell you what's right for you and quite another to listen to people you respect, think about what they say, and then make your own decision based upon your own feelings.

Sometimes it will be tough to stand up to everyone and be who you are. So many people try to tell others what to do, what to wear, what to say, how their hair looks best, and so on. The day you believe that it's your body, your clothes, your hair, and your right to make your appearance feel good to you, is the day you'll not let other people rule your feelings.

You want a perm really badly? If your parents say okay, then why not try it; that's the only way you'll find out if it's right for you. You want to let your hair grow to see what a different style looks like? Why not!

It was real interesting talking with Jeannie, age thirteen, who had a new hairstyle that all her friends hated. Three weeks after they teased her, one, then two, then more, decided they wanted to try that style too.

Chances are whatever style you wear will be comfortable, easy to manage, and flattering for you. Enough said!

## More About Perms

If you want this kind of a curly look, it's a good idea to find a beauty salon that will take the time to explain to you and your parents exactly what they plan to do to your hair. Perms should last about two to four months, depending upon how long your hair is and how fast it grows.

## Combs and Brushes

They're those things with handles on one end and teeth or bristles on the other. The idea is to pull them through your hair regularly. Even a great hairstyle can look like a mop if you don't! Be sure to clean your combs and brushes regularly. If they're dirty, they can help create unwanted scalp conditions. Besides, dirty combs and brushes look gross.

## A Personal Word About Taking Care of Your Own Hairstyle

It's real helpful for you to learn how to do your own hair. If you depend upon your mom, dad, sister, or brother to do your hair for you, one day they won't be home and you'll be left wondering how you will ever face people if you have to do it.

My doing-your-own-hair story is this. My mom always used to do my hair for me. Until one night she decided that it was time that I learn how to do it myself. She refused to help me and said I should try my best.

I cried and yelled and blamed her for the fact that I would be ugly in school the next day. But none of my begging helped. She was sticking to it and I was forced to try.

To my surprise I was able to do it. And from that night on, I've done my hair myself. It didn't take very long for me to feel that I was the only one to be able to do my hair the way I really liked it.

It's interesting how we sometimes have to be forced to learn. I encourage each of you to at least try to do your hair on your own. Try on the weekends, for starters—if you wish. But start. That way you'll soon be able to be responsible for your own hair care.

My mom told me afterward that it was such a hard thing for her to do. It would have been so simple to just come out of her room and set my hair for me. But that wouldn't have helped me learn.

## Taking Care of Your Nails

First of all, never cut, pick at, or bite your *cuticles* (Q-ti-kulls). These are the areas of thin, sometimes hard skin that peek out from around the back of each nail. It's good to push your cuticles back, but this should only be done when they are wet, like after a bath or shower. This can be done with a soft Q-tip or towel. You can injure the cuticle or nail bed, which is right behind each cuticle, if you push them back when they are dry.

Your nails will grow faster if you regularly move your cuticles back off your nail. They will look nicer if you keep them clean and try to let them grow as long as it is comfortable for you. Keep your hands clean too. Of course, no nail biting, please!

Nails should be filed straight across. Don't file into the corners. Both boys and girls should keep their hands and nails groomed. A good hand cream will help to keep your hands softer, especially after you've been in windy, cold weather, in the sun, in the water, etc. Using a moisturizing cream on your face is also a good idea to help prevent dryness.

It wouldn't be fair not to mention your toe nails. Please cut them straight across too. Are you one of those people who cuts his or her toe nails or one who lets them grow so long that they're about to cut through your socks or maybe even your shoes? Well I know I've given you a lot to think about, but see if you can remember your toes too.

## Athlete's Foot

It's a good idea to dry in between your toes so the area doesn't stay moist. This will help prevent an infection called athlete's foot, which is caused by an organism called a *fungus*. I've already told you that some infections are caused by bacteria. This is another type of infection.

*Fungi* (fun-jie, many fungus), love moisture and darkness and may try to grow there. Lots of kids and adults get this. (You don't have to be an athlete to have it!)

Athlete's foot causes the area in between your toes to itch and sometimes peel. Because this can be spread, it's wise to use your own towel and make sure it's cleaned. Even if you don't have it, other kids might, and they may not know to cover the infected area (by keeping their socks on or by wearing shoes). They may not even know they have it! Or they may be embarrassed to let anyone know they have it (by protecting their feet) and will still go around barefoot. To lessen your chance of getting athlete's foot you might consider wearing thongs any time you're in a public shower area or locker room.

There are special creams and powders to treat athlete's foot. So tell your parents if you even think you might have it and they'll help you to take care of it as soon as possible.

## Pimples or Acne (ak-nee)

Hillary, age ten, looked in the mirror one morning and said, "Is that a pimple? It better not be. I don't deserve it!"

Well, Hillary, even nice people have pimples. In fact it's probably safe to say that pimples visit most people at one time or another. Pimples are an expected part of puberty, not one of the best parts, but at least kids who have one, a few, or tons of pimples can know they've got lots of company.

Pimples show up because pores of the skin get plugged up with waxyish oil. So often pimples result because the oil and sweat glands in your skin are changing. They also can result from unclean washing habits. But just because someone has pimples doesn't mean he or she doesn't wash. They may have very clean habits but still get pimples. Some girls get pimples around the time of their periods.

Besides appearing on your face, sometimes pimples cluster on your neck, back, and even your buttocks (rear end or behind). This can possibly happen due to irritation from underwear, tight jeans, or the laundry detergent that is used to clean your clothes. Sometimes it happens in the summer when you sit around in wet bathing suits.

Usually pimples will show up as whiteheads or blackheads. Black-heads appear as blackish pimples on the surface of the skin. Whiteheads happen when the waxy oil shows under the surface of the skin and appear whitish when they come to a head and open up on the surface.

Neither whiteheads or blackheads should be *squeezed!* If you apply a hot washcloth to the pimple (as hot as you can stand it), this will help to bring all the pus to the surface. Then put on some alcohol and let it dry itself out, being careful not to puncture it.

If you squeeze your pimple, part may be squeezed out, but there probably will be another half or so that can squeeze inward (back into the surface of the skin) and cause a hard knot underneath. Sometimes squeezing a pimple can cause an infection in your entire body (because the pus can cause bacteria to travel through the body).

Medicated acne (pimple) creams can be used at night. Antibacterial soaps and pore cleansers can help prevent and treat pimples. If pimples are bothering you, make sure you speak with your parents. They can also get advice from the pharmacist or your doctor.

All you have to do is look at the faces of kids whose bodies have started to develop and change. Keep looking from day to day. Only some of the kids who don't have pimples will get away with not having them at all. Most kids will have at least a few. Pimples are kind of sneaky. They'll appear one day, disappear in a few days, only to appear again—maybe in the same spot, maybe in a different spot. You really can't count on a pimple to do what you want it to do.

Thirteen-year-old Janie said, "As soon as you think your face has cleared up, they can come back to haunt you again. I hate the way they make me look."

Rodney, age twelve, said, "I don't mind a couple of pimples. They're just a part of adolesence." (A-doe-less-sense, the period of years between childhood and adulthood).

Rodney, Janie, and so many kids that I've spoken with have different attitudes and feelings about pimples. Some accept them and treat them and don't get hung up on having them. Others really are embarrassed, feel like their friends are looking at their pimples all the time and thinking how awful their face looks.

If you also have been embarrassed by your pimples, it's very natural to feel that way. Maybe you, Janie, and any other kids who might get pimples in the growing-up years would be less embarrassed if you realized there are loads of other kids who have this problem too. Hardly any kids are completely pimpleproof.

If you *don't* squeeze and *don't* pick at them, they'll have a better chance of healing quickly without leaving any marks on your skin. Remember to use lots of hot water to open up your pores.

Pimples will go away on their own time and have nothing to do with what food you eat (even chocolate and french fries can't be blamed for pimples). Some will stay longer, others will seem to disappear very quickly. For each person, pimples will be slightly different.

So much for pimples! Let's move on.

## Using Makeup

Fourteen-year-old Jennifer told me, "I was allowed to have my own lipstick in the seventh grade. After all those years of watching my mom use hers, it felt great to have my own. But I'm still not allowed to use eye makeup. Some of my friends started to, but my parents are really strict about it."

Laurie, age twenty-five, talked with me about her mom's "wet test." Her mom wouldn't give her permission to wear eye makeup. Said Laurie, "Most of my friends wore makeup and I didn't want to feel left out. So, I had to sneak putting it on after leaving my house in the morning. When my mom asked me if I was wearing it, I said no. Most of the time I got away with it, except when she gave me the wet test. She'd put water on my eyes and if makeup came off, she'd know I was wearing it and wasn't telling the truth. Then she'd give me some kind of punishment and get upset with me. It was really hard, though. I didn't want to lie to her but I didn't want to feel left out either."

Danny, age eleven, said, "I think some girls look stupid the way they put on so much makeup. I don't think it's right until about the eighth grade." Erin, age eleven, agrees with Danny about eye makeup but thinks it's okay to use a little lipstick at "special times."

Beth, age thirteen, said her mom lets her wear eye makeup if she wants to, as long as it's not too heavy. Debra, age twelve, said, "Even if my mom or dad gave me permission, I wouldn't want to wear it anyway. None of my friends do and I think it's silly for kids my age to start."

So many different feelings. The decision to wear makeup is very personal. Using it seems to depend on three main things: when you are ready, when your friends are ready, and when your parents give you permission to use it.

## How Much is Too Much?

I guess if kids start mistaking you for someone who should be in the circus, you'll know you look more like a clown than the regular old kid that you are. If you look in the mirror and wonder who it is staring back at you, that would be another clue that you might have used too much. But it's also possible that the "new" face in the mirror may take a little getting used to. So give yourself a little time to think about your feelings. The nice thing is that you can change your mind.

## How Much is Enough?

Only you can answer that for yourself (with the guidance of your parents). I feel that enough means using as much as you need to make you feel that bit more attractive—an accent, a touch, so that it shows in a very soft, flattering way. More than that really makes me question what you're trying to say about yourself.

Many kids use heavy makeup to try to get others to pay attention to them. Many use too much because it makes them look tough, cool, and maybe even older.

I think it's very important for you to realize that your clothes, whether or not you comb your hair, how neat you are, how clean you are, how much makeup you use, all make a statement about who you are as a person. Even when you don't say a word, people will look at you and get a certain *impression* (im-press-shun), a feeling about you. Not that you're dressing or acting the way you do for everyone else, it's just that you need to look yourself straight in the eye and be happy with what you see, no matter what your friends think or do. If you're honest with yourself, then probably you'll be able to answer if you feel good looking that way or if you think it's just not for you.

*Real important:* Make sure whatever makeup you do use is quality makeup. Your skin is soft and sensitive. If you're using eye makeup, be careful not to go too close to the inside of your eye. And don't go to sleep at night with your makeup on. Cleanse or cold cream it off each day then put it on again in the morning, if you wish.

### It's Important to Exercise

It's very important to make time for physical activity. Whether you run, swim, dance, skate, or play sports with other kids, try to fit some kind of exercising into your schedule a few times a week. This is a great goal to have all throughout your life.

It's healthy to balance work—(and TV)—with exercise. It's great for your body, great for how you feel, can be very relaxing, and can be lots of fun! You don't have to be a super athlete to be able to enjoy activities that feel good to you. Go at your own rate with what you like to do. If you're not sure about what you like, try a few activities until you find one that's fun.

Some people make the mistake of thinking that if they only have fifteen minutes or half an hour, it's not enough time to bother trying to exercise. After all, what could be done in such a short period of time? The answer is, "More than you think!"

Even if you jump rope (a good one to get has ball bearings in the handles), do sit-ups, or walk or run around your block a few times you'll be surprised at what a difference it can make in how you feel. When you return to your studying, or whatever, you'll be refreshed and probably much more able to concentrate.

If you already exercise, terrific! If you don't, how about taking the first step? At least think about what you'd like to do and when you might fit that activity into your schedule—then you're on your way!

## Eating Properly, Getting Enough Sleep

Eating right is not only very important to how you look and how your body grows but also to how you feel and how much energy you have.

Not taking in enough food or the right kinds of food is like trying to run a coal furnace without supplying it with enough coal. How do you expect your body to do all that you'd like it to do without giving it the necessary fuel? Food is fuel!

Did you ever fall asleep in your morning classes at school? If you didn't fall fast asleep, were there ever any times that you had to fight to keep awake? Did you or didn't you have breakfast on those mornings? My guess is, "Probably not!" Of course the other question to check out is what time you went to bed the night before?

Starting the day off with a good breakfast (not only one that tastes good, but one that's good for you) is most important. A healthy breakfast might include a citrus fruit, like an orange or orange juice, some whole grains, like bread or cereals (minus the sugar; if you want to sweeten your breakfast cereals, you might try adding fruit), and milk. You might also consider having eggs a few times a week. All it takes is a decision to care about yourself enough to get up a few minutes earlier so you can eat before going to school. Try it!

Scott, age ten, told me he loves to cook. He really wanted to make himself french toast in the mornings, but his mom said he couldn't cook while she was sleeping and she didn't want to get up! I suggested to him that he ask his mom to let him show her how he cooks later in the day when she's up. Then he could prove to her that he's responsible and can handle cooking in a safe way on his own. You guessed it! He now has permission to cook breakfast and he feels great about it.

As far as the rest of the day goes, people seem to eat for lots of different reasons. Some people are actually hungry, but many others are bored, nervous, eat because the food is in front of them, don't know what else to do. . . .

It would help to begin to take notice of exactly what you're eating, when and why. It can be real interesting to write down everything that you eat for several days. Even tiny bites of things—no cheating! Then you can see what kind of eating habits you have, what's in your diet, and whether you are getting enough of the important fuels.

Healthy eating means including lots of different types of foods in your meals (be sure to include whole grains and vegetables). You can also cut down on foods that have high fat content (less crunching on the fat of your lamb chops) and try to cut down on adding extra sugar (honey is a good sweetener to use). Since water is important for the healthy functioning of your organs, try to drink several glasses of water each day.

Healthy eating also means staying away from fad diets, such as the ones that tell you to starve yourself for periods of time. Rather than starving or cutting out certain basic foods that your body needs, you are better off eating balanced meals and watching out for too much in-between meals. (Be smart about your snacks!) Combine good eating habits with exercise and you'll probably feel and look terrific.

Good, sensible eating habits are not hard to develop. They simply result from deciding to care and learning as much as you can about the food you eat, and what foods are more or less healthy.

For more detailed information about eating properly, you and your parents can speak with your family doctor, school health educator, or nurse. You can also go to the library and ask for books written about nutrition (nu-tri-shun).

Are you eating the same exact thing each day or are you eating lots of different things? Do you have heaping portions or smaller ones? How many seconds and thirds of dessert do you have?

Have you looked in the mirror lately? Do you consider yourself overweight, skinny, sort of in the middle? Just right? Does the way you look make you feel good about yourself?

If you're heavier than you'd like to be, it may be that your body will thin out as you begin to develop. It also may mean that you've got to change some poor eating habits.

If you're honest with yourself and decide you wish to try to change, talk with your parents so they can cooperate with your new eating plan.

Perhaps you can help them make up a new menu for family meals. You can also talk about what kind of snacks are good for you.

You'll find that you've got to combine good eating with exercise and the right amount of sleep. Sleep adds to your strength and is very important.

A good way to tell if you're sleeping enough is to be aware of how tired you are during the day. Some kids find they can stay up later, others find they need to go to sleep real early. Not sleeping enough can help to run you down and make it easier for you to get sick.

Only you can answer how you feel, how much energy you have, if you seem to get very tired by late afternoon or can't seem to keep your eyes open all morning. Since each person's sleep needs are different, it would be impossible for me to tell you how many hours of sleep is right for you.

It's up to your parents to help guide you about what bedtime might be right for you. It's up to you to be honest with them and with yourself about how tired you are.

Believe it or not, the health habits you have now will have an affect on your health as an adult. So it's very important to think about what you do and what you don't do about your own personal care.

Just remember that your habits took time to form and will probably take time to break. Even if you understand what and why you should change, it can be hard to change right away. So be patient with yourself but be strong about what you now know is good for you.

In the next chapter I'll talk a bit more about the different shapes and sizes and some other changes that can be part of puberty. You might want to grab a snack before going on to the next chapter. (You might want to grab a shower too!)

# 11
# Different Shapes and Sizes

## Does Your Size Make a Difference in How You Feel?

Are you skinnier, fatter, taller, shorter, more developed, or less developed than your friends? How does this make you feel?

If you're happy with your weight, size, and stage of development, then you'll probably feel really good about yourself. If you're not happy about those things, you might not feel as good. You might even feel miserable!

I know that I've told you over and over again that you can't help what size you are and you can't speed up or slow down your development. But I also know that no matter how much you understand that, it still can be pretty hard to accept your size and feel good. Kids always seem to compare themselves with each other, forgetting that each person can't help the way he or she is.

Cari, age eleven, grew taller than her friends at an early age. She told me, "At first, I was embarrassed when everyone started calling me 'too tall' and making fun of me. I felt comfortable with my size but their teasing made me uncomfortable. I just started calling them names back and then I told them to stop. They listened and I didn't have any more embarrassment."

Heather, age twelve, said, "When we had to do pull-ups on the rings in gym class, my gym teacher always used to say things like, 'We'll have to make this one lower for the shorter people. Some short people can't reach this.' And she'd always look straight at me. I was so mad and

129

embarrassed because there were a lot of people in my class who were much smaller than me and she just picked on me and my shortness. Also whenever I answered her, she always mimicked my voice in a high tone as if I was a munchkin. And my voice really wasn't that high!"

Jimmy, age ten, wanted to know, "How can I help my friend from being teased about his height?" Peter, age eleven, wanted to understand why his friend was so short.

Eddie, age fourteen, is still quite small. He finds that when kids choose up sides for baseball, unless they know him and how he plays, they'll usually pick him last because he's so much smaller. They figure that small means "not as good." But he shows them how wrong they are when he starts to play. Then they're sorry they didn't pick him first! It's very frustrating to him because he seems to always have to prove himself to kids who are bigger.

Marion, now thirty-five, remembers how great she felt because she was so much taller than all of her friends. It made her feel very grown-up. Said Marion, "No one dared to tease me! The only problem sometimes was when my parents expected more from me because I looked older."

So many feelings. So many different sizes and shapes!

If you have feelings about your size and development, it might help to write down your feelings. Put down what about yourself makes you feel good and what doesn't. Then try to decide if the things that disturb you can be changed. Or do they have to do with development that you cannot control?

If you can change something, then begin to think about how. For example if you feel that losing a few pounds would make a difference, then you can try to eat more wisely. Have a salad instead of mounds of potatoes with gravy. Have a piece of fruit for a snack instead of three cupcakes. Try eating one piece of bread instead of two. With a new attitude and better understanding of how your habits can affect you, you'll begin to see results.

You can help control your weight, how clean you are, the way you wear your hair—but how tall or short, how developed or undeveloped, that's not up to you! So try to keep the teasing down and the understanding up!

If your parents (or those around you) seem to expect too much of you because your development makes you appear older, or if you feel you're

being treated as if you're younger because your size is small, remind them of your age. They may not realize they're doing this.

If you hear anyone making comments or fun of anyone because of things you know they can't help, maybe you can spread this understanding to help others feel good about themselves too.

### A *word of caution*
Certainly kids (and adults) who feel they're too heavy have a distorted (not the way things really are) view of themselves. They think they're too heavy but they're really quite thin. Because they don't want to gain any weight, they try to starve themselves or eat very little. People who feel and behave this way are called anorexics (an-or-eks-iks). The condition they have is anorexia nervosa (an-or-eks-ee-a ner-voe-sa).

Some people make themselves vomit their food after meals (they often eat a lot then vomit) just to make sure they won't gain any weight. This condition is called bulimia (buh-lee-mee-a).

Both anorexia nervosa and bulemia can be very dangerous. Even though people with these problems lose more and more weight, they still think they're not thin enough. If they lose too much weight, they will not allow their bodies to get the nourishment needed to stay healthy. Sometimes it is necessary for them to be put in the hospital so that doctors and nurses can make sure they eat or are fed what their bodies need. Depending upon how undernourished they are, they may need to be fed through a tube that's placed down their nose, or intravenously (in-tra-vee-nus-lee), which is done by placing a needle underneath the skin, usually on the inside of the person's arm; the needle is connected to a long tube through which liquid nourishment flows.

This needle way of feeding is used a lot in hospitals when people have operations or when they're too ill to be able to eat on their own.

*Another caution*
Some kids (and adults) who are much heavier than is healthy for them to be find that they eat more and more. This just makes them heavier. Usually this kind of eating is not because they're hungry. They may think or say they're hungry, but really they eat because they're upset or concerned about something, want attention, or just don't feel good about themselves. There can be many different reasons. The name that is often attached to this kind of eating is "compulsive overeating."

*Note*: Even though parents can often be a great help to children with any of these conditions, it's sometimes very important to speak also with doctors, counselors, therapists, or any other professional who is specially trained to offer help and guidance. Getting this kind of help is not a sign of weakness. It takes a lot of strength to admit that you have a problem that you can't seem to handle so well by yourself.

If your mom or dad (or both) suggests that you speak with a professional person trained to help you understand your eating or any other type of problem, try to realize they're saying this because they care about you and are concerned. Also, it takes strength for parents to admit that neither they nor their child can handle the particular problem on their own.

Although it may be tough to be honest about your feelings, if you care about yourself you'll try to cooperate and allow yourself to be helped. If you don't care about yourself, it's all the more reason to begin to understand why.

You deserve to feel good. And, there are people all around you who will be happy to help you if you need them. First, *you* have to make the decision that you want to feel good.

## When It's Your Turn to "Sprout"

Sprouting or growth may come on suddenly. This is often talked about as a growth spurt. You may grow several inches in a real short time (like over a few months). In the beginning of puberty boys will sometimes need a year or more to catch up in height with girls of the same age.

Your feet may play "knock, knock" with the tips of your shoes; the bottom of your pant legs might move higher and higher above your ankles. You may find yourself feeling a bit awkward, gawky, uncoordinated (almost like you're going to trip over your own feet) for a while until you get used to your new size. Your nose may seem like it's on the wrong face. (Sometimes the nose does grow before the rest of the face. Then the face catches up and all looks right again.)

*Not to worry! This is all very natural!*

## New Moods, Feelings and Emotions

You may find there will be times when you will be cranky, irritable, easily excited, sad, edgy, moody, or even feel like crying without being able to figure out why you feel this way. You might also feel fine again without understanding what made you feel better.

These mood changes (changes in your emotions) are influenced by your hormones and the many feelings you might have about yourself, your body, and the people closest to you. Such moods are considered a natural part of the growing up years.

In time you will learn to be able to handle your emotions in a way that will reflect your growing maturity. Some boys and girls will experience more noticeable changes in their emotions than others.

Changes in feelings and emotions may also relate to the excitement, confusion, and frustration that often goes along with learning to become independent (no longer depending on your parents for everything, taking on new responsibilities). While you might find it wonderful to feel more grown up, you also may find there will be moments when you'll wish you could hold onto childhood a little longer.

## Puberty, a Time of Change

New shapes, new curves, new growth, new feelings, moods, even new braces and eye glasses, you will change in your own special way. You'll have your own feelings, your own concerns and frustrations, your own excitement and happiness, your own hopes and dreams.

You're the only you that there is in the entire world! Isn't that incredible? That's especially why you deserve to feel as good as you can about yourself.

I hope the information I've offered in the first eleven chapters has cleared up any questions or confusions you might have had about all the physical changes that are part of puberty. I hope I've helped you understand and feel better about your body and how to care for yourself. I hope by now you realize that you're not alone in so many of your feelings and concerns. And if your concern is different, that's okay too! Even best friends won't feel exactly the same way on everything.

I'm excited about sharing the remaining fourteen chapters with you. More feelings, of course. I'll start with friendship. . . .

There's lots to say, so let's go!

# GROWING UP FEELING GOOD ABOUT YOURSELF

# 12
# Friendship

## Friendship is One of the Most Important Parts of Growing Up

Friendship means caring about another person, being able to trust them, getting to know them, and learning about them—what makes them laugh, what bugs them, and even what their favorite ice cream flavor is.

Friendship means understanding. You don't have to pretend with a friend. It's okay to be who you are. They'll understand when you're sad and be happy with you when you feel good.

True friends tell each other secrets and know that they won't be spread all over. True friends won't make fun of you if you get a bad grade on your test. They won't tease if you're the first to have braces or the last to grow. They'll tell you if your fly is open, if they think your hair is too short, or if you need a bra. They'll try to help you with your homework before school, if you had trouble doing it the night before. They'll cry with you if your pet dies.

Friendship is special. This chapter will give you a good chance to think about the friends you have, the friends you'd like to have, and the friends you wish you didn't have.

Some kids have a lot of friends, some have just a few, others don't have any. The same is true with adults. It's not that there are any rules about numbers of friends. In fact even when certain people seem to have many friends, they can be very lonely.

My feeling is that it's much more important to think about *who* your friends are than how many you have. One or two very good friends can mean much more than a bunch of kids who just *act* like they care but when it comes down to it really don't.

The friendships that are made while you're growing up are ones that are often kept, or at least remembered, for a lifetime. If you don't have any friends (you're not alone—lots and lots of kids have talked about this) or would like to make another friend, you can start thinking about it right this minute!

## Have You Ever...

Have you ever looked at someone in your classroom, in your lunchroom, at a club meeting, walking home from school, on the school bus, etc., who looked like he or she would be nice? Maybe even like the kind of person you might want to have as a friend?

What did you do? Did you go over and say "hi"? Did you tell the person your name and ask what lunch period he or she has? Did you say, "Let's sit together on the bus!"? Or did you do nothing, wishing you could be confident enough to do something?

Many people feel it's not the easiest thing to just go up to someone and start talking. Adults as well as kids get the jitters. Boys and girls of all ages have said to me, "I'm shy... and I don't know what to do."

Getting started at trying to become less shy, and making the decision that you want to find a new, or especially a first, friend takes *guts*. Everyone has them inside.

If you're one of the many shy people, even you have guts! Your guts may have been taking a rest for all these years, but that will probably just make them stronger as soon as you decide to poke them a little (a lot?) and let them know you need them.

It's time to realize that being shy or scared doesn't have to prevent you from being able to enjoy all the special things that friendship can mean. You deserve to have at least one close friend. And, whether you believe me or not, someone out there will be very lucky to have you as theirs.

Here are some steps you can follow to try to find a new friend.

## How To Make a Friend

The first step is to realize that you want to make a friend.

The second step is to think about who you might like to have as a friend. This may take a bit of time. That's natural since it's not such an easy decision. The exciting thing is that you've made up your mind to do something for yourself. That's great!

Look around carefully. Try not to judge people by their clothing, how they wear their hair, how developed they are, how fat, small, or very tall they are, what street they live on, or whether they almost flunked gym! These outside things don't tell you all you need to know if you're thinking about becoming someone's friend. You must learn about how that person is on the inside.

It's more important to find out if the person is nice, if you can have fun together, if you feel comfortable together. Are there things you can enjoy doing together? Would you be able to trust this person? Could you be honest with the person? That kind of learning will take some time.

Until you get to know this person, it's really not fair to make any decisions on the type of person he or she is. You'd just be guessing. You might be right. But you could also be very wrong.

Pay attention at the bus stop or walking to and from school, in the lunchroom, and at recess. Take a good look at the kids in your classes. Watch who walks with whom through the halls. Notice who seems to be alone much of the time (they may be shy too). After-school clubs and religious classes might give you the chance to meet different kids. The more people you're around, the more choices you have. Keep looking. . . .

You'll be ready for the third step when you've picked one person out who you think might be nice to know.

The third step is to let that person know you're alive, if they don't know already. Usually, it will be someone you've seen in school and know a little about. Sometimes, the person or you will be "new," perhaps because one of you has just moved to a different school or into a new town, new club, or new activity.

If you've never seen or spoken with the person before, a good start would be to ask them their name and tell them yours. You might say, "Hi, I think we take the same bus in the morning. My name is ——." Or, "Hi, I'm ——. What's your name?"

You might also take a chance and say, "A group of my friends are going into town after school, do you want to come?" Or, "How about eating lunch together?" Or, "That's going to be a tough test tomorrow. Do you want to study together this afternoon?" Or, "How about coming over my house (apartment) this afternoon or one day this week?" Or, "I see we walk home the same way. Do you want to meet after school and go together?" Or just, "What did you think of the math test?", "Wasn't that concert great?" You don't always have to ask them to actually *do* something with you. A beginning can be just talking with them if you never have before.

By now you might be thinking, "I can't just walk over to someone and start talking! What if they don't talk back?" (What if they do?)

Well, this is the tough part. You may think that your knees will shake, your face will get all red, and you'll "die" of embarrassment. But what's the most awful thing that could happen? That the person says "no." Or worse, they walk away and totally ignore you! This is called *rejection* (ree-jek-shun), and it can feel rotten. But . . .

An old Ellen Rosenberg belief is that you haven't lost anything by trying. You may hurt for a little while, but you still have everything that you walked up to the person with. You have you and that's very special. If you groan and moan and feel sorry for yourself, that won't help. Besides, it's better to try to feel sorry for the person! Just think. He or she is missing out on getting a chance to know you!

Repeat five times: "It's their loss!"

The trick is not to let rejection stop you. If the answer is "no," it doesn't mean that something is wrong with you. It's just that not everyone likes everyone else. Not everyone relates to everyone else. Even if the person seems to like you, you may find that you don't like being with him or her. That's life.

If you are rejected what happens next? You move on to the fourth step. Find a new person and start again.

*Special advice:* Sometimes it helps to approach that other kid—when you can do it—privately. If you ask in front of the kid's group of friends, he or she may say "no," even if they want to say "yes."

The fourth step and beyond: Keep trying. You may have to try many kids before finding one that says, "Hey! I'll look for you later. Oh, my name is ——, what's yours?"

I'm not pretending that this will be easy. And I'd be lying if I said you'll feel terrific if kids reject you. Rejection can be very painful. You might begin to think that the easiest thing would be to give up. But if you stop trying, you're choosing to give up on yourself. So the lesson here is that you shouldn't stop. Go on to the next and the next, as tough as that may be.

Someone (maybe your twelfth, maybe your twentieth pick) will be so happy you came over. Someone will be so relieved that you had the guts to say "hi" first.

Take a chance. The hardest will be the first try. You may really have to force yourself to get the words out. But do it. And see what happens. Once you get back a smile, a hello, or a "Yes, I'd love to come to your house or walk into town with you"—you're on your way. Things will just fall into place after that.

Remember to be patient with yourself. Building confidence and learning that you're special too can take time. I believe that there's someone out there for everyone.

## What About the Friends You Have?

As I talk about the many questions that boys and girls have asked me about friendship, you'll have a good chance to think about your own concerns and situations.

*"What if friends act one way when they're alone with you and another way when they're with the group?"*
So many kids have talked about this. For instance Scott, age eleven, told me that he has this really good friend. When they were alone, things were real easy between them. "He wasn't loud or show-offy or anything like that. But when he was with the whole group, for some reason, he had to show off. He teased; he was loud; he wasn't even nice, sometimes."

Thirteen-year-old David told me pretty much the same thing. His friends were great when he was with them one at a time. But as soon as they got together, they acted up and even teased him.

The reasons for this are probably different for each friend. Very often kids act this way because they're not sure of themselves in a group. They may feel they have to prove themselves, show off, and get extra attention in order to be accepted.

When they're alone, there's usually a trust that doesn't exist in the crowd. They don't have to prove themselves in the same way. They can just be who they are and don't have to put on an act.

Stacey, age ten, said, "When people are in a crowd, they're more nervous about what they're saying. If they say something wrong, they're afraid kids won't like them. When they're alone, they know just one person will hear it, and they'll speak more freely."

If you find that you're bothered by how much any of your friends change when they're not alone with you anymore, it's important for you to talk about your feelings with them. You might also ask them if they realize how different they act when you're alone together. If they're fooling around too much or teasing you, let them know it hurts and you don't think it's funny.

They may not have any idea that they're hurting or bothering you. Once you tell them, they'll probably try to stop—if they care about you and the friendship you have. If they don't stop, you may have to tell them a few more times until they believe you're serious.

If they still act very differently and it's still bothering you, then you may have to do some thinking about whether you want to remain their friend. It may be time for you to make some changes.

*"What if you want to be someone's friend, but you don't want to belong to the group they hang around with?"*
It would be sad to give up the friendship and unfair to be pressured (feel forced) to be with kids you really don't like.

What you can do is talk honestly with your friend. Say that you care about him or her a lot and want to be friends. But say you're not comfortable or you don't have the same feelings for their crowd. So you hope he or she will understand that you're not going to join in when the group is around. When he or she can be with you alone, great!

If your friend can't deal with that or doesn't understand, then you may have a choice to make. To be friends, care about each other, but not see each other very much. Or, to be friends and hang out with his or her group, even though you don't want to, just so you can be together. What else do you think you might do?

It's not completely up to you, though, since the friendship includes both of you. Even if *you* can deal with this situation, they may not be able to.

Friendships don't always work out, even if both people want them to. There are sometimes other things that one or both of you have to deal with that make being together difficult.

## When friends are in different crowds

Tammi, age eleven, told me, "I'm friends with another group of kids and I'm friends with my group. I'm in classes with both and can be with either group when I want to. I don't feel like I'm in the middle. I can be friendly with who I want."

That's great! Sometimes when friends are in different groups one can be jealous of the other. Janie, age ten, said, "When I'm with one friend, the other one gets mad at me and thinks I don't want to be with her. They're not in the same crowd and it's not fun to be with them together. I'd rather see them by themselves. I always feel like I have to choose between them. I hate being in the middle."

Have you ever felt this way? Did you do anything about it? One suggestion would be to speak to both friends, privately. Tell them you like them both and want to be good friends with each of them. But you always feel pulled if you spend time with one instead of the other. Ask them to please understand that it's easier for you to be with them alone separately, and it would help if they didn't make a big deal about it.

## "What about when friendship changes, when your feelings change about a friend?"

Susie, age fourteen, shared, "Nothing really happened between us. We didn't fight or anything like that. But my friend spent the night at my house last weekend, and I found out things about her that I didn't know. Things I don't like. She uses words that I don't like to hear. She talks about doing things that make me feel uncomfortable, that I'm not ready for. Maybe we shouldn't be such close friends anymore. I thought I knew her but I guess I don't. It makes me upset."

Andy, age thirteen, feels, "Friendships change over long periods of time. Not seeing the person can cause this to happen. Even best friends can stop being best friends because they fall in with new people, or they try things that you're against. I find this mostly with girls. They seem to change their best friends much more often than boys."

Sheryl, age thirteen, told me, "Last week I just found out that one of my best friends smokes [cigarettes]. When I heard this, I cried and cried. I never would have thought that she'd do a thing like that. But I have another close friend who talked with me for hours and helped me see that it really is her choice, not mine. I can only choose for me. She's not trying to pressure me to smoke, either. In fact, she's hidden her smoking from me all this time. Maybe she thought I wouldn't be her friend if I found out. The truth is, the first thing I thought of is that I don't want to be her friend anymore if she smokes! How could a close friend of mine smoke? But I guess maybe this is what she needs to do right now. I'll have to think about it. Maybe it has nothing to do with me."

Sheryl was shocked and upset. I think a big part of her reaction was that she thought she knew her friend so well. So did Susie. Friends change. Even best friends! Maybe they would have changed anyway. But often the change is because of pressures at home or at school, wanting to be accepted by different people, or new experiences.

You can't know (wizards don't work here, either) when you start being close with someone in kindergarten or first grade that by junior high or high school or even by the end of elementary school if they'll begin to smoke or drink, get involved with drugs, cheating, or stealing.

When you find out about these changes, it can be really tough to deal with. It can be confusing and sometimes painful. Usually you're not prepared; you never thought about your friend in that way. You never expected him or her to be different from when they were with you.

You end up having to make another choice: "Do I keep on being friendly with this person, even though he or she has changed? Do I stop the friendship or stop seeing them as often as I have for all these years? I don't know if I can accept what they've become or what they're doing. I don't want to be exposed to it. I don't want to be pressured. I don't want to deal with it. I don't believe in it. Should I stay away? I don't want other people to think I'm that way or that I do it too. Getting involved might even turn out to be dangerous."

Though the love between you and your friend may not change, the difference in how they act, what they say, and the kinds of things that have become important to them may prevent you from being able to be as close with them as you were before. Staying away from someone who you care about when both of you really don't want to lose the friendship is very very hard to do.

If you want to keep on being friends with that person, you'll have to work at accepting them the way they are with their changes and know that if they have to do what they have to do, it doesn't mean that you have to do it too. As long as there's an understanding between you. First comes acceptance. And that can really be tough.

## When friends hurt your feelings

Sometimes friends say things to be funny and don't realize you're going to feel bad about it. But other times friends can say things on purpose to be mean. I'm not sure what kind of a good friend they are if they want to hurt you, but maybe he or she got mad and that was the only way this person knew how to get you back. Or maybe you're the only person he or she could take his or her anger out on, even if it had nothing to do with you.

More from Stacey, age ten (you can tell I had a long talk with her!), "If one of my friends said something I knew she really didn't mean, I'd discuss it with her and make her understand why she hurt me."

That's a real good way to deal with hurt. It's true; friends don't always know how you feel. So it's up to you to tell them what hurts you and what doesn't. That's how they learn to become more thoughtful and sensitive to your feelings. When your friends are honest with you, that's how you can learn to be more caring with them.

If you don't tell your friends how you feel, then you can't blame them for hurting you again in the same way. You might say, "I really felt hurt when you did that or said that." Or, "You probably didn't mean to hurt me, but I didn't think it was funny."

If you find that your friends still put you down or tease you after you've told them how bad you feel when they do this, then maybe that means they don't care about you as much as you thought they did. Maybe it would be smart to start looking around for other friends.

## "What if something really bugs you about a friend?"

Did you ever have a friend who drove you crazy when he or she did something or said something? What did you do? Did you keep quiet about it or did you say something to your friend? Or did you talk to a different friend about how you can't stand what that other friend did?

Lisa, age thirteen, told me about a friend of hers who "drives her up a wall." Said Lisa, "She embarrasses me and tries to act so cool. I hate it when she comes up and kisses me in public, and I get so embarrassed. But if I'd tell her, she'd only get mad."

Craig, age nine, said, "I have a friend who I don't like anymore. But I'm afraid to tell him because he'll probably beat me up."

Keith, age twelve, said, "I used to spend a lot of time with this friend. But I don't want to be with him as much anymore. He tags along and always asks me what I'm doing after school. I don't want to hurt his feelings, but I don't want to play with him either."

The big concern seems to be how to let someone know how you feel without getting the person mad and without hurting him or her. The problem is sometimes you can't help hurting the people you care about, even if that's the last thing you want to do.

If you tell your friend or write a note, being kind and sensitive at least can help to make whatever you have to say hurt a little less. The person may not like hearing it and may feel very badly, but at least he or she will be able to trust that you're saying it because you care, not to be nasty or mean.

You might begin by saying:

"It's really hard for me to say this to you."

"I would never want to hurt you. . . ."

"I love you but you really bug me when you . . . " (Instead of "bug me" you could say: "drive me crazy," "get me angry," "embarrass," "upset," "disappoint," whatever you feel.)

"Please listen before you get mad. I want you to understand something, and it's not easy for me to tell you because I don't want to end up fighting."

If you have a friend tell the person instead of you, he or she is still going to feel bad, and may even be more hurt and embarrassed because you couldn't tell them yourself. If you keep quiet and let things be, you're taking the chance that you'll get more and more bugged. That can't be good for the friendship.

Being honest about fun, happy things is easy. But dealing with hurt and things that don't feel so good can be an even better test of a friendship. Finding out that you and your friend can talk about the harder, sometimes painful things as well as the laughs can often make you closer.

## *When friends fight*

Jeremy, age twelve, told me, "If my friends get mad, I just figure they liked me once and they'll like me again. I don't really worry about my friends, or whether they like me or not. I just know they do. Other people don't feel that way with their friends. Like my sister, if her friends say 'I don't like you,' she gets all upset. If my friends say that, I just say, 'Good!' And the next day we'll all have forgotten about it."

It's a real good feeling to be able to trust that your friends will still be there even if something goes wrong for a little while. Maybe Jeremy's sister will feel less upset as she realizes that it's pretty natural for friends to fight (argue) sometimes. Fighting doesn't have to mean the end of a friendship. It could mean that, but usually fighting just blows over and is forgotten about until the next thing comes up.

Lynn, age eleven, said, "Three of us are very good friends. Whenever I have a fight with one of them, the other usually sticks by her and stops paying attention to me. Then when I talk with her privately, she's really different. She says she likes both of us and just wants to stay friendly with both. But why does she takes sides then?"

It's possible that she may be more sure of her friendship with you than her friendship with the other girl. Since she doesn't have to worry about you, she sticks close to the other girl. It would help if you told her how this makes you feel. Maybe she will stop taking sides or at least seem like she is.

Thirteen-year-old Andy feels that his friends seem to fight a lot. He remembers recently when an entire social group got into a fight. "That happened mainly because the telephone can be a deadly weapon. Because rumors are spread back and forth, and you end up going to school having a grudge against somebody and they have absolutely no idea what's going on."

Andy continued, "I think girls get into more fights with their friends than boys do. A lot of girls fight with their friends about girl friends and boyfriends and stuff like that. With me if my friends and I get into a fight, it almost turns into a joke. After it starts out being really serious, even if we insult each other, with us it's only a game. None of the grudges are held over until the next day."

James, age fourteen, said, "I find there's not much fighting between good friends, at least with friends in my grade. When I was younger, there seemed to be a lot more fighting, but I don't even remember what it was about."

There are so many reasons that kids have given me as to why friends fight: boyfriends, girl friends, being jealous, rumors, telling secrets, misunderstandings, forgetting to meet at a certain time, not calling back, leaving someone out, hurt feelings, being embarrassed, buying the same exact sweater. . . . I'm sure you can add to this list.

Since no two people are exactly alike, each friendship is different. Each fight will be a little different—even between the same people. But the one very important thing that can help all friends, no matter what the fight is about, is to try very hard to talk things out. Some kids have told me they're afraid to do this because what if the friend won't listen?

As I said before, the only way you can be sure someone knows how you feel is if you tell them. Explain why you did what you did. If you hurt them and didn't mean to, say you're sorry. If they embarrassed you, let them know so they'll learn not to do it again. If a rumor was spread, make sure they realize it wasn't you who started it. If they left you out, ask them why they forgot about you. Clear up any kind of misunderstandings, the sooner the better.

You can say, "I don't blame you for being angry with me. That was a stupid thing I did." Or, "I'm so sorry. I didn't realize it would bother you so much." Or, "I can't believe you would have done that to me if you knew how I felt. Why . . . "

If it's hard to begin, once again say that. "It's really hard for me to say this." Or, "Please don't say anything until you hear everything I need to say." Or, "I hope I don't start crying in the middle of this. . . ." Or, whatever you feel!

If your friendship is important to you, gather up at those guts and take another chance. Ask them to forgive. Tell them you want to try again (if you do). If it's worth it to both of you, with luck the fight will be over quickly so you can get on with your friendship.

Just remember if you decide to wait for the other person to say something, you may be waiting for a long time. Silent wars are no fun. So no matter who started the fight, if you want it stopped, you may have to be the one to talk first.

## When friends don't keep secrets

Said Katie, age ten, "It really can hurt if you tell a friend something very private and the next day you get to school and everyone is talking about what you said!"

I don't blame anyone for getting upset if a close friend blabbers a secret. Most of the time it's either embarrassing or painful to learn that other people know. The hurt part is that you thought you could trust that friend. And you couldn't!

How many times has someone said to you, "You promise not to tell anyone? You better not let anyone find out I told you this 'cause [so-and-so] will kill me." One person tells the next not to tell; the next tells someone else. And by the time they're all finished, tons of kids know what they shouldn't know.

That happens a lot. The problem is that you can't be completely sure you can trust someone unless you test the trust out a little bit. You may think someone is close with you and find out they can't or won't keep

your secret. But you can't find that out until after the secret has been passed around.

Jamie, age fourteen, suggests that you test if kids can keep a secret. "Tell them something that you don't care about so it won't matter if they tell. That way, you can see if they keep their promise not to let it out."

An interesting idea, Jamie! Roz, now age fifty-two, remembers, "There were always certain people we knew would tell everyone everything. My friends and I used to make up rumors just so we could tell them to this girl in our class who never kept her mouth shut about anything. We called her up and said she better promise not to tell anyone about it. Then we used to time how quickly the rumor spread around the school and laugh and laugh and laugh."

According to Cori, age thirteen, "Most secrets are not kept. You can't expect them to be. It also depends on the subject. If it was really important and really, really heavy, like 'My parents are getting a divorce; what can I do?' or 'My best friend smokes; how can I deal with that?,' then probably there'll be less talk. But if it's who likes who or who is breaking up with who, that will always get around."

What can you learn from this? That certain people can be trusted to keep their mouths shut and lots of others are blabber mouths, gossipers, or snitches! It may or may not depend upon what the secret is.

So the next time you have a secret, think carefully about who you want to share it with. Think even more carefully about how you'd feel if it got out. Then make your decision.

If you're wrong about trusting a friend with something private, that will teach you not to share with them next time. It doesn't mean your friendship has to change. Rather you know that much more about them and can make better decisions as to what you want to tell them and what you don't.

When you're right about trust, you'll probably feel even closer to that friend. It's a good feeling!

## When parents don't like your friends

It's possible that your mom or dad (or both) won't like one of your friends or even the whole crowd you hang around with. It can be tough to stay friendly with those kids when this happens.

It's one thing if your parents tell you why they don't like your friends—maybe that you should watch out for certain things that they don't trust or think are a poor influence. But that can make seeing your friends a bit uncomfortable because now you might have a question in your mind about them. But it's the toughest when your parents tell you not to see certain friends anymore, and you still really like them.

What would you do if your parents said that to you about one of your friends? Would you listen to your parents and stop seeing them? Would you tell your parents you'll listen, then sneak and see your friend in classes at school? How guilty do you think you'd feel if you had to sneak?

Randi, age twelve, told me:

> I was very friendly with a boy who lives around the corner from me. We spent a lot of time together since the third grade. All of a sudden his parents started getting on his back for spending time with me. We did every school project together that we could. We always signed up for the same committees. I really think his parents thought that their son was doing most of the work and I was just getting a free ride, but that was never true. So they forbade him to do any more projects with me. I knew he wanted to, but it was just because of his parents. I soon stopped going over to his house and felt funny about calling him if I knew his parents were home. Now it's been a while since his parents became so strict about him being with me. Even though we still see each other at school, something has changed. Slowly we've been getting more and more apart. It's sad because we were really close.

Thirteen-year-old Andrea talked about her parents and how they all dealt with not liking one of her friends. "My parents don't like my friend, but they let me decide if I still want to be close with her. I agree that certain things about her are not like me, but other things are. I can't stand it when they say, 'She's not your type!' I don't have to do what she does just to be her friend. It's not what my parents think. It's true that she smokes. But I don't want to and she doesn't make me feel funny about not smoking when she's doing it."

It's important to respect that your parents are probably trying very hard to look out for you. They don't want you to get hurt. They'd like to see you with friends that are, in their opinion, right for you. And they may just see something that you're not able to see.

You can listen to them, think about what they're saying, and then see how you feel. With luck your parents will trust and respect you enough to allow you to make up your own mind. Of course if they really think someone will be a danger to you, you may not have a choice.

One more thing: if you find it's really hard to listen to your parents about not seeing a friend and you don't want to sneak, talk with your parents about how you feel. I would hope they'd rather you be honest with them than be forced to go against their wishes behind their backs. Maybe you can work things out. They may not have any idea that not being with your friend bothers you that much. Remember they can't know for sure what you're feeling unless you tell them.

### How to deal with two-faced friends

Michelle, age twelve, explains, "Friends are two-faced when to your face they're your friend, but behind your back they go against you."

It's got to hurt when you find out that somebody you think is a true friend, really isn't. I would let them know that you know, and that you're very upset to find they're not the good friend you thought they were. See what they say.

Even if they apologize and promise not to go behind your back anymore, it may take a long time before you feel you can trust them. The good thing is that at least you'll know that they weren't honest and you can be more careful about what you say or do around them.

### Liking someone whom hardly anybody likes

Cathy, age ten, asked, "What if my friend and I don't want to play with a girl because nobody likes her and she can ruin our reputations? Then nobody will like us. Sometimes we like her and sometimes we don't like her at all."

Probably the times that Cathy and her friend like the unpopular girl are when the other kids aren't around. They're afraid that other kids will find out they like her and maybe won't be their friends anymore.

Their friends may even say, "If you're the kind of person who hangs around with her, then you can't be my friend too." That can make it harder to stay friendly with her. I think it comes down to making a choice (of course!). As with all the other choices, it helps to understand what each might mean.

If you choose to keep seeing someone that nobody likes, then you're taking a chance that your usual friends may not want to be with you, if they find out. But who do you think should decide how you spend your free time? Your friends or you? Do you think you should be able to like who you want to like?

If you spend time with that other person, your friends may tease you about it. And they may tease the other person with you or without you around. When that happens, you'll have to decide if you want to go along with any teasing or comments or if you're going to stick up for that unpopular friend.

If you stick up for him or her, your friends may stop and respect what you're saying. Or they may tell you to bug off. Or, they may even invite her to join them, if they know it's that important to you.

You'll have to follow what your brain and especially your heart senses as to what you should do. Think of the other person's feelings. Be kind. But also be honest about how important your usual friends are to you. This is getting into something called peer pressure (when friends pressure you to do something that you really don't want to do), which I'll talk about in Chapter 15.

## When friends use you or try to buy you

Steve, age twelve, told me that his friend's little brother "always used to come over to play with my brother's computer game. He spent lots of time at our house. When the game was broken, he stopped coming over. When it was fixed, he came back. Then he got his own computer game and hasn't come back since."

That's a real good example of using. He came over for the game not for the person. It's also like when someone asks you to come over for lunch or dinner and instead of saying "I'd love to," because you want to be with them, you might first ask "What are you having for dinner?" Using would be if you came because you liked the dinner and said "no" just because you didn't. You'd be making the food much more important than the person, just like the computer game was to Steve's friend's brother.

When you're younger, kids might want to come over to your house because of a toy that you have and they don't. Or if your mom (or dad) bakes great cookies. Or if they're not allowed to have candy or soda in their home and you can have all you want. So they can come over to your house and pig out.

As you get older, kids still use other kids, but the reasons seem to change. Sometimes they're friendly with you because they like a certain boy or girl and you're the way they can get close to them. Or if you understand science and they don't, they might want to copy your homework or have you spend time explaining theirs to them. Or they may just want to get an invitation to the party they know you're going to have in a few weeks.

If your mom or dad is always around and is able to take you places and pick you up, someone might just be your friend to come along for the ride. As you get even older, people might be friendly with you because you or your boyfriend or girl friend have a car and that's cool. It's also easier than walking. . . .

Besides being used, there are many kids who try to buy friendships. Bobby, age nine, remembers one boy in his second grade class who used to give him things. Bobby finally understood that the kid just wanted to be his friend and thought he had to do that to make Bobby like him. Bobby said, "I didn't like taking all that stuff from him. It was nice, but it made me feel weird. I knew something was not right about it."

Some kids will come over to you and say, "Want to come over to my house? I just got a great thing." Or maybe they'll be the one to approach you with, "You want me to help you study for French this afternoon?" Or, "Do you want to swim in my pool this week?"

While some kids make these offers because they really want to be nice, it's sad to me that certain kids feel that they have to use the offers to "sell" themselves. It means that they don't have enough confidence in themselves to believe that someone else will like them for who they are rather than needing to con them with swimming pools, sodas, or things.

It's also sad (and rotten!) that kids use other kids. I imagine that some people don't realize they're doing it on purpose. It may only be when the game breaks that they find out they really don't have such a good time with that person. But it's different when they know they're taking advantage of someone. I don't feel that's very nice. It's even sadder when the other person knows he is being used but wants the company badly and lets it happen.

Can you think of any times when other kids tried to use you or your friends? How about buying friendship? Have you ever felt the need to do anything like that yourself?

*What can you do for others who always seem to be left out?*
As important as it is to feel good about yourself and your friendships, it's also very special to try to show other people that you care about them.

Now that you have a better understanding of how difficult it can be for some people to try to make friends, why not go over to someone you notice by themselves a lot and start a conversation. If you say hello first, it would probably be much easier for them to talk with you. Your talk might help them feel more confident with others. As you already know getting started can be so hard.

It may take practice to be able to do things for other people, not because of what you'll get in return, but just because you care enough to be nice. There are always chances to show someone you care, if only you look for them. Besides approaching someone who is often left out, you can say hi to a person who is new in your school and doesn't know many people yet, pay attention to someone who seems quiet, shy, or sad. Do something nice for a friend or classmate (or anyone you know) who is ill.

You can practice caring with people of all ages. Many older people would probably feel so good to have the chance to talk with someone your age. Try showing different people you care.

*What if you don't have a lot of friends and you feel left out?*
If you feel this way (lots of kids do), then this would be a great time to start looking around for someone who seems to be nice. Go back to the beginning of this chapter and reread the part that talks about how you might try to make a friend.

Remember it may be a little scary to go up to someone and ask them if they want to meet you in the lunchroom or come over to your house after school. But not trying to do anything about those left-out feelings would be worse.

*Anyone* who feels left out can *decide* to do something about it! If you feel you're on the outside, you can try to make your own inside.

Try not to be fooled when you see a whole bunch of kids who hang around together and wish you could be a part of their group. Sure it can be great to "belong." But there are also kids who appear to belong who have told me about how "lonely and unsure of themselves" they really are. Being invited places and a part of a big group is not always the answer.

As I'll talk about more in the next chapter on Being Popular, I feel that the friend or friends who you care about make up your crowd. Each person has his or her own crowd, even if it is just two people. Lots of kids that I've spoken with all over the United States agree.

The exciting thing is that you don't have to sit around and wait for a friend to find you. *You* can look for *them*. If you feel left out, you can decide to do something about it, now!

It's up to you. . . .

# 13
# Being Popular

## What Does Being Popular Mean?

Twelve-year-old Susan thinks, "Being popular is being liked by just about everyone." Rosey, age thirteen, states, "Being popular means being massively socially accepted!" Eleven-year-old Steve feels, "Popularity means that a lot of people like you and know you—not just from your own grade but from the other grades too."

I agree with Susan, Rosey, and Steve. Being popular usually means being well liked, accepted, having lots of friends. Being popular can be really important to some kids. Others don't seem to care.

What are your feelings about popularity? Do you think you're popular, unpopular, or somewhere in the middle? How does that make you feel about yourself? Come on, be honest! How important is popularity to you?

I asked those same questions to kids of all ages and found there are so many different feelings and concerns that can go along with being popular. As we take a look at some of their answers, think about whether you've ever felt the same way.

## Feelings About Popularity

Johnny, age nine, shared, "Being popular is great. It makes me feel really good. I don't have to worry about having someone to sit with in the lunchroom or who I'm going to play with after school. There's always someone to walk with; people always say hello to me in the halls. It makes me feel important."

Angela, age fourteen, stated, "Being popular is really important to me. But sometimes I feel more pressured than good. I feel I always have to be on my guard. I watch everything I say. I try sometimes to act in ways that are not even me. I don't understand it. I wonder whether just having a few friends, instead of worrying about the crowd all the time, would be better."

Lysee and Rachel, identical twins, feel that popularity is not that important to them. They have their friends that they care about, and it doesn't matter if that means they're popular or not.

Rosey not only doesn't think it's all that important to be popular, but also he doesn't even believe that popularity exists in his grade at school (eighth). He says, "There's no such thing at my age [thirteen] because of the way our school is set up. There are at least six or seven groups in my grade. The people in one group don't have much to do with the people in the other groups. If that's true, how could there be a popular group? Each kid is popular within his or her own group. But some people are friends with everybody. They're based in one group but also have friends elsewhere. Not good friends but friends."

Kevin, age thirteen, said, "I'm one of the most popular kids in my unpopular group! It feels great! Like I belong. I know people care about me, and I don't feel lonely like I used to. I'm never bored, because I always have someone to do something with."

Mrs. A told me her twelve-year-old daughter wanted so badly to be in the popular group. "She's been trying to get into that group for a long time. They finally accepted her this year. One night I found her up very late. She was writing down what she was going to say the next day when she was with them. I know how important it is to her to be with those kids. But now that she's 'in,' I think there's more pressure to stay in than there was to get in!"

Another parent, this time the dad of one of the popular boys at a middle school in the Midwest, said, "I guess Peter is just one of those kids who gets along with everyone. Our house has been filled with his friends since he was little." In answer to my question about whether he thought Peter was pressured by his popularity in any way, he answered, "The only pressure I can think of is finding the time to be with his friends. I guess that's a good kind of pressure."

Andrea, age eleven, said, "I could be with a lot of kids but still feel very lonely. Maybe that's because I'm never sure if I'm really part of them, or if they're just being polite and don't know how to tell me how to get lost."

Jeremy, age twelve, told me, "Sometimes kids don't even like the person who's popular, but because they're popular, they'll just hang around with them. Then other kids will think that they're popular too."

As you can see, being popular has its pressures along with the rewards. Some kids find it very easy to make friends and be "liked by just about everyone." They don't have to put on an act to be popular. They can just be themselves and know they'll be accepted.

Others find that wanting to be popular can force them to do things they wouldn't normally do or be with people they might not even like. It can take them a long time to get into a group and be tough to keep up with the group once they're in.

## Why Are Kids Popular?

Kids are popular for lots of different reasons. Here's a list of whys made by a group of boys and girls in the sixth, seventh, and eighth grades. The marks are next to reasons that I feel kids can't help. Think about what you would add or take off the list, and see if you agree.

    *good athlete
    *good looking
    *if you're developed
    *you have a brother or sister who's popular
     you have lots of friends
     most people like you
    *you have a certain toy or other possession
    *because you're rich
    *you have nice clothes
     you get the best grades
     you're fun to be with
     you're a good person
     you don't lie or cheat
     you're dependable and reliable
     you're a good friend

you're skinny
you're friends with someone who's very popular
you're going out with someone who's popular

## A Few Thoughts About the Reasons for Being Popular

Take another good look at that list. Maybe you already noticed that I put extra marks next to certain things. Can you guess why I think they're different than the others? Time's up!

You may or may not agree, but I feel these are the things that kids can't control. For example it's not their fault that their parents are rich and are able to buy them nice clothes. They can't help it if they're good looking or not. They were born that way.

It might be interesting and fun to choose someone like a TV or movie star who most of your friends know and see how many people think he or she is good looking and how many do not. (If you pick someone at school, it may be embarrassing.) I think you'll find that some will think he or she is gorgeous; others will think "eh"; still others will think "yich!" Since good looks are so personal and people can't help how they look, do you think it's a fair reason for some kids to be popular?

I've already spent a lot of pages talking about how kids can't control their development. They also probably have little or nothing to do with how popular their brother or sister is. Toys, electronic games, or anything like that are usually, if not always, bought by parents, not kids. And yet people think these things are important enough to make someone popular or not.

Twelve-year-old Jeremy feels, "Being good at sports is so important for popularity that even a person who is not nice can be popular just because they're a good athlete."

Jeremy continued, "There's this boy in our school. Not many people really like him but it *seems* like everybody does. He's really popular. He's a really good athlete and plays all kinds of sports. He's not all that great at school but everybody likes him, I guess, because he's a good athlete. Being a real good athlete is sometimes even more important than grades for popularity. You have to be really nice to be popular if you're not a good athlete. If you are a good athlete, you don't have to be nice at all and you'll still be real popular!"

Mrs. M. told me that her thirteen-year-old son came home the other day and said, "I don't feel very popular right now." He had been on the football team and just missed making the basketball team. When she asked him why, he said, "All the girls seem to go for the guys who are on the team. Well, I guess I'll just wait until I make the baseball team!"

How do the attitudes among the kids in your school compare to those that Jeremy and Mrs. M's son talked about? Are most of the popular kids that you know also good athletes? Do you think they'd be popular even if they weren't good at sports?

The mark I put next to "you get the best grades" is not the same as the others. That's because I feel that this is partly in your control and partly not. You can control how hard you study, whether your work is completed on time, how well you pay attention, and anything else that you may *choose* to do in order to try to get high grades. What's not in your control is your mental ability. You also can't control having a disability that might limit your learning ability.

Each person's ability to work and get good results is a little different. Some kids seem to get high grades without even working. Others can only do well in school if they study a lot. Some kids work very hard but still get lower grades. But those lower grades may be the highest they are able to get! Of course, there are also kids who get low grades who don't try and don't care. Do you think kids should have less of a chance to be popular if their grades are lower but they're trying their hardest and are doing the best they can?

Being skinny goes along with looks. If a person is healthy, he or she usually can eat in order to weigh as much as they feel is comfortable and looks good. Remember, exercise and proper diet can help to make you look and feel good.

If a person is popular because he or she is going out with someone who's popular, or he or she is friendly with a popular person, what do you think might happen when the person stops being friends or stops going out with that other person?

I have a feeling that most kids are popular because of all the rest of the things on the list—being friendly, nice, easy to be around, fun, a good friend, honest, and so on. It might be interesting to think about the personalities of the "popular" people in your school. Check off which qualities they seem to have that are on my list and add anything that I missed.

If you're not as popular as you'd like to be, taking a closer look at what makes different people popular can help you understand what you might want to try to change in your own personality.

## What Makes Someone Unpopular?

Here's another list of whys to think about. Once again a bunch of kids helped me make up these reasons. Remember, the marks are next to reasons that I feel kids can't help. See which ones you agree with and which you don't.

showing off
being a spoiled brat
never doing their work
*not athletic
*if they have raggedy clothes and are poor
*being ugly
if you're too fat or too skinny
if you're not developed
*if you get bad grades
if you borrow something and don't give it back
if you're unreliable or undependable
if you lie
if you cheat or are dishonest
if you're not responsible
if you're a pest
if you hurt someone that everyone likes
if you tease
if you say you'll do something and then you don't
*if you're crippled or something like that
not being nice or considerate

Take another look at the reasons I didn't mark. They're the ones that I feel kids can work at and change. Kids can decide not to lie, cheat, or tease. They can stop bragging or showing off and can start being nice. They can stop being pesty and stop hurting other people.

They can stop. But—even if they want to change—some people find it really hard. Though some kids do tease and hurt just to be mean, many kids do it because they feel it's the only way they can get attention. That's sad to me, but it sure doesn't make it right. It just might help if you try to understand. (You might even say to someone, "You know, I like you anyway! You don't have to bother saying something like that.")

Reasons that I did mark, such as being crippled (disabled), poor, not having nice clothes, being ugly, getting low grades, are things that often prevent others from even trying to get to know a person. People seem to be so quick to judge. They see someone with something a little different about them, and they make a decision that they don't want to know them or they don't like them—without knowing anything else about them.

Not having the use of an arm or leg, not being able to see or hear,* not being able to get good grades, having to be placed in a separate learning class, not having enough money to get nice clothes, not being handsome or beautiful, being too fat or too skinny, doesn't mean that a person can't be a special friend or well liked by a lot of people.

I've already spoken about how being a good athlete can often make you more popular. Lots of kids have talked about what a horrible feeling it is to be picked last for a team, or for other kids to laugh or get angry when they miss a ball or something.

It would help if kids would learn that each person is different. Some are better than others at things, but it doesn't need to have anything to do with the kind of person you are. All of us need to work hard at accepting ourselves and others for who and what we and they are—instead of spending so much time wishing we were someone we're not.

## Feelings About Being Unpopular

Twelve-year-old Liz shared, "I watch all the popular kids running around together, doing things, laughing, and whispering in the halls. I hear them talking about the parties they're going to on the weekend, where they're meeting after school, not to forget to call tonight. And I feel like crying. I wish, just once, someone would ask me to come along with them into town or go to one of their houses."

Kenneth, age thirteen, told me, "I know that I'm not very popular. I don't play sports and I don't really like any girl. My grades are good

---

*If you've ever stayed away from someone who has a physical disability, my guess is it was because you might have been uncomfortable about it, didn't like the way the disability looked, didn't think you knew what to say, were scared. You may not ever have been taught that disabled kids have the same kinds of needs that you have. They're not as different as you think! I'll talk more about this in Chapter 23, Being Disabled.

though. It doesn't seem to be enough. I wish I had something else about me that would make me popular."

Cary, age nine, told me, "There's someone in my class who has a problem walking normally. She sort of leaps like a frog because she has to raise her leg in a strange way while walking. Everyone calls her Froggy, including kids from other grades. It makes her a laughing stock, and she's not popular at all. It makes me sad that people make fun of her, because I had to do a report with her and she really is nice."

Twelve-year-old Stephanie talked about how embarrassed she feels every time her teacher tells the class to pick someone to work with on a project. Said Stephanie, "All the popular kids pick each other and I always have to wait for the teacher to ask us to raise our hands if we don't have a partner. That's the worst part because everyone knows that I'm one of the ones not picked. I feel like shrinking when that happens!"

(I suggested to Stephanie that she talk with her teacher about her feelings. Maybe next time she'll just assign partners and can even put Stephanie with someone she'd like to get to know better.)

Twelve-year-old Debbie states, "I really don't care that I'm not with the popular group. I'm not going to do what they do just to go around with them!"

Peter, age twelve, said, "In elementary school I was very popular and I had three best friends. When the kids in all the schools combined into one school, my best friends just left me and went into another group with the popular kids from the other schools. I hardly ever see them anymore. I get very lonely sometimes."

Dana, age thirteen, said, "The thing that really hurts is when everyone is talking about a party and I know that I'll never be invited. In elementary school kids used to give birthday invitations out in lunch because they weren't allowed to give them in class. My heart would always pound so loud as I watched, hoping I would get one too. But I didn't . . . except once. And my mother is very friendly with her mother so I know she made her invite me."

For some kids being unpopular is embarrassing and pretty lonely. Others don't really care if they're popular or not. They've got a few good friends, and they're very happy. They're also relieved not to have to keep up with anyone.

## What Might You Do If You Want to Become More Popular?

More than anything else I'd have to go back to saying, "Take a chance and be yourself!" That's the only way you will be liked for who you are. Not for the pizza you think you need to buy for the whole group, not for helping with social studies homework, not for the clothes you wear, not for where you live, not for what you look like.

Some people are afraid to let others know them. They always stay on guard. They feel they have to put on an act to impress people, to make people like them. They're not confident that people will accept them just the way they are.

The problem is when does the act stop? How long would you have to keep it up until you feel you can try to be yourself? How many pizzas do you think kids buy for the crowd until they feel that maybe they'll be accepted without buying anymore? How many times will a boy or girl have to say "You want to copy off of my paper?" before he or she is confident enough not to need to buy the friendship or popularity anymore?

It might help to think about the many reasons that kids think people are popular. Are there any qualities that you think you can try to work on changing? Why do you think people might be staying away from you?

You can try to smile and say "hi" to more people. Learn some new names and tell others yours. Instead of staying in the background, where it might seem safer, start to let people know you're around.

As I've already said, it can be a little scary and hard to take a chance on yourself. What if people don't like you back? But how much will you feel you need to change yourself in ways that aren't you, just to be accepted and popular? Even if you were popular that way, would you be happy with yourself inside?

Just think! You're all you've got! And the sooner you begin to believe that's special, the stronger and more confident you'll become. If you start out letting people know you as you really are, then you've got a great chance to be happy within yourself and happy with your friends, because at least you'll be sure they care about you because you're you—whether you have one friend, two, or twenty.

# 14
# Boyfriends and Girl friends, Going Out

Depending upon where you live, you may use other words than *going out* to describe having a girl friend or boyfriend. Maybe you and your friends call it "going steady," "going with," "having a boyfriend," "having a girl friend," or "hanging around with." They all mean pretty much the same thing.

## What Does Going Out Mean?

Christa, age thirteen, said to her mom, "Mom, I'm going out with Andy!" Her mom replied, "Where?" Christa said, "No, mom, you don't understand, we're not going anywhere. We're just going with each other, get it?"

Until eighth or ninth grade *going out* is just an expression, a saying. It usually means that you're that person's girl friend or boyfriend. Starting in about the ninth or tenth grade, when someone asks to "go out" with you, it usually means for one date not for keeps.

Notice that I have written the ninth grade twice? That's because I'm really just guessing. It's so hard to know when going out and not going anywhere will stop, and going out on a date will start. It may be earlier or later than the ninth grade.

Fourteen-year-old Jeff raises an interesting point. "It depends where you live. When you ask a girl out here [suburb of a big city], that does not mean you have to go any place. But I could ask out a girl that I know who lives in the city to go to a movie with me. That doesn't mean we're necessarily going out; that means we're on a date. There's a difference between what goes on here and what goes on in the city. Kids seem to start dating earlier in the city than out here."

Besides thinking about what the words *going out* mean, it's interesting to take a closer look at what having a boyfriend or girl friend means. You'll probably find, as I have, that a boyfriend or girl friend means different things to different people at different times.

## In the Beginning

Valerie, age thirty-three, remembers when a boy walked her home in the sixth grade. That meant they were going out! Said Valerie, "We hid a special rock in the garden and only the two of us knew what that meant."

In the beginning going out or having a boyfriend or girl friend is a way of testing or practicing what it might be like to have one special person who you care about. It's a way of learning if you like to *focus* (foe-cuss) or give all your attention to just one person instead of a lot of people at once. It's planning what it might be like when you get older.

According to fifteen-year-old Keri, "If you went out in the fifth or sixth grade, you felt great about yourself. In the seventh and eighth grade you went out so other kids could think highly of you. It almost didn't even matter who it was. Now, in the tenth grade, not as many people are going out with each other. People seem to go out because they want to, not to impress anyone else."

Glenn, age thirteen, states, "In the fourth grade it was marrying on the playground. In the fifth grade more marrying but really nothing. In the sixth grade people started going with each other. In the seventh grade dating was important and exciting. I'm in the eighth grade, and it's just sort of there. Not that many kids are going out with each other. The only people who are excited about it are those who never dated before and are just starting."

Monica, age thirteen, said, "Having a boyfriend or girl friend in the fourth grade was a joke. The important thing then was getting married, getting divorced, who was having kids first (we made up families). In the fifth grade people went out with each other mostly to impress people. Things changed about in the sixth grade. Now, dating is very important [eighth grade], not for impressing but just for me personally."

Joanne, age forty, remembers, "We started having boyfriends in the fifth grade. By sixth many of us were going steady. I think sixth was even more social than seventh or eighth. Maybe because we went to a new school after sixth and up until then we all knew each other. In seventh we had to start all over meeting people."

Jeff, age fourteen, says, "In fourth grade it was—hey, there's a girl, what do I do?' In the fifth and sixth grade it was all sports, no time for girls. In seventh grade, it was sports? I don't want to play sports! I'm going out with this girl. In eighth grade total concentration on girls. So dating got a lot better. A lot more serious too."

While Keri thought having a boyfriend impressed people in the seventh and eighth grade, Monica thought that happened more in the fifth grade. Joanne was more social in the sixth grade; Jeff is "really concentrating" on girls in the eighth grade. Glenn says that seventh grade was the time when kids really were excited about going out.

So many different feelings. What does going out with someone mean to you? If you don't have an answer, don't be concerned. You don't have to know how you feel. Maybe you're interested in the other sex; maybe you're not. Maybe you haven't even thought about it and don't care; maybe you've just been planning but really haven't done anything about your new feelings. This is normal!

As with physical development there's no set time when your feelings about the other sex can be expected to change. It will just happen whenever you are ready. Just because you're going out doesn't mean your feelings have changed. Maybe you feel you have to go out, even if you don't want to or are not ready.

## When Will "Liking Someone" Start for You?

Keith said to me, "I'm eleven years old. When am I supposed to start liking girls?" Well, Keith, I wish I could give you an answer. But, once again, I'd have to guess.

You may start liking someone of the other sex as early as elementary school or perhaps not until after high school. You never know. Each person becomes interested at different times.

Being ready depends upon how you feel, how your parents feel, what your friends are doing, and even has to do with your hormones.

Greg, age twelve, thinks, "The kids who were first made the rest of the group go faster." Heidi, age eleven, agrees. She says that her other friends began to change because she and another girl started liking boys last year. "At first they teased us and said we were silly, but then they started liking them too."

Gene, age thirty-nine, said, "I was always scared stiff of girls. I didn't know how to act with them. Most of my friends were interested in girls at least by junior high. But I didn't have my first date until I was twenty-three! My friends understood that I wasn't ready, and I understood that my friends were. It didn't bother my friendships."

I've heard mixed feelings about whether being interested or not causes friendships to change. Gene's friends stayed the same even though he didn't date and they did. Other boys and girls have told me that they didn't spend as much time with their friends when their interests were no longer the same. I think that much depends upon how close you have been and how much each of you respects that everyone has his or her own feelings—even best friends.

Traci, age thirteen, said, "I'm interested in boys but my parents won't let me go out with anyone until I'm in the ninth grade. What a bummer!"

Jimmy, age fourteen, said, "My parents think it's okay for kids to date at my age. They always ask me who I like and will say that someone looks cute if we go to a school concert or something. But I couldn't care less about girls right now. I wish they'd stop bugging me about it."

As you can see, some boys and girls are ready before their friends and parents, others not until way after. Some get interested (sometimes pressured) to begin dating the other sex because their friends have started; others feel more free to do what feels right to them. Of course lots of friends can become interested all at once. It doesn't always have to be at different times.

Some kids are ready but their parents aren't. Others are not ready, but their parents are. Have you ever discussed going out or dating with your parents? We'll talk more about this later.

The big question is how you feel about all of this. Even if you've been going out with someone for years, it might be interesting to think some more about how you felt when you started. Who else of your friends was also interested; who wasn't? Did anyone tease or give you a hard time?

If you haven't yet begun, it might help to keep telling yourself, "It's okay that I feel the way I feel." Try not to rush yourself. But also watch that you don't hold yourself back, even if you feel shy and a little scared. Think about Gene. He waited until he was twenty-three; not because he wanted to, but he just was so nervous that he couldn't try.

It's very natural to be nervous. Keri, age fifteen, shared, "Before I went out, I didn't know how to act with just one boy. I always had lots of friends that were boys, but we all usually were together in a group. It's much different when you're alone. Most of my friends are scared of boys. You always think about what it's going to be like and what you're going to do. I think if you date even once, you won't be as scared the next time. I grew up so much even from one date."

Maybe if Gene had pushed himself, he would have got more comfortable earlier. But you can't always expect to be comfortable with everything you do. If that were so, lots of people would be waiting their whole lives to get started. Besides you've got a right to start when you choose.

Just because your friends are interested doesn't mean that you have to be. You may want to be interested, but think twice if you feel forced. It may not be as much fun for you if you let others tell you what to do and when.

## How Can You Tell If Your Feelings Have Begun to Change?

When you look at the girl who has been sitting in front of you for three months and realize you've never really seen her before, and she's kind of cute.

When the boy who has been grabbing your scarf and throwing it around to his friends at recess decides to stop grabbing, and you wish he would do it again.

When you notice that the girl who has been the only girl allowed on the boy's baseball team has started looking more like a girl and less like one of the boys.

When you look at someone and think, "Oh, I'd just 'die' if he or she would come over and talk to me."

When you start taking more showers and begin to pay attention to what you look like.

When you start noticing other peoples' appearances too.

When there's more teasing, more phony phone calls to boys from girls or girls from boys (usually, that means more interest).

When you feel a desire to get closer to someone, perhaps even to touch them in a different way.

When you'd rather spend the afternoon with one girl or boy than be with your friends.

When you think a lot about someone and write his or her name on your books or on a secret piece of paper that only you or your close friends can see. When you dream about someone special. . . . When you get all fluttery when you see that person, maybe even blush.

When you go out of your way to make sure that you "bump" into him or her while walking through the halls at school.

When you spend even one minute hoping that he or she would call you, or wishing that you'd have the guts to call that person.

You and your friends might be able to add some more whens of your own to this list.

*Important Note:* You needn't be concerned if you have never felt any of these feelings. Maybe your time for being interested in the other sex has not begun yet. Remember that each person's feelings are different. There aren't any rules about "when."

Try to be patient with yourself. Try to accept the way you feel, no matter how much interest your friends have. If they're really your friends, they'll respect your right to feel and be who you are and they won't try to push you if you're not ready. If they do push you, tell them to lay off. If they don't leave you alone about it, maybe you need to look for some new friends.

It's possible that you'll spend a little less time with your friends if they're with the boys or girls and you really don't want to be. But you might choose to hang around and just see how you feel with them. Maybe the feelings won't have started inside of you, but if you try being around them, you might find it fun. Do whatever feels comfortable for you.

Once you're interested, you'll be that way for the rest of your life. So be patient with yourself. What's another month, or year or two? You've got time to think about it.

## How Can You Let Someone Know That You Like Him or Her?

When you decide to let someone know you like them, you're deciding to take a chance that they'll like you or at least will think about it. It might help to remember that if you don't try, he or she may never know how you feel. If you'd like them to know, then you have to make sure—somehow.

Before you read these choices, it might be fun to try to make your own list of how you can let someone know.

Eleven-year-old Hillary suggests, "Just tell him!" While this is certainly the most direct way to make sure he (or she) knows, I've learned that this is one of the hardest for kids to do.

What's the concern? Once again, rejection. What if they say, "Thanks for telling me but no thanks." What if they don't like you? What if they laugh? Actually they just might laugh if they're nervous—especially if they do like you.

If you don't think you can get up the courage to tell them yourself in person, on the telephone, or in a note (watch what you say in notes; they have a sneaky way of getting around), then maybe you'll want to try something else.

Jody, age thirteen, says, "Tell your friend and have your friend tell him." Lots of boys and girls seem to feel this way is easier. Brian, age eleven, thinks that a good way is to tell their brother or sister that you like them and have them find out if he or she likes you back.

Twenty-four-year-old Judy remembers, "The way everyone found out who liked who was when we passed notes around in class. You know, Judy likes Jimmy and so on. The only trouble was that you could get caught! Once a teacher took away a note I was passing to my friend and asked if I wanted everyone to know what it said. I was so embarrassed thinking she would read it out loud, but she never did! The boy I liked was in the same class and didn't know I liked him yet."

"Spread a rumor," said Danny, age ten. "Rumors usually spread all around the school very fast. You can tell your friend to start it." While it may be easier for you to let other kids tell your feelings instead of you, you're not as in control of what's being said. By the time a rumor reaches *the* person, it may not even be what you wanted to say. So be careful about whom you trust to tell.

Jennifer, age twelve, thinks it's a good idea to ask *the* person if they want to go into town (or to someone's house or anywhere) with you and your friends. "That way it will be a group and not as personal. Sometimes it's easier to start that way."

Danielle, age fourteen, said, "You can also flirt with someone you like. Tease but be cute or funny about it."

Pay more attention to them. Ask them questions about what they're doing so you can show them you're interested. Let them know you notice them and do what you can to make them take notice of you. Smile!

Choose a way of letting them know, that feels best to you. If one way doesn't work so well, try another and another. Or mix a few ways. Experiment! The more you try, the easier it will probably become.

## How You Might Know If Someone Likes You

Just take all the suggestions in the section you just read and turn them around. Instead of you doing something to try to let someone else know how you feel, they'll have to try to let you know how they feel.

Here are a few tips to remember.

When it seems like someone really is not interested in you because they're always teasing, that's the time to wonder if they really are interested but don't know how else to show it.

If it seems like someone is hanging around you and may like you, you might try to help them out. Understand that it may be very hard for them to talk to you about how they feel. The more sensitive and nice you are, the easier it will be for them. In fact if you like them and they're not saying anything about liking you (but you think they do), instead of waiting you can talk about it first.

## Choosing Someone to Like

Just like you can look around for a new friend, you can also look around for a girl friend or boyfriend. Remember to watch out for judging things like clothes or looks that may not really tell you what kind of person they are.

I know that if, for example, a girl wears a lot of make up, that might color your opinion of her. You may not care what kind of person she is, if you don't like the way she presents herself. So it's tricky to decide what's important to consider and what really isn't. It's very personal.

Cindy, age seventeen, told me, "There was a boy in the sixth grade who dressed really shabbily. He was clean, but he didn't dress in the coolest clothes to come to school. My friends and I couldn't figure out if we really liked him because of the way he dressed. Yet he was nice. And I know that the way he dressed really stopped me from wanting to like him. Then we invited him to a party. He came dressed in the greatest looking sweater and pants. No one was even sure if it was really him. He was gorgeous! When he told us that he didn't wear his good clothes to school because they were for special occasions, we were all really sorry about judging him." So you never know.

Some kids are so good looking that many people feel they can't ever go up to them. Tommy, age thirty-one, shared, "I was very lonely when I was growing up. I was too shy to ask any one to go out with me, and I think because of my looks people were afraid I would reject them."

The steps I suggested you try in order to make a friend are the same for going out. If someone says no, go on to the next and the next. Tommy's loneliness might help you realize that no matter what a person looks like, *try*. They may be so happy that you did. And if they're not, it's their loss! You don't lose anything by trying!

## Liking Kids Who Are the Same Sex As You Are

It's common during the growing up years for you to feel that a person of the same sex is very special in your life. They can mean a lot to you. You'll probably want to do everything together. Sometimes you might get jealous when they pay attention to anyone else.

It's possible that you will find it hard to have a boyfriend or girl friend because your feelings are so strong about this close friend. You might want to spend more time with them than anyone else.

Most of the time, you'll outgrow these feelings toward this close friend and become very interested in kids of the other sex. But sometimes, your feelings will grow even stronger for your friend or a person just like them. They might make you feel very good. But if these feelings confuse you, I suggest that you speak with your parents, a favorite teacher, school counselor, religious leader or other trusted adult.

## How To Let Someone Know You Don't Like Them Anymore

I think it's very important for you to tell them yourself (in private), rather than have a friend tell them for you. Understand it will not be easy for them to hear that you don't like them as a boyfriend or girl friend anymore. If they liked you a lot, you can expect they'll feel upset about breaking up, even if they don't show it. So be honest, but be kind.

You might say, "I've been doing a lot of thinking. And I really feel I'm not ready to only go out with one person. I hope we still can be good friends." Or say, "I really like you and everything, but I don't think I want to be boyfriend and girl friend anymore. Can we just be friends? I hope you understand."

The key is how you say what you say. Be sensitive and show that you care. Then go ahead and say what you must. For you to keep quiet and continue a relationship that has already ended for you would not be fair to either person.

Sometimes you can't prevent hurting someone's feelings, even if you don't want to. That's an important lesson to learn. It not only affects your girl friend or boyfriend relationships but will help you be more honest with your parents, teachers, and friends.

## "What If You Like Someone Who Your Friends Don't Like?"

Tim, age eleven, said, "I like this girl, but my friends all think she's ugly and want me to go out with someone else."

That's an example of the judging that I've been talking about. Maybe if Tim's friends allowed themselves to get to know the girl he liked, without letting her looks get in the way, they'd think she is nice too.

Pressure from friends can be very strong. Would you stop going out with someone you like because your friends didn't like his or her looks? Who do you think should decide who you like, them or you?

If you're strong about your own feelings, I would hope your friends would respect you. The thing to ask yourself is, "What do I feel?" Then make your own decision.

## "What If You Don't Have a Boyfriend or Girl Friend and Most of Your Friends Do?"

Marni, age twelve, talked about how out of it she felt in the seventh grade. She wanted a boyfriend so badly but no one seemed interested in her. Most of her friends had boyfriends. Said Marni, "They would talk about their boyfriends at the lunch table all the time. They would hang out together in the afternoons after school. They'd go over to one person's house or walk into town together. But since I didn't have a boyfriend, I didn't go along. It felt awful. Finally, I found a boyfriend. I really didn't like him that much, but it was better than not having anyone at all."

How do you feel about wanting a boyfriend or girl friend so badly that you take on whoever seems to be interested just to belong? It really can be painful to feel left out. But you can't always magically produce a boyfriend or girl friend just because you're ready! You've got to look around, find someone interesting, and try to get to know them first.

If you allow yourself to need a boyfriend in order to feel good about yourself with your friends, then you're forgetting that it's not the boyfriend that makes you so special; it's being who you are. With or without a boyfriend your importance doesn't ever have to change.

I can understand that it might feel awkward going to someone's house if everyone there is paired off. I guess it depends upon what they're doing. If everyone is together with each other, you can think about being there too. If they're just together with their boyfriends, you're probably better off finding something else to do.

Walking into town with a group of your friends and their boyfriends or girl friends might not make you feel as left out as you think. More than likely you'll all know each other. You probably even grew up with many of the boys and girls. So why not join them? If you don't already know them, it would probably be nice to meet them. Have they said anything to you to make you think you should stay away?

Another way to deal with this is to find some other friends who don't have boyfriends or girl friends either. I'm not suggesting you give up your friends. It's just that you might find you'll be spending less time with them until you find a boyfriend or girl friend or they give up theirs.

There's also nothing wrong with taking a chance and just asking a boy or girl if he or she wants to come into town with you and your friends.

### "If You Like a Boy and That Boy is Going Out with Another Girl, Should You Tell Him Your Feelings for Him?"

As always you've got several things to think about before choosing what to do. First, whether or not the other girl is a friend of yours, flirting with him and letting him know you like him would probably be thought of as a ratty thing to do.

Second, realize that anything you say to him might be told to her and many others. That might be embarrassing and could give you a reputation as a boyfriend stealer (not a good thing to be). Thirteen-year-old Andy states, "I don't think you should even hint at it. Because if anybody else finds out, then it will get around. That could be embarrassing to you and to that other person."

Jamie, age fourteen, feels, "If someone is going with someone else, you don't have to totally go in the background. You can get to know that person and be friends, but don't let anyone know you're making a play for them. You just have to wait!"

You never know. If you're nice and fun to be with, he just might look at you differently. You don't have to flirt to catch his interest. And there's no rule that says you can't be friendly. Just be you and hope he doesn't take too long with that other girl.

Most important is how *you* feel. No matter what cautions I or anyone else have offered, you may feel so strongly about him that you want to tell him, no matter what. As long as you understand and are willing to accept what might happen if you tell him your feelings, then go ahead and choose what you think is best for you. You have a right to make your own decision.

## "If You and Your Friend Like the Same Person, What Should You Do?"

At your age boyfriends and girl friends usually come and go. But the friendships you make can last forever. It would be sad to let liking the same boy or girl (or anything) interfere with your friendships.

I suggest you talk with your friend about who you like. With luck, both of you will have good senses of humor! Maybe one of you likes that person more than the other.

While you can even flip a coin to choose who can keep liking him or her, you still have to wait to see who he or she likes. Maybe you won't have to choose, after all. Maybe he or she already likes one of you more than the other. Maybe he or she doesn't like either of you!

## "What If Your Boyfriend or Girl Friend Goes to a Different School?

Darren, age fourteen, shared, "I have a girl friend but she doesn't go to this school. And all my friends have girl friends. I feel that when we have activities involving boys and girls, I won't have anyone to go with. I don't like anyone in this school as a girl friend, so I feel I'll be left out." It often depends upon what the activity is. A lot of the time it doesn't matter if everyone's girl friend or boyfriend is there, because you're all there together. And if you're really good friends, they'll be happy you're with them, girl friend or not.

If you're concerned about being with someone, there's no reason not to ask a friend who's a girl or boy to go to those activities with you. Then you'll have company. As Jeff, age fourteen, shared, "I asked a girl who's a friend of mine to go to a movie with me. We're not going out in school; we are just friends going out."

As you can see, going out doesn't always have to mean that you're boyfriend and girl friend. You can still go places with other friends that are going out with each other and not feel left out.

## Parties

Boy-girl parties can begin as early as third grade with some groups of children. Have you ever gone to a boy-girl party? If you have, were most of the kids paired off or all together?

Katie, age twelve, shared, "I was really embarrassed and bored at the party my friend had last weekend. Everyone except me and another girl was with a boyfriend. There was one boy there without a girlfriend. The three of us stayed in another room while the others turned the lights out and had kissing contests. I couldn't decide if I should have my parents pick me up or stay since it didn't seem to matter that I was there."

If most of the kids at a party are paired off in couples, it can be awkward to be one of the only people who is alone. I think in Katie's case, the fact that they turned off the lights made it more difficult to be there. If all her friends were just hanging around together, listening to music, dancing, and talking, she probably would have felt good about being there.

Sean, age twelve, told me how he felt pressured because he's friends with a group of kids who have had girl friends for at least two years. They started having parties in the fourth grade. Sean just started going out with someone and felt very funny at the last party he went to. He said, "All my friends have had girlfriends for at least two years, but this was the first time I was with a girl. I felt funny being there when the lights were turned low. It was embarrassing. The other kids look like they were kissing and holding each other close. I didn't want to do anything like that. Besides, I didn't really know how. So I asked the girl I was with if she wanted to go into the other room so we could just talk."

Wise move, Sean! As you can see, even if you're paired off, you can feel a bit funny depending upon what everyone else is doing. The best idea is to follow your gut sense as to what you'd like to do. Try to think of your choices, and then pick something that seems comfortable. In Sean's case he chose to leave the room where the other couples were "kissing and holding." In Katie's situation she and two others stayed in another room but weren't sure what they wanted to do. Sometimes it's harder to decide than other times.

## Parents and Parties

Fourteen-year-old Alexis shared, "The only problem with having a party is that my parents come down so many times to check that no one is doing what they shouldn't. While I understand they have to check up every once in a while, they don't have to do it that often. They never allow us to have much privacy. It embarrasses me in front of my friends that they come down so many times. I'm always glad to go to parties at other kids' houses, so I won't have to worry about what my friends will think."

It would be a shame not to feel good about inviting your friends to your home. You owe it to yourself and your parents to let them know how you feel. It's hard for some parents to realize that their children must be given a little space and privacy. Perhaps the fear is that if they were to leave you alone "with all that's going on among kids today" you or your friends would do something you'd all be sorry about. They've got to work at believing they can trust you, just like you've got to prove to them you deserve their trust. Perhaps an honest discussion with them will help to ease any concerns.

"My problem," said Peter, age twenty, "was when my friends showed up and my parents weren't home, and I had to tell them they couldn't come in. My parents made a rule that no more than three kids could come over to our house if they weren't home. And no girls! But it was really hard. What do you do when your closest friends are outside saying that your parents will never find out, and they can't believe you're actually going to listen? But I always worried about being caught, or that

something would break, or they'd try to take my parents' booze. So I would shut the door and feel awful about it."

As hard as shutting the door might have been, I feel Peter was correct in respecting his parents' limits. It's his parents' house and their right to make the rules. He may not be happy about following them, but he can't always be happy about everything (sad but true!). If his parents found out he didn't obey, they might have had a hard time trusting him about other things.

It would probably have made not letting Peter's friends in easier, if he had explained his parents' rules before. That way his friends wouldn't have been surprised that he couldn't let them in. Peter could have just said, "Sorry, they're not home!" And his friends might have had an easier time accepting what they already knew to be a rule. If he believed the rules were too strict or hard to keep because of his friends, then it might have helped to talk with his parents.

## Parents and Going Out

Kenneth, age thirteen, said, "Every time I tell my father and brother who I like, they make fun of me and tease me about it. They don't realize that I'm serious."

Kenneth, I think it's very important for you to tell your father and brother how you feel. Let them know you are serious and feel bad every time they make fun. You might say, "I don't think you realize how serious I am. Every time you make fun of me I get very upset. If you don't stop, I won't share with you anymore."

Samantha, age twelve, said, "My parents won't let me date. They think the seventh grade is too early." Laurie, age eleven, told me, "My parents don't care!"

Kim, age eleven, said, "I'm afraid to talk to my mom or dad about liking someone. I'm afraid they're going to tell me that it's too early, that I have to wait."

Well, Kim, the fact is they may just tell you that. Different parents have different ideas about when going out or dating should begin. But you won't know what your own parents feel unless you take a chance and ask them. If you think they're being old fashioned or unfair, tell them your feelings and see if you can reach some agreement.

One boy told me he spent two hours trying to convince the mother of a girl he liked to "let them go out with each other." Said Carl, age thirteen, "But she wouldn't budge an inch. She still feels her daughter shouldn't date until the ninth grade. We're in eighth grade now. We can be friends and be together in school. But I can't really say that I'm dating her. What a bummer!"

Some parents are more strict than others. Have you ever talked to your parents about going out? It might be very interesting and important for you to ask them when no one is rushing off and you'll have time to stay and talk with each other for a while—perhaps at the dinner table one night.

Even if you're not interested in going out with anyone yet, you can still ask your parents their feelings about when it's okay for you to start. You might be surprised to find that your parents also had crushes and first dates when they were your age.

It's good to be able to talk with your parents about this. They can probably help you understand your own feelings better. Talking with an older brother, sister, teacher, or older friend you trust can also be helpful.

# 15
# Peer Pressure, Making Choices

Before reading this chapter please take a few minutes out to think about whether you have ever done anything that you really didn't want to do but did anyway because your friends were doing it? That's what peer pressure is about.

It can affect your friendships and decisions about going out, using drugs, smoking, drinking, having sex, dress, and how you treat your family. Since making choices can often be difficult and confusing, I hope this chapter will help you better understand what peer pressure is and how it affects your choices. The more you understand, the healthier decisions you will make.

## What's Peer Pressure?

If you take the two words separately, you'll find that *pressure* is the feeling of being forced, persuaded, or influenced by something. It can give you an uneasy feeling and sometimes cause you to do things that you really don't believe in and wouldn't usually do. A peer is someone who is about the same age as you are. *Peers* is another way of saying "your friends." Peer pressure is felt when your friends try to influence you to say or do something, even if you don't want to. You feel you need to do it so you can stay friendly with them.

You may still be wondering, "Yes, but what is it?" Maybe if you think carefully about each of the following questions, you'll begin to get a better idea of what peer pressure means. You'll probably be surprised to realize how many different ways your friends have influenced you, even if you weren't aware of the pressure at the time.

Have you ever:

> Wanted to do something just because your friends were doing it, thinking if you didn't go along with them, they wouldn't accept you as much and you wouldn't stay their friend?
>
> Wanted to do something that no one else wanted to do but felt funny doing it because you didn't want anyone to call you dumb, silly, or say they wouldn't be your friend?
>
> Wanted to do something that all your friends were doing but couldn't because your parents wouldn't let you?
>
> Not wanted to do something that everyone was doing but did it anyway? (And didn't let anyone know you didn't want to do it, because you thought your friends would laugh, be angry, or not think you were the type to hang around with them anymore?)
>
> Not wanted to do something, told your friends you didn't want to, and found they said things like, "Oh, come on, why not?", "I don't know why we're friends with you if you won't come with us," "Oh, try it, just this once..," "What, are you chicken?," "You're such a baby.... Why don't you just go home to your parents?"

If you said yes to any one of these considerations, you have felt peer pressure! Most kids, if not all, have felt it at one time or another. Adults have too. You might already have found that some pressures are easier to deal with than others.

## Dealing with Peer Pressure

Peer pressure can be very confusing and sometimes painful. But it also can challenge and strengthen your confidence, help you learn more about who you are and what you believe, and teach you which friendships are real.

At times you'll probably find that friends may not be as kind as you would like them to be, especially when you don't go along with them. So you'll end up having to make a choice between their feelings and yours.

You may find it confusing to even figure out what your choices are. But trust that they are there if you think hard enough. And realize that you have the final word (of course, figuring in what rules your parents have set for you).

Sometimes you may have the confidence to do what you feel is right, no matter what your friends think (even your best friend). Other times you may feel that the pressure is too much and it's better to give in than fight it. Each choice will be up to you.

Dealing with peer pressure forces you to take a chance and see if your friends will respect your right to decide what's best for you. First you have to respect yourself.

Peer pressure can be felt in many ways. Even the same pressure in the same situation with the same friends will be felt differently by each person. It would be great if everyone learned that the only decision a person has a right to make is his or her own. Friends can give advice and tell you what they think, but it's not fair for them to tell you what to do and how to do it and expect for you to listen. If you allow them to make your decisions, you have only yourself to blame.

This is a tough message, but if you don't learn to be strong about saying no (or yes) when you must, then you can end up being pressured into doing something very dangerous. The sooner you take charge of your own decisions, the easier it will be to act according to what you believe.

Let's take a look at some of the different ways in which other kids have felt peer pressure. Maybe you've been in similar situations. In each case I've suggested ways the boy or girl might have acted differently. I hope the lists of other choices will help you better understand how each situation can be taken apart in order to figure out what you want to do. As always, it would be great if you can add any extra choices.

Tommy, age eleven, told me his parents are very strict and don't let him go to R rated movies like his friends. His friends always tease him about not being as mature as they are, and they make sure to talk in front of him about the movies they've seen. That only makes him feel worse. Whenever he can, he tries to change the subject.

What else could Tommy do?

> Instead of changing the subject he could tell them how he really feels.

He could tell his friends that he knows they're talking in front of him about the movie on purpose.

He could say to his friends that he can't help what rules his parents make. If he were allowed to go, he'd love to (so bug off!).

He could let his friends know that their teasing and movie talk make him feel worse, and he'd like them to stop. (If they're really his good friends, they will.)

If they don't stop teasing, he could start to look for some non-R rated friends!

He could talk with his parents about the fact that he feels he's old enough to go to that kind of a movie. Maybe they would agree to let him try one as long as they went with him, so they could be sure to answer any questions and see that he understands.

(Note: If Tommy's parents won't even think about it, Tommy will have to try harder to accept that he'll have to wait for a while.)

Jeannie, age thirteen, shared that she felt pressure when a girl she wanted to be friends with her asked her for answers during a test at school. She'd never cheated before and didn't want to then, but had a hard time deciding what to do. Since she wasn't very popular and wanted to make friends badly, she went ahead and let her copy.

Some thoughts about why Jeannie did what she did:

She was worried that saying no would make the girl not want to be her friend.

She thought that saying yes would be proof that she was a good friend to have.

What else could Jeannie have done if she didn't want to let her cheat?

She could have said, "Quiet! We'll get in trouble. I'll be happy to help you with your homework after school if you still have any questions."

Another possibility is, "I'm sorry, but I don't want to get into trouble."

Or, "Please don't ask me anything, I really need to think."

And she could have ignored her.

What do you think you would have done?

Richard, age twenty, said, "One afternoon when I was in the eighth grade, I was at my friend's house with a group of other kids. They decided to try one of his parent's cigarettes that was lying around. They passed it from person to person, and when it came to me, I passed it on to the next person without trying it. (I knew it was wrong and didn't want to get in trouble.) They couldn't believe that I was such a wimp and kept telling me that for the rest of the afternoon. I don't know why I stayed."

Let's hear it for Richard, he had guts.

It must have taken a belly full of guts for Richard to have passed the cigarette without trying it (A lot of kids would have been pressured into trying it).

Richard had the confidence to take a stand for what he felt, even if it hurt to have his friends call him names all afternoon.

I'm willing to bet there were other friends who wouldn't have tried smoking that afternoon, if they knew someone else wouldn't try it too.

If the name calling got bad enough, Richard could have left.

What else could Richard have done?

He could have left when they first began to talk about taking the cigarettes.

He could have told his friends from the start that he didn't agree with what they were doing and would not go along with it.

He could have tried to convince them not to smoke.

Thirteen-year-old Mindy's story is another example of how friends can influence your decisions. She shared, "A couple of weeks ago my mom bought me a great pair of purple overalls. Purple is my favorite color. I loved them and couldn't wait to wear them to school. As soon as I got to school the next day, kids started saying things like, "That color is gross," and "I like your overalls but why purple?" I had a hard time stopping myself from crying. I was so embarrassed and so angry." Mindy decided she would only wear them at home and when her family went visiting.

Some purple truths:

Even though she wanted to wear her overalls to school, how her friends felt about them was more important to her than how she felt.

Her friends' remarks pressured her into keeping her new overalls private.

What could Mindy have said to her friends?

"You may think they're gross, but I love them!"

"Now that I know how you feel, you don't have to keep saying it."
"I love them, and I'm the one wearing them. I'll remember not to
lend them to you."

Jeremy, age twelve, shared, "I don't like going down really steep
places fast. Like, say I'm skiing. I like taking my time and going slowly.
When I'm riding my bike with my friends, they will sometimes go down
some very steep place. And even if I'm really scared and I don't want to
do it at all, I'll go down it. Even if I hate it the whole way, I'll do it."

(Jeremy told me he mainly does it because he hates being teased and
doesn't want the word to get around that he wouldn't do it.)

What could Jeremy have done besides go down the steep hill with his
friends?

He could have said, "No way! Go ahead if you want to but I won't!"
He could have told them, "I'll meet you at the bottom. I hate going
down really steep places fast."
He could have asked his friends to go somewhere else or told them
that he would lead the way as soon as he realized where he was
headed.

How about trying to make your own list of choices for the next few
situations. It might be interesting and fun to ask your friends to make
their own lists too. Then compare and talk about your answers. Pen or
pencil ready? Here goes.

Scott, age fourteen, said that he felt pressured when all his friends
wanted him to go out with a certain girl, and he didn't like her. What do
you think Scott should have done? What could he have said to his
friends?

Craig, age nine, felt pressured when the kids he was with wanted to
sneak through his neighbor's yard and his parents had already told him
not to do that. What might Craig have told his friends? What would you
have done if you were Craig?

Liz, age fourteen, would have been very happy not getting a bra. She said she didn't even need or want one. But most of the girls in her gym class wore one and she felt she had to get one too. Would you have felt the same thing? What would you have done if you were Liz?

Alan, age twelve, feels very embarrassed that he's not allowed to go to the candy store a few blocks from his house. Alan shared, "My parents think that too many rough kids hang out there, but most of my friends can go. It drives me crazy when we ride our bicycles home from school and my friends are making plans to go there." Is there something that Alan could say to his friends so that he doesn't have to be driven crazy hearing their plans? What might Alan say to his parents about his feelings? What would you do if you were Alan? Would you listen to your parents?

Rob, age thirteen, said, "I get very embarrassed sometimes when I go into town with my friends. They get bigger allowances than I do, and my parents don't believe in giving me any more money if I spend it all at once. A lot of my friends can't understand it when I can't have a second piece of pizza. Maybe it would be easier if I just say I'm not hungry." Do you think that would be a good thing to say? How else could Rob deal with this?

Charlene, age ten, loves to put peanut butter on her tuna fish sandwiches. The first time she brought one of these to school, the kids at her lunch table said, "Gross me out! That's disgusting. How could you eat it like that?" Charlene answered, "Because I love it." Her friends said, "Well, you're crazy!" Charlene decided that she would only eat peanut butter–tuna fish sandwiches on the weekends, and she'd eat plain tuna fish during the week at school. Would you have still added peanut butter no matter what your friends thought? Would you have only put a tiny bit of peanut butter on so they couldn't notice that much? What could Charlene have said to her friends to let them know how she felt and stop them from saying her sandwich was gross?

Now that you've had some practice in figuring out choices in many different kinds of peer pressure situations, the next step is to look closer at what your choices might mean.

## Just Knowing You Have a Choice is Not Enough, You've Got to Look Ahead to What Your Choice Might Mean

Looking ahead means to *anticipate* (an-tiss-i-pate) or try to guess what the results of your choice might be. Think to yourself, "What will happen if. . ." For example:

This is what might have been rolling around in Richard's head as the cigarette was being passed around to him.

If I decide to smoke that cigarette,
a) I'm going to hate myself for giving in.
b) My friends will think I'm cool.
c) I could get into trouble.
d) I might look dumb or foolish, since I don't know what to do.
e) Maybe I'll cough a lot or get *nauseous* (naw-shuss: when you feel like you need to vomit).
f) If my friend's parents find out about this, they could tell my parents. And that could mean trouble.
g) Maybe I'll really like it. Then what would I do?

If I don't try to smoke when the cigarette is passed to me,
a) I'll really be doing what I think is right.
b) My friends will probably try to convince me that I should try it.
c) My friends will learn that I can be their friend but not feel I have to do what they do.
d) My friends might tease me and give me a hard time.
e) My friends might respect me and just keep passing it among themselves without trying to push me to do it.
f) My friends might feel I shouldn't be hanging around with them if I won't do what they do.
g) My parents would probably be very proud of me if I told them I didn't smoke when I could have tried.
h) I'll feel good about myself.

If I leave before they start smoking,
a) I won't be in an uncomfortable situation.
b) I'll feel relieved not to be part of something I know is not right.

c) Maybe my friends will talk about me when I leave—that I'm chicken or whatever.

d) I'd be taking a risk. Maybe they'll think I'm not cool enough to still be friends with them.

e) I won't get into trouble.

If I try to convince them not to try smoking,

a) They might think I'm a real goody-goody.

b) They might listen.

c) They might laugh at me for trying to stop them.

And so on. Get the idea?

No matter what the situation or how much you're pressured, it's very important to get your facts straight first. Then think about your choices and ask yourself, "If I do or say this, then what could happen?" When you've considered all the possible feelings and reactions that might result from each choice, then you'll be much more ready to make the decision that's best for you at the time.

Here are some more questions you can ask yourself before making a choice:

How will your decision make you feel?
(proud, embarrassed, disappointed in yourself, ashamed, confident, left out, relieved, etc.)

How will people react to what you say or do?
(with surprise, anger, relief, happiness, disappointment, respect, maybe they won't want to be your friend any more, etc.)

*Important note:* Just because you understand your choices doesn't guarantee that your decision will be the right one. If you make a mistake, it will just prove that you're human like the rest of us. What a relief!

All you can do is try your best, say you're sorry for being wrong, and learn from what you did, so you don't make the same mistake next time.

## Taking Charge of Your Own Choices

Your parents (or anyone else) can tell you not to cross a busy street, not to go to a certain store, not to hang around with a certain group of kids, not to smoke, not to drink, not to cheat, not to use drugs, or not to have sex before you're an adult and are more ready to make that choice. You can know and understand what you've been taught. But when it comes down to actually being faced with the situation, you're the one who will have to decide what you will or will not do.

It will be *you* going down that steep hill, *you* taking the chance that you might fall, *you* risking that you'll be left out, *you* chancing that you'll be caught, *you* facing the possibility that your friends will not talk with you for a few days, *you* taking the chance that what you're doing might be dangerous to you, *you* risking that your parents will be angry if they find out, *you* who will have to deal with any guilty feelings from doing something you know is not right for you. You will have to decide. And you will have to live with your decision, its *consequences* (con-si-kwen-ses), or results—what happens when you do something—and with luck you will learn from it for next time.

If you respect yourself strongly, then I hope you'll be very careful about going against your *values* (val-use), or what you feel is right or wrong and important or not important, unless you're sure that the time is right to do so. Not only because someone else is pressuring you, but also because you've had the freedom to think of all the reasons why you should or shouldn't and then made the choice yourself.

## Sometimes You May Be More Easily Pressured Than Other Times

Have you ever wondered why it is that sometimes you're more likely to give in to pressure than other times? It usually has to do with the way you feel about yourself at the moment. If you feel confident and good about yourself, you'll probably not give in so easily. If you are not confident and don't feel so good about yourself, you'll probably give in more easily. Most of the feelings you have about yourself come from the way you relate to your mother, father, brothers, sisters, and friends.

For example, even if your mother and/or father really love(s) you, if you feel unloved, then you might not feel as important. Maybe you'd think that your parent's bad feelings were your fault. Maybe you'd think if you were just a little bit better as a kid, it would make your parents happy.

So since you might have difficulty making your parents happy (with you), you might try to at least make everyone else happy, like your friends. That's one of the reasons peer pressure can start, and you may give in to pressure that you might not agree to if you felt stronger and better.

Also if you've had a bad experience because you made a decision that didn't turn out right, you might be more likely to let other people make a decision for you—so you don't have to be concerned about being wrong again. Remember each decision will teach you something, whether it's right or wrong! All you can do is try your best and be honest about your feelings.

## Making Choices Will Become Easier
## As You Learn More About Your Values

It's hard to know exactly what you will do if your friends pressure you for any reason. Making choices will become easier as you learn more about your own sense of values. Sometimes what's right or wrong will be clear to you; other times you may not be so sure. Try not to rush into anything especially if you feel you need more time to decide. If you can't make up your mind, it might be smarter to wait.

You'll probably end up staying away from or saying no to situations that are too dangerous or are much too different from the way you feel. For example, you might give in and go to a movie that everyone else wants to see, even if you don't wish to see it. But you may not join your friends in teasing the retarded boy who lives on your block.

You may decide to wear a certain kind of shirt, beads on your sneakers, or the same jeans that everyone else seems to have (even if you don't like the style that much and you miss your purple overalls). But you may not choose to smoke or drink in the afternoon at your friend's house, just because the other kids are doing it. If you say no and find out that your friends don't respect your decision, maybe they were never your good friends in the first place.

You may be wondering, "Why the big deal about making choices, respecting myself, and learning about my values?" Throughout your life you'll probably find that many people will try to tell you who you are and how you should behave. They'll even try to tell you how you should feel. Peer pressure never ends. Though the situations will change and you may feel pressured for different reasons at different ages, your values, inner confidence, and self respect will be tested each time.

The stronger you are about what you believe, the stronger you'll be about making the choice that seems right for you. The more you understand how to take each situation and figure out what choices you have to consider, the more likely that you'll find a choice that is healthy for you and makes you feel good.

# 16
# Sexual Feelings

This chapter will deal with sexual feelings, more pressures, and more choices. Since there's little room for mistakes when it comes to making sexual decisions, it's important that you pay close attention to the many ways you might handle these feelings.

The tingly feelings I spoke about in Chapter 9 were sexual feelings that can be felt when a person is alone. In this chapter, I'll talk about when these feelings are felt for another person and shared.

## How Can You Tell When You Have Them?

When you have the desire to touch someone in a caring, personal way.

When you want to share yourself with another person and allow them to touch you.

When you have a case of the tinglies just looking at that other person.

When you feel a warmth in your genital area just thinking about them.

When you want to be held by that person.

When you want to hold them.

When you want to be close.

## When Can You Expect To Feel Them?

Once again, because each boy and girl is so different, it's impossible to say when. The most honest answer I can give you is that you'll feel them when you feel them, whenever that may be!

You may have been "going out" for some time and not have felt those feelings. You may not be "going out" with anyone and might already feel them toward a special person, whether or not that person even knows it.

As with all other changes of puberty (both physical and emotional), some boys and girls will have sexual interest in the beginning stages, and others won't have these feelings until much later. Your hormones have an influence here, too.

Since you can't predict when your sexual feelings will start, it wouldn't be fair for you to sit around expecting them, wondering why they haven't begun and worrying if something is wrong with you because they haven't yet appeared.

Many boys and girls have shared how frustrating it has been for them to listen to their friends talk about what sexual things they did or would like to do with someone, and know that they've never had any of those feelings. Very often, in fact, they didn't even know what their friends were talking about!

John, age thirteen, said, "A lot of boys talk about wanting to do something with their girl friend. I don't really think anyone has done anything. But I haven't ever wanted to do anything like that and I wonder when I'll get those feelings."

## How You Might Let Someone Know
## You Have Feelings For Them

Holding Hands: One of the ways kids (adults, too) show that they like each other in a special way is to hold hands or put an arm around each other.

Linda, age thirty, said, "It used to be such a big thing if a boy held your hand. Then you knew he "liked" you and you always hoped people would see you walking together."

Jimmy, age fourteen, shared, "I haven't gone out with girls that much and it gets me nervous to try to hold a hand. What if they don't want to hold mine?"

Jimmy, this is the same type of concern that I talked about in the Friendship chapter. It's called rejection. What if she doesn't have the same feelings you do? It may help to realize that she might want to hold your hand in private but may be too embarrassed about these new feelings to want to hold your hand in public. I can only remind you that you've got nothing to lose. Try it if you wish. Chances are if she's showing any kind of interest in you, she'll be happy to hold your hand. If not, you might as well know it sooner than later.

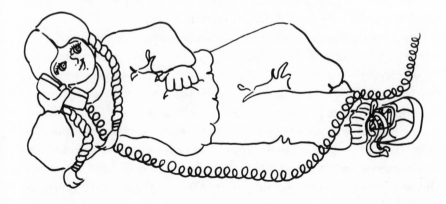

Becky, age thirteen, said, "I love holding my boyfriend's hand. He's too shy to take my hand so I just take his!"

Many boys are relieved when girls take the first step. Though old rules of etiquette (eh-ti-ket: social manners) state that girls should wait for the boy to act first, fewer and fewer people still believe that to be true. Many kids today are realizing that whoever feels the wish to approach the other person is the one who should. There doesn't have to be a rule. It's easier that way and takes pressure off the boys. Also, girls don't have to sit around waiting; they can ask, too.

*Note:* The same with telephone calls. I remember sitting around not wanting to leave the house just in case "he" called. Today, many girls just pick up the phone and call the boy themselves.

## Kissing

So many boys and girls have asked me when is the right age to start kissing the person you like. Since I've been told about Spin the Bottle games that were played as early as third grade, it would be hard to give you an age to go by.

Sometimes Spin the Bottle and other kissing games are practice to see if you'll like kissing someone for real. There's a difference between kissing games and "kissing" someone who you call your boyfriend or girl friend. Often in early kissing games no one really kisses anyway.

Think back to the "going out" chapter when I talked about when kids said they started having boyfriends or girl friends. Sixth, seventh grade? Usually when you have reached the point where you're "going out" and have picked one person that you'd like to be with more than anyone else, you might be ready to kiss that person. But, there isn't any rule since many boys and girls are not ready until much later.

Besides, it doesn't matter as much when other kids are ready. The important question is, "What about you?" You'll be ready when you're ready, no matter when anyone else is ready. As far as when it's okay for you to be ready, that's a good question to talk about with your parents.

Spin the Bottle is one of the very early kissing games (if you mention it to your parents, they'll probably smile and tell you some funny old stories). That's when a bunch of boys and girls sit around in a circle and one person spins a soda (pop) bottle in the middle. If a girl is spinning, the nearest boy that the bottle points to is "it." If a boy is spinning, the bottle has to point to a nearest girl. The person that spun the bottle and the person who's "it" then go to another room or behind a door or wherever, and are supposed to kiss. Or, as eleven-year-old, Stephanie, said, "You just run over and kiss. It only takes a couple of seconds!!"

Mark, now twenty, remembers his first game of Spin the Bottle. Mark said, "I was so scared. I didn't know what to do. I thought of ducking or getting up to get a snack or something, but it was too late. The bottle pointed to me and my heart started beating so fast. The girl I was supposed to kiss went with me into the back room of my friend's basement and I told her I didn't know what to do. She said not to worry, just go like this (she puckered her lips to show me). Then she touched my lips with hers. That was my first kiss. I remember thinking, 'Hey, this is great! I like this! I hope I get picked again.' "

Judy, age thirty-two, shared, "One time, I was invited to a party at a girl friend's house. And they did all those things like Spin the Bottle and Postman where the person who got the "letter" was supposed to go behind the door and kiss the postman." Judy said that when she was picked, the boy who went behind the door with her said, "Let's pretend we're kissing!"

Danny, age thirteen, said, "The big thing at our parties was kissing contests. We all sat around and timed how long the couples who were going together could kiss."

That kind of kissing, though lips were touching and the people were going out together, is more like a game. It's one of the ways that kids can find out if they want to think differently about kissing. It's also one of the ways kids lead into more tingly, sexual, one-to-one type kissing. When will these feelings happen? Only you can answer that.

Bobby, age fifteen, shared that his first "real" kissing was with a girl friend at a party in the basement of his friend's house. All the lights were out and everyone was with someone. Bobby said, "We were holding each other, but no one really knew what to do. We were too scared to try anything else but kissing and it was nice to feel close. I remember peeking out from the corner of my eye to see what other people were doing."

## Touching
Often times kissing real hard and being close can cause you to want to touch other parts of each other's bodies. Touching places like the breasts and the genitals is called petting.

This kind of touching can make boys or girls feel very aroused (tingly) and can lead to orgasm. Many kids are not sure what to do with these sexual feelings if they have them. Such feelings can be exciting, confusing, and scary at the same time. Exciting, because they can stir up inner warmth, especially in the genital area. Confusing, particularly when boys or girls have never felt that before. They may not know where the feelings will lead and might not be sure if they should even be having such feelings. Scary, because when two people have allowed themselves to go that far sexually, the feelings can start to build and get stronger. The stronger the feelings, the harder they will be to control, and the harder it will be to stop.

Too many kids are positive they can handle these feelings and will stop when they want to, but they really can't or won't. It would be sad for any boy or girl to find themselves in a situation where emotions are telling them what to do instead of brains!

One tingly feeling can lead to another and another and another. It takes a very strong boy or girl to reach the point of having such feelings and be able to say in the middle of having them, "I think we better stop!"

Too often kids think that sexual intercourse (Chapter 2, p. 34) is where all sexual feelings have to lead. Now you know this is just not true. There are other ways to express sexual feelings that are more appropriate for your age.

## What About Sexual Intercourse?

Sexual intercourse is an adult thing to do and has too many possible unwanted results for you to have to deal with at this time. A very important risk to think about is that having sexual intercourse can result in pregnancy (an egg can be fertilized if present in the fallopian tubes around the time of intercourse).

Having a baby is a twenty-four hour a day responsibility. Real babies are not like dolls. They can't be put away when you're finished playing with them. Besides being loved, babies need to be fed, clothed, and cared for completely. A baby's needs are more important than (and may keep you from) school, homework, parties, vacations, sports, movies, or anything. And, you've got to have enough money to pay for a child's needs.

Being pregnant and having a child can be wonderful when the experience comes at the right time in your life (as an adult). Pregnancy and all the responsibilities of having and caring for a child can be a very sad, scary experience that's much too much to handle if it occurs much earlier than when you're ready.

Therefore, if you risk having sexual intercourse and become pregnant, you'd not only have to deal with the pregnancy, but also how having a baby would change your life. You'd also have to deal with the fact that you'd be pregnant without being married. And you'd also have to deal with your parents (who I hope would help you even though they would probably be very upset if you were in this situation). A better idea would be not to risk getting pregnant in the first place.

Another important possible unwanted result from having intercourse is getting a sexually transmitted disease (a disease that can be passed on from one person to another during sex). You might also have heard these referred to as venereal disease (ve-near-ee-al), V.D. or sexually transmitted diseases. Examples are genital herpes (her-peez), syphilis (sif-i-liss), and gonorrhea (gone-er-ee-a). Many veneral diseases can be very uncomfortable and can cause permanent damage if not treated properly.

Some young people think that they can avoid unwanted results of intercourse by using contraceptives (con-tra-sep-tives: birth control devices that can be used as protection against becoming pregnant or causing someone to become pregnant). Examples are the condom (also called a rubber) and the diaphram (die-a-fram). Often times contraceptives work very well. They work best when the person using them knows exactly what he or she is doing. Most kids don't know enough about contraceptives to use them properly (too many kids who are risking sexual intercourse don't use them at all).

Some girls think that even if they do get pregnant, they'll just get an abortion (a-bore-shun: when a woman chooses to have a doctor remove the fertilized egg from the wall of the uterus so it won't develop any further). A woman who decides to have an abortion doesn't wish to be pregnant anymore.

Too many teenagers and young adults think having an abortion is no big deal. They aren't aware of the emotions and difficulty that can be involved with such a decision. They forget that an abortion is an operation. And having an operation carries with it possible medical risks.

*Note:* Many religious groups are angrily against abortion and feel it should not be legal (allowed).

Many people feel very strongly that it is important and right for a woman to have the freedom to choose to have an abortion if she wants. They believe that abortions should be legal.

Many people feel that having an abortion is like killing because they feel a human being is formed as soon as the egg has been fertilized.

Many people feel that abortion is not like killing because they feel the developing egg is not considered a person until birth.

There are many different feelings about abortion as it is a very emotional topic. It would probably be interesting for you to talk about this with your parents.

If having sexual intercourse is so serious a decision because of all the possible unwanted results, then why is the number of teenage pregnancies so high?

It's disturbing to suppose that so many thousands of teenagers must not have been taught about respecting themselves, being able to deal with sexual pressure, understanding choices, being able to say NO, and recognizing when they're taking too much of a chance if they go further sexually. I suppose also that a lot of teenagers think, "It (unwanted results) won't happen to me." Besides everything else, many facts about intercourse are not understood properly.

## Making Sexual Decisions

How far is it right to go? How much touching? Where? At what age?

Your sense of when you will be ready to allow yourself to touch and be close will probably be based upon what you have been taught by your parents, religious leaders, teachers, and what your friends are doing (or talking about doing). Being close is a personal decision and depends very much on your values and self-respect. It also has to do with how comfortable you are with that other person and how much trust there is between you.

I think what helps to make sexual decisions confusing is that it's common for movies, magazines, radio, books, and TV to give the mes-

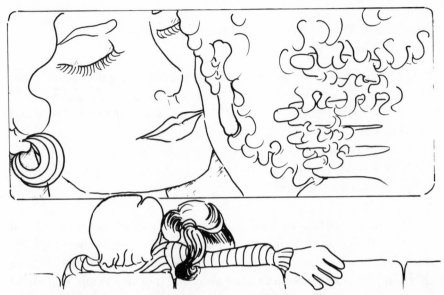

sage "sex is okay." Parents, teachers, and religious leaders are likely to be telling you that sex should be saved until you're married or at least until you're an adult and can deal with the emotions and such closeness in a responsible way. And there you are, in the middle, wondering what's right.

More pressure and confusion can come from all the talk about sex. Even when kids aren't even "doing anything," they often feel the need to sound like they do a lot. Sexual talk often causes pressure to be felt by others who have nothing to say or don't understand what's being said.

Some boys and girls have talked to me about being upset (or wondering if they should be upset) that they aren't interested in going out with anyone and certainly don't care about being close. They feel pressured to be like many of their friends but they just don't have the same feelings. That's okay! For both boys and girls, each person's time of readiness for wanting to be close is going to be different. You may be interested about the same time as your friends or not until many years later.

When you do feel ready, perhaps a good guide that will help you decide how much sexual sharing is appropriate is to answer for yourself: "Am I about to do (or doing) what I truly believe is right for me, according to my values and what I was taught?"; "Am I caring about myself?", "Am I respecting myself and the other person?"; or, "Am I being pressured into doing something that I'm just not ready for or don't want to do?"

## Sometimes People Are Forced Into a Sexual Act Against Their Will

Being forced to have sexual intercourse against your will is called rape. This is considered to be violent, not sexual, because it's not closeness wanted by both people. It's usually a very disturbing experience and could be dangerous (physically as well as emotionally).

Very often, a person is raped by someone they know. As you get older, it would help for you to be aware of not teasing someone into believing that you're interested in having sex when you don't mean that at all.

It's also important to keep your eyes and ears open for verbal and non-verbal messages from people. For example, if you're being guided into an area where no one else seems to be around, try to avoid going there. If you move someone's hand away and they don't stop, that might be an alert signal. Be careful who you trust.

It might shock you to know that many girls are raped by older brothers, fathers or uncles (or any other parent-like adult). This happens more than you think. In fact, some girls even agree to have sex with them (or their friends) because they're threatened or are told this is a proper thing to do.

You probably can't imagine sexual activity with a relative happening, but it does. Or, perhaps you know only too well that this can happen. Just in case anyone tries to convince you it's natural, it's definitely NOT! The name for this type of sexual activity between family members is *incest* (in-sest). Incest can also be between sons and mothers or aunts and even between brothers and sisters. This is not natural either.

If you are being forced to have sex against your will or are being abused sexually in any way by a stranger, someone you know, or a family member, it's very important that you tell someone, even if you were warned not to do so. Tell your other parent, a grandparent, or other relative, a special teacher, your religious leader, guidance counselor, a friend's parent, or any other adult you trust. If that person doesn't believe you the first time, tell them again and keep telling them.

If a certain family member has had sex with you or you are raped, it would help if you realize it wasn't your fault. You're not to blame and don't let anyone blame this on you!

## Respecting Your Feelings

If you're clear about how you feel, then hopefully you'll have the confidence and strength to go as far sexually as seems right according to your own values. Sharing sexually is a choice. No one has a right to make that choice for you before you're ready to choose for yourself. If you're not sure, WAIT! If you are, then at least be sure you understand what you're doing and be ready to take responsibility for your actions.

If someone doesn't seem to care about your feelings or values and tries to make you feel uncomfortable, guilty, silly or "not with it" for feeling the way you do, my guess is that they probably don't respect you. When this happens, it can be tough to do what you know is right for you, especially if you want to continue to go out with that person or if you're concerned that your private feelings (or actions) might be spread around your school.

If you are saying to yourself right now, "If anyone pressured me into doing anything sexual, even kissing, before I'm ready, I'd just tell them to forget the whole thing!", it can be very hard to follow through and say something like that when you're right in the middle of the situation.

One of the most important things is for you to respect yourself and your right to be who you are and feel your own feelings. If you are strong about your self-respect, then others will be more likely to respect you in return. If they don't, then maybe it's time to look for someone else who will.

## I Want To Keep Going Out With You, But...

If you're just doing something sexual to make someone like you or to prove that you like them or to try to be popular, then take a step back and ask yourself, "Is it really worth it?"

Although such sexual sharing might be nice while it lasts, unless you really thought about respecting your feelings before saying yes you may have some doubts about how you feel about yourself afterwards.

If your decision to be close is based upon your own free choice and respect for your own feelings, you'll probably be able to look yourself straight in the mirror afterward and feel good.

If someone likes you for being you, then hopefully they'll accept that it's your right to decide what you're ready to do and they won't try to push you (no matter what their friends or your friends are or are not doing).

## What Can You Do When You Feel Pressured Sexually?

Jill, age fourteen, asked, "What do you do when boys want to have sex but you think it's wrong?" Leslie, age thirteen, asked, "How do you deal with boys that want to have sex and you don't?" Many girls have asked me how to deal with sexual pressure felt when boys want to touch or see parts of their bodies that they're not ready to share.

Boys have talked about pressure, too. Much of this pressure has to do with thinking they were expected to "make a sexual move" or "try something sexual," whether or not they wanted to, were ready for it, or even knew what to do. Some boys talked about finding it hard to say no when girls put sexual pressure on them.

Many boys and girls talked about not knowing what to say or do in order to stop once the feelings were started.

Here are some possible ways to say NO:
    "NO!"
    "NO!"
    "NO!"
    "NO!"
Get the idea?

Here are some possible ways to say STOP:
    "STOP!"
    "STOP!"
    "STOP!"
    "STOP!"
This can also be used with "Please" or "Let's".

You might also say:
    "I hope you understand but I'm just not ready."
    "I really don't want to right now."
    "Please don't push me; I don't want to go any farther."
    "I really want to but I'm afraid I won't stop."

"Cut it out!"
"This is much more than I can handle."
"Enough!"
"I'm really not interested in getting involved right now."
"If you really respect me, you'll stop."
"Keep your hands off of me!"
"I THINK I BETTER GO HOME!"

Another way to let someone know how you feel is telling them with motions instead of words. This is called communicating or speaking nonverbally (non-ver-ba-lee). Instead of saying "stop" with your voice, you can put up your hand, push a hand away, or even shake your head no. If your motions are clear, they'll get the message.

If you have already felt feelings of sexual pressure, you'll probably find it easy to understand what I've been saying. If you can't relate to and have never felt sexual pressure, you can file this information away in your mind to be used at a later time.

*Note:* If you do feel good about what you are sharing with another person, it's nice to let them know. You can say something like, "That feels good," or "I like the way you did that," or "I really like it when you hold my hand."

## Caring About Others

As important as it is to respect yourself and your own values, it's also important to respect and care about others. Just as other people do not have the right to pressure you into choices that aren't comfortable for you, you need to be concerned with how you treat other people.

Try to be sensitive to other people's feelings and accept their right to their own values and beliefs just as you hope they accept yours.

It will help to remember that it's often hard for people to share their true feelings. Especially with sexual sharing, it's common for people to keep their feelings in rather than admitting them aloud. Listen carefully to what they're saying verbally and nonverbally. If you sense their discomfort or concern, you might help them out by saying, "You seem uncomfortable, is everything okay?" "Is something bothering you?" "Do you want to stop?"

If you are not sure about what they're feeling, care enough to ask.

## Parents and Sexual Feelings

Though lots of kids think if there are four children in the family, their parents "did it" (had sexual intercourse) four times, three children, three times, and so on, it might interest you to know that parents can continue to share themselves sexually for the rest of their lives together.

You might be saying to yourself, "Not my parents! I never see them even hold hands in front of me." I'm not making this point to interfere with your parents' privacy. But if you realize that your parents are sexual people, too, perhaps you'll feel that much more comfortable talking with them about things you never knew you could.

Here are some examples of how you might start a conversation with your parents:

"This is hard for me to say."

"I'm embarrassed to ask you this."

"I know we've never talked about these things before, but I'd like to."

"Please. I need to talk with you. I know you might get mad if I say this, but please listen. I'm scared and I don't know what to do. Please help me."

"I know you might not think I'm old enough to talk about these things, but everyone talks about them on the playground and I'm not sure of what they mean."

Whatever you're feeling, remember to try to turn your feelings into words.

Give your parents a chance if you haven't already. They would probably be so happy to be able to help you, offer advice, or at least be a caring "ear" for your concerns. They'd be even happier that you trusted them.

If your parents have been silent and have never talked with you about sexual facts and feelings, it's possible they're uncomfortable, too (they may never have spoken about this with their parents). Even if they're very interested and want so much to talk with you, it may seem strange and awkward for them to be talking with their own children about such grown-up type things. They may not know how to approach you just like you may be unsure of what to say to them.

Also, some parents worry about children knowing too much too soon. If your parents hold back information, it might help for you to understand that this might be their concern. If you feel you need more information and sense they're not giving you the full explanation, ask more questions and let them know YOU know there's more.

Those parents that worry about how much their children learn might think that as soon as their child knows about sexual feelings and sexual intercourse they'll probably run right out and try it. They may not realize that the only way for their child to make responsible decisions is if he or she understands the facts, feelings, choices, and possible wanted or unwanted results, as well as what all of these might mean.

If anything, not knowing what sexual feelings are and where these feelings can lead and not understanding facts about intercourse has a greater possible risk for you to do something you don't realize is not appropriate for you at this time.

If you have tried to talk with your parents and they refuse to discuss sexual topics with you, you might tell them once again how much it means to you to be able to go to them with your concerns rather than to anyone else. Sharing this section, the whole chapter, or any other part of this book might also help to open up conversation between you and your parents. If you still have difficulty talking with them at least you will have tried very hard to make them understand. Perhaps you can try to talk with them again in a few days.

If this is your situation you might consider talking about your feelings, questions, and concerns with an aunt or uncle, grandparent, older sister or brother, a friend's parent, trusted teacher, your religious leader, family doctor, or another trusted person.

Be careful when taking facts from your friends. Sometimes they'll be correct and sometimes not. If you still need more information about any topic, you can also ask your school or public librarian to help you.

# 17
# Comparisons and Competition

Have you ever felt terrific because finally your grade was as good or higher than the class brain's? Have you ever looked at someone and said to yourself (or to others), "It's disgusting that her hair looks so perfect all the time," and wondered, "Why isn't mine?"

Have you ever stopped yourself from trying out for cheerleading, a part in your school play, or an athletic team because you felt other people would probably get picked instead of you? Have you ever felt "out of it" because you didn't have the same sneakers that "everyone" was wearing?

It's natural for you to compare yourself with others. It's another way to learn about who you are and where you stand among your peers. If you think you measure up, you'll probably feel great about yourself. If you think you don't measure up, you might make the sad mistake of wishing you were someone else instead of accepting who you really are.

Competition is a part of everyone's life. It can make you try harder and be able to do things better than you might ever have done. It can also make you feel you shouldn't try at all.

This chapter will give us a chance to talk about the different ways making comparisons and competing can influence how you feel about yourself and how you might judge others.

## Clothes

Clothes can make you look dressed up, grown-up, sloppy, sexy, comfortable, stiff, silly, handsome, beautiful, rich, poor, with it, or out of it. Some kids don't care at all about clothes; others are just beginning to realize it might be fun to test out a new look. Still others think clothes are very important. What do clothes mean to you?

Many times kids will judge others mainly by their clothes never fbothering to learn about the person inside. But clothes can only tell so much about a person. And those kids that think clothes mean everything are in for a surprise. While clothes can give hints about how neat a boy or girl is and whether his or her tastes are similar, they can't tell what kind of friend a person would be. Someone who is beautiful inside may not have clothes that reflect that beauty.

Still there's a lot of peer pressure about clothes, a lot of comparing. For example some kids think if they wear jeans with designer labels on them that makes them better than someone else who doesn't. And those kids who want very badly to be accepted think if they run out and buy the same jeans with the same labels, then the "better" people will like them.

It's too bad more kids don't realize that better labels don't make better people. Some people are not as beautiful as their clothes! Besides it's not the clothes you become friendly with, it's the person inside the clothes. When was the last time you threw a ball to a uniform, told a secret to a T-shirt, or asked a sweater to go for pizza?

Some kids have the courage to wear whatever they wish, even if it's different. Many others try to dress like everyone else—labels or not— hoping that will give them a better chance to be accepted.

As you read about the many different feelings kids have shared with me about clothes, try to take a few guesses as to why they feel the way they do. It might give you some extra understanding about your own feelings.

Maggie, age eleven, shared, "Most of the time I wear jeans and sweat shirts to school. But my mom bought me a mini skirt outfit that I've been wanting for a long time. When I wore it to school, one of the girls in my class said that my shoes didn't match my mini skirt.

"I was so embarrassed and wondered how many other kids also thought my shoes didn't match. Some of the kids in my school seem to have a different pair of shoes for each thing they wear! Well, I have my sneakers and one pair of shoes. I just couldn't wear my mini to school again. I didn't want to think that kids would be checking to see if I matched.

"My parents say they spent too much money on it for me to leave it in my closet. I told them I'd save it for when we go visiting, but I just can't wear it to school. It makes me sad—angry too. But I can't."

Peter, age thirteen, told me, "I've been paying more attention to how I look. I can't believe that I, the shopping hater, asked to go shopping a few weeks ago. I think my parents must have freaked after all those years of arguing with them when they forced me to go for clothes. Maybe it's because of the girls. I don't know. But all of a sudden I care about how other people see me. It also makes me feel good to look good."

Barry, age twelve, said, "I always loved getting hand-me-downs from my cousins. Even though they weren't new, it made me feel good to have some different things to wear." Jessica, age ten, said, "I hate getting hand-me-downs. I never get to pick what I like. I never get to wear something new. I understand there are a lot of kids in my family and clothes cost a lot of money, but sometimes I wish just once I could get a whole bunch of clothes that are mine and no one else's first!"

Lawrence, age thirteen, said, "I've heard some kids say, 'Oh, John? He's so popular, he could wear anything he wants.' If he wanted to wear a skirt to school, I don't think kids would tease him!"

Mrs. H., age forty-five, said, "My daughter drives me crazy with her clothes sometimes. It's so hard to say no to her because I know she'll probably storm out of the room and make it unpleasant for everyone else in the family to be around her. But there's a limit to what she can get. She tries to make me feel guilty by saying things like, 'Oh, please, everyone is wearing it, and I want it so badly. It's not fair. It's going to be your fault if everyone doesn't think I look good.' "

Christine, age twelve, said, "All the girls who have nice clothes think they're such hotshots."

Bobby, age twelve, said, "I don't pay clothes much attention. When I wake up, I just grab whatever is at the top of my drawer and put it on."

Susan, age ten, told me that she thinks clothes are important and carefully plans what she's going to wear the next day in school. Each night she lines up her clothes very neatly near her bed. Sometimes she has fun making the clothes look like they're on a make-believe person.

Nancy, age fifteen, remembers a time in the sixth grade when she was really growing out of her old jeans and badly needed a new pair. Her mom finally got the chance to take her shopping, and it took a long time to find a pair that fit well.

It happened to have a designer label, but she bought it because it was the best fitting pair not because of the label. She felt great when she arrived at school the next day. She knew her jeans looked good, and the feeling made her smile to herself.

As soon as she put her coat in her locker, kids started commenting on her jeans. They teased her about the label, called her snobby, and it didn't take long for her inside smile to turn to inside tears!

Said Nancy, "After I felt so hurt, I started to get angry. I know why I got them. They fit better than any other pair in the store. And they were more comfortable. Why does everyone always have something to say about everyone else? Anyway, I decided that I wasn't going to let them make a big deal out of this so I told them to shut up about it. After a couple of days, they left me alone."

Isn't it interesting how one scrunched-up nose or a few words can make someone not want to wear something. The kids that can take the judging are usually those who feel pretty confident about themselves. Others who feel less sure, probably wish they could run right back home, open their closet door, jump in, and stay there!

If you're one of those kids that thinks hanging out means hiding in your closet, think again. So maybe your family doesn't have the kind of money to buy you T-shirts in every color or fifteen new pairs of shoes to match each skirt. Maybe while you're waiting for hand-me-downs, your jacket from two years ago looks like it's ready for that big clothes rack in the sky. Maybe that's embarrassing to you and doesn't make you feel very good about yourself.

Remember when I talked about things you can control and things you can't? You can't help it if your parents don't have the money to buy you hotshot or any other type clothes. Even if they did, you'd find that after a while, the clothes wouldn't mean as much as who you are. That, you can control.

It's just too bad that when parents choose to buy their children tons of clothes, they often forget to teach them respect for others—no matter how much they have. Just like with the designer labels they think having a lot makes them better than someone else with only a little. (We'll talk more about this in When People are Different, Chapter 25.)

So, how much importance do you place on clothes? Here are some questions that will help you think about your answer:

How much checking do you do to see how your clothes look compared to everyone else's?

If kids that you wanted to be friendly with were all wearing the same thing and you didn't have it, would you feel it important to ask your parents to buy it for you?

If you liked wearing clothes that are a little different than those around you, would you be confident enough to wear them anyway? (How concerned would you be about people making comments, teasing, or looking at you as if you had six eyebrows?)

How important are clothes when you're trying to decide whether or not you want to be friendly with a person? Would a person's clothes prevent you from wanting to get to know someone?

Much of what you might feel can result from the influence your parents have on you. Sometimes it's not the boy or girl who thinks of comparing, it's the parents who ask, point out, and make it important to talk about how much money clothes cost. It's hard to separate what you feel from what your parents feel and are teaching you.

Sometimes your parents and friends have a strong say in the kinds of clothes you wear. Even when you don't realize you're letting them choose for you, there may be a little tiny voice in your head that's saying, "Oh, come on, pick this style. You know the other one's just not 'you.' "

But that may not be your voice. It may really be theirs, but you think it's yours. Or you know it's theirs, but you believe that they know what's best for you. So you listen.

The truth is, along with changes in your emotions and your body, it's likely that your tastes will change too. If you're a sweat-shirt person but have a secret feeling you'd like to see what a frilly blouse looks like, or if you always wear football jerseys or T-shirts and you wonder how you'd look in a crew-neck sweater with a shirt underneath, take a chance. Experiment. At least allow yourself to try it on, so you can see how it looks and feels.

Your friends may kid you and ask if you're going to church or something. But if you know you feel good, that's what counts. In time they'll get used to your new look and may even decide to try it.

## Grades

Eleven-year-old Leslie said, "There's one girl in my class who always gets hundreds on everything in social studies. When I ask her what she got, she tells me one hundred, and I give her a look. I say, 'of course.' And then she gives me a look."

Mindy, age nine, told me, "We have a lot of smarty pants in our school. . . . People who get hundred averages in everything. Some of them are nice but a lot of them brag about their grades."

Tommy, age ten, said, "I hate it when my teacher reads the grades out loud. I get pretty low grades, and she always ends up reading mine last or almost last. I know the kids in my class think I'm stupid compared to them. I think so too."

Cindy, age thirteen, told me, "Sometimes I feel like lying because it makes me feel funny to always get one of the highest grades in the class. Then people look at me and make faces and say to each other, 'I knew it!' I'll bet they think I'm the teacher's pet or something."

Scott, age twelve, said, "My friends and I always compare grades after a test. If I got a low grade and everyone else did too, I don't feel so bad. Then when I have to tell my parents, I can tell them that the class really didn't do that well or that I'm not the only one to have got a grade like that."

David, age thirteen, told me, "I'm in competition all the time for grades with this kid in my class. My father always asks me about my grades. I tell my dad and he always asks what did that other kid get. If he does better than me, my father always asks why. It just drives me up a wall. Sometimes I'd just rather forget it."

I asked David if all the pressure is from his father or if some of it is from himself. David answered, "Sometimes I pressure myself just as much as my parents pressure me. I always try to get better than him. Every time I get a better grade than him I'm always very happy because he's a genius. He stays home every day and studies. And I don't even do close to that because half the time I'm out in the afternoon."

"I always feel awful when I have to take tests," said Bonnie, who's eleven. "My sister had the same teacher three years ago and got very good grades. I always feel that the teacher compares me to her and expects my grades to be as good as my sister's."

So often kids feel the higher the grade, the better the person—sort of like designer labels on jeans: better label, better person—not so! They're always asking each other, "What did you get?" or "Let me see your paper."

If your grade was high, you probably wouldn't mind showing it. In fact, you might tell your classmates before they've had a chance to ask. A high grade can make you feel proud, relieved, really good, and make you not have hassles with your parents. You, your classmates, teachers, and parents might think that higher grades make you a better person.

If you get a low grade, you may not want anyone to know. (You'll probably wish you were absent the day the grades were handed out!) Those are the test papers that kids sometimes try to stuff in someone else's garbage can on the way home, praying that the teacher won't call their parents to tell them what the grade is. (That's probably why many teachers ask their students to bring the paper back signed by a parent.)

Lower grades can make you feel frustrated, embarrassed, confused, upset—and dumb. Kids who get mostly lower grades often do not have a high opinion of themselves. They may not think they're as good as everyone else. They may even say they hate school (really, they hate how it feels to do poorly) and stop trying.

Did you ever think that maybe your 75 percent is the best you can do? That's not to say you shouldn't try to get a 77 or an 80 or even an 83 or 85. But maybe you'll never get in the 90s! Probably it's unfair and unrealistic to expect that you should. It doesn't mean you're a bad person and everyone else who gets higher grades is better than you. It simply means that's the level that you're working at. Each person works at his or her own level. The problem comes in when people compare and think they should be working at everyone else's level but their own.

The next time you find yourself about to comment on a friend's low grade, stop! If your friends bug you about your grade, tell them to bug off. The next time you start getting down on yourself, remember that you're not your friends; you're not your brother or sister, you're you. If you can honestly say you tried your best, that's all you can hope to do.

So instead of stomping on your good feelings and letting yourself believe you're not as good as others, realize that you do have the power to learn from your mistakes (ask your parents or your teacher to explain them to you, if you're not sure why you made them). You can hope to do a little better next time. The only person you can fairly compete against is yourself. Challenge yourself to do better next time. And if you want to compare, check back and see if you improved your own grade.

If your parents tell you how disappointed they are in you and start telling you how well your older sister or brother is doing and asking why you can't do the same, perhaps it would be a good time to tell them your feeings about being pressured and compared. Maybe instead of spending so much time talking about what you're not able to do, it would be more of a help for them to teach you better ways to study.

Just because someone is brainy doesn't say anything about how much fun they are to be with, if they're kind or if they would make a good friend. It simply means they may work hard and might be very bright. It doesn't mean that they care about their grades any more than you do. Being better is something that anyone can be, no matter what their grade.

Maybe if friends, parents, sister, brothers, and teachers would try harder to accept that each person is different, there would be less teasing, fewer bad feelings, less pressure, and more freedom to try harder the next time.

## Sports

Most boys and girls love sports. The problem is that only some kids are good at them. Others are okay. And still others are what lots of people call uncoordinated. These differences have created many kinds of feelings and pressures.

Robert, age twenty-nine, shared, "I never had someone to play ball with when I was growing up. My father was always too busy, and my older brother wasn't an athlete. He was always playing his guitar or going on dates or hanging out with his friends. I missed it."

Joan, age eighteen, told me, "The first time I tried to play volley ball in gym class, I was in the seventh grade. I couldn't get the ball more than halfway up toward the net. I was smaller than most of the other kids and everybody laughed. They didn't even hide their laughter. Every time it was my turn to serve, I couldn't do any better. Every time I stepped up to try, they started whispering and laughing again. Even though the teacher told them to be nice, I became the class joke."

Abby, age twelve, said, "When we pick teams, I'm one of the last to be picked. It's not that I'm bad at sports. It's just that I'm not one of the popular kids. Most of the time they're the captains or they'll whisper to the person who is the captain."

Mrs. T., age sixty-three, said that when her son was in eighth grade, he played Little League baseball. He wasn't a good athlete, but he liked the game. "The coach's son, David, came to the door one day, just before it was time to sign up again in the ninth grade. He said, 'Hi, Mrs. T., do you know if Charlie [her son] is going to play ball again this year?' I told him I was pretty sure he wasn't. David said, 'Good. He was the worst on the team!'" Neither of them knew that Charlie was standing right behind his mother and heard every word.

How do you think David's statement would have made YOU feel if you were Charlie?

Richie, age thirteen, said, "I'm really nervous about making the basketball team this year. I was on it last year, but I just blew tryouts. I have another chance later in the week. I'll be so embarrassed in front of everyone if I don't make it again and kids from a lower grade make it instead of me."

George, age thirty-four, said, "I remember standing by the backstop at my elementary school playground, watching kids yell at each other or pick on some boy for not being a good player. I never understood why kids were so cruel. The bad player was really nice but just couldn't play baseball."

Danny, age fourteen, said, "Since I made the team, people seem to be acting differently toward me. Some of the popular girls actually talked with me at lunch yesterday."

Barry, age fifteen, said, "In the sixth grade, it was the 'in' group that played semi-hardball before school. That was *the* group! If you didn't play, you were not part of the crowd. There was always a lot of pressure about that."

Lenny, age twenty-nine, said, "I think if I were more into sports, I wouldn't have got into so much mischief. I just never felt I was good enough to play. So I hung around with the gangs instead."

Alan, age thirteen, said, "I was playing first singles for my school tennis team last fall. The kid I was supposed to play walked onto the court and my friends and I looked at each other and had a hard time holding in our laughs. He was kind of fat and we were sure he wouldn't even be able to run for a ball. I figured the match would be a piece of cake! Well, he beat me. I guess you can never tell by looking at someone how good they'll be."

Robin, age eleven, said, "People were always making fun of me when I played after school sports, so I stopped playing. My parents said I could take dance lessons. I'm doing really well. Now, even if kids tease me about not being good in gym class, it doesn't make me feel bad because I know that I'm good at my dancing."

Mary, age ten, told me, "I was playing goalie at our play-off soccer game last week. We beat that team already but couldn't make a goal this time. That was okay because neither could they. So the score was tied at zero to zero. Just before the game ended, they tried to score again and I don't know what happened. I just couldn't stop it. So they scored and won the game. Everybody was saying things like, 'Didn't you see it coming?' and 'I can't believe you missed it!' I felt awful."

If you're a good athlete, you already know how important sports ability can be. Even if your grades are poor, somehow being good at sports wins out. You're still respected, often envied (that means people are jealous of you), often very popular, just about always included, and never picked last.

If you're not good at sports, you probably understand the pain of being left out, the embarrassment of being teased, the feeling of being laughed at, or overhearing teammates say that they would have won the game if it wasn't for you.

While good athletes seem to play whatever they want, poor athletes may choose never to play at all, even if they want very much to play. It takes a lot of guts to get out on a court or a field and know that you can't completely trust yourself to catch the ball. But you don't have to catch it every time. Even professional athletes drop balls every once in a while! Not everybody is good at everything. But everybody can try. And every person has a right to be on a team, if he or she is interested.

Certainly, if you can't make a school team, there are plenty of chances in gym class, in after-school sign-up sports (often called intramurals), and with your friends at a playground or in the street. You can also get together with kids who are not the top athletes and have a game at your own level, where there might be less pressure. Just because you're not a super-jock (slang for good athlete) doesn't mean you shouldn't play at all.

If you don't want to play a team sport, you can play what's known as an individual sport—one that you can do by yourself. You can jog and no one need judge how you run. You can swim without judges. You can

roller skate or ice skate. You can take long walks and just take in the fresh air, think a little bit, and feel refreshed. You can go fishing. You can try golf and all kinds of dance. You can work out and do many different types of exercise for your body. You can also hit a ball against a wall by yourself and practice your tennis arm. You can try to ski.

Sometimes recreation centers offer free or low-cost lessons in many different activities. Even if your parent, older brother, or older sister isn't an athlete or doesn't have time, you might be able to ask one of your friends, another relative, a neighbor, a friend's parent, or a teacher to help you learn a skill. Sometimes you need to let your parent, sister, or brother know that you're interested. Don't expect them to magically guess what you wish they would do.

Perhaps one of the most helpful things to remember is that even though everyone is different, everyone has a right to enjoy playing. Once again a good athlete doesn't have to mean "better person." It's who you are, not how you play, that makes you so special. If someone calls you a clod (uncoordinated), tell them it's part of your charm!

## Looks

Everyone can be beautiful. But not everyone believes it. People often look at others to check and make sure about their own looks. They compare. Depending upon how other people look, they may still think they're beautiful, decide that they're less beautiful, or maybe think they're not beautiful at all. In fact, many people really believe they're ugly!

That's very sad. If you think you're ugly, you probably don't feel so good about yourself. You may shy away from people. You may keep to yourself. You may not ever give yourself and others a chance to appreciate how special you are.

There are some people who look physically beautiful and yet because they may not dress so cool, because they're not particularly good at sports, because they tend to be quiet and shy, or because they're not around enough people so that friends can say to them, "Hey, you know something, you're really very pretty!" they don't think they're good looking. When kids don't get this kind of *feedback* (when someone gives you information about yourself), they often don't feel that their body and face is as good as anyone else's. So, they think they're ugly because no one ever tells them they're pretty.

Lois, age thirty-three, remembers that when she was in junior high school, one of the most popular girls had short stubby legs and blond hair. She said to her friend one day, "So-and-so has got the nicest legs! They're short and fat. I only wish I could have short and fat legs. Then maybe I could be popular."

Sometimes kids who don't look good on the outside are very popular. This might make kids who are not in the popular group think that if they had a particular feature that the popular kids had, then maybe they'd be popular too.

When Lois got to high school, she looked at that girl's legs and thought, "How could she have been popular with those legs?" But in junior high she thought, "Maybe if I had those kind of legs, I'd be popular too."

Sometimes when boys or girls don't feel so good about themselves, it's hard for them to see the truth. While your body is in the process of growing, it may just be that your arms or legs are a little bit lankier and longer. During the time your body is getting used to the changes that have taken place, you might even find yourself tripping over your own feet. If you're thinking that you're ugly, it may just be that you're not as graceful as you once were and will be again when you get used to your new size and shape.

Every person can have an inside beauty no matter what his or her outside looks like. If people are beautiful on the outside, that might make them nice to look at, but it won't mean they're nice to know. They may be nice but not because of their looks. Feeling good about knowing them has much less to do with their face, their hair, their body, their clothes, and much more to do with what kind of person they are on the inside. What makes a person beautiful is something that can't be seen!

You may be saying, "But I'm really ugly." If you're talking about the feeling that you're outside looks are ugly, well, maybe it's time to deal with that feeling a little differently.

First of all is it your ears that you don't like? Your eyebrows? Your chin? Your cheekbones? Your neck? Your hair? Your legs? Your rear end? Your thighs? Your hands? Are you overweight? Skinny? Are your knees kind of funny looking? Do you have piano legs? Too many pimples? Do you feel you're too short? Are you too developed or not developed enough? Is your nose too wide, too long, too bumpy, too pointy?

Though it may be hard to be honest about this, can you figure out exactly what it is that gives you the uglies? It might help to write down your own private ugly list, so you can understand your feelings a little better. Think carefully about what you write down (or think about) and then try to decide which things you might be able to change and which you can't.

Since it wouldn't be fair or helpful to pressure yourself to change everything at once, pick one thing to start with and imagine what you can do to turn that ugly feeling into a sense that you're beautiful too.

For example do you think you would feel better about yourself if you lost a few pounds? If so, you can decide to change your eating habits and ask your parents to help by buying and guiding you to eat the right things. Maybe a new hairstyle or a change in the type of clothes you wear would freshen up your look. Getting involved with some kind of physical activity might also help.

If your ugly list is mostly made up of things you can't change, then you've got some work to do. A can't change example would be that you can't switch your legs for new ones, stretch your neck, or speed up or slow down your development. But you might be happily surprised anyway. Just realizing what you cannot change can be the relief that will allow you to stop dwelling on it and go on to other things.

You've got to start, even if it's little by little, trying to accept each thing that you cannot change as the part of you that's always going to stay the same, no matter what you do about it. If you don't, you may never feel good about yourself.

So which will it be: feeling ugly forever, or finding the beauty in you that nothing on the outside can touch? You can start looking right this minute if you want to.

Though I just talked mostly about people who don't have good feelings about their looks, there are lots of people who do. Those are the people that feel beautiful inside as well as outside. Yet, there are some people who look beautiful but don't feel very beautiful. They don't see themselves as beautiful.

Vicki, age thirteen, said that her mother always told her that she was so pretty. But she never believed her mother because Vicki was 5 foot 8 inches tall, had long and swinging arms that were very gawky, and was a twig. She used to walk with her shoulders slouched so that no one would see she was not developed. She wore glasses and some people called her "four eyes." Very few of her friends said she was pretty and she didn't feel pretty. Her ugly inside feelings made her outside looks and personality kind of dull.

It took Vicki until high school to realize that she could grow out of gawky feelings, wear contact lenses instead of glasses, get a sensational haircut, and learn how to apply makeup. It was her inside confidence that made her outside looks and personality sparkle and come to life. She started to feel beautiful inside and outside.

Other people may be very happy with the way they look compared to everyone else. But they're not happy with themselves. Even with their good looks, they may be lonely.

You see, people need more than looks to fill emptiness, more than looks to make friends. As you read the different feelings shared by boys and girls as well as adults, you'll get an even better idea of how outside looks can affect how people feel about themselves and others.

Patty, age thirteen, said, "I'm pretty conscious of the way I look. I've broken my nose a few times. There are really queer people in my school. They stick notes in my locker and call me birdie and stuff like that. If there's a kid that I like, I feel like covering my nose."

(We may see ourselves differently than anyone else sees us. A nose that seems too long on our own faces may be passed right by without a blink by others.)

Patty doesn't realize that her nose is not who she is. Besides if people can't see past the end of her nose, they're probably not worth it anyway.

Gerard, age eighteen, said "Sometimes I wish I wasn't so good looking. I get the feeling that people are afraid to come up to me because their looks are not as good as mine. Maybe they think I won't talk with them. Even when I go up to them, they seem to get a little nervous, like they have to watch how they act or what they say."

Maureen, age ten, said, "My friends always tease me about being fat. What really hurts is that they do it behind my back. Sometimes I hear them talking about me. They say I eat three candy bars at lunch, when I really don't. They eat more candy bars than I do and none of them are fat. It makes me feel horrible, and it's also not fair that I eat less and am fat and they eat more and they're skinny."

Billy, age twelve, said, "I hate it when the kids tease this girl in my lunchroom. She has white hair and is kind of weird looking but she's nice. I had to do a project with her."

Samantha, age eleven, told me, "I wish I could have hair like my friends. Mine is kinky and like Brillo. My white girl friends have soft, silky hair, and mine is never going to be like theirs. Sometimes it makes me feel so ugly, but at other times when I corn roll it, it's really funky and I love it."

Andrea, age forty-eight, remembers feeling very embarrassed about her legs. Said Andrea, "They reminded me of tree trunks. That's why I hated gym. We had to wear a silly looking short gymsuit that made my legs look even worse. I made excuses not to play whenever I could."

Craig, age fifteen, said, "When the girls come over to our lunch table, I know they're coming to see my friends and not me. The guys I'm friendly with are really good looking and I'm kind of puny next to them."

Chris, age fourteen, said, "I am extremely short and need to grow. Everyone calls me Pee-wee. It's sort of become like a nickname by now and I really don't like it. But everybody thinks I do."

Diane, age fourteen, said, "I get so angry when I wake up with pimples on my face. They make me feel so ugly. Until they're gone, I just feel like burying my head or wearing a mask whenever someone talks with me close-up. I wish we got them on our knees instead of our faces!"

"My best friend is so beautiful," said Marni, age thirteen. "All the boys follow her around. I know I'll never be beautiful. I don't know whether to love her or hate her sometimes."

As you can see, too many people don't understand that outside beauty is not as important as a person's feelings and who they are. They tease, often cause embarrassment, and help to create ugly feelings.

If you think that outside beauty is all it takes to be beautiful, what happens to the person who is born with a birthmark covering much of his or her face? How about the person who is injured and has a permanent facial scar? How about the person who loses a leg, is paralyzed and must remain in a wheelchair, or has a deformed arm or any other disability? Does that mean the person can never be beautiful? No! Everyone can develop their inner beauty, if they believe they can.

It's hard for kids (and many adults) to realize that beauty is such a personal thing. No two people see things quite the same way. What one person may believe is beautiful, another may not. Isn't it a shame that so many people only see themselves through other people's eyes? They allow other people to judge if they're beautiful or not. And they judge themselves by other people's beauty.

If only more people could realize they have the power to like themselves better, and to work at accepting themselves no matter what their shape, size, or how they look on the outside. If only they would try . . .

## A Special Note About Permanently Changing Your Looks

In this day and age with people being able to walk on the moon, with the technology to take talking pictures and instantly see them on a screen, and with the knowlege of how to reattach arms and legs, send messages across the world in a matter of seconds, and put artificial hearts into bodies, it's no wonder that doctors can perform special surgery to change just about every possible part of the body in order to make it appear more like you wish it would be.

This surgery should not be considered lightly, as if you were just going out and changing a pair of jeans. And, like all surgery, there are risks and there are benefits.

I would strongly suggest that you sit with your uncomfortable feelings about your nose or any other body part for a long, long time in order to make sure that having such surgery is really what you want to do. (Of course, this must be discussed with and arranged by your parents.) Wouldn't it be sad to find out after surgery that it wasn't ever your nose that was bothering you, but instead that you were unhappy with yourself inside?

## Competition During Tryouts

Tryouts, whether for a part in your school play, getting on a sports team, becoming a cheerleader, becoming a school officer, being elected representative to student government, or getting a solo in a chorus concert, can be a real test of how good you feel about yourself.

Tryouts test your confidence; they test your cool. Some kids who are really good at what they're trying out for are a disaster at tryouts! That's probably because they choke or "take the apple." As thirteen-year-old John said, "I always fold in tryouts."

"Tryouts make me nervous," said Donna, age twelve. "Tryouts can really be embarrassing because everyone will be watching you and maybe everybody else will make it and you won't," said Allison, age twelve. Robby, age eleven, said, "I always worry that everyone will be better."

With all the talk we've done about trying not to judge, that's just what tryouts set out to do. When you sign up or appear for a tryout, you are asking to be judged. You're taking a risk. You're saying, "This is me; this is what I can do; these are my talents; this is how good I am, now judge me!" You're allowing yourself to compete and be compared with everyone else who wants to get the same position. Tryouts can be very exciting and very scary. Tryouts take guts!

Yes, everyone may be better than you at the tryouts. Yes, most of the kids might be picked instead of you. Yes, it can be scary and even embarrassing to put yourself through such a test. But just because tryouts are not the most comfortable thing to do, that doesn't mean that they're not good for you.

To be able to get up in front of judges and your peers and at least try, says a lot for the kind of strength and confidence that you have. As I've said so many times, each person is different. Each person has his or her own abilities, and some people are better than others at certain things. But everyone can try.

Some people who want very badly to try out, don't. They're the ones who don't feel very confident. They may not want to deal with worrying that other kids will laugh at them or spread around the school how poorly they did. So they stay away. My guess is if people respect them and like them as people, then no matter how poor they are at tryouts, they'll be loved anyway. Others will probably even feel, "Good for them that they had the guts to be here."

You might hear someone say, "I'm not going to try out because I'm not going to make it, anyway. So it's stupid to try out." Well, the interesting thing is that if they don't try out, they definitely will not make it. If they try out, at least they have a chance. And since they don't feel they'll make it, they won't be disappointed or surprised when they don't. So why not try? They have nothing to lose and might just gain!

Tryouts can teach you a lot as well as be fun; some kids love to watch how everyone else does. Proving to yourself that you can actually get up in front of a group of people and take the chance can help strengthen your confidence. I spoke with a girl who ran for vice-president of her school several months ago. She wanted to win but really didn't expect to. When she found out she lost, she wasn't so upset because she felt so good about having the guts to run. She proved to herself that she could try. That was even more important to her than winning. She had never done anything like that before.

Trying out lets you see what skill level the other kids seem to have (even though some kids "fold" and aren't really showing the judges how good they can be). Some people are surprised to find that they're not as bad as they thought they were. In fact, they're pretty good, compared to the other kids who tried out. All this time they never thought they could come close. So the experience of trying out gives you a chance to compare your skill level and get a sense of where you stand.

If you try out, you can also learn more about what the judges are looking for. By watching the other kids perform and learning who is picked, you can put the two together and figure out what was important to the judges and what wasn't. Then you can practice what you know for sure will be tested and can be much better prepared next time.

It might help to realize that sometimes judging isn't as fair as you'd like to think it would be. Since we're dealing with judges who are human beings, there are personal human feelings that can get in the way of fair judging. As thirteen-year-old Marcy said, "Some teachers will give kids parts because they like them and have them in class, not because they're better than the other kids who tried out."

Even though I'd like to believe that most judges try to be fair, sometimes kids are picked who shouldn't have been picked, and kids are left out who should have been included. That's called LIFE! Who ever said everything was going to be fair?

Here are some other feelings that kids have shared about tryouts.

Fourteen-year-old Mitchell said "At the younger grades usually the most popular kid is voted for representative or school office. Even if they're not good. When kids get a little older, it doesn't matter as much if the person is popular, people are more likely to pick the better person for the job."

Donna, age fourteen, said, "I can't believe it. I practiced all last year and the beginning of this year to try to make cheerleading and I screwed up at the tryouts. I was so nervous!"

Jessie, age thirteen, said, "It's really bad when you make a team and everyone knows—and so do you—that the only reason why you made it was because you're the teacher's pet or your sister was good."

Patricia, age eleven, said, "Sometimes it's hard to decide if you want to try out, even if you know you're really good and will probably make it. If none of your friends make it, then you won't know anyone else on the team."

Charlie, age twelve, said, "It's embarrassing when you tell everyone that you know you're going to make it and someone else won't. And then you don't make it and they do."

Bobby, age fourteen, said, "I can't stand the pressure at tryouts. Especially when everyone expects you to make the team. I wish no one else would have to watch."

Susie, age twelve, told me, "My friends got really jealous when I was picked for cheerleading and they didn't make it."

Nine-year-old Seth said, "If you start bragging about getting on the team and you spread around school that you expect to get it, then you might be embarrassed if you don't get picked."

Thirteen-year-old Andy said, "One of the problems with tryouts is the waiting, knowing that the list is going to be posted after fourth period."

Hank, age thirteen, said, "I was really angry that this kid got picked instead of me. I know I'm better than he is. I just can't understand it."

Gail, age eleven, told me, "Everyone thought the girl who was running for president would get it because all the boys would vote for her. She has tits! But she lost, anyway."

Now that you have a better understanding of the different ways people compare each other and how they make judgements from their comparisons, I think there's one more thing you need to consider.

That is sometimes you can judge yourself more harshly than anyone else judges you. So the next time you find yourself thinking, "They're better than I am. . . ." maybe you'll stop and think some more about what you're really comparing. Remember that there's a big difference between what you have and who you are, what you look like and who you are, and what your talents are and who you are.

The more you accept yourself for who you are, the more others will accept you too.

# 18
# Growing Up Drugged Up, Drinking, and Smoking

## Growing Up Drugged Up

As you know by now, growing up is loaded with all sorts of things you need to learn how to do in order to feel good about yourself, like how to be friends, how to make your own decisions, how to let someone know your feelings, how to talk about sticky issues with your parents, and how to deal with peer pressure and competition.

It can be really hard to make the right choices, can't it? Sometimes making choices can be very confusing and painful. Often when people feel confused and pained about things that happen in their lives, one of the ways in which they deal with them is to use drugs.

## Risk Taking and Drug Use

Using drugs means taking risks. Yes, that means all drugs. Over-the-counter ones (like aspirin) that can be bought without a permission note from a doctor and the ones that doctors give you (called prescribed drugs or prescriptions).

Sometimes the risks of taking these drugs are small, for example getting an upset stomach after you take aspirin when you haven't eaten anything (on an empty stomach). And sometimes the risks are large, such as if you were to lose your hearing because you took a commonly prescribed antibiotic (a drug that fights bacteria).

In our society, all of us take drugs. We are a drug taking society! It seems that in the United States we take drugs for just about everything. Our medicine cabinets are filled with drugs from the drug store. Yet all drugs should be used with great care.

Some drugs are necessary for getting us back to health. Some that are supposed to get us back to health can make us even sicker. Over-the-counter and prescribed drugs are used for our well-being. When used properly, they can help us lead long, healthy lives.

Yet there are other drugs, many intended for getting us healthy (some legal, others against the law), that are used for changing our moods, feelings, and attitudes about ourselves. Maybe you know some of them by name: *marijuana* (mara-wana), alcohol, uppers, downers, and hallucinogens—the drugs that get you high. Many of these drugs carry major risks, especially when you use them while you are trying to grow up and feel good. Unfortunately, they make you grow up drugged instead.

## Reasons for Getting High

Sometimes using drugs seems like a good idea at the time. Many kids will not really be able to tell you a specific reason for wanting to get high except that drugs were available, their friends were using them, and there didn't seem to be any consequences for using the drugs. So drugs seemed good at the time.

This way of using drugs is often called experimentation. Fourteen-year-old Mara shared how she unexpectedly began to experiment with drugs: "I always said I'm never going to do it. I'm never going to try it. But this year I knew some people who were smoking pot [marijuana]. One close friend did it a lot. I would always tell him not to smoke, but he'd always say it's so great. I guess I just wanted to see what it felt like. The first time I smoked nothing happened to me. The same with the second and the third time. So I just kept doing it until something happened. I think the fourth time I did it—I felt it. I think I was scared because I'd smoked a lot and felt very weird. I thought I was out of control.* But then I just tried to relax, listened to some music, and was okay. After that I made an agreement with myself."

*This feeling of being out of control is called rushing. It's almost a sense of panic.

I wasn't going to go look for it, but if someone had it, then I'd do it. What happened was there was a lot of pot available to me. Kids could buy it pretty easily if they knew the right people.

So I started doing it more and more. I got very caught up in it. I thought about it [smoking pot] all the time. It was constantly on my mind. I was constantly waiting for the next time I was going to do it, thinking about when, where, with who? . . .

But then I said I've got to stop. The stopping started with me when I realized how much it had taken me over. But what forced the stopping was my parents. I got punished because they found pot in my drawer. That was the worst thing that ever happened to me. Now they don't trust me anymore. My parents said if they ever saw it again, they'd punish me for an even longer time. The most important thing to me is my freedom to go out with my friends, and my parents grounded me. I couldn't go out to parties and I had to come home right after school.

I wanted to stop or at least cut down. I knew it was better for me. I got no pressure from my friends when I stopped. If anything they were telling me I'd better not smoke anymore. They gave me a lot of support.

Now we almost never do it. Once in a while, but hardly ever. I would never have believed I could have gotten so caught up with smoking pot. I didn't realize what I was getting into until I was there. It just happened. I didn't even see it happen and then didn't really know what to do about it. I always said it would never happen to me! Now I'm fine. My grades are even higher. I can't say I'm not going to do it anymore. I might. But I'm never going to let it control me again. It will be my choice, not because I think I have to use it. I'll be controlling it.

## It Hurts To Grow Up

If you've been reading this book faithfully, you have already seen in so many ways that growing up is no easy task. Sometimes we must make choices in our lives that we would prefer not to do. And yet we really must because making choices is a part of growing up.

Sometimes there are situations that we face in our homes and with our friends that we don't have very much control over. We may not like the things that happen between ourselves and our friends or parents.

Sometimes death, divorce, parental drinking, fighting in the home, absence of friends, and feeling lonely can make it very painful to grow up. I'll bet you won't hear any kids say that they use drugs because it hurts to grow up. It's hard for someone to understand that this might be the reason.

James, age thirteen, talked about his friend who smokes pot during and after school every day. His grades used to be in the 80s. Now he's getting 60s in every class. Said James, "I know his parents know. They gave him permission to smoke in front of them but haven't said anything about stopping! I wish they'd pay more attention to him. Maybe he wouldn't smoke so much if his parents paid more attention to him and showed him they were concerned about him. Maybe he wouldn't smoke so much if they showed him he was important enough to try to get him to stop."

Many kids become very angry at their parents for neglecting them and making them withdraw from their families. They want love, affection, attention, and above all to communicate with their parents. Even if they say that's not what they want, it is what they want. It really does feel special to have someone care about you and tell you so. When your parents don't care, it can hurt so much.

If parents are not there for their child, he or she might end up using drugs as a way of getting someone to pay attention. Kids are often really disturbed about having to do this. Many don't even want to. But to them some attention is better than no attention. Their drug use can really be a cry for help.

### Hanging Out and Boredom

A lot of times kids say that they started using drugs because there was just nothing better to do. They hang out and feel bored. Sometimes drugs become their activity. So these drugs are their recreational drugs since the activity of using the drugs gives them something to do.

Although drugs may change the way you feel, they very rarely give you the desire to do anything else. We all go through periods of boredom. We cannot expect every single minute to be filled with excitement and pizzazz. Boredom is a fact of life that everyone has to deal with no matter who they are.

Lots of times there are many things we can do. Several choices are available to us. But we don't make the effort to get started. We get cranky and irritable. We want other people to provide entertainment for us. It's at these boring moments that some people can get all screwed up and find themselves saying, "We've got nothing better to do; let's get high!"

John, age fourteen, told me when he's bored, he always asks his friend, "What do you want to do?" His friend asks back, "I don't know, what do you want to do?" John then says, "It's not up to me. I don't know what to do. What do you want to do?" Someone always ends up asking, "Does anyone have any grass?" (Grass is another way of saying marijuana.) "Let's get high."

There are plenty of things you can do to stop boredom. The first thing is sit with it. Sit with being bored for a while, even though it doesn't feel so good. Then realize that just getting started at something can help break down the boredom. Even though you don't want to do it, start an activity. At least try it.

Here are some ideas: walking, hiking, jogging, swimming, going to the movies, getting a group of your friends together and playing some sports, taking sports lessons, taking art lessons or just taking some art supplies and trying to express yourself on paper or in clay, taking musical instrument lessons, reading a book, getting together with a friend or several friends, baby-sitting, doing homework with a friend, volunteering to help out somewhere in your town (like at a hospital or nursing home, or coaching a kids' team), cooking something yummy, and there are lots more!

## Experimentation

Some kids will only try smoking grass or using other drugs once or twice. They'll then make a decision that they don't like the way it makes them feel; they don't like the possibility of getting caught; they don't like hassles with their parents, and overall, they don't like the *head* (what it does to their mind and senses) they get from it.

Other people experiment with drugs and like the feelings they produce. (More about this in the section Drugs Take You, Not the Other

Way Around.) Experimenting with drugs that you know nothing about can often put you in a situation where you're getting more than you've bargained for.

Zelda is now seventeen. When she was fourteen years old, she went to her girl friend's boyfriend's house to get high. (It was her third time getting high.) The boyfriend was a drug dealer and sold marijuana to the kids at their school. When she went up to his room and smoked a *joint* (a marijuana cigarette), there was a *bust* (the police barged in and caught them). Over the next few years Zelda went through shame, embarrassment, and was placed on probation by the police and spent much time in court. She lost a lot of time in school and felt that experimenting caused her more grief than it was worth.

Some other kids experiment and are lucky not to suffer any consequences for their experimentation. They have enough guts to be able to decide about using the drug instead of having the drug make a decision for them.

## Drugs Take You, Not the Other Way Around

If you decide to use drugs, after the first few times and not really knowing what you're doing, you might find that you feel good and maybe even a little guilty for having those feelings and doing what you're doing to get them.

Those good feelings that you can get when high last only a very short time. After a while you might want that feeling good feeling (some kids called this feeling mellow) to last longer. So you'll think you should take more of the drug to make the feeling last.

Unfortunately, since drugs are chemicals (even if they do come from certain plants), the attitude of "if a little is good, a lot is better" does not work. While a little of the drug can make you feel mellow, a lot can usually make you feel sicker, spacey, dizzy, tired, out of it, like your words are coming out funny, like your body is moving without you, and generally weird.

After time passes, you may want to make the original good feelings happen more often and last longer, in spite of all those feelings just mentioned. If you continue to use the drugs, no matter what kind of drug you use (be it alcohol, marijuana, uppers, downers, etc.), your emotions will be so stretched, it will be hard for them to go back into place.

Many friends will start to notice that you're not the person they knew. You may be withdrawn (keep more to yourself), angry, nasty, unfriendly, filled with fear, and have emotions that you just can't explain to anyone else or yourself.

Isn't it interesting that when the drug was first taken, you wanted to capture good feelings? Unfortunately, bad feelings also captured you. You don't even recognize yourself now. This is called being drug dependent.

## What's So Bad About Drugs—Learning About Growing Up While Being High

The problem with using alcohol and other drugs a lot is that you learn many of your growing up tasks high. This is called state dependent learning. That means, your learning is dependent upon the state you're in, which can be straight (not under the influence of drugs) or high (under the influence of drugs).

Drugs and alcohol can change and stretch out your emotions. They can make you sleepy, happy, giggly, filled with fear, *paranoid* (thinking everyone is watching you and talking about you), make you have false courage or take it away, make your anger turn into violence, make your sadness worse, and make your loneliness deeper. They can change all your feelings. And yet, at the same time, you may still feel very much a part of your group that's using drugs.

The problem comes in when you've done your growing up high. If you were high when you practiced asking girls out, took a test, made friends, took dares, played a sport, and made decisions about what to do, where to go, how to act, how to feel, the drugged you has acted—not the real you.

If you've grown up high, over time it will become difficult to do things straight. You know what it feels like to do things high, but the more you do your daily activities high, the less practice you get doing them straight. This can become very scary. Let me give you an example. If you've ever broken your leg and were in a cast, you know it's very difficult to learn how walk around in that cast. But like most things, you learn to adjust. You manage to walk around with the cast, impaired as you are, hard as it is. Imagine that this is similar to getting used to being high.

Once the cast comes off (once you stop using drugs), it's difficult to walk again. You have to exercise the leg and strengthen it because it's weak and has been out of use. Well, after using drugs for a while and then stopping your personality is weak and it's difficult to trust the decisions that you're going to have to make.

You'll have to learn how to make choices, pick and choose wisely, and deal with more confused emotions than you ever had to before using the drugs, because you are continuing to grow up. It will be hard to trust your judgment because your normal self has been hidden for such a long time and you're not used to practicing how to make choices.

If you started using drugs and alcohol at twelve and stopped using them at fifteen, there are three years of your life in which you did everything as a drug-dependent person. So, as far as your emotions are concerned, when you stop using drugs, you have to continue to grow up starting back where you left off at age twelve.

## Different Drug Effects

### Marijuana
Also called pot, grass, or reefer, it's a drug that is in the grouping of a *hallucinogen* (ha-loose-in-o-jen). It comes from a plant that is illegal to grow in the United States, and people usually smoke it to get high or stoned.

The problem with smoking marijuana is that since it is illegal and can be gotten from many different sources, very few people know what's actually in it. They don't know whether it is mixed with something else that can be dangerous (that's called laced), if it is sprayed with some pesticides (used to kill insects, bacteria, or harmful animals) that can be very hazardous to your health, or if it is stronger than they even suspect it should be.

If you smoke marijuana, you may get that rushing feeling (like feeling you're nauseous and floating in the air and are not able to stop the feelings from happening). It becomes difficult to concentrate on what it was you wanted to say to your friends. It becomes hard to put thoughts together, hard to know what you just said.

Often times, if you get a bad feeling in your head while smoking pot, it's hard to get rid of those bad feelings—they seem to stay with you for a very long time. You can also get paranoid (see page 241). This of course is not real, it's just the effect of the drug.

Smoking pot will also give you a case of the munchies. If you're concerned about gaining weight, you might consider the fact that marijuana can put extra pounds on you because it makes it difficult not to raid the refrigerator and everything around it!

The last real problem with smoking pot is that it makes you feel like doing nothing. It may be that you've got nothing to do, so what's the harm? However, all of us have responsibilities, whether they be cleaning our room, mowing the lawn, taking care of our brothers or sisters, baby-sitting, delivering newspapers, working on relationships with friends and parents, and/or going to school.

All of these things to do take motivation (you've got to want to do them). Smoking pot really prevents you from doing these things. That's why smoking pot over a long period of time can be so damaging to your mind.

It first was believed that there were very few physical consequences of smoking pot. However, new facts seem to suggest that smoking pot may cause lung damage that equals the damage of cigarettes on lungs and that it may have an effect on hormone levels, sperm count, and sexual functioning.

Although marijuana is not physically addicting (which means when you try to stop taking the drug, you go through terrible withdrawal symptoms, like shaking, sweating, vomiting, etc.), you may develop a real affection for the drug. This feeling might make the drug a best friend and make it very difficult to give up when you know you have to go on in life. It may be hard to leave such a close friend behind.

## Alcohol and Downers or Depressants

One of the most interesting things about alcohol is that it's a depressant drug that slows down the central nervous system (brain and spinal cord). In small amounts (like one or two beers), it makes people feel mellow, relaxed, giggly, and talkative. That's why it may seem like a stimulant. Yet it's really putting to sleep the policeman in your brain (the part that makes you listen to reason). Maybe this is why alcohol is so popular among adults. It's the one legal way they can get away from everything!

The more a person drinks, the more you can see that the drug is really a depressant. It's likely that a person's speech will become slurred, they'll have difficulty in walking, they'll think they're very funny when they're really making fools out of themselves, they'll talk louder than they have to, and they'll just be plain rowdy.

Sometimes the alcohol can cause difficulty beyond your control. You may have acted and appeared normal while drinking, yet you may have no memory of what you did while you drank. This is called a blackout and can happen if you drink heavily.

You may even become unconscious. This is your body's way of preventing you from doing it harm. It's screaming, "NO MORE!" If you're unconscious, you can't drink anymore (clever body!). Another way that your body may protect you from doing it in, is to cause you to vomit everything up (nature's way of saying slow down) to prevent the alcohol from getting through your stomach. So sometimes your body has more wisdom than your brain does.

You may be wondering how to put yourself (or your friend) back into the condition you left your house in. People have some interesting ideas to make a person sober up more quickly (get back to normal or no longer be under the influence of alcohol).

They mistakenly think that if you take a cold shower or drink lots of coffee, you'll get rid of the alcohol that's in your body more quickly. This is not correct. Coffee will make you wide awake and drunk, and the shower will make you wet and drunk.

The only thing that you can do to help yourself is to go to sleep, pull the covers over your head, and pray that the next morning you're going to feel much more like the person you normally know.

The body can only get rid of one drink (a can of beer, a glass of wine, or one glass of the hard stuff mixed with water or soda) every hour. There is nothing you can do to speed this up. Even taking yourself on an evening jog will not help.

These very same type feelings can happen when you use drugs that are called depressant drugs. They are really alcohol in extreme form because they act the same way as alcohol does on the body.

They're called downers and also slow down and depress the central nervous system, and have the same effect as alcohol. There's one major problem that you ought to be aware of. If you mix downers with alcohol, you may be in for some serious trouble.

Here's the problem. In mathematics we're taught that one and one equals two. But one and one does not equal two when you are dealing with drugs. The effect of one downer and one beer is like the effect of four depressants on the brain instead of two.

What happens is that once you start to feel so high, you may not know how much you have taken or when you last took anything. Therefore, without wanting to, you could cause your own death.

When people mix alcohol with other drugs, this is called *potentiation* (po-ten-she-ay-shun) or *synergism* (sinner-jizem).

Unlike marijuana, alcohol and downers have one extra property. The more you use of these drugs, the more you're going to need of them to get the same effect, even at low levels. So, if you've been used to drinking two beers every day for one week, you may need to drink two and one half beers the following week in order to get the same feelings you got from two beers the week before. This is called developing a tolerance for the drug.

As your tolerance increases, your body may start to physically crave the drug. This happens when you are using alcohol or downers very often and you're using heavy amounts.

If you stop taking these drugs, you might find yourself shaking, feeling hyper, sweating, feeling irritable, feeling nasty, having a rapid pulse, and perhaps having convulsions (like a marionette puppet that's gone crazy). These are the withdrawal symptoms I mentioned before. Withdrawal can be very dangerous and can result in death.

Therefore, if you think that you've been abusing alcohol and downers and want to stop, it's very important that you speak to your parents and your doctor privately. You can't stop by yourself because the withdrawal can kill you.

## Uppers

Uppers are drugs that can stimulate the central nervous system and make you feel as if you were walking on air. They pep people up, make them awake, talkative, less bored, and feel that they have the power to do anything they want.

The problem with doing uppers for a long period of time is that it becomes impossible to sleep. That's why so many people who use uppers drink alcohol to go to sleep, take uppers in the morning to wake up, use alcohol to go to sleep, and so on. You can see where this might lead—to the morgue (a place where they put the dead).

Often if you are using only uppers, like cocaine, *amphetamines* (am-fet-a-means), or diet pills, and you want to stop using them, what may happen is that your body will crash. Crashing means that your body can no longer keep up at the pace it's been operating on, and you need to sleep for many days.

Taking uppers can cause major problems with your heart and lungs. It can also cause mental problems: make you feel edgy, anxious, nervous, and not be able to tell the difference between what's real and what's not.

Just like with alcohol and marijuana, anyone who feels the need to keep using uppers may find themselves becoming dependent on them and needing more and more of the drug in order to get the same effects. Having to leave the arms of the drugs can sometimes be very hard.

## Growing Up Drinking

All people drink. We drink water, soda, fruit juice, and a variety of other beverages. They quench or satisfy our thirst. And yet alcohol is not drunk to quench thirst. People put up with the taste of alcohol because it makes them feel high.

Many companies that make alcohol are making alcoholic beverages in malted form, and kids really like the taste of these. Keep in mind that no matter what form it's in, it is still alcohol.

Alcohol is probably the most popular legal drug available to adults. Each state has its own laws about at what age a person is allowed to buy alcoholic beverages. You may know kids who can get alcohol from older brothers or sisters, or by asking people to go into liquor stores for them.

Because alcohol is legal, parents often would rather think of their kids drinking alcohol than smoking pot or taking other illegal drugs.

Mary told me that when she was fifteen years old, her older brother who was in the bar business, told her if she wanted to get high, she should go into his bar to get high. He felt that at least he could keep an eye on her, and she wouldn't be taking those other dangerous drugs.

You should know that Mary is now recovering from alcoholism. Alcoholism is a disease where a person feels an emotional craving for alcohol (a drug), may be physically addicted, goes through changes in his or her personality, and gets into all sorts of problems as a result of drinking.

Millions of people each year are affected by the drug alcohol. There are a lot of related accidents in the home and on the highways. Divorced, broken, or angry hostile homes, lost jobs, failure at school, illnesses, and death can also result from using alcohol.

The decision to drink alcohol, how much to drink, and the consequences of drinking are all in your hands. Sometimes decisions about your happiness, when it comes to drinking, are made for you. In some families one or both parents suffer from the disease of alcoholism, which can cause very painful feelings for all the kids as well as the healthy parent in the family.

The decision about your parents' drinking is not in your hands, because they are the ones who are doing the drinking. But what is in your hands is how you feel about their drinking and whether or not you will go to someone for help to deal with your feelings about living in a family that drinks too much.

## Growing Up in a Drugged Family

When the chief rule maker in your family (usually your mom or dad or both) has a drinking problem, this causes the other parent and the kids to cope with the unfair rules in the best way they can. The rules are unfair because the drugged parent is not really in a position to think straight. After all his or her feelings and emotions are stretched out from using alcohol or drugs for quite some time.

Even if they make a rule when they are not under the influence of alcohol or drugs, their thinking is still affected by the many times they have used the alcohol or drugs.

Just because you are coping deep down inside with painful feelings because the rules are unfair, doesn't mean that the way you are going about it is the best way for growing up feeling good. Every kid in a drugged family has his or her own way of coping with unfair rules. The oldest will often make things better by being the best in school, being most popular (although he or she may not want to bring friends home), being the best in sports, and being, generally, an all around super person. They hope that maybe because of their efforts, their mom or dad (or both) will stop drinking.

What they might tell themselves is, "Boy, a kid who does this well in school and with friends can't really come from such a bad family."

Growing up with trying to make mom or dad not drink is a real burden. It can hurt a lot! The family gives so little good stuff back while you keep feeding them with the wonderful things you do. The hurt feelings get buried, and the world only sees how good and responsible you are.

Lisa, age twelve, the oldest child in an alcoholic family, felt that by being a cheerleader, cleaning her room all the time, and being daddy's favorite, she could in some way get him to stop drinking. She so badly wanted the family not to fight and to be okay. She wished she could bring her friends home. The more she tried to make her family better by trying to stop fights and pleasing her father by getting good grades in school, the more she felt unable and helpless to do anything right. Even though Lisa feels she is smart, she has this nagging feeling that she hasn't done enough.

Sometimes the second child in the alcoholic family seems not to be able to live up to the first, unless they have talent and skill that is very, very different from the first. Like if the first one loves music, the second one might be a soccer star. If the second kid just does not seem to be able to measure up to the first, this kid can start getting into trouble at school, begin to use drugs and alcohol, run away from home, get pregnant, get into trouble with the law, and if they're "real bright," be the leader of a troubled group of kids (a bunch of rowdies).

What's real sad is that deep down inside, they feel awful about themselves and do not like what they are doing.

When this happens, the mom or dad who is drugged can easily say the family mess is because of their troubled kid. Don't you believe it! It's the other way around. This troubled kid is angry about having to get their attention by leaving the family and using drugs and trouble as a way of getting attention.

The truth is they would love for the family to get better. They would love mom and dad to be like other moms and dads. They would like mom and dad not to drink.

Patrick, age nineteen, always remembers hating his older brother, who could do no wrong. Patrick thinks that his parents thought that the moon, sun, and stars set on his brother's head! Patrick feels guilty about not loving his older brother but feels it was a bummer being number two. When Patrick used to make his father, who was an alcoholic, get him out of bed in the morning, come down to school after he was thrown out, or go to court to help him after he broke store windows, at least he felt he was getting some attention.

But his father's drinking never changed. Patrick started to use drugs and alcohol very heavily and all the family problems were blamed on him. Patrick is still very angry at his father for being so two-faced. He says, "My father can only see my problem; he can't see his own. I hate him for that."

Meg, age seventeen, spoke about always running away from home, even if it was just for half an hour. She hated her house. If she could live underneath her bed to escape the family pain (the yelling, screaming, and fighting), she would have. She could do nothing as well as her older sister. So she decided, without being aware of it, that she would make her own way in the world.

She decided that having a life with her boyfriend was where she was going to get her attention. She started using drugs heavily, got pregnant, ran away from home for good, all the while knowing that she hated herself for her behavior. But she could see no way out of it.

Although Meg is back at home and understands that her behavior comes from living in an alcoholic family, she's still too angry at her mother to do anything about her own behavior.

Sometimes the younger kids in an alcoholic family may find themselves playing alone, spending most of their time in their rooms, and not being sure of what's really going on in the family. Very often no one seems to worry about them because they're so quiet. However, just because they're quiet and seem to be behaved, doesn't mean they're not feeling anything. They're often fearful deep inside, and may have little success in making friends because they spend so much time alone with their imaginary friends. (It's less embarrassing to bring an imaginary friend into a drugged home!)

Nicole, age eleven, stays away from the fighting in her house and sits in her room watching television with her dog (who is her best friend). She does this all the time. Even when it's sunny out and all the kids are playing outside, Nicole feels that her room, television, and dog are her best friends.

No one seems to pay very much attention to her. They figure because she's so quiet and doesn't give anyone trouble, she has no problems. When you ask Nicole how she feels about her father's drinking, she shrugs her shoulders and says (with her face down), "It doesn't bother me."

Nicole wishes she could really have a best friend besides her dog.

Sometimes the last child in the alcoholic family can look like the child who has no problems in the world. He or she often is the class clown, is usually joking, and is sometimes unable to sit still. The last child may not know about the drinking and the drugging in the family since he or she is so young. And family members may take great pains to protect the youngest from the major family secret.

Because they feel that the family members are trying to protect them by telling them that there is nothing wrong in their family, deep down inside, they may feel very anxious and scared that maybe there really is something wrong that no one is telling them.

Because they are so nervous that something might be wrong, they can appear to be busy cracking jokes and running around like chickens without heads. Every once in a while, family members might like to laugh at the youngest child's jokes. The problem occurs when no one takes them seriously, and they really can't tell anyone about their nervousness.

Mark, age seven, the youngest child in an alcoholic family, can't sit still for one moment. He's either spilling milk, making silly faces, or driving every adult in the house crazy. He's cute and loving and every one likes him. But no one takes him too seriously.

## What You Can Do if Your Family Is Drugged Up

The number one rule in families that are drugged up seems to be that you're not supposed to talk about what's going on in the family: not with other people in the family and not with outsiders.

Sometimes you hear this rule from your mother and your father, and sometimes you know deep down inside that's the way it's supposed to be (it's unspoken). What this rule does is to prevent you from getting help with your painful feelings. It also prevents the family from having a chance to get better.

You might be saying to yourself, "My family is the only family where this is going on." You should know that growing up in a drugged up family is probably one of the major family problems in the United States.

Many kids have the exact same feelings as you. The problem is, so many of these kids have the same rules. So it becomes very difficult to break the rules and find out that other kids are suffering too.

Kids with courage, kids who are fed up, kids who are asked by their teacher or the courts "What's going on in your family?" are the kids who usually break the family silence by finally telling someone what's going on. Other kids may not say one word, even to their best friends, and may really think the family's problems are all their fault.

I hope that by reading this chapter you will understand that if you live in a drugged up family, the best thing you can do for yourself and your family is to break the rule of silence. It is important for you to tell your mother or father (the one who's not drinking) that you are unhappy, confused, sad, fearful, and nervous about the family situation, and you think that the *family* needs to get help—not just the drugged person.

If this is too much of a risk, you must get help for yourself and those family members who want to come along. You can speak to a school counselor or social worker, a favorite teacher, a religious leader, or your family doctor.

The best thing that you can do would be to pick up the telephone and call Alateen. Alateen is an organization of kids that understand what it's like to grow up in a drugged up family, because that's what happened to them. There are meetings of Alateen in every community. Many mothers or fathers who live with the drugged up person go to Alanon meetings so that they, too, can talk about what it's like to live with a drugged up person. If the drugged person makes the decision that he or she can no longer live with stretched out emotions, doesn't like what's happened to their personality, and doesn't want to create any more problems for themselves or their family, they can get help by going to Alcoholics Anonymous (AA).

These meetings can be found in every neighborhood in the world. Just look for the telephone number in your local phone book or dial 0, for Operator, and ask how to get Information. There are all sorts of meetings and plenty of wonderful, good, loving people who will reach out to help you when you walk through the door.

Sometimes things that are best for us to do aren't the most comfortable. But that doesn't mean you shouldn't go ahead and do them. Take the chance on yourself to grow up and feel good. You're worth it!

## Drinking and Driving

While you might not understand or relate to what it's like to live in a drugged up family, you may have been touched by the effects of alcohol in a different way.

Although you're probably not old enough to drive, and it's certainly not legal for you to drink, you may suffer the consequences of someone who is old enough to drink, old enough to drive, but puts the two together. How is this possible?

Robert, now twenty-eight, shared, "When I was in the ninth grade, my good friend and his father were spending a Sunday afternoon together. They were sitting in their car at a red light, standing absolutely still, when a drunk driver speeding from behind crashed into them. They were doing nothing and were both killed. The drunk driver wasn't hurt at all."

Camile, age eighteen, started to cry when she talked about her sister, a new driver, who was hit in the rear by a nineteen-year-old guy, a drunk driver, and how her sister's car was smashed into a tree like an accordian with her sister's body crushed inside. To make Camille's anger worse the nineteen-year-old drunk driver was given a slap on the wrist and had to pay a small fine. Camille felt that something more should have been done to the driver.

This is a harsh reminder that even if you don't drink, you can be seriously affected by someone who does. The responsibility for this decision is not only to yourself but to everyone around you.

The problem comes a little closer to you when you need to take a ride from someone you know that may have been drinking. Steven, age fourteen, shared, "I didn't know what to do. Last weekend my older brother said he'd pick me up at my friend's party. When I heard the horn, I looked out to find that my brother's friend was driving instead of my brother. When I got closer to the car, I saw there were beer cans all over the front seat and I knew they had been drinking. His friend who was driving seemed okay, but it bothered me. I got in the car anyway, hoping we'd get home without hitting something."

Betsy, age seventeen, said that there were times when her boyfriend had too much to drink and she felt scared driving with him. She thought he'd feel badly or get mad and not want to go out with her anymore if she told him she'd rather walk or call her parents to take them home. So she got into his car and hoped they'd get home safely.

You may get home safely the first time, or the second, or the third. But the more you drive with someone who has been drinking, even if they're not drunk (polluted, bombed, smashed) but just mellow, the better your chances that you may not get home the next time.

When you get a driver's license, you may think that the best way to not hurt someone and not get arrested for drinking and driving is to let someone else who has been drinking drive home. You may not get arrested. You may not hurt someone. But if the driver gets into an accident, he or she may take you along.

Mark, age twenty, shared, "My friend was driving my pickup truck and we both had some beers. The ride home was pretty straight and easy. It was just our luck that we ran into the only parked car off the road. My pickup truck was wrecked! I spent the night in the hospital, and my friend spent the night in jail. My friend and I were very lucky. The fact that two girls from my high school died in a drinking-driving accident earlier in the year didn't have as much effect on me as when something actually happened to me. I'm really starting to look at things differently."

A lot of people who have been drinking and feel that they are mellow, not wrecked, think that they can make it home, because their home is such a short distance away. Did you know that most drunk drivers are picked up by the police within one mile of their home?

Some people feel it's too embarrassing to admit that they can't drive home because they've been drinking. They may be concerned that their friends are going to laugh at them about not being able to handle drinking and driving at the same time.

Others are embarrassed in front of a boyfriend or girl friend, especially since they don't want this person to think less of them. Still others don't have a problem with embarrassment. They may think, "If I brought my car here, I have a responsibility to get it home, no matter what shape I'm in."

Even others think that there's absolutely nothing wrong with drinking and driving and will continue to drink until they get caught. Did you know that people who say they will not drink and drive until they get caught usually continue to drink and drive even after they are caught? In spite of injury to themselves and others, embarrassment, shame, a possible jail sentence, guilt, or money trouble, some people never learn. Maybe they have a very big problem with alcohol.

## What You Can Do About the Drinking-Driving Situation

Many kids are finally starting to look at the drinking and driving problem very seriously. Usually these kids have been personally affected by this problem.

Doug, age eighteen, talked with me about his two closest friends who were killed last year. "Their car smashed into a tree off a winding road on the way home after a night of partying and drinking a lot of beer. Both were great guys, liked by everyone. Both were seniors in high school, really cared about their grades, and we were all looking forward to graduation. We went to school together each morning, partied together, spent a lot of time together. They were my closest friends. I really think as many people as possible should learn from what happened so they won't have to go through the horrible grief I experienced."

Doug and his friends started a driver-doesn't-drink rule and haven't broken it since. This rule means that the driver for the night (or day or whenever) doesn't drink even a sip of an alcoholic beverage and is responsible for getting everyone home safely.

Said Doug, "My friends are now really aware of drinking and driving. So is our whole high school class for that matter. The problem is that's where it stopped. The younger classes, I'm afraid, just did not learn. I hope many people read your book so they'll know."

Another way that you can prevent drunk driving is to call a parent. There are many community groups where parents have gotten together with the police and have arranged a special force of people who will be on call for any kids in their town who need to be picked up because they feel they should not drive home alone or with someone else who has been drinking.

You can also spend the night with your friends and call your parents to let them know that you're okay. The reason you're not coming home is because no one is able to take you home and your friend's parents will look after you for the evening (that's important for them to do).

It takes a lot of guts to do the next prevention measure. And you usually need two friends to help! If a friend of yours wants to leave a party and you think that the friend is in no condition to drive, have two friends

walk arm in arm with the sloshed person while you remove the car keys from his or her hand or pocket.

Convince them to spend the night even though they tell you everything is fine or might even be yelling at you. Call their parents to tell them that they are okay and don't pay much attention to how much they say they hate you. They'll thank you in the morning.

You might be thinking that bad people do these things. Being bad has nothing to do with growing up in a drugged up family and nothing to do with drinking and driving.

Even if you work hard in school, love your parents, always baby-sit for your little brother or sister, are a good friend, say your prayers regularly, and have wonderful dreams, trees aren't choosy. Neither are parked cars. Hospital visits are not as good as dates and parties. And funerals are not fun places to be.

Drinking and driving affects all of us. We all are responsible and we all must do something about it. Isn't it sad that most of the people who make sure to do something about the drinking-driving problem are those that have been personally touched by it?

We all must do everything we can to take care of the problem before the problem takes care of us!

## Growing Up Smoking

Take a few minutes out to think about how you feel about smoking. How you feel about the smoke going in and out of your nose and lungs, how you feel about being in a smoke-filled room when you don't smoke, how you feel about being in a smoke-filled room when you do smoke, how you feel about your parents smoking, how you feel about your friends smoking, and whether or not smoking would have any consequences for you.

## Risk Taking and Smoking

Unlike drugs and drinking, the risks of smoking cigarettes might seem far, far away from your day-to-day life. Yes, you are correct if you believe there are consequences to inhaling the chemicals in tobacco into your body. Yes, you are correct when you say that the chemicals in tobacco can:

- lower a person's energy.
- make a person's blood vessels (roadways through which the blood travels around the body) constricted or narrower so that the heart has to work harder to pump the blood through.
- cause lung damage. (Cigarette smoking is believed to be the main cause of lung cancer in human beings.)
- cause heart problems.
- cause breathing problems. (Many people who play sports have noticed that smoking has made them out of breath sooner than

before they started smoking. But I'm also talking about breathing problems that cause people not to be able to even walk up a flight of stairs!)

- possibly lower the weight of a newborn baby born to a woman who smoked during pregnancy.
- cause smoker's cough. (This is often *chronic* [kron-ick] or lasts a long time, doesn't heal, and stays with the smoker.)
- possibly take *years* off a smoker's life.

You may be saying, "I know all of this!" But these consequences seem far, far away. And if you smoke now or are planning to start, it's hard to think that these physical problems are real for you in your life right now.

You probably hear your parents and other people wishing that they had stopped smoking years ago. You might have heard people say, "If only I had not picked up that first cigarette."

And yet, in spite of all the physical changes, in spite of listening to older people talk about how much they hate their smoking habit, in spite of your teachers telling you about the dangers, you might still smoke.

## Feelings and Pressures Related to Smoking

As with everything else there are so many different feelings and different types of pressures related to smoking. The more you explore these pressures, the more ready you will be to deal with them if they ever happen to you.

Steve, age thirteen, said, "I always saw my parents smoke and have wanted to try smoking since I was little. It seemed like the big person's thing to do!"

Beth, age fourteen, told me, "Some of the kids I hang around with started smoking. I'm not sure what to do because I don't want to feel left out, but I really don't want to smoke."

Vicki, age nine, said, "I don't ever want to smoke. My mother and my father smoke and I hate it when the smoke goes in my nose. I don't know how they can sit there with the smoke in their faces all the time."

Sammy, age eleven, shared that he's upset because his father smokes so much. His father coughs all the time and still smokes. Sammy's very worried that the smoking will make his father's cough worse.

Sharon, age fifteen, said, "I smoke because I like to, not because it looks cool or anything like that. My parents won't let me smoke in front of them, so I have to sneak."

Roger, age forty, said, "When I was younger, my parents told me I could smoke in front of them if I wanted to. I think they took all the fun out of it by giving me permission. I never smoked until years later."

Betsy, age twelve, told me, "I'm really afraid of what's going to happen in the girls bathroom at the junior high school next year. I've heard people say that you can get pressured to smoke if you walk in there."

Carol, age thirty-eight, remembers, "I was one of the first and only people to have a car in high school. Every morning a lot of the kids sat in my car and smoked before school started. I didn't smoke and didn't feel pressured to smoke even though they did. I admit that for a while, it was important to let them use my car because they were my friends and I didn't want to say no to them. But finally I told them. I hated the smoke and didn't want them to smoke in my car anymore. I said they'd have to find somewhere else to smoke.

"It was really interesting. I found out who my friends were. Some of the girls used me and didn't have much to do with me after I told them to stay away from my car. Other girls continued to be my friends."

Alexis, age fourteen, who always hated smoking and whose parents never smoked but whose aunt did, started smoking. Even though she was coughing a lot and hated it, she did it because a boy she really liked smoked.

She felt that in order to get him to like her better, she should do the same things that he did. So she continued to smoke in front of him. She would never smoke alone.

Then her girl friends, who were feeling the same way she was feeling, started to smoke in front of each other but still not alone. Now a new pressure was added. Not only did Alexis smoke in front of her boyfriend, but she felt she had to smoke in front of her girl friends. Little did she know they were all feeling the same pressure.

After a while Alexis started doing a lot of her activities with a cigarette in her hand. She started to feel grown-up like her aunt. In time she decided that smoking was not for her. But she never really felt it very strongly.

So when a new boyfriend came along who always had a cigarette hanging out of his mouth, once again Alexis felt the need to smoke. The smoking started to become a real habit. She smoked—needing to—not wanting to.

I hope by now that if your friends are smoking and you really don't want to, that you'll have a better idea about how to say no. (For a quick review of what you might say or do if you feel pressure to smoke, turn back to Peer Pressure, Making Choices, Chapter 15.)

## Living In a Cloud of Smoke

Since the physical dangers of smoking are far, far away, they don't seem to really bother you now. You can still run, play sports, be physically active, climb up stairs like you always could, breathe easily, go without headaches, and feel really good (although you may feel dizzy and nauseous when taking the first few puffs due to the poisonous effect of nicotine, one of the chemicals in cigarettes), you may now be asking yourself, "So what's the big deal about smoking?"

The truth of the matter is, if you are like so many other people, you may think what you can't see probably won't hurt you. People often use this slogan in order not to look honestly at their harmful behavior.

If you smoke you are probably saying, "I'll give up smoking when and if I can see that it has caused some harmful consequence to my body." But years from now saying prayers and promising to be good by not smoking any more in the hopes that you can once again do all the physical activities that smoking has already taken away will not work.

So what are the consequences for living in a cloud of smoke now? Living in a cloud of smoke has some social and physical results that you may not have thought of.

First of all let's talk about the lingering odor in your hair. You may spend hours each day trying to get your hair to look and smell nice. Yet the smoke in cigarettes, cigars, and pipes manages to get on your hair and stays there until washed again.

Smokers' hair often smells like old sweat socks that have just been used to clean out ashtrays. If that sounds gross, that's what it's like to be around smoker's hair. Gross!

Next, let's deal with breath. Phew! Lots of kids don't like to kiss smokers because their breath smells like a cesspool that has backed up. Get the picture?

When everyone starts running for nose clips after you've smoked a cigarette, now you know why.

A smoker's clothing often has that lingering smell of stale cigarettes. And even if you wear cologne or perfume, your body may smell like perfume on the old sweat socks that have been used to clean the ashtrays.

The unfortunate part is that many smokers have no idea they smell so badly. That's because two of the consequences of smoking are that it can lessen your senses of smell and taste. Therefore, many people have to put up with the way a smoker smells and tastes. Smoking also can cause fingers to smell and fingers and teeth to be stained a yellowish color. Yuck.

Lauren, age sixteen, finds it's very difficult to tell her girl friends that they stink. She wants to be their friend and doesn't want to push them away, but her other nonsmoking friends have just about had it with the way her smoking friends smell. She likes her friends but hates their odors.

Allison, age fourteen, decided that she doesn't want to kiss her boyfriend anymore. He used to smell so nice but now he started smoking and uses breath spray to cover up the odor of tobacco. Allison gets nauseous from the breath spray and tobacco. Her feelings are beginning to change toward him.

Jason, age thirteen, can't stand when his father, a cigar smoker, tries to kiss him. He loves the fact that his father wants to kiss him and really would like to kiss him back. But he makes the excuse that he's too old for kissing and would rather shake hands. His father's cigar smell turns him off.

Sean, age ten, heard his brother, a nonsmoker, fighting with his girl friend about her smoking. His brother said that his girl friend was starting to become a turn-off. Even though she thought she looked cool and glamorous, getting close to her was disgusting. She always stank of tobacco chemicals and it was hard to be physical with her.

Wouldn't it be nice if you could be strong, charming, popular, attractive, and independent without one of those ugly chemical sticks hanging out of your face?

I should warn you that the people who advertise cigarettes and alcohol are doing the best that they can to make you think that drinking and smoking will make you sexy, popular, desirable, successful, and the best. They're very clever in their commercials. They would like to keep you drugged in a cloud of smoke. See if you can open your own window, let the fresh air in, and keep it flowing!

# 19
# Your Parents

Many kids say that they feel great about their parents. One nine-year-old girl said, "We get along. We're very close. I can say anything I want to them and they'll listen. They spend a lot of time with me. They don't pressure me. They're great!" Kids who feel this way are usually secure, happy, calm, confident. They feel loved.

Too many other kids have told me that they wish they could feel closer to their parents. A young friend of mine said, "I can't talk with my mom and my dad. They don't understand me. They're always bugging me about something. They're hardly ever home. I don't think I'll ever be able to talk with them." Kids who feel that way are often unhappy, insecure, lonely, angry, scared, frustrated, and very sad. As much as they might love their parents, and as much as their parents might really love them, these kids may not feel loved.

How do you feel about your parents? Are you happy with the relationship you have with them? What do you wish you could change? What have you wanted to say but have just not been able to get out the words? What about your parents makes you feel good? What makes you feel bad?

This chapter will give you a chance to think about all the feelings you have that relate to your own parents. Trying to understand these feelings and learning how to deal with them better is very important. So get cozy and really try to concentrate. For now, forget about the homework you might not have finished. Promise not to let any phone calls interrupt.

263

Just think about you, your parents and how you feel about your relationship with them.

If you haven't been writing down your feelings in a notebook as you read, this might be a good time to start. That way when it's time to talk with your parents about anything, you'll have all your feelings in front of you and you can make sure not to leave anything out.

## Talking with Your Parents

If you can talk openly with your parents and trust they'll care enough to listen, that's very, very special. The sad thing is that most of the boys and girls I've spoken with can't talk openly with their parents.

Sharings such as, "I'm nervous when I have to talk with my parents"; "my parents don't understand about how I feel. I try to talk things over with them but they treat me like a baby"; "I'm afraid to talk with my parents"; "I have trouble talking to my mom. I don't know what to say to her"; "I have a question to ask my mother, but I think that she'll say I'm too young to know"; and "I can't talk to my dad" can give you a clue as to why so many feelings stay hidden. Maybe you've had some of these feelings.

Even when kids want very badly to talk and parents want very badly to listen, there still can be silence. Why? Well all too often, children and their parents don't know what words to use or what questions to ask.

It might be a relief for you to realize that the words are always right inside of you. So you never have to be stuck for what to say—not with your parents, your friends, your teachers, your boyfriend or girl friend, not with the President of the United States, or the man (woman?) on the moon, or anyone! Just think about how you feel and then turn your feelings into words.

If you feel embarrassed, you can say, "Mom or Dad, I'm really embarrassed to say this. . . ." If you feel scared, you can say, "Mom or Dad, I'm scared to tell you this. . . ." If you're concerned they won't take you seriously, you can tell them, "I'm concerned you won't realize how serious I am about this. . . ." If you're worried that they'll be mad, you can say, "I hope you won't get mad when I say this. Please don't be mad. . . ." If you're ashamed, you can tell them you're ashamed. And so on.

Sometimes your parents may say and do things that cause you to have some strong feelings. Since they may not realize that they've embarrassed you, hurt you, blamed you unfairly, or anything else, it's very important for you to let them know about your feelings. Here are some more suggestions:

If your parents embarrassed you, you can say, "I don't know if you realize how much you embarrassed me. . . ."

If they hurt you, you can say, "You know, you really hurt me. . . ."

If you think they were unfair, you can say, "You weren't very fair. . . ."

If they blamed you for something you didn't do, you can say, "I don't understand why you blamed me for that when I didn't even do it! . . ."

If you feel they don't understand, you can say, "Mom, Dad, you just don't understand how I feel. . . ."

If you think they're going to say you're too young to know, you can say, "I know you're going to think I'm too young to know, but if I'm old enough to ask, I'm old enough to get an answer! . . ."

Anything you feel can be turned into words. Even if you can't figure out how you feel, you can say, "I don't know what to say," or "I don't know how to tell you this," or, "Is it okay that we don't talk? I need time to think about how I feel. I'm not sure."

So if you're ever not sure what to say, listen for a moment to what you're feeling. Turning the feelings into words will become easier and easier. The feelings are always there, you just have to know to pay attention to them. Your parents can do the same. (Mention this to them in case they don't already know. It might help to make it easier for them to share their feelings with you.)

### Being comfortable

Now that you know how you might approach your parents (or anyone) and what you might say, it might help for you to think more about what topics are harder to discuss than others.

Lots of kids have told me they have difficulty talking with their parents about their bodies (sometimes your parents' faces will be more red than yours), their development (your parents' faces may get redder), sex (they're almost purple now!), dating (no change), and death (the red has turned to white). This is very natural.

Parents are people just like everybody else. They may get embarrassed and uncomfortable about a lot of topics that you'll want to talk about. But that doesn't mean you shouldn't try to talk with them about these things.

### Needing all the answers

I think it would help for you to understand that some parents don't feel good talking with their children about certain things because they think they need to know all the answers.

Your parents would probably be relieved if you told them, "I know you probably can't answer all my questions. But that's okay. I'm really happy I can ask. Maybe we can find out the rest together."

## *Your mother, father, or both?*

Which parent can you talk with more easily? Maybe you're one of those kids who can talk with either parent. Maybe you can talk comfortably with your mother, maybe only with your father.

This may surprise you, but there's no family rule book that states who should speak with whom. The best thing would be for moms and dads to speak with sons and daughters.

The more I talk to kids, the more I find that girls continue to think that it's kind of strange to talk with their dads about periods, bras, and things like that. Boys often feel the same way about talking with their moms about wet dreams and erections, and so on. Not all boys and not all girls feel this way. But many do.

With so many kids living in single-parent households, there are going to be girls who only live with their fathers and boys who only live with their mothers. (And girls will continue to have men teachers; boys will be in classes with women teachers.) The earlier you realize that dads know about girls' development and moms know about boys' development, the earlier you'll take a chance on sharing feelings and asking questions—not only because of living with single parents but especially because parents are usually so happy when their child shares in that way with them.

Perhaps the next time you find yourself holding back, you'll push yourself a little to try to say what you think you can't. Remember, just because you're not comfortable doesn't mean you shouldn't try. Say it quickly if you have to but say it! You might be so wonderfully surprised at how much closer you'll feel with that parent.

## *Talking can be nonverbal* (without words) *as well as verbal* (with words)

You're giving messages all the time, both verbally and nonverbally. Sometimes the nonverbal messages are much louder than the verbal ones.

For instance, did you ever see someone act really upset? They might have a deep frown, tightened up mouth, and seem as if they're holding back their tears. And when you ask them "What's wrong?" they say,

"Nothing!" Well, you know very well something's wrong, they're just not telling you.

Or if someone gives you a huge smile and a great big hug, the message is love. They don't really have to say anything after doing that. They've already given you their message loud and clear. That's a good thing to remember in case you feel funny saying "I love you" out loud. Now you know you can give an "I love you" message without words. (If you wanted to say "I love you" with words and haven't for years, you could say "I know I haven't said I love you for so long, but I just want you to know, I do!" You see? You can put your feelings into words about anything.)

You'd be surprised how much you can learn about your parents and how much you are telling them, perhaps without even realizing it. If they're paying attention, parents can probably sense when you're happy or sense when something is wrong with you, even if you don't tell them a word. If you pay attention, you can probably learn a lot about what your parents feel if you sense their feelings from how they act, the expressions on their faces, and whether or not they seem tense. If you're not sure about what you're sensing, or if you're upset or confused, ask them if everything is okay. Tell them your feelings! Maybe there's something to be concerned about but maybe not.

## When You Can't Talk with Your Parents

While most parents would do anything to be able to talk with their children in a meaningful way, the disturbing truth is that some parents really don't care. I can't pretend that all do. That can be very sad and deeply painful for the child who wants their parent so badly, who wants to reach out and know their parent will be there.

But all you can do is express your pain and let them know how much they're hurting you, how much they mean to you, how much you want more of a relationship with them. They're the ones who'll have to make the decision to change, to pay more attention, to set more time aside so you can be together. You can stamp, slam doors, kick, scream, and cry yourself to sleep every night, but nothing will matter unless they decide to change themselves. You can't do it for them.

The more you try to get your parents to love you and the more you don't succeed, the more you may feel that you're not lovable. It would be helpful to remember that even though your parents may not be able to talk with you that doesn't mean you're not lovable or special. It just may be that there is nothing you can personally do to make the feelings different between you.

Sometimes parents spend more time with their friends and much less time with their own kids. They can spend hours and hours on the telephone or with friends who have come to visit, and when you want to talk with them, somehow they're always too busy. The message is that their adult conversations are much more important than you and your conversation. The message is, they just don't care!

When Sharon was thirteen, she said that her mother would spend hours in the kitchen drinking coffee with her neighbor. Every time Sharon wanted to talk with her mother about anything, her mother would "shh" her and say "Can't you see I'm talking? Don't interrupt me!" Sharon would wait for hours to get to talk with her mother because it seemed like any time she approached her would be an interruption. It got to the point where Sharon realized that her mother thought her friends were truly more important than Sharon and her problems were.

To tell your parent that you'd like to talk with him or her more, sometimes writing your feelings in notes can be easier. Then you can take the time to say all the things you need to say, without feeling like you're interrupting. You can give your notes to your parent and hope to talk together after they've been read.

While you're waiting and hoping to talk, you can reach out to the other parent, an older brother or sister, a loving grandparent or other relative, religious leader, a trusted teacher, school counselor, or even your friend's parent. They won't take the place of your parent. No one can. But at least you'll be able to get guidance in how to deal with your situation in a way that will be helpful to you, and you'll be able to feel loved and more secure in knowing there are other people who care.

Sharon decided from that point on that her older sister would be the best person to talk to about all the small and big things in her life. In time she realized that her mother was never going to change.

## When Parents Don't Listen

There are several different ways that parents don't listen. Johnny, age eleven, told me, "I can't stand it when I'm trying to tell my father something important and he keeps on reading his newspaper. When I ask him if he's listening, he says, 'Of course. I can do both things at once!' But I never get the feeling he's really hearing me."

Joanne, age thirteen, said, "I wish my mother would listen more. She hardly ever looks up from her book when I talk with her (she's always reading). She says things like, 'Ummm,' 'hmmm,' and 'oh,' and then ends up saying 'I'm sorry to hear that.' But then says nothing else."

Pete, age twelve, said, "I know my parents try to listen to me. But my younger sisters and brothers always need attention and it's always so noisy. I hardly ever get a chance to talk with them by myself."

Nancy, age ten, said, "Sometimes I have to say things five times before my father will look up from his TV program and give a grunt."

In every one of these situations Nancy, Pete, Joanne, and Johnny can let their parents know how they feel. Maybe their parents don't realize how much it would matter if they made the extra effort to pay more attention. See if you can put their feelings into words.

Sometimes, even when a parent really would put down the newspaper, turn off the TV, and take the time to look you straight in the eye and listen, they just can't.

Your mother or father may work long hours out of the house and may not be able to see you very often. They may hardly ever come home for dinner, or maybe they travel a lot. Even if you feel close and comfortable with each other, it's hard to share if they're not around.

At those times you can write down your feelings in a note to them so they can read it when they come home. Maybe you can set aside a certain time over the weekend, like Sunday morning breakfast or Sunday evening after dinner, as a catch-up time. Though you'd like to talk with each other more often, knowing that you're doing your best to use the time you do have will help to make you feel good.

Sometimes when your parents are around and do listen, they may just not "hear" you. They might say, "Oh, it's ridiculous for you to feel that way," or "you shouldn't let that bother you!" When anyone, even your parent, says that you shouldn't feel a certain way and you know you do, that's when the sirens need to go off! Just tell them, "It doesn't matter what you think I should feel, this is how I do feel. Now could you help me? . . ."

## Spending Time with Your Parents

Many kids have told me that they wish their parents would spend more time with them. Sometimes this is impossible, but many times it just takes being smarter about the time you do have.

Too often you only have ten or fifteen minutes, so you think it's not enough time to do anything. But it's plenty of time to walk around the block, sit in your yard, kitchen, or living room to talk, catch up, and let each other know about the day you've had so far. It's time enough to give a hug and tell someone you miss them and wish you could spend more time together.

You might find yourself jealous of other kids whose parents are out in the street playing ball with them for hours at a time. You may be sad when your parents aren't able to come to back-to-school nights, school concerts, or sports events.

But if you love your parents and know they love you, then you've got something so special. There are probably plenty of kids whose parents can spend time who would trade all that time spent in a second if they could only feel such special feelings as you do toward your parents.

*Important Message:* With all the talk about communicating with your parents, sharing your feelings, sharing your time, it's important to point out, if you haven't noticed already, that it's natural for kids to want to spend more and more time with their friends. Even if that takes away from some of the time they could spend with their parents (and family).

That doesn't mean they love their parents any less. It's simply a part of growing up.

Also parents may find their children aren't telling them as much as they did when they were younger. Here, too, it probably doesn't mean that their children trust or love their parents any less. And it doesn't mean that they have failed as parents. As children get older, it's natural for them to want to share certain things with friends, often instead of sharing with their parents. (Hopefully, if there are any serious concerns, a boy or girl will realize how important it can be to let their parents know.)

As long as you feel you can and will share with your parents when you want to or need to do so, then that's fine. It's not fine when you want to share and don't feel you can.

If you're wondering how your parents feel about the time you spend with your friends, ask them. If you're feeling guilty about wanting to accept your friend's dinner invitation instead of having dinner with your family, talk with your parents about your feelings.

If you're upset about something and would rather talk with your friends about it at that time, just be honest about your feelings. You can tell your parents that you're really upset, but need to talk to your friend very badly so you can straighten it out. Tell them if you need them you'll let them know, and you feel good knowing that you can come to them. You can even thank them for understanding and give them a hug.

## When Your Parents Fight

Robin, age eleven, shared, "I'm very upset about my parents. Lately they've been fighting more and more and this worries me. Does a lot of fighting mean they might get a divorce? When I hear them starting, I go to my room and turn up my radio real loud, so I don't hear them. This helps, but the trouble is that I still know they're fighting. My brother says not to worry about it, but I can't help it."

Though there are plenty of parents who have gotten divorced after too much fighting, fighting doesn't have to mean divorce. It's natural for people to fight sometimes. Most kids fight with their sister, brother, or friends every once in a while. That doesn't mean they don't love each other and don't want to be friends anymore.

If your parents are fighting more than ever, it may mean one (or more) of several things. Either one or both of your parents could be tense about something that has little or nothing to do with their marriage, but they're just taking it out on each other. Or, they could really be upset with each other. Whatever it is may take a little while to work out. Breaking up their marriage may not even be a thought although their fighting may sound awful.

I don't agree with Robin's brother. I think if you're worried about your parents' fighting and what it means, that worry will probably stay with you all or most of the time. It's so hard to just turn it off.

The truth is, it's also possible that your parents really are having a rough time with each other, and that they really are thinking about divorce.

It's very important that you let them know how upset you are about their fighting and that you think it's getting worse. Tell them that you're worried all the time and need to know the truth about what's going on between them. (Divorced parents will be discussed in Chapter 20.)

## When Your Parents Punish You

Some parents punish; others don't believe in it. Some are more fair than others. I guess that's to be expected. Perhaps the most helpful suggestion about this would be to deal honestly with any feelings you have about punishments that are given to you.

If you don't think your parents are being fair, say so. Maybe you can come up with a suggestion that you think is more appropriate. Taking away the use of electronic games, being grounded, lowering curfew (when you have to return home after being out), not having friends over, not watching TV, or making you go to bed earlier seem to be among the most popular punishments from parents.

One boy said, "When my parents punish me, I think they don't love me." Although I suppose that's always possible, usually punishment is because a parent doesn't love what you've done. It has little to do with not loving you! The love for you will be there, whether you're grounded or not.

It's interesting how some boys and girls are relieved to be punished. Somehow it gets really tough to be able to say to a friend, "I can't meet you tonight," or "I can't go out." It's easier to blame the controls on the parents.

As much as Mara (from Chapter 18) hated being grounded from seeing her friends after her mom discovered marijuana in her drawer she admitted to me that she was happy she didn't have to make up excuses. Being grounded was the control that she couldn't place on herself, at least at the beginning.

If you're ever punished and don't understand why, ask your parents to explain why they did what they did. If you know what their rules are ahead of time, you might find it easier to avoid being punished. If you know the rules and choose to break them anyway, then you only have yourself to blame for any punishment. You'll have to live with the consequences of your choice (sound familiar?).

## When Parents Don't Make Rules

Patricia, age twenty, told me that she never really knew what was expected of her because her mother never told her when to come home, what to wear, how to act, and what was good or bad behavior. Patricia was left to decide all her own rules. She realized that she made up rules for herself that were more difficult than any rules her parents could have made her follow. She always felt guilty when she broke one of her rules and always felt that she had to be perfect. She only wished that her mother had given her guidelines to follow. She said, "I'm harder on myself than my mother would ever be."

Most kids who have spoken with me about this said they'd rather have rules than not "as long as they're fair" and "not too old-fashioned." The limits often make it easier to make decisions.

Sometimes it's the child whose parents do not enforce any rules who cries out for attention (like James' friend who smoked so much pot in Growing Up Drugged Up). Kids seem to get the message that parents care more if they bother to set limits.

If your parents have not given you any guides for your behavior, and you feel you want and need them, let them know. If your parents have set limits that you feel are fair, they would probably feel great hearing that from you. If you think they're unfair, you owe it to your parents and yourself to tell them. They may not realize how you feel and may reconsider their rules. If they still don't change, at least you know you tried your best.

## When Your Parents Blame You for Something You Didn't Do

So what do you do if you're blamed unfairly? By now you ought to be an old pro at figuring out what words to use! How about, "Mom, Dad, I really don't think you're being fair. You're blaming me for something I didn't even do!" Or, "Why do you always blame me when it's not my fault? You don't even give me a chance to explain. You only listen to them."

Sometimes you can know that you've been blamed unfairly and there's very little you can do about it. If your brother or sister get to your parents first or yell the loudest, your parents may side with them instead of you. It's really helpful when parents don't side with anybody. But, as you might have already found out, that's often not the case.

Sara, who was the oldest, used to get blamed for starting all the fights between her and her middle sister. Her sister would go running to Sara's mother and say that Sara picked on her, hit her, was being mean, didn't want to play with her, left her out, was being nasty, pinched her, took her doll, and locked her out of the room. Sara's mother would always take her kid sister's side. She'd yell at Sara, give her a slap, tell her she was rotten, ask how she could do that to her younger sister, and say she should know better.

Sara's younger sister used to watch her mother scream and beat Sara up. She sometimes felt delight that Sara was getting beaten up, but most of the time she felt guilty because, after all, Sara was her older sister and wasn't always that bad to her, anyway.

There was very little Sara could do to prevent herself from getting blamed in this situation. Her younger sister was the only one who could call off the war. Sara was angry for a very long time at her mother and her sister for being a team against her.

Sometimes the oldest child in a family gets blamed because parents expect them to know better. They expect more of them. If younger brothers and sisters get you in trouble all the time, it's important to let your parents know. Though at times they may not listen (like Sara's mother), maybe they'll be able to help you figure out a plan so the blaming will stop ( or at least be less).

I'll talk more about brothers, sisters, and being the oldest, middle, youngest, or an only child, in Chapter 21, Family Feelings.

## When Parents Don't Agree

"If one parent says no about going out and one parent says yes, which one do I listen to?" That question, asked of me by a girl in the sixth grade, is a great example of how confusing it can be when parents don't agree.

Who do you listen to? Well, I guess many kids would say, "Listen to the parent who says what you want to hear!" But it's usually not as easy as that. Sometimes there are guilt feelings, like, "If I listen to my mom, then maybe my dad will think I love her more." It can become a game. Sometimes parents test to see who their child listens to. But in that kind of game there are no winners. There are only more confused feelings.

This situation doesn't have to turn into a game of who loves whom more. It's very natural for parents not to agree on everything. In fact I'd be surprised if they did. Think of your own friendships. Do you really agree with your close friends on everything? (You're supposed to say, "No!")

It's important that you let your parents know how confused you get when they don't agree. Tell them you're not sure who you should listen to when they disagree, and ask them what they suggest you should do.

If they're allowing you to make more and more decisions on your own, perhaps you need to listen to both of them and then think more about what you feel. Then make up your mind.

## When Parents Embarrass You

When you were little, do you remember learning nursery rhymes or starting to count? Did your parents say, "Oh, Debby learned how to say another rhyme this week. Say the rhyme, Debby!" And you (make believe you're Debby) said, "Okay, Mommy or Daddy, rhyme, rhyme, rhyme . . . "

When you got a little older, maybe they left nursery rhymes and went on to asking you to play the piano for company or telling you to explain how well you did on your report card. Some kids love to perform like that. Maybe you did. Maybe you still do.

But others hate it! What a bummer! As soon as their parents come toward them and they know they have company over, they run the other way because they know that their parents will ask them to do something.

In those situations you can privately tell your parents that you hate being asked to perform. Tell them it embarrasses you and would they please stop. Explain that you'll be happy to come out and say hi, but ask them please not to ask you to do anything.

There are other ways parents can embarrass you. They can fight when your friends are over. In front of a friend, they can yell at you and say personal things that you don't want anyone to hear. They can tell a new friend how much you've been wanting them to come over. They can talk too loud in a restaurant or in a department store, be more dressed up than anyone else, be drunk in front of your friends, get in a fight with a person at a store, make you come home earlier than anyone else, make you wear your boots when everyone else doesn't have to. I could go on and on, but I think you get the picture.

The key is communicating your feelings of embarrassment. If you don't let them know, you can't blame them for doing it again and again.

## When Parents Abuse You

Just in case you're not sure, it's not normal for a parent to frequently beat you, pinch you, push you, make you go long hours without food, make sexual advances at you (this you know already), or do anything else that can be called abuse.

Part of the problem in dealing with such abuse is the fear of the parent finding out you told someone. (Remember the code of silence in Chapter 18?) The other part is finding out who to tell so you can get help. Aside from your school counselor, guidance counselor, trusted teacher, religious leader, friend's parents, family doctor, each state in the United States has its own agencies. In many towns you'll find child abuse or neglect hotlines. If you can't find one, you might look in your yellow or blue pages for any type of child protective services. Under state agencies you might try youth or children's services, social services, family services, health or mental services. They can probably direct you to the right person to call. If you can't find a listing, dial 0 for operator and ask.

Once again many kids don't break the silence. It's up to you to decide whether how your parents treat you feels good, bad, or just plain dangerous. If you realize you're being abused, you deserve not to be treated that way. Take a chance and call someone who will help you!

## When Parents Are Overprotective

Sean, age thirteen, asked, "How can I get my parents to stop treating me like I'm younger than I am? They tell me to act my age and then they treat me like a six-year-old."

Fifteen-year-old Aimee said, "Everyone hates the way their parents always ask where are you going, what are you doing, who will you be with, how long are you going to stay there, when will you come home? My parents aren't on my back too much as long as I call and tell them where I am."

Gary, age sixteen, shared, "My parents are worried about me driving with teens because of all the accidents that have been happening. I'm at the point lately where I don't drive with people anyway. But how do I tell them to lay off with this pressure?"

If your parents are overprotective, it may be that they won't let you cross a street by yourself, won't let you go fishing alone with your friend, won't let you go to the candy store hangout, won't let you travel by bus or train to the nearest big city by yourself, or won't let you stay out as late as most of your friends.

But they can also be overprotective in different ways which are not always as easy to see or understand. Karen's story will give you an example of what I mean. When Karen was thirteen years old, she went shopping with her mother (as usual) for a special dress for her aunt's wedding. Before her mother could decide on which dress to buy for Karen, she asked eight ladies in the dressing room which dress looked best. Karen has become very used to allowing strange ladies in dressing rooms to decide what clothing she should wear.

Her mother does this because she's so concerned that everything Karen wears and does be just right. She leaves little or no room for Karen to even try to make her own decisions—this is overprotection. When it comes time for Karen to make choices, she usually checks with each of her friends just to make sure she's doing the right thing.

By being overprotective Karen's mother has not given her the chance to learn how to be responsible for her own actions, even if they turn out wrong. As a result Karen has become fearful of making a mistake and lacks the confidence and practice in being able to think through each choice in order to figure out which one may be better.

Overprotection can also take the form of shielding a daughter from getting hurt by her boyfriend. When Ann's boyfriend broke up with her, her mother spent days sitting with her telling her that the boyfriend was really a creep, was really no good, wasn't good enough for her, and was a downright bum! Ann didn't really feel that way about her boyfriend. She knew he was wrong to break up with her the way he did, but she felt her mother was trying to take her side too strongly—overprotection. Maybe Ann would have gotten stronger sooner if she wasn't so protected.

Some parents don't know how or when to let go in order to allow their child the room to grow more independent. Some parents find letting go hard because they can't imagine their little girl or little boy is growing up.

Too many parents don't realize that you must feel all kinds of emotions, even the ones that hurt, in order to gain confidence and learn how to cope with all life's experiences. Life isn't all fun, games, and laughter. There will definitely be times of hurt and sadness in all of our lives. If Ann doesn't learn how to handle hurt now, she'll continue to have a hard time as an adult, when there may be no one there to sit and hold her hand.

If you feel your parents aren't giving you any room to breathe, talk with them about your feelings. Maybe they'll be able to back off a little bit. But at least you will have tried. Just understand it may take a while for your parents to become used to the idea that you're going to disappear around the corner (whether on your bicycle or in your girl friend or boyfriend's car), go about your day or evening on your own, and return home at some later hour. As much as they want to trust, it may be very hard for them to do so (that's why your parents might be waiting at the window when you return!).

It may take a while for you to prove to them that they can trust you. It may take some figuring to reach a good balance between your parent's comfort and your freedom. As Aimee said, "most parents at least want to know where you are and when they can expect you home." If you know you'll be late, it's just plain courteous to call and let them know so they don't worry. It's also very smart! They'll know you're respecting their feelings.

Parents can be especially overprotective if you're disabled, and they feel they have to protect you because your disability won't allow you to care for yourself. I'll talk more about this in Chapter 23, Being Disabled.

Still other parents are overprotective because a sister or brother has died and they want so badly to hold onto you in order that nothing happen to you too (they may be *extra* strict about where you can go and who with).

## What if Parents Bug You?

"Don't bug me!"

"My hair's okay."

"I can pick out my own clothes."

"Keep my brother out of my room."

"Why do I have to eat everything on my plate?"

Bug, bug, bug. . . . If you're bugged by your parents, how does that make you feel? If you're like most kids I've spoken with, you probably can't stand being bugged! Did you ever stop to realize that parents can't stand bugging their kids?

Do you think it's pleasant for a parent to say "Clean up your room!", "Did you do your homework?", "Don't hit your sister!" or "Comb your hair!" over and over again? Do you think a parent feels great knowing that every time he or she has to remind you about the same thing, you're going to be bananas? Huh? Huh?

Well maybe a truce is in order. Maybe you can sit down with each other and say something like, "I know you probably don't like bugging me, and I hate being bugged. So what can we do? How can we deal with things a little better?"

## When Parents Go Out of Town
## and Leave You in the Care of Others

Before your parents leave be sure to get the rules straight with your baby-sitter, grandparents, or anyone. Be sure you get permission ahead of time for anything you might need or want to do.

Think ahead! That way you won't find yourself in the middle of conversations like:

You: "But my mom and dad always let me do that."

Baby-sitter: "Well, they didn't tell me you could, so you'll have to wait until they come home."

## When Both Parents Work Outside the Home

Lots of changes have taken place over the past few years. More mothers are working outside the home than ever before. With the prices of food, clothing, and everything getting more and more expensive, with unemployment such a difficult problem and with the rise in single parent families, their income is usually a must. But even when money is not a concern, mothers may choose to work out of the home because it's something they want to do for themselves.

That might mean you will have to make your own breakfast, lunch, and, at times, even dinner. When you come home from school, you may be coming home to an empty house. While lots of children like being independent, there's a lot of loneliness, a lot of frustration, a lot of anger, a lot of resentment. Even though many kids are proud of what their parents are doing, they'd like them home, especially right after school. It's tough not to be able to spend time with your parents like you want and need to. But, unfortunately, you can't always have what you want to have, as much as you and your parents would wish things could be different.

What you might be forgetting is that it's also tough for your parents to balance their time. Very often they feel frustrated too. Perhaps it would help for you to understand how some parents feel about their working situations and how they feel it affects their children.

> I work with 'special' children all day long and find I have the patience of Job. When I get home, my two children arrive home from school [one of whom is handicapped] and all my patience goes out the window! What to do?
>
> I am the single parent of three children [ages four to ten], and I work full time. When I get home, it seems my children all want to talk at once. So no matter how I try to give each one a chance, the others keep talking. How do I get each one to listen to the other?

What can I do to lessen the guilt feelings I have because I work until five o'clock?

My four kids [ages four to eight] are so excited to see me when I get home [five o'clock]. By that time I'm tired from fighting traffic, rude people, and other things. I need to unwind before I hear the excitement and screaming and fights for attention. Sometimes I feel like sneaking home! They get very upset and un-understanding if I don't devote my entire attention as I walk in.

I've suggested to these parents (and any other parent who has similar feelings) that they talk with their children about their feelings. That they tell their kids how frustrated they are, how they want so badly to be there for their children, and how hard it is to do everything. Also how they often need to calm down and relax just a little bit before being ready to listen.

If your mom and dad work away from your home and their schedules keep them away for long hours, it's important to tell them how you wish you could spend more time with them, if you feel that way. Maybe you could all figure out when to set aside time over the weekend to be together.

It would probably help you a great deal if you tried harder to understand what your parents might be feeling. It would definitely help your parents if you could be more sensitive to how hard it can be for them to balance their time and how pressured they might feel.

If they rush in from their job, rush to make dinner, and seem like they're tense (remember to check out those nonverbal messages that are coming in loud and clear), you can just go over to them and give them a huge hug and say, "It's okay. You don't have to rush so much. We can wait a couple of minutes for dinner. Can I help you?"

## When Parents Are Unemployed

If your mom or dad has lost her or his job for whatever reason, that may make them pretty tense. They may be edgy, upset, worried, and just not their normal old selves.

They may or may not try to hide their concern, depending upon how old you are and how much they usually share. They probably will be careful not to make you overly upset about the money situation.

Even if they don't say a word, if you sense that something has changed, if you sense (especially if they're sleeping much later than ever before, are around more when you get home from school, or are drinking more alcohol—clues) that there is a problem, it would be very helpful to you and to them if you mentioned what you sense.

It's often a relief to parents to be honest about a family situation. That way they don't have to pretend. They can tell you straight out that there's really no extra money for the movies this weekend, or maybe you better wait until next week or the week after to buy a new pair of shoes.

Parents who are unemployed often think that they're not worth as much as they used to be. They tend to get down on themselves. But sometimes job loss has nothing to do with their skill or intelligence. It's often a matter of luck, like if a factory is going to stay opened or close, if the company is not doing as much business as it used to. . . .

It would be very helpful to give a lot of messages that mean, "I care. Even if you lost your job, you're still special to me." You can say that verbally, with words, or nonverbally, with hugs and looks or maybe a comforting hand on the shoulder.

## When Parents Are Single

This may be a result of separation, divorce, or death of the other parent. It's also possible that your parent never got married in the first place.

I'll talk about the feelings and concerns both parents and children might have about this in the next chapter.

## When Parents Are Ill

When a parent is ill—not just with headaches (which can sometimes be pretty bad) or a passing cold but the kind of illness that makes you worry about them all the time—additional stress can be put on the family. Illness may require your parent to go into the hospital, make your parent weaker than usual, keep him or her in bed or at least in your home for many months, in extreme cases result in death.

First of all I just want you to know that I know this is not such an easy topic. It can be very painful and scary. No one likes to see their parent ill, no matter how old you are, no matter how old your parent is. Sometimes parents are confused as to whether they should even tell their children about their illness. They don't want to upset them.

Though I imagine there are children somewhere who would rather not know, I have found that most children would rather know than not know. As upsetting as it can be to know the truth, it's worse to have to guess because that can sometimes make the illness seem worse than it really is. And sometimes the illness is more serious than you can guess.

An eleven-year-old girl shared, "My mom has a ruptured disc and she might get an operation that's new to the doctor that's going to do it. She might be allergic to the stuff that they are going to inject into her. If she is, she might not survive. I'm scared! Without my mom I don't know what I would do!"

I told her, as well as the other children at the program, that this is the kind of fear that words may not be able to take away. Don't let anyone tell you this is not scary. It *is* scary to know how risky the operation might be. It is scary to think about what life will be like if the operation doesn't go well. It is scary and painful to imagine not having your mother with you. In fact, she probably can't imagine how it would be. That's the kind of thing that can only be fully learned when the time comes.

But since her mother's health and survival is in the doctor's hands there's not much more (which is very frustrating) this girl can do but talk with her mom, tell her how much she loves her, and even tell her how scared she is. Her mom would probably be so relieved to be able to talk about this with her daughter.

Seanne, age twelve, told me that her mother has been very ill for the past three years. She's been in and out of hospitals. Every time the doctors think they've found out what's making her so sick, they realize it's probably something else and they have had to do so many tests. And so many operations. Things have been very tense. Seanne said, "In all this time I've only seen my mother cry once! I just can't understand why she hasn't cried more. I always go into my room to cry, so I don't upset her. But I felt so much better when I saw her cry."

I suggested to Seanne that she talk with her mom about how she always needs to hold back her feelings. There's no rule that says you can't cry in front of someone you love. Yes, it may make her mom cry if Seanne cries in front of her. But you know what? That also might make them even closer and more free to talk about what they're really thinking and feeling instead of always trying to hide their emotions.

*One more thing*: All you have to do is turn on your radio, read a newspaper, listen to the news on TV, and you're bound to hear about another accident, another illness that resulted in death. We wish we could keep the people we love forever. As hard as it may be to try to accept, life isn't forever: not for your parents, not for you, not for anyone.

But knowing that we all have only a certain amount of time together doesn't have to be so sad. In fact, that's the greatest, most wonderful challenge of all. The challenge is to make each day as special as it can be. Though we can't control the amount of time, we can control how we spend it with each other.

Let people know you love them. Actually say "I love you" every once in a while. Try harder to share your feelings. Try to appreciate even the little things. Learn as much as you can about each other. Share all that you can share.

Then if someone close is taken from you earlier than you ever expected, at least you can smile knowing that you lived each day with them as fully as you could. You don't have to look back and say, "I wish I had said —— to them," or "I wish I had spent more time."

(P.S. If you find yourself saying "Oh, if only we didn't fight. I feel so guilty," just remember that it doesn't mean you don't love someone if you fight. Fighting is normal every once in a while. One day might be a little more special than another. That's okay too. It's hard for every day to be special. But at least now you'll know to try.)

The last thing (I promise) is that you may not think you can live without one parent or the other. But the fact is, if the situation happens, you will. You know why? You'll have no choice. You'll have to. You can get strength from the special memories and wink at your parent's picture every day. You can get strength from your family and friends who will be there with you so you can talk about your feelings and know you're not alone. You can gain strength from all your parent taught you, all your parent shared, all your parent gave to you of themselves. So that even though you can't hold onto them, you'll always carry a part of them around with you. That part can stay with you forever.

What did I leave out? Only you can answer that. Think about your own parents. Think about what you love about them, think about what you wish you could change, how you wish they would change. Writing down these feelings can be very helpful.

The next step will be to poke some of those sleepy guts that are inside of you so they can give you some extra strength to talk privately with your parents about what concerns you.

If you're one of those lucky children who already knows the warmth and close feelings that can come from being open and trusting with a parent, also know that no matter how close you are, you can always become closer and closer.

Remember, no matter what it is you need to say, if you say it respectfully, if you say it in a caring way, then they're more likely to listen and understand.

If you hold back and think you shouldn't say something because you may hurt them, just know that hurts are part of life. You can't prevent them. You can only try to be as kind as possible. You'll probably be surprised at how many things you can talk about that you never thought you could say.

# 20

# Dealing with Separation, Divorce, Single Parents, and Stepfamilies

This chapter will help you better understand the hurts and the changes that are so much a part of separation and divorce.

If your parents are apart or are talking about separating, I hope my words, along with the chance to learn how other children feel, will help you strengthen your ability to accept what you cannot change and realize how you must try to find happiness in new ways. That's only if you can allow yourself to let go (put behind you) the bad family feelings that aren't working out as you had hoped.

## Separation and Divorce Hurt

Pain, loneliness, sadness, frustration, fear, anger, guilt, confusion—if you're one of the thousands of children whose parents have separated or gotten divorced, you've probably felt most of those feelings. If you haven't felt them yourself, chances are you know someone who has.

Mindy, age twelve, asked, "How can I express my feelings to my parents about how I love them so much and I don't want them to get a divorce?"

Stephen, age eleven, shared, "My mother and father are divorced and my mother is married again. I haven't seen my father in two years and he never calls. I'm not sure if I should love him or not. Right now I think I hate him."

Joe, age thirty-nine, told me, "I came home from work one day and found that my kids were next door and my wife was gone. There were things leading up to this but she never told me she was leaving. It was a very emotional time for me as well as the kids. A few days after my wife left, my son woke up and said to me, 'Mommy's never coming back.' I'll never forget hearing that. I didn't want to believe it. Neither did he. And all we could do was just sit there together and cry."

Separation and divorce hurt. They hurt the parents who no longer can live together in a way that feels good. And they especially hurt the children.

## It's Not Your Fault; It's Not Within Your Power

Wouldn't it be great if kids of unhappy parents had the power to make their parents happy again? Lots of kids try but end up blaming themselves for not being able to make their parents stay together. They often feel guilty because they think that all the fights must be their fault. After all why would their parents have gotten married in the first place if they didn't love each other? They think "It must be me." Or, "It must be because of my sister or brother. I hate them." Or, "Maybe if I loved them more." Or, "Maybe if I were a better person. . . ." Perhaps you have felt the same way.

But no matter how much you love your parents, how high your grades are in school, how much you help clean the house, or how much you baby-sit for your younger brother or sister, you don't have power over your parents' relationship.

Eric, age eleven, said, "My parents are separated and sometimes I feel left out or not cared for. I always want to be with both parents but I can't. How can I change it?"

Eric, I wish I could tell you what you want to know. But I can't. What happens between your parents is not up to you. It's only up to them. The truth is something that you probably don't want to hear. The truth is that you may never have your parents back together again. If they do get back together, it won't be because of anything that you can do. Change has got to come from them. Your wanting it so badly is not enough.

It's very sad to imagine that any boy or girl would make the mistake of blaming themselves or their sister or brother for difficulty that is so beyond their control. It's a shame so much energy is wasted trying to change something that's not theirs to change.

Parents can become unhappy with each other all by themselves. If anything is going to change, it's the parents who will have to work out their differences.

## But Kids Have a Different Kind of Power

Though kids don't have the power to get their parents back together, that doesn't mean they're completely powerless. They do have power within themselves. More power than they might think they have, especially when everything seems like it's crumbling all around them.

It comes from those tough old guts that hang out in their insides, just waiting to help. In this case they can offer extra strength to deal with all the hurt and all the changes. All a kid has to do is realize they're in there (and then poke a little in case they're taking a snooze).

A boy or girl's inner power can get even stronger if it takes in more "fuel." The fuel is information about what's really going on, understanding why their parents are having difficulty getting along, and the ability to realize that they're not as alone as they think. Lots of other kids are hurting for the same reasons.

## Separation Can Be an Ending or a Beginning

Parents may decide to separate for so many different reasons. Maybe they have been fighting for years and finally decided that they've had it. Maybe there's never been fighting and they really still love each other as people but just can't live with each other as husband and wife. Maybe the father or mother has changed so much from who they were when both got married. Maybe the mother or father can't live with who the other has become.

Maybe one parent did something to break the other's trust. Maybe they've become strangers to each other. Maybe there are money problems that are coming between them. Maybe there's jealousy. Maybe there's no longer any kindness. Maybe there's hardly any communication. Maybe they don't know how to talk with each other. Maybe they don't want to try. Maybe they just don't have the same values anymore.

Maybe one parent is sneaking off to see another man or another woman behind your father or mother's back (maybe your father or mother knows). Maybe one parent is taking a lot of drugs or drinking heavily and is ruining any chance of a good relationship. Maybe it's too painful for the other parent to stay around and watch while they destroy themselves.

Sometimes parents talk openly with their children about the possibility of separation. Sometimes it comes as a great shock the day or night before one of them is going to leave. Sometimes a child doesn't have any clue until he or she walks into their home and finds bags packed or the other parent sitting there with reddened eyes.

Very often a child can sense the strain between his or her parents. Remember, nonverbal messages can be very loud. But just because you sense a strain it doesn't mean your parents are about to split up. It may mean there's pressure at the office, money pressure, someone who is ill, or they might be tired, and so on.

The best thing to do is be honest about what you feel. Sometimes parents try to protect their children by not including them in personal problems. When the child brings up the concern, it's often a relief to everyone and much less of a worry than the child may think.

If there's really trouble between them, they often don't know how to tell their kids. So they don't say anything until they have to, which may mean the day one of them walks out.

Separation can rock any child's sense of security. It can mean a broken home, broken dreams, confusion, anger, hurt, and maybe some of that guilt I spoke about. But let's take a closer look at what else separation can mean.

Separation can give each parent just the space or distance they need to sort out their feelings and decide that they really do want to try again. Separation may give them the private time they need to figure out what went wrong and realize they need to make changes if the marriage is ever going to stay together. They may return after a few days or not until weeks or months later. In this case separation may have shaken each parent up enough to make them want to work even harder to make their marriage feel good.

But while you can hope that a parent will return or that the parent who stays will want the other parent to come back, you can't count on it.

Separation has no guarantees. Even though it's possible for separation to force a new beginning, it also can signal the end. That's the part that's toughest to accept.

The parent who left or even the parent who stayed, can decide that he or she would rather stay separated. Even though the parent is sad about the breakup, even though he or she wishes the marriage would have worked, even though he or she is pained that it has to have a troubling effect on any children in the family, the parent would rather be alone than be together fighting. Or he or she would rather be alone than with someone he or she can no longer respect, trust, and love. Or the parent would rather be alone than with someone who doesn't share in working together to make the relationship a happier one. Or?

As you probably have learned from your own friendships, a relationship must work two ways. If only one person cares, then it's hard to keep up the friendship. If only one person tries hard to get to know the other person better, or if only one person decides to share more personal things, then it's hard to be close. If only one person is honest, then it's too hard to trust.

Sometimes marriages are like that. Only the mother or only the father may be the giving partner. The other may not give at all or at least not very much. So it's only when both parents decide they want to try to become more sensitive to each other, only when both parents decide they're going to work at communicating better, will there be hope of working out differences.

Are you beginning to understand better why children don't have the power to make their parents get along?

## Sometimes It Will Help To Walk on Tippy Toes

Justin, age ten, shared, "My mom and dad are separated and my mom is an old grouch! What should I do?"

It's very hard to talk with anyone while they're upset or angry. Maybe it's not fair to expect that your parents are going to be their old, normal, nongrouch selves during this very hard time in their lives.

If they're fighting, don't bother them. You'd be wise to tiptoe around, helping out with the chores, helping out with the other kids in your family, just doing whatever you can to keep everything else calm, even though your parents are not.

You can also turn up the TV or radio very loud, go in the shower, take a walk or jog around the corner, go out and shoot baskets, jump rope, or do any kind of physical activity to keep your mind off things and help you get your frustrations out.

Try not to get in the middle of their fighting. Try not to let them involve you. If they ask you to take sides, tell them you love them both and don't want to be involved. Walk away if you have to. This may be very hard to do.

You may even find that you'll have your own case of the grouchies every once in a while, especially if your parents fight a lot or you're very, very upset and scared about what's happening and especially if you're very angry. If you accidentally blame your sister or brother for your parents' problem, you may find yourself hitting them extra hard or yelling extra loud at them. Neither you nor your sister or brother may realize that the hits, screams, and yells were really meant for your parents. (It's just easier to hit a sister or brother than a parent. Get the idea?)

Depending upon how lonely you feel and how much you wish someone would just hold you and tell you everything is going to be okay, depending upon how angry you are and how much you need to lash out, depending upon how much attention you need, you may just find yourself sitting in the principal's office for throwing spitballs at some kid. The sad thing is, no one (not even you) may have understood that the spitball was really aimed at your parents.

Probably you'd be wise to put up your antennae and keep them up. Be sensitive to those moments that are more calm. That's when it will be okay to try to talk with either parent or at least the parent who you're living with.

Don't be surprised if you find your parent crying. Don't worry about holding back your tears if you feel like crying too. That's very natural and is a great way to get out your emotions. If you're worried that you'll upset your parent if you start crying, just remember that the more you can honestly share the closer you will be. Your parent might feel better that he or she no longer has to pretend about how upset he or she is. Some things in life are very sad.

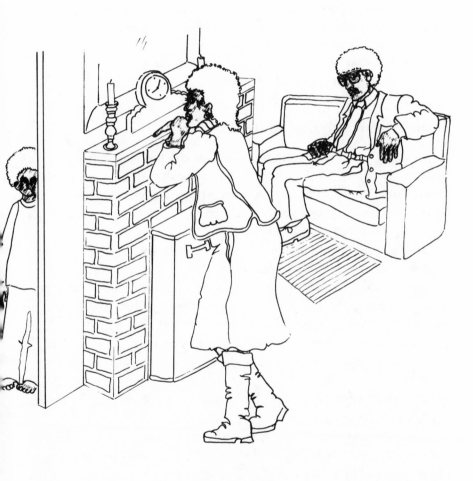

### Very Important Message

Just because your parents are not getting along,
  that doesn't change their love for you.
Just because your parents don't love each other anymore,
  that doesn't change their love for you.
Just because you're angry at them and might even say you hate them,
  doesn't mean you don't really love them deep down.
Probably, you love them very, very much;
  you just don't love their separation or divorce.
I've never met any child who does.

## Talking About This Can Be Hard

If you find there are no calm moments, or you just can't talk with your mother or father, it's important to try to speak with an older brother, sister, aunt, uncle, grandparent, trusted teacher, guidance counselor, school counselor, social worker, religious leader, friend's parent, or another person you respect and trust.

Though the talking may not change your parents' situation, getting your feelings out can be a great relief. Many children wonder if they should tell their friends about their home situation. That's a very personal decision. There aren't any rules. It would probably be helpful to have a friend your own age who you can turn to when you feel like talking or just being near someone who cares about you, even if you're silent.

It can be a special comfort to know that you can speak openly with a close friend who you can trust. A trusted friend will understand that it doesn't mean your parents are bad people just because they're having trouble getting along.

A close friend whose parents are already separated or divorced can be a great help as they can share their own feelings with you and let you know what you might expect. They'll also remind you that you're not the only person in the whole world to experience those feelings.

It's always good to write your feelings down on paper. You can even write a poem, if you like.

If you're very confused and find you're getting more and more upset, or if you're having trouble getting your feelings out, it might be important to talk with someone who is trained to help children with such feelings. They may be able to offer guidance that will lessen your confusion and help you get along better each day. Your school psychologist or counselor might be helpful. If you can, try to let your parents know how bad you feel, and maybe they can arrange for you to speak with the right person.

Remember, admitting that you're having trouble with your feelings, is not a sign of weakness. It takes a very stong person to admit such a thing and a smart person to know when he or she can't help themself.

## When Parents Are Divorced

While a separation may mean there's hope, a divorce must be considered final (there are some parents who get back together after getting divorced, but you can't expect this to happen). All the feelings I've mentioned so far belong here too.

Divorce makes it official and legal that parents are not going to be married anymore. Here, too, some parents tell their children from the very beginning of difficulty, and some parents don't tell them until the divorce is in process.

Marlene, age eleven, shared a very sad experience when she was away at summer camp three years ago. Said Marlene, "One of the girls in my bunk got a letter from her mother telling her that her parents had gotten a divorce. She told her in a letter! The girl didn't even know that her parents had had any problems. The whole bunk was so upset for her. She started crying, and we all started crying with her. I didn't know how to help her. On visiting day her mother brought her up so many presents and so much food that they couldn't even fit on her bed. I think she was trying to make up for the divorce."

My guess is that it was easier for the mother to wait for her daughter to go to camp than to tell her in person. Marlene said the letter came about two weeks after camp started. Do you think the girl's parents knew about the divorce before she went to camp? You bet they did!

Someone should have taught them that running away from painful situations is not the answer. There's very little that's going to soften the blow of being told your family is about to split apart. That girl would probably have felt better crying in her parents' arms than in her bunk away from them at camp.

It would help for parents to tell children as early as they know. That way the whole family can deal openly with the situation. Each family member can talk about his or her feelings and the children can get involved with plans that must be made.

I know there are children who don't want to hear that their parents are having problems. They may shut them out, not listen, maybe even try to run away. But no matter how far they run, just like if they take drugs or drink alcohol to run away, the problem will still be there when they get back. Though it may be very painful, probably the best thing to do is to stay and face it.

Oh, I almost forgot. You know those presents piled up on that girl's bed? Well, her mother is one of many, many mothers and fathers who try to make up for the hurt, try to win their child's love, and try to feel less guilty by giving presents. Some parents even try to outdo the other parent to make them seem better.

Why doesn't anyone tell parents that candy, clothes, movies, vacations, toys, money, and food—things—can't take the place of them being together? I know, I know, that doesn't mean that presents are not nice to have but just open your eyes to how much is being given to you and how often you get gifts. That can teach you a lot about what your parent might be feeling. Maybe you can even talk about it.

## Who Will You Live With?

Sometimes parents agree about who should care for the children after they get divorced; sometimes they end up having an angry custody battle in court (that means they're fighting about who should have legal control of the children). Still other times parents give their children a choice of which parent they want to live with. Such a decision can be very painful and confusing, especially when you want to live with both.

Jimmy, age twelve, said, "My mother and father got a divorce a few years ago. Now my father is getting married again and he wants me to live with him. Who should I go with, my mom or my dad?"

Go with who can take better care of you. Go with who it feels better to be with. What's your gut feeling, Jimmy?

Cathy, age twenty, was visiting her father when I met her. She and her mother, stepfather, and six-year-old stepbrother live in a different state. Cathy said, "My parents decided to split when I was twelve. They gave us a choice of who we wanted to live with. My younger brother and I went to live with my mother. My older sister [she was seventeen at the time] went off on her own. My other sister went to live with my father because she could never get along with my mother. I visit my father and stay with him for a few weeks every chance I can."

Scott, age eleven, shared, "My father and mother got divorced when I wasn't born yet. I didn't see my father until I was seven. Last year my mother couldn't handle me and my sisters so she turned us over to my father. They had to go to court but my mother didn't show up and they had to arrest her for a little while. Now my father won't let me or my sisters call her or see her. I think she is dead. My baby brother lives with my mother. I wish I could see them. I love both of them a lot. I would like them to come back together and get married again. But my father married another lady already and she is all right. But I love my father and my mother a lot. My sister hates my mother now. But I love her a lot."

Do you think it's any wonder why Scott has trouble concentrating on his school work? I can't even begin to imagine the pain he feels, the sadness of wanting to see his mother but not being able to. Maybe if he spoke honestly with his father and told him how much it means to him to at least speak with his mother, he might let him call her.

A girl in the fifth grade shared, "My mother and father are divorced. I live with my granny. I have problems talking with my father and mother."

Sometimes grandparents, aunts, uncles, or even a parent's close friend may take over custody if neither parent is able to.

In some cases, like Joe's, there's no choice to be made. His wife left seven years ago, leaving him to take care of their two sons. Joe feels that he has grown closer to his sons in a very special way. So even though the divorce was hard to deal with, a lot of good came out of it.

As you can see, there are many different kinds of arrangements. Each one is a little different; each brings with it different feelings. Though all new arrangements will take some time to get used to, some aren't as tough to deal with as others. Being able to talk about your feelings, even when they hurt and might make you cry (remember, crying is great for getting feelings out), will be very helpful.

*One more thing*: Lots of kids who have to choose whether they want to live with their mother or father really do know their answer. But they're afraid to tell their parents because they don't want them to think they love one more than the other. They don't want to hurt their parents' feelings and they certainly don't want to make them mad. So maybe they'll just say "I don't know," when deep inside they really know.

If you're given such a choice, remember to put your feelings into words. It may hurt to say certain things out loud but think about how much more it will hurt if you let your parents make your decision for you and you end up with the one you didn't want to live with.

If you have feelings, let them be known. If you don't share how you feel, you may be sorry for the rest of your life.

## Where Will You Live and
## How Often Will You Visit Your Other Parent?

Depending upon which parent has custody, you might stay in the home you've always lived in or move out. Sometimes the move is to another, often smaller, home (possibly to cut down on expenses) right in the same town. Sometimes the move is much further away.

Where you live and how far the other parent moves will affect how often you see that parent. Seeing him or her will also depend upon what visiting rules might be in your parents' written divorce decree (order of the court). For example, if your mother has custody, the decree might say that your father is allowed to visit with you every weekend, every other weekend, every Tuesday and Thursday, on certain holidays, during the summer, and so on.

Donna, age ten, asks, "How can I talk with my father? My parents are divorced and my father is in California." Since she lives in New York, it's very difficult and expensive to visit with him. She told me she's been very upset that he hasn't called her very often. He told her that it's expensive to call. I suggested she write him, which she did. But he didn't answer her letters. Both Donna and I had a hard time accepting that he didn't realize how much he was hurting her and how badly she wanted him to show her he cares.

As much as I hate to say this, some parents really don't care. They just want to do their own thing, start all over, try to forget, and run away from their responsibilities.

Dayna, age fourteen shared:

My mother left us because of her career and because she wanted to be her own person. She wanted to have more freedom to come and go, go to classes, and go to work. Ever since she started her job, we felt we lost her. It was too late. She knew that she wanted to leave and she didn't want to have a family anymore. She'd come home and make dinner. Then she'd leave. She saw her friends and other men. She was hardly ever home. We saw my mother maybe one night a week. She never gave us a lot of attention. She never hugged us or kissed us. Never even a pat on a head.

She left the day before finals. That really screwed us up! But we're okay now. My father is seeing a woman. She's the nicest person in the world, and she's trying to make up for all the hurt.

When some parents leave, they stay away forever, even if that means they won't see their children again. While they probably still love their children, this may just mean they can't deal with any part of their life the way it was and they have to get away. I'm at a loss to offer words that can ease the sense of loss children must feel when this happens. It's natural for this to make children feel very sad, very angry, and very alone.

If your parent leaves, it will be most helpful to be able to talk about your feelings openly with an adult you trust. Since you can't bring them back, at least you can try to understand and gain strength to try to live your life as normally as possible without them.

But many parents try to stay close to their children, at least while they're growing up. Even if they aren't close by, they really try to keep in touch and arrange to see them whenever possible.

A friend of mine who has joint custody of her sons—even though she and her husband are divorced, they still share in raising their sons—said that her sons are free to travel back and forth between her home, where the children live, and her husband's home, about one and one-half hours away. They know how to travel by bus and train, and see their father quite often. They have no strict rules about when. They just go and come when they wish. It's very easy that way and everyone still gets along. In fact they all spent last Christmas together. Not all divorces have to be nasty.

Gary, age twelve, told me he sees his father every weekend. But he hates it when his father's new girl friend is there. He wishes he could be with him alone, even though she seems nice.

Michelle, age fourteen, says, "Now that my parents are divorced, at least my father has to make time to see me. I spend more time with him than I ever did when my parents were married. We've gotten closer."

If your parents are divorced and you want to communicate with your other parent more, it may help to realize that even if you don't see them, you can talk with them on the telephone or write them letters, poems, or anything you wish.

Don't expect them to guess what you're feeling unless you tell them. Don't expect them to know how you want so badly to see more of them. Even if the visiting rules won't allow more visits, you can tell that parent how much you miss them. It's okay to say you're sad. It's okay to say you're unhappy about everything. It's okay to cry. I never met a child who was happy about his or her parents' separation or divorce—relieved maybe, but not happy!

## Visiting Can Be Confusing

Mrs. P. has custody of her son. Her son lives with her and her new husband (his stepfather) during the week and visits his father every weekend. She told me that every time her son returns from a weekend with his father, he's upset and often seems very angry with her.

Sometimes a child's anger can be from not being able to accept their parents' divorce. A child may blame one parent or another for breaking up the marriage, especially if one parent tries to influence the child to believe the other is at fault. One parent might try to turn their child against the other parent. That can make them very confused (and even angrier).

I already mentioned that presents are often given to make a parent feel less guilty, to bribe, or try to make it seem that they are more loving than the other parent who hasn't given as much.

Sometimes values are different in the mother's house and the father's house. One parent may let their child stay up all night if they want to; the

other parent may say, "Lights out at ten o'clock!" One parent may say it's okay to watch a sexy movie; the other may think you're too young.

While parents can feel differently, even when they're not divorced, usually they try to work out their feelings and decide together what they'll teach their children. In a divorce situation one parent will not necessarily check with the other about what's being taught. The parent will do what they believe is right and may even think that allowing extra privileges or being less strict will make the child love him or her and want to visit more. There can be a lot of competition and comparing between parents too.

Learning completely different ideas about what's right and what's wrong and living by a different set of rules with each parent can be very confusing. It may be hard for a child to keep track of which rules go with which house.

What do you think a boy or girl might say to both parents if they were confused or upset about the differences?

## It May Take Some Time To Get Used To Being Single Again

Whether because of divorce or death of their husband or wife, a man or woman who becomes a single parent may take a while to get used to the idea, especially if they've been married for years.

When people are married and their relationship is special, the husband and wife not only share their love, they are best friends. They trust each other with the most private secrets, they love to spend time together, laugh, and have fun. They can talk with each other about anything and sit together in silence without worrying about having to speak. They can count on each other, can share their sadness, joy, dreams.

When the relationship is no longer special, and they grow apart to the point of separating or getting a divorce, it may take a while before they're ready to even think of sharing so closely with another person.

Each person will take his or her own time getting used to living on his or her own. It would be impossible to guess how much time it will take each person to be ready to begin looking for another friend, someone to be close with again. Because they felt such hurt from their marriage, they may go very slowly with other relationships. If someone is single because their wife or husband died, it may take them even longer to reach the point of being ready to share again.

It will help for children to be patient with their single parents. At a recent lecture a single woman told me her children can't understand why she isn't dating. Her ex-husband (the man she divorced) has been dating for a while and even introduces his dates to his children. She just isn't ready yet and doesn't want to be pushed. Yet her children won't stop asking her why.

It will also help for children to try a little harder to understand that their mother and father probably spent a lot of time together. Just like children need their friends, it's important for a mother or father to have a relationship that feels good to her or him.

So if you find yourself a little selfish and not wanting to accept your parent's need to find other adult people to be with, try to remind yourself that adults can be lonely too. Just like adults can't completely fill in your loneliness if you don't have that many friends, you can't fill in theirs. You need people your age, and your parent needs someone who's also an adult. It doesn't mean they love you any less because they need a friend. If anything, when they feel good about themselves and their new lives, they'll be able to give you more.

## When Parents Start Going Out: Your Parent's Girl Friend or Boyfriend

No part of divorce is easy. Perhaps this is one of the harder parts since it makes it even more real that parents aren't together anymore. Boys and girls whose parents have started dating have said it's very strange to see their mother or father with a different man or woman.

If your mother or father has started to go out with other people, you probably have felt lots of different feelings about it. You may resent their date, even if the person is nice, just because you don't want to see your parent with anyone else but your real mother or father. You may be jealous that this man or woman is taking away some of your private time. You may be scared that your parent will end up marrying this person. You might even find that you're having a hard time being nice.

Maybe you need to know that parents are often scared too. They wonder and worry about how their children are going to feel, since they know that dating someone else makes their divorce seem even more final.

Resentment, jealousy, anger, and being scared or frustrated can naturally interfere with being nice. It can also be confusing to know how to introduce your mother or father's date to a friend. You may find it embarrassing for other people to learn that your parents aren't together anymore. When your parent starts to date, the divorce becomes more public, more known.

Perhaps it would help to think about how your parent might be feeling. No doubt they, too, will feel very strange, especially if they were married for many years. Dating is something they probably haven't done since they were much younger.

Maybe this is the first time in months—or years—that they were actually able to have a pleasant time with someone who respects them, is truly interested in being with them, and makes them feel good.

When a parent has dated someone for a while and likes them very much, they may decide it's time to invite them home to spend the night (sort of like having a sleepover but in a grown-up way).

Many parents are not sure how their children will react to their decision to share themselves in that way. Many parents are confused about what they need to explain to their children so that they'll understand why this is important to them.

Stacey, age twelve, is an only child. Her parents got divorced several years ago and her father moved away. Since he left, Stacey and her mother have gotten very close. With her father gone, Stacey felt free to come into her mother's bed and sleep there for the rest of the night in case she had a nightmare. In fact she kind of looked forward to going into her mother's bed. It made her feel safe and close to her mother.

When Stacey's mother's boyfriend moved in with them, everything changed. Stacey no longer felt she could go into her mother's bedroom. Her mother's boyfriend had taken her place. She was jealous and very upset. She especially resented him telling her what to do around the house. "After all," said Stacey, "he's not my real father. He has no business telling me what to do."

Stacey tried speaking to her mother about this and things got a little better. She still felt like she wasn't as important as she used to be when there was just the two of them (Stacey and her mother).

Stacey admitted that it wasn't really the boyfriend who bothered her. It was the whole idea of having to share her mother. She didn't want to. She had given up too much already.

Holding in any of these feelings will not be as helpful to you or your parent as will talking about them honestly and openly at a time when both of you can be alone with each other. If you can't talk with your parent, you'll know to go on to your list of other trusted adults.

## When a Parent Gets Married Again

If your parents are separated or divorced, have you thought about what you might feel if either parent marries again? (Think about this now if you haven't already.)

If your mother or father has remarried, what were your feelings when you first learned they were getting married? What are your feelings now?

It's normal to be confused, scared, and even resentful. It's also normal to be excited, very happy, joyous, and feel wonderful that you're going to have an extra parent who will live with you, care for you, be there for you, and get along in a loving way with your mom or dad.

Notice I said extra parent. That's because a new marriage doesn't mean that your real mom or dad will now take a backseat. It simply means you have one more parent, called a stepparent (the name given to the person your mother or father remarries). He or she doesn't replace your original parent. No one can. Rather a stepparent is taking his or her own place in the hope that all of you will have a better life together than you would have if you had remained apart.

## Stepparents and Stepfamilies

Some kids find it hard to give their new stepparent a chance. Some are confused as to how to act toward them. They wonder if it's okay to try to like them.

If the parent who you're not living with gets married, you may be concerned that if you like your new stepparent too much, your parents will decide you should live with them instead of staying where you are.

If you like the stepparent too much, you might feel guilty or concerned that your real parent might be jealous or worried that you like the stepparent more than your real parent.

Boys and girls are often not sure what to call the stepparent. Mom? Dad? By a first name? That's something that needs to be talked about.

There are stepparents who will be kind, caring, and will love you as if you're their own child. Others are not so loving.

A girl in the sixth grade shared, "I have a stepmother. She doesn't like me and she treats me awful. She has children of her own and none of them likes me. She always lets her kids do everything. But not me."

What would you do if you were this girl? One of the important choices to consider would be to speak to your father (privately). You could also speak to your stepmother and ask her if you've done something to make her upset with you. You might tell her that you didn't ever mean to get her upset and maybe you can try to get along better.

Talking about getting along won't always make the bad feelings go away. The truth is sometimes kids don't get along with their stepparent, just like some kids don't get along with their natural parents. As you know, relationships must work two ways in order for them to feel as good as possible. If you're trying hard and your stepparent doesn't care, the sad thing is that you may never feel good about your relationship with your stepparent. And they may continue to treat you unfairly. But, your real mother or father probably will do his or her best to help make them treat you better.

Once again violence should not be considered acceptable or natural. It's not natural. Besides telling me about her parents's divorce, twenty-year-old Cathy also talked about how scared she is of her stepfather. He's an alcoholic and beats her mother a lot. Sometimes he tries to beat her. But when he starts in, she just hides. She said she's afraid to move out but would really like to. She's afraid of what her stepfather will do to her mother if she's not there.

I suggested to Cathy that as much as she may not like it and as much as it may seem wrong, her mother has made a choice, at least for now. Just as her mother has to take responsibility for her own life and her own choices, so does Cathy have the right to choose for herself. As painful as it will be to leave, knowing how her mother is treated, how long do you think it fair for Cathy to live at home so she can protect her mother? Cathy said she's saving up money so she can move out someday. She'll see. Cathy might find it helpful to call Alanon or Alateen.

I'd like to believe that in most cases, a stepparent wants a good relationship too. It's just not so easy to fill in the gap of all the years they didn't know you. It will take you and your stepparent time to learn about each other and become sensitive to each other's feelings. It will take time to learn what each other expects, as each family has been living by their own set of rules. Many of these might be different. It will take patience and the ability to forgive each other for not knowing what will hurt and not knowing how to handle situations that are new. Everyone will need time to learn to get along.

As far as your stepbrother(s) or stepsister(s) are concerned, there are families who come together who can get along beautifully right away. Especially when a child has always wanted a brother or sister and will now finally have one. Or, for the first time, they'll have someone to live with who's closer to their age. But it's also very natural for them to feel jealous, resentful, and angry. It's not always so easy for two families to come together and expect to get along.

Sometimes in order to fit everyone in one home, kids have to share rooms that they had all to themselves. They may not like that. It may crowd their space and invade their privacy.

Comparisons and competition can easily get in the way of friendship. If a stepsister or stepbrother feels you are better looking, smarter, more popular, a better athlete, a better piano player, or whatever, they might be jealous or resentful.

If they feel you are taking away some of their mother or father's love, they may even say they hate you (you may say you feel the same way about them). While I suppose it's possible that you really hate each other, I'm willing to bet that it's not so much the stepsister or step-brother who's hated but more the whole idea of change, being forced to live with someone and call them family, and no longer having your parent all to yourself.

Some stepfamilies get along more easily. Others may take a while before everyone is able to learn to live together in a way that feels good. If your stepfamily is having a lot of difficulty in getting along, you can talk about this with your mom and dad, stepmother or stepfather. You might find it helpful to have a stepfamily meeting so that everyone can rap together about what they like, what bugs them, what they wish could change, and other problems.

If your family still can't get along, it might be very important for your parents to check out what kind of counseling for stepfamilies can be offered to you in your town. In some communities there are stepfamily organizations that can offer extra guidance.

## While Divorce May Seem Like the Worst Thing
## That Could Happen, It's Sometimes a Blessing, Even for the Kids

If parents are fighting much of the time, if there's a lot of pressure, if your parents really don't want to be together, if they're really miserable being married to one another, if they just want to get away from it all, or if they still care very much about each other but just can't live together as man and wife, then maybe separation or divorce will be a blessing. Yes, even if separating hurts.

Joe, age thirty-eight, shared, "During the first two years after my wife left me, I thought being divorced was the worst thing that could have happened to me in my life. By the time the third year began, I knew it was the best thing that could have happened to me."

As much as you want something to work, you can't force it. It goes back to what I said in the beginning of this chapter about relationships needing to be two way. If they're not, then how long do you think it would be worth staying married to someone if they stopped loving you, stopped wanting to work at being able to communicate better, stopped wanting to please you, stopped wanting to be sensitive to your needs, stopped wanting to accept you for who you are?

Sometimes marriages don't work because one or both partners expect so much of the other person that they're sure to be disappointed. Their expectations aren't fair or real (just like sometimes your parents or teachers or friends expect too much of you and then are disappointed that you didn't live up to what they expected). So the husband or wife is never satisfied.

Since each person is different; each relationship is different as is each reason for staying together or splitting up. Since I'm not a believer in wasting time, my guess is that people are not so wrong to go ahead and make a tough change if they feel their lives will be happier and have more meaning.

*One more thing:* If your parents or older sister or brother get separated or divorced, that doesn't mean that if you get married someday, you'll get divorced too. (Divorce is not hereditary.) Just like your parents are responsible for their own relationship, so will you be for yours. No one else's marriage need affect yours.

You're not your parents; you're not your brother or sister or close friend. You're you. If their marriages don't work it will be because of something they and their husband or wife did or did not do. What happens with them is their responsibility. The future of your own relationships will be up to you and the person you care about.

Everyone has the ability to work harder to try to make their relationships special. And if after trying your hardest, you find the relationship is just not right, life is too short to stay just because it's too scary to leave. Even if there are children.

# 21
# Family Feelings

Your family feelings aren't just from today. They come from years of sharing many different experiences with all the people in your family, some which have made you smile, others which are sad, and still others which probably have made you wish you had huge fangs so you could run around and growl at everyone.

Think back as far as you can remember and try to pick out special family moments that have made a difference to you, moments which have affected your family feelings. Things like, climbing into your parents' bed so they could protect you from the thunder, visiting your grandma and smelling the special aroma of her super-terrific-grandma-type chocolate cake, the first time you saw your baby sister or brother, the first time you were allowed to drive the tractor by yourself, going fishing with your dad or grandpa, finally learning how to ride a two-wheel bicycle, a special birthday party, holiday dinners, been sent to your room for being bad, being told your pet was very sick, family outings, and more.

Some of these may be on your list of memories. But the best thing to do would be to make your own list. Take a few moments now to think. Along with each experience that comes to your mind, try to imagine the feelings that went along with it. You might have felt happy, excited, surprised, sad, disappointed, angry, scary, proud, grown up, and so on.

As I've been writing this, suggesting that you write your own list, things keep popping into my head—my own grandmother's chocolate cake and her second-day chicken soup, being homesick for my parents the first summer I went away to camp, the day we were supposed to go to the amusement park and my father had to work again at the last minute and we couldn't go, the time in the third grade when I pushed someone off the top of the monkey bars on the playground because she was teasing my sister, the day my grandmother died when I was in the ninth grade, my mom's chocolate chip cookies, being scolded for squeezing my sister's arm and cursing at her, my dog's bad breath, playing tennis with my uncle, the comfort of being able to knock on my parents' door at any time in the middle of the night if I was upset and felt like talking, being so scared when my father got very badly burned, singing with my sister when we did the dishes, when my grandparents took me (by myself) on a real airplane to visit my cousins who lived far away, throwing dolls across the room at my sister in the dark, secretly hanging upside down at the top of the stairs with my brothers and sister so we could hear my parent's friends tell dirty jokes, dressing my little brother up in funny clothes.

It's amazing how every one of us has our own list. No two lists can be exactly the same, even if you're a twin. That's because each person has his or her own feelings, reactions, and memories. Some of the memories are wonderfully happy ones, others still cause you to ache. But all the experiences have helped to make you and me who we are today. What we feel for our family is like no other emotion in the whole world. Our family can make us feel secure, special, loved, happy, and make us have a deep sense that no matter what, we belong and will be cared for.

But not all children (and adults) have such family feelings. Some lists will be filled mostly with sadness, dreams that never came true, love that wasn't shared, loneliness, distance, and fighting.

I've found that when a boy or girl feels good about his or her family, they can enjoy their friends, concentrate on their work at school, and fully participate in other activities. If they're pressured, worried, scared, insecure, or unloved at home, everything else seems much less important.

It seems underneath everything is the need for family. Even if children run away from their families, my guess is that they wish they didn't have to feel that way. They wish they could be closer and feel good, so they could stay. Even if parents are not close with their children, or if sisters and brothers stop talking with each other, I've never spoken with anyone who hasn't at least wished it could be different, even though it's not.

## Family Means Different Things to Different People

Some people have family feelings for others who are not related, but they feel and act like they are. It seems that whoever can give you the caring, time, love, and security that is so important to your feeling good can become like family and share family feelings.

Even orphans, who don't have any parents and often live with other orphans in special homes for children without parents (called orphanages), find that the other orphans as well as the adults that care for them can feel like family.

There are stepfamilies who enjoy closer family feelings with each other than they ever did with the family members who were born together. Families with adopted children, many from all over the world, have the ability to develop family feelings that are special. So many foster parents take other people's children, raise them, and love them as if they were their own.

One woman in her sixties, whose sister and brother are no longer talking to her, feels that certain friends have become like sisters to her. She said about her friends,

There is nothing that we wouldn't have given up if we needed each other. That's dedication, a feeling of true loyalty, a feeling that if your hand is out, you know you can count on each other. But my own sister and brother never gave me that feeling. Because you're a sister doesn't mean that you're going to have family feelings. I once was at an airport when a man was waiting to see his brother who he hadn't seen for twenty-five years. The brother was not allowed to leave his country during these years and had just gotten permission to get out. When his brother came off the plane, they embraced; they cried; they yelled; they hugged. It was the most emotional experience I have ever seen. There's nothing to replace flesh and blood if the feelings are there. But if the feelings are not there, it doesn't matter if you're flesh and blood or not.

She and her friends are closer, spend more time together, are more trusting, and are more there for each other than she and her real sister and brother ever were. Her friends have become her family.

Just because someone is related to you, doesn't guarantee that you'll be able to have warm, close family feelings with them. That would be nice. But that's not the way things are for everyone. All you have to do is think about the divorce rate, the kids that run away, or the kids who feel they need drugs or alcohol to drown their loneliness so they don't have to deal with it, and you'll know that being able to feel close and secure is a gift to be treasured.

## When Family Feelings Are Not Good

Though it's sad to admit, there are some families that will probably never feel good, no matter how hard anyone tries.

Those might be the families where there's:

| | |
|---|---|
| constant fighting | drug or alcohol problems |
| money pressures | illness |
| failure | unemployment |
| neglect (nobody pays attention) | abuse |
| no communication | loneliness |
| little kindness or understanding | jealousy |

Some parents never really wanted to have a family in the first place. Others who really love their children may just not be capable of taking care of them in a way that feels good to anyone.

Boys and girls growing up in a home where family feelings are not good will probably find it hard to be happy. They may not be able to concentrate in school, bully other kids, show off, or misbehave in class. So often they do this to try to get the attention they aren't getting at home. Some will not even show up at school. They'll hang out in the streets and just try to survive.

Some kids from homes that don't feel good will just get unhappier, angrier, and lonelier over the years, especially if their family situation doesn't change. They may run away from home at an early age or get married earlier than they normally would (even if they aren't really in love) just to get away from their parents and their unhappy family life. They may turn to drugs, alcohol, and may even commit crimes— because they're so angry, hungry, or whatever.

Some children from unhappy homes are able to find happiness with other families. Gary, age nineteen, shared,

> When I was growing up, I loved going to my friend's house for dinner on Friday nights. I never felt good with my family. My older brother was always out with his friends and my parents. . . . Well, my father drank a lot, and my mother was so afraid of my father that it was miserable even being around them. I felt sad. I didn't want to be there. But it was different in my friend's house. He had two little sisters who became very attached to me. They always wanted to sit on my lap, and I loved reading to them. He had a younger brother who always teased him. But I loved hearing it because it was fun to be with what seemed like a normal family. I became very close with his mother and father and was always welcome there. I don't know what I would have done if I didn't have them to go to. They were like my adopted family. But they felt more like my family than my own family did.

One woman shared that her friend (we'll call her Joan) had a baby-sitter who started baby-sitting for her three sons from the time she was ten or eleven. Her baby-sitter's mother had died of cancer, and her father physically abused her. Finally, because of all the abuse and unhappiness, the baby-sitter just couldn't live with her father anymore. Joan, her husband, and her children had grown to love this girl and decided to legally adopt her as part of their family.

That was many years ago. This girl is now expecting a baby of her own, and will most likely have learned that there really is goodness in the world. Sometimes it's just so hard to find.

Another woman talked about a girl who was loved by her mother but was very neglected. Her father had died and her mother, who was a child, herself, was just not capable of taking care of her three children. Though the girl had been a very good student, she started dropping out of school. She slept in basements, garages, or wherever she could instead of going home. A teacher at school realized there was a problem and tried to reach her and encourage her to come to school. At least if she was in school, he could give her support, talk with her, and try to keep an eye on her, which he did. This girl touched him. And as time went on his feelings about wanting to help her grew even stronger. One day she came home with him, supposedly to baby-sit for his children, and she has never left. She's been a part of his family ever since. Though her mother loved her, she was more than happy to have someone take the burden of caring for her off her hands.

According to this woman, "There are all different types of love. To say 'I love you,' doesn't mean 'I want to care for you, be with you, or spend time with you.' "

How lucky these two girls were to have such special people reach out and bless them with the warmth, care, and love that is so much a part of family life that feels good. Their new families became closer to them, gave them the time, and answered their needs in a way that their real families never could.

Unfortunately, not all children who are unhappy at home are lucky enough to have loving families to visit whenever they wish or to be taken in and raised by families who love them as their own. But all children who feel frustrated, sad, angry, unloved, neglected, lonely, or troubled about any part of their family life can at least try to better understand their feelings and learn new ways to cope with their family situations.

If you have such feelings, it is important to talk with someone who cares and is trained to listen and offer guidance. I know the list of whom you might go to for help keeps repeating itself, but maybe if I write it often enough, you'll begin to really believe that there are choices.

No one need deal with these difficult situations alone. You can speak with an aunt, uncle, older brother or sister, grandparent, trusted teacher, religious leader, guidance counselor, school psychologist, school social worker, friend's parent, or other trusted adult. You can also check your local telephone book to find children's, family, or social services that can help.

If you're from an unhappy home, it may help to remind yourself that it's not your fault. If your parent is ill, or there's very little money, or there's failure, or your parents don't get along, or your parents neglect you, or they have an alcohol problem, or they get into trouble with the police, it's not your fault. It doesn't mean you're not special, it just means you weren't so lucky.

## Some Families Who Think They Can't Feel Better Really Can

Though certain families may never feel better, others who think they can't really can! In order to feel better family members first have to admit that they don't feel good and they'd like things to be different. Then they have to agree to work together so that change can take place and feelings can improve.

Trying to change will take a lot of teaching and honest talking. It will probably mean taking risks and taking chances to say things that might hurt so that family members will learn to be more sensitive. If you teach each other what doesn't feel good, then it will be easier to understand what does.

Change will also require patience. If you figure it's taken years to develop the bad feelings you have, you've got to respect that it will take time to change to better feelings. Even if you seem to only be taking teeny-tiny baby steps forward, just remember moving forward in any way is better than standing still with bad feelings—or worse, moving backwards. Any change takes time.

Some families find family counseling (when the whole family gets advice from someone who is trained to listen and offer guidance) can be very helpful.

## You Can't Choose Your Family

Have you ever said to yourself or heard someone say, "Oh, if only my mother was like that." Or, "I wish my brother would switch places with my friend's brother. Why do I have to be so unlucky?"

Well, family is different from friends. While you can choose your friends, you're kind of stuck with family! You can't switch brothers, change mothers, or go shopping for a different sister.

Like it or not, you got what you got! So, you might as well try to feel as good as you can about the way they are, instead of spending so much time wishing they were different or someone else. The day you begin to accept them for who they are, maybe you'll begin to feel better about them. They're not someone else and never will be!

## Brothers and Sisters

If you have a brother or sister, think about what he or she means to you. Do your thoughts make you feel good, sad, frustrated, angry, cheated, or do they give you a bad case of the yucks? How do you think your brother or sister feels about you? If you're an only child, what are your feelings about not having a brother or sister?

Brother-sister feelings are affected by many things, such as who was born first; who's in the middle; who's the youngest; how many years are between you; how your parents treat you and how your parents treat them.

If you were several years older when your sister or brother was born, you were probably very excited about having a new brother or sister. You most likely couldn't wait to help feed, dress, diaper, bathe, and play, play, and play with him or her. You probably thought your new little brother or sister was so cute (much better than even your best doll or stuffed animal) and felt great about being such a number-one helper to your mom and dad. If you didn't feel that way, how did you feel?

If you were closer in age to your new brother or sister, you may have been excited and happy, but you also could have been very jealous. Now your mom and dad were going to take all the attention that was supposed to be for you and give it to your new brother or sister. You might even have felt you hated him or her!

"When Carol was born, I was three years old," said Elaine, now age thirty-four. "Everyone was paying attention to her. I didn't realize why I felt so jealous at the time, but I thought it would be fun to stick her finger in the closet door! I took her out of the crib, and when no one was watching, put her on the floor, stuck her hand in the closet, and closed it. I guess I thought that the baby's hand should have a new shape. Then I told my mother and said that I did it. She said, 'You didn't.' I said, 'I did it.' And then she said, 'It was an accident.' She didn't want to believe I could have done such a dangerous, horrible thing on purpose. And I kept saying, 'No, I did this. I did this.' I really hated my sister. If I could have beaten her up, I think I would have."

Not all kids go as far as to put baby's fingers in the closet door. But, if you check closely, what looks like tickling and patting may really be pinching and powing. (Lots of nonverbal messages!) Maybe you remember doing some of this yourself. Maybe you're still doing it.

## Fights and Feelings

Some brothers and sisters hardly ever fight. They have strong feelings of love for each other and show it in many ways. They really look out for each other and are quick to take each other's side if someone tries to be harmful in any way. They're very good friends and aren't jealous if one gets a red lollipop and the other one gets a yellow.

Sheilagh, age thirty-two, has always been close to her twin brother. She has always been very protective of him. Even when he was sent upstairs without dinner, she made sure to sneak him a peanut butter sandwich, so he wouldn't go hungry. Today they're as close as they've ever been and are still looking out for each other.

Kent, age fourteen, said, "I've never fought with my sister. She's six years younger than I am, and I have always loved the way she looks up to me as her big brother. She's also very cute and has always been very small for her age. I'm very tall and I think she'd never get up if I hit her. I never would. Besides, my parents would kill me if I did."

## Some Fighting Is Natural

Other brothers and sisters have love feelings for each other but fight anyway (just like friends and parents do.) Unless the fights are very violent and harmful, day-to-day arguments are pretty natural. In fact, there are parents who have told me they'd be concerned if their children didn't fight at least a little.

Allen, age thirteen, remembers a time when his younger sister was totally wising off. He shared, "She got me to the boiling point! I chased her into her room. She slammed the door and locked it. I started banging into it with my shoulder, screaming, and daring her to come out and play. She was hysterically crying. My dad came in, took me downstairs, and told me to wash my face. I was so mad that as I was washing, I broke a piece of soap in my hands without even realizing it. My mom went upstairs and brought my sister down from her room, holding her hand. I could have killed her [my sister]! But when I saw her face, all my anger drained out of me and I gave her a hug."

Bonnie, age eleven, said, "Even though I always say I hate my sister and wish she wasn't around—sometimes I even say I wish she were dead—I really love her. Because when she was in the hospital, I was really scared she was going to die."

Samantha's "shark story": Samantha told me that when she was twelve, her middle sister was nine, and her youngest sister was six. They all shared a room together. She and her middle sister used to make believe the carpeting in their bedroom was the ocean. They used to push their little sister off into the "ocean" on their carpet and say, " 'There are sharks and the sharks are coming to eat you! Here they come. They're eating your leg. Now they're eating your arm.' We'd make big, shark-type chomping sounds. This would make our sister cry hysterically, and we thought it was so funny. She was a real pain, anyway. She was always crying.

"Now that we're all older, we're much closer. We haven't thrown her to the 'sharks' in at least fifteen years! But we look back and smile [though her smile is not quite as wide as mine and my middle sister's]. No wonder she cried all the time."

No matter how much scratching, growling, "I hate you's," and shark eating goes on each day, most brothers and sisters have a secret supply of feelings for each other. Underneath the hateful shouts, the slamming doors, and the "it's not fairs," the close feelings are always there. But they may only show themselves at certain times, like when a brother or sister is bullied, or one of them is upset, or if something serious happens.

Close feelings may only show themselves after brothers and sisters have become much older. The age differences that seem so great when you're little, usually become less of a concern when you're older.

R., age thirty-three, told me that he and his brother were worlds apart when they were younger. Said R., "It's hard to be close when you're seventeen and your brother's eight. While he was growing up and playing with his toys, I was trying to figure out where I wanted to go to college. But now that he's twenty-four, I think I understand what he's going through right now. In fact, he's coming to stay with me in a few

days. He wants to interview me about my work and may be interested in the same type of thing. It may be the first time that we'll be able to talk about something that we're both interested in that's got more to it than cars or the beach."

No matter what the differences in age or anything else, the fact is that brothers and sisters share so many different personal experiences over their growing-up years that they are able to look back together and relate to things that no one else in the world can.

Maybe that's what makes those brothers and sisters who really do have the good feelings underneath try so hard to become closer, even if they have to wait until they're older. That's also what might make them so sorry when they can't relate to each other and see each other (because of differences, being far away, or perhaps marrying someone who doesn't like the brother or sister), even if they want to.

## No Matter How Deep You Dig

Unfortunately, some brothers and sisters who really sound like they can't stand each other really can't. The hateful or resentful feelings on the outside are also on the inside. No matter how deep you dig, no love can be uncovered underneath. There's jealousy, resentment, and lots of comparing.

The other person's piece of cake is always bigger. Sometimes parents are the ones who take sides and cut the slices unfairly. Sometimes even if the pieces were carefully measured with a ruler, you will think and believe that yours is the smallest. (That has very little to do with the cake and much more to do with those inside feelings.)

The following experience was described to me by Mimi, age fifty-three.

My parents brought up a monster. If she didn't get her way, she would throw a tantrum. She'd actually throw herself on the floor and kick, scream, and yell, so she could get her way. She was so strong, my parents just didn't know how to handle her. My mother used to say, "Please, please, give it to her. Give it to her. Give her whatever she wants." I remember when I was a little child, she pushed and pushed until she got her way.

I'll never forget the time I had gotten a new coat as a gift from my aunt. My aunt also got one for my sister. She picked a tan coat and I picked black. I hadn't worn it yet and my family was getting ready to go out to a religious service together. My sister decided that she wanted to wear my new black coat. When she started raising her voice, my mother said that black was an older color, and she's the older sister, so I should let her wear my coat. So I never got a chance to wear it for the first time, she did. I've never forgotten it.

It's funny. I don't ever remember resenting my mother, even though I felt awful that I had to give up my brand new coat. I think I felt so sorry for my parents that they had to deal with my sister. And yet, even though our childhood was so difficult, I kept up a decent relationship with her for years and years. Until we reached a point where nothing was enough for her. She was jealous of everything. It was too painful to try any more. We haven't spoken to each other in several years.

Maybe Mimi and her sister would have been closer if their parents could have been stronger and handled her sister differently. No one will ever know. . . .

If the underneath feelings are good, time and maturity will probably make them even better. If they're not good, like with Mimi and her sister, all the sharing and all the years together may not be enough to prevent a brother or sister from becoming the most distant strangers to each other, even enemies.

## If You Think You're Not As Good As Your Brother or Sister

It may be that your parents always say to you, "Look what Beth [make believe your older sister is Beth] was able to get on her test. She got another ninety-five. I don't understand why you're having such a hard time with your studying. No child in our family is dumb. If it's easy for Beth, it should be easy for you, if you would only work a little harder."

Those kinds of comparisons can kill. They can kill the confidence that comes from knowing your parents accept you for who you are, for your own abilities. They can kill your strength to accept yourself as you are, because you're always believing you should be better; you're always believing you're not good enough; you're always believing you should be like your sister. They can kill any chance that you will relax and be able to concentrate when you take your next test, because you're so worried about doing at least as well as Beth (you may even feel forced to cheat).

And such comparisons can also make you want to "kill" Beth! Not really dead-type killing but feeling like you wish she just wasn't around. (Things would certainly be a lot easier for you.) Even if you and Beth really love each other, these kinds of comparisons can interfere with close feelings between you. The sad thing is that it's not Beth's fault that your parents always compare you to her.

Because you're angry, you may purposely forget to give her telephone messages, spill her perfume, stick her brush in the toilet (only kidding), hide her stationery, or even try to embarrass her in front of her friends. But doing those kind of things will only make the feelings worse between you and Beth.

Because you're frustrated, you might decide that since there's just no way you can get those high Beth-type grades, you might as well stop trying. It's not worth trying so hard and knowing that your parents will never think what you get is good enough. It's too painful. You may start talking and fooling around more in class, because there's no point to paying attention. At least if your grades are really low, there's not even a chance they'll get close to Beth's. So maybe your parents will leave you alone.

What to do? Since you're the one who feels resentful and frustrated, it's important to let your parents know how you feel when they compare you. Look back in the beginning of Chapter 19, Your Parents, if you're not sure how to turn your feelings into words.

Since you're the one who might not think very much of yourself because you don't think you measure up, you can begin to work harder at accepting yourself for who you are (whether you get a 70, a 75, an 80, or a 95—just like Beth). That doesn't mean you shouldn't work to improve your grades or at least keep them at a point where you're satisfied with them.

You can try harder. Maybe instead of spending so much time comparing, your parents would be more helpful if they sat down with you and talked about study habits and ways to organize your work so you can improve. Then maybe on the next test you'll be able to get a 73 instead of a 70. The truth is maybe you'll never get a 95, no matter how hard you work. Maybe that's just not you. But by comparing yourself to yourself you'll be able to go as far as you can for you and not be so pressured to be like anyone else. You'll probably be amazed at how much better you'll start to feel about yourself.

And since you're the one who now realizes that Beth has little to do with this (it's really because of your parents' unfair expectations), then maybe you and Beth can have a private talk. Maybe you can give her a chance to be the friend she might already be, but until now neither of you has been free enough to let those underneath feelings come out.

You need to remind yourself that you're not your sister (your brother, your cousin, your friend). You're you. Whatever your sister does that's so great—good for her. It would be nice to have the freedom to be proud of Beth.

You have your own things that you can do, and you have a right to do them in your own way. If you always try to be like your sister, you may be disappointed for the rest of your life. How sad to spend all that time wishing you were someone else. You can't be like your sister or anyone else. You *can* be like yourself.

That goes for comparing how good you are at sports or how well you can bake, sew, sing, play the piano, or how many friends you have, or whether or not you're popular, or your looks, hair, or if you're interested in a boyfriend or girl friend. You can only be you. It's time for your parents to learn that if they haven't already. And it's certainly time for you.

### If It's Hard to Talk with Your Parents About Their Comparisons

If you're finding it hard to tell your parents how pressured and resentful you feel because of their constant comparisons, you might ask them to read this section and say you've been feeling a lot like Beth's sister.

If you really don't think you can say even that, you might leave this book on their pillows, opened to the section about Beth with a little note attached, "Please Read: Hint, Hint!"

Remember, you may not always be comfortable with what you want to say, but that doesn't mean you shouldn't say it. It's very important for your parents to realize how much their comparisons hurt you and how much they interfere with good feelings for your brother or sister. They may never know unless you tell them.

## Sometimes It's Not the Parents Who Pressure and Compare

Some boys and girls just love competition. They compete whenever they can with their friends and classmates, so it's natural for them to compete with their brothers and sisters (and their brothers and sisters compete back with them). Lots of times the competition is healthy. Other times it may cause bad feelings and pressures at home.

Even if parents don't say a word, children might think their parents are comparing them. They feel their parents' pressure; they feel the competition, and they act in response to it. These feelings might make the children feel better or worse about themselves. These children often continue to believe that their parents are comparing them even when they haven't checked to see if their parents feel that way.

Sometimes it's your relatives or the kids at school who do the comparing. If you find you are aware of a pulling or tugging at your insides because you think your sister or brother is better than you are, or that your parents, relatives, or friends think they're better, it's time to catch those feelings before they go any further and take a good, hard look at what you're doing to yourself.

If you really think your parents are comparing you, even if they don't talk about comparing out loud, ask them. Also, be careful about pressuring yourself even more than anyone else might: those tuggings may be a signal that you have to work harder at accepting yourself.

## So What Does All This Mean?

Well, whether you're younger, older, or right in the middle, you're you. Many kids have feelings about each position. Some say they'd like to switch places in their family, and others want to stay right where they are. But since you can't switch, you might as well make the best of it. (It would be more helpful to think about why you wish you could switch, so you can begin to change what's possible to change and accept what you must. Sound familiar?)

We spent Chapter 17 talking about how people make judgments and compare many different things, like clothes, grades, looks, sports ability, and other talents. You saw how the comparisons and competition can cause resentment, jealousy, and bad inside feelings.

The same thing can happen in families between brothers and sisters. Sometimes the comparing is done between the brothers and sisters themselves. Other times it's the parents who create the pressure and competition.

Think about your own family life and try to figure out the many ways in which each family member compares and competes with the other. What jealousies and resentments do you feel?

## Why Isn't My Lollipop the Same as Theirs and Other Jealousies

"He's allowed to cook breakfast, and I'm not."

"He's allowed to stay up later than I am. It's not fair!"

"How come she can go with you, and I can't?"

"Why do I have to stay home and do chores when they can just go out and play with their friends?"

"My older sister gets real good grades, and I don't always."

"Everyone always tells her how pretty she is, but they never say anything about me."

"My younger sister always gets away with everything."

"My older brother always gets away with everything."

"Everyone else's piece of cake is bigger than mine."

"I'm so jealous of my sister. She's so popular, and I hardly have any friends."

"All the relatives pay more attention to her than to me."

"My brother knows how to bake and I don't."

"How come my sister is such a good athlete, and I can't even throw a ball. The guys tease me that I should take lessons from my younger sister."

"Why did my brother get the looks and the brains?"

"My younger sister is more developed than I am."

"You only buy what he likes and not what I like."

"You only make her favorite cake and not mine."

"Why does Uncle M. only take her out to play tennis and not me?"

"How come I always have to be the one to get hand-me-downs?"

"He always gets away with things, and I always get blamed."

"You only make time for him never for me."

"You don't love me as much. . . . "

"You listen to her, but you never listen to me."

"He always hogs the talking during dinner."

Do any of these things affect you? What else would you include on your own list? You may be surprised to realize how much comparing you really do.

Now that you understand more about the need to be yourself, that each person is special in his or her own way, that each person has his or her own abilities, and that no two people are exactly alike (even twins), I hope you'll be able to start crossing unfair comparisons off your list. I hope you'll start liking yourself even more and resenting others less.

But remember not all competition is bad. In fact, it can be fun, healthy, and make you strive to be better in a very positive way. It's only bad when you don't realize, accept, and respect that each person is different.

One more thing: Many problems on the preceding list can be changed, if you just let your family know how you feel. For example, if you want to cook breakfast, talk about it with your mom and dad. Just prove to them you know the safety rules and maybe they'll let you.

## What If You're Older, Younger, or in the Middle

Many oldest children in their family have told me they feel they get blamed the most (because they should know better), have the most responsibility, have to live up to high expectations, have to set the example, and generally are very pressured.

But not all oldest children feel that way. I know I loved being the oldest. I felt special, don't remember any competition pressure, and feel that my younger brothers and sister looked up to me (most of the time). I don't remember being resentful of them and feel my parents must have worked very hard at making us understand that each one of us was (and is) special but different. Sometimes they got; sometimes I got. But the getting was always fair. I owe my parents a lifetime thank you for their love and for teaching us to love each other.

I think how parents handle their kids, and what kind of feelings there are in the home really affect how kids relate to each other. Just like with Mimi and her sister. Who knows with different parents things could have been different between them.

As much as I'd like to think otherwise, not all parents treat their children fairly. Some really do have favorites and don't try to hide their feelings. It's got to hurt a child who sees that a parent really doesn't love him or her as much as the others. It's got to cause resentment of the others too.

But sometimes resentment has nothing to do with how parents deal with their children. Even when parents love each child and try hard to show it, sometimes the resentments that are inside a child are too deep for a parent or even a child to handle and get rid of. Sometimes help from a trained professional will offer understanding and guidance in how to ease the anger and reduce the competition.

One mother of two teenage sons said, "The younger one would love to be friends with the older one. But the older one only 'saw red,' only reacted with a lot of anger and resentment toward the younger one. The anger seems always to be there and has come out in many different ways."

Some younger children have told me that they resent the fact that the oldest gets more privileges. They sometimes think their older sister or brother gets more attention, gets to spend more time with their parents, seems more important, and is often the favorite. Other younger children look up to their older brother or sister, miss them when they're off with their friends, and almost regard them as a second parent. The thought of favorite doesn't even enter their minds.

Many middle children have shared that they think they're always blamed and that the oldest and the youngest are more special than they are. One parent, now in her forties, told me, "No matter how I try to convince my daughter that I'm not playing favorites, she won't believe me. She's our middle child and thinks that we treat her differently than her older sister and younger brother. No matter how equally we treat them, she will always see her portion as less than theirs or her present as not as nice. I hope one day she realizes we feel she's just as precious as they are."

From family to family the feelings between sisters and brothers can be so different. Even in the same family some brothers and sisters are closer than others. Again age differences may have a lot to do with having these feelings. Their relationships depend on so many different things.

## Sharing Your Room

If you're sharing a room with your brother or sister right now, and you're thinking "What a pain!" maybe you'll smile and figure you're not so bad off when I tell you that Ann, age seventy-three, told me stories about when she and her two sisters not only shared a room, but they had to share the same bed! (Are you smiling?)

The following stories will give you an idea of what can bug brothers and sisters as well as what can feel good when they share their room.

Betty, age thirty-seven, told me, "I had no privacy when I was growing up. I would clean my room and my sisters would mess it up. I wanted them out when my friends were over, but I couldn't get rid of them. They were scared to bring their friends home because I was in the room. I never had moments alone for my own thoughts. I couldn't listen to records when I wanted to. When their friends did come over, they touched my things and spilled my perfume bottles. One of my sisters put soap in my goldfish bowl. The worst was when I walked into our closet and stepped on my sister's turtle because she was playing with the turtle in the closet and left it in there."

Meredith, age thirteen, said, "I feel like I don't have much privacy. If my sister and I would have our own rooms, maybe we wouldn't fight as much. We're constantly using each other's clothes and stationery. If we had separate rooms, we would have more and would keep our own things. Sometimes I really get mad at her and I'll write signs on everything that's mine and say, 'Do Not Touch. This is Meredith's.'

"Sometimes it's good. If I get scared at night, my sister is always there. She comes over and stays with me until I fall asleep. If I have trouble with my friends, she gives me good advice.

"I feel like we have a very close relationship because we share our room. She can see how I feel. We can read each other's emotions better because we see each other more often.

"We're not that far apart in age, but the years still make a difference. Sometimes she comes to me with problems that didn't happen to me yet so I don't know how to answer her."

Beth, age sixteen, shared, "I really need to be by myself a lot. But there's no place for me to be alone. My sister sometimes doesn't understand. One time I was on the telephone and she heard something very private. That friend was over one day and she said something. I don't think the friend has ever forgiven me.

"Sometimes when I tell her something, I don't think she wants to know. She judges me. I just want her to accept what I say. We're very different. We have really different relationships with our parents. I think sometimes she's really jealous of mine, and I'm jealous of hers.

"With our bedrooms together I guess she sees me at my worst times. I don't think we're closer because we share a room. Maybe it's good in a way that we share. Except for wanting to be alone sometimes, she's pretty good about it most of the time."

"It stinks!" said Jim, age nineteen. "I have no privacy. He's older, so he thinks he runs the room. And he comes first, so he gets to put the stereo on, and he gets to listen to what he wants first. If I'm not in bed at a certain time and I wake him up, he gets ticked off. You know, things like that. It doesn't seem like I have many rights. But now he only comes home on weekends, because he goes to college. So weekdays I have the room all to myself, which is good. It's better than before he went to college. There was just no privacy. He still acts like it's his room and I'm not even in there.

"I think we're less close because we share a room. He's extremely different from me. He's very conservative. He's into boring music, I'm not."

Feeling good about sharing rooms seems to be influenced by many things, such as the difference in your ages, your interests, your respect for each other's things, how much privacy you need, your study habits, what time you go to bed, what time you wake up, how neat or messy you are, and, of course, turtles.

Now that you've read about other people's feelings, it's a good time to write down your own (if you share your room). Make a column for what bugs you and a column for what feels good. Put down everything you can think of, and, then, at the right private time, give your brother or sister the list to read.

Blaming won't be as helpful as just plain talking about what you'd like to change. See if you can figure out what each of you can do to make living together more fun. You might even ask your sister or brother to write his or her own list that you can read. That way both of you can deal with your feelings and try to work out any differences.

## It's Better to Slam Your Pillow Than Your Brother or Sister

Depending upon how angry you are, you may have a hard time controlling how you let it out. Some kids slam doors; others stomp around on the floor as loud as they can; others curse and yell; still others smash their sister or brother.

The only problem is if you catch your sister or brother in the wrong place it can be dangerous. As much as you might be saying to yourself that some action is deserved I'm not so sure you'd be happy breaking an arm, busting a nose, or making a bruise that they'll remember for too long.

It's natural for you to get angry every once in a while. The only concern is how you get angry and what you do with your anger. Next time you're about to wind up and sock your sister or brother, think again.

Especially think twice if you were about to hit your sister or brother in the face.

Here are some other things you might do which won't put them in the hospital:

Yell as loud as you can "I'm so angry at you! I feel like smashing you in the face!"

Smash your pillow as hard as you can at least twenty times (you can make believe the pillow is her or his face, as long as your sister or brother's face is not on the pillow when you're smashing!).

Tear up paper into as many little pieces as you can.

Run around the block.

Go out and shoot baskets or throw a ball against a wall.

Go outside and throw a ball up into the air as high as you can. Do that at least ten times.

Take a shower.

Slam your fist into a punching bag.

Take out a piece of paper and just start writing.

Get the idea?

If you want to settle your argument, remember to wait a little while until everyone is more calm. It's almost impossible to talk things out when you're in a rage. (That's good to remember when you're dealing with your parents, friends, and teachers too.)

## Feelings About Being Twins

In case you're wondering how twins become twins:

*Fraternal twins* can be two boys, two girls, or one boy and one girl. They're not identical and often don't even look alike. That's because two separate eggs are released by a woman's ovaries instead of one, both eggs are fertilized separately (only one sperm can enter one egg), and both eggs plant themselves separately on the walls of the uterus in order to grow into two separate babies.

*Identical twins* must be either two girls or two boys. They result when a single egg is released and fertilized. That single fertilized egg splits into two separate, identical egg cells that will plant into the wall of the uterus and develop into two separate, identical babies who will look exactly alike.

*Siamese twins* must either be two girls or two boys. Everything starts the same as with identical twins, but when the one fertilized egg splits, it doesn't completely split. That's why Siamese twins are attached at some point on their bodies. They develop in the uterus from two identical eggs that are not quite separated. Depending on where the babies are attached, doctors may or may not be able to separate them after birth (for instance, if they're sharing an organ and each needs its own).

*Triplets* (three), *Quadruplets* (four), *and more*: Just increase the numbers I gave you describing twins. For example, if triplets are born, there could be three separate eggs released at about the same time, three eggs fertilized separately, each planted separately on the wall of the uterus, and you know the rest. Triplets could also result from two separate fertilized eggs. In that case, one egg would split (making two identical children) and one would remain unsplit (one fraternal). If a single fertilized egg splits into three parts, the triplets would be identical.

Barry, age forty, father of identical twin girls, shared, "It always annoys me when people hear you have twins and say, 'Oh, double trouble.' I always answer them, 'No, double love.' "

If you aren't a twin, it will be hard to imagine what it would be like having a double, someone who looks exactly like you or at least someone who was born at the same time as you, even if you don't look alike.

David, age fourteen (an identical twin), said, "I think it's good being a twin. You always have a playmate. There's always a friend there. I always have a person to study with. We play against each other in sports and help each other out if we're not doing something right. Michael's my best friend. But it bothers me when people make mistakes about who is who all the time. It's a pain in the neck, and that's frustrating."

Michael, his twin brother, said, "We're very much alike. We have the same feelings. Sometimes we ask each other 'What are you thinking,' and very often we're thinking about the same thing. People always try to find ways to tell us apart. Kids at school ask us who we are in the beginning of the day, so they can tell us apart by the clothes we're wearing. But I don't think that we look so much alike. When I think of myself, I don't think of myself as a twin. I think of myself as my own person. I don't see that I look like David, I just look like myself. We look so different. We are different."

It might interest you to know that Michael and David also said their grandparents have trouble telling them apart, "and they've known us all our lives."

Rachel, age ten, is an identical twin. She told me, "Sometimes we dress the same, usually we don't. But we feel the same whether dressed like each other or not. When we dress alike, people say it's cute. But when we're not, we're just regular people."

The issue for twins is that they are two different people. Besides the frustration that's felt when other people aren't able to tell identical twins apart, there are too many people who just think they're the same.

Linda, age forty, mother of identical twin girls, said, "I don't think of them as twins. To me they're two separate people. The only time I get reminded that they're twins is when they dress alike or if someone makes a comment to me."

Like everyone else twins have their own feelings—even though many of them may be very alike—their own personalities—though sometimes they're similar—and their own dreams—though sometimes they're also the same. That's not unlike how brothers and sisters who aren't twins might be. It just happens that twins were born at the same time, but they're different people.

Yet there's a specialness about being a twin that I heard from each twin that I've spoken to. Sheilagh, age thirty-three, has a twin brother. (She was the one who snuck peanut butter sandwiches up to her brother when he was punished.) She told me, "Just being with each other for those nine months, something must have clicked. There's absolutely a bond between us. I often think if I'm sad, I wonder if he's sad. Or if I'm troubled, I wonder if he must be troubled too. I don't stop what I'm doing to call him and find out, but I do think about it. I truly believe it's a miracle when you have two individuals born at the same time. It's magical."

A mother of identical twin boys shared, "The boys are special people. It's hard to say how much of that comes from the experience of being twins. It's such a unique experience. As close as we ever feel to them, it's interesting as a parent to know that you're not the closest. They're depending more on each other than on you."

What about competition? Of course, each set of twins will have different feelings, just like each brother and sister who are not twins will have their own feelings.

Sheilagh remembered identical twin girls who went to high school with her. She said, "I was friends with one of them. They fought over clothes, fought if one of them got something extra. They were vicious with each other. They'd fight if one got a date before the other, if one got her period before the other. I think I would have died if I had to deal with that all the time."

Sheilagh didn't have that with her brother. They were very close, hung around with the same friends, and there was very little competition between them. The only thing she remembers that was hard for her brother was when she passed her driving test before he did. Said Sheilagh, "Imagine, gosh, you're a boy and your twin sister gets her license before you! And she has to drive you around."

Dana, age forty, is an identical twin. She shared, "There were never any competition issues that I remember. We were a little bit different; our personalities were different. We had no boyfriend competition. I don't think we ever liked the same boy. We dressed alike up until the sixth grade but in different colors. (I guess then we got smart and realized if we had different clothes, we could have a much bigger wardrobe.) We were always in different classes. My parents never brought us up to compete. I have to credit my parents for that. They never showed any favoritism while we were growing up."

Fourteen-year-old Michael said, "I don't like when people say to you, 'Who's the better athlete;' 'Who's smarter;' 'Who's stronger.' What do they expect us to say?"

Ten-year-old Lysee (Rachel's twin) shared, "My parents treat us equally. Some of my friends are her friends, and some of her friends are my friends. The only time I feel yuck is if she gets a better mark in school." (Lysee, maybe you would feel better knowing that Rachel told me you have a harder teacher and she has an easier one.)

Besides the natural competition between twins, a lot seems to have to do with parents; what they expect, how much they try to teach each twin and the other children in the family that each is an individual. Each person is different. If parents expect the same things just because children are twins, that's just as unfair as expecting it from any child.

If you're a twin and feel people are treating you together instead of as individuals then it's time for you to have one of those special private talks. Whether it be your relatives, friends, teachers, or your other brothers and sisters.

But most of all it would help for you to remember that you are you. You're not your twin, just like you're not any other sister, brother, or anyone else in this world.

One more thing, though the twins I've spoken with happen to be very close, I'm sure there are twins who are very, very different and are not close at all. If you are a twin and wish you could be closer to your twin brother or sister, no matter how old you are, it's never too late to try. Just turn your feelings into words and hope they'll care enough to listen.

If you're a friend of a twin and are having a hard time separating being friends with one and not so much with the other, then it might also help to talk about your feelings. You don't have to feel the same way about them both, they're not the same person. But you do have to deal with your feelings, so you can at least enjoy the relationship you want to enjoy.

And if you're the brother or sister of a twin and you feel your parents are playing favorites, it is important to talk with them about their actions. Or if you'd like to have a better friendship with one or both of the twins, then talk with them about your feelings. Maybe you can all try harder.

It would also help to realize that as close as you can be with your twin brother or sister, it may have nothing to do with their lack of love for you if they seem so close with each other. They may really love you very much. But what you might see between them that makes you never think they feel that way about you, may be that special bond that seems to come from the miracle of who they are.

## Feelings About Being an Only Child

Jennifer, age twelve, shared, "I think since my mom and dad are really great, I have a better time with my parents. But sometimes, like on weekends, when everybody's gone away, then it can get kind of boring.

"Some of my friends have older or younger brothers and sisters. I see how they really have fun with them, and then I feel kind of sad because I don't have any. But then I think of all the other things and I'm not sad anymore. Like, I think of how much fun I have with my parents. Sometimes I hear my friends saying that their moms are kind of boring, or their dads only play with them sometimes when they come home from work. So I feel happy with my family because my parents spend a lot of time with me.

"If I had the choice of having a brother or sister now or not, I think I'd stay being an only child."

A fourteen-year-old boy told me, "I guess it seems that only children want to have brothers and sisters, and people with brothers and sisters want to be an only child! When I talk about this with my friends, they envy me because I'm by myself. I don't see why. They're not lonely sometimes, like me. I only have a dog to keep me company.

"My aunt and uncle have three kids. They're all younger than me. I guess I feel like they're my brothers and sisters. I always like to play with them. I'm going to sleep over there this weekend. Sometimes I envy my cousins. They seem to have everything . . . happiness, a nice home, a great family. I feel that they do more with their parents than I do with mine."

John, age thirty-three, said, "Maybe there was a time or several times when I had a desire for another sibling [brother or sister]. In the long run it hasn't made a difference. It would have been nice to have a live in playmate. I was lucky enough to have two very intelligent parents who always gave me a lot of reading material and spent much time with me. I went shopping with my mother, played ball with my father, and they never smothered me or overburdened me with attention.

"I read huge amounts, and I guess my imagination was running full swing when I was little. I could turn anything into a game, like a cardboard box from a grocery store. It became necessary to be creative. I had to make up my own fun."

Ten-year-old Ken said, "I wish I had a brother or sister. Even if we fought, it would be better to fight then not have anyone around at all."

One thirty-year-old woman told me, "I learned how to keep myself busy when I couldn't see my friends so I didn't miss having a brother or a sister. But I did always feel as though I was in the middle between my parents, and that keeping peace in the house was my responsibility."

Ellen, age forty, shared, "Being an adopted only child, I wish I had a brother or sister. I was told that when I was three years old, my parents were offered a chance to adopt another child. It turned out that it was a boy. My father didn't want a boy only another girl. So they said no. I asked them, 'Why didn't you adopt whatever you got?' A boy or a girl would have given me a brother or sister. I can't understand why my father couldn't see past girl. I feel terrible that I don't have a brother or sister.

"I don't have a real family. That part of it is really hard. Maybe that's why I relied so much on my parents. I couldn't ever say, 'I hate that little kid,' or 'I wish I were my older sister.' I wish I had the choice to love or hate. If I had a brother or sister, maybe I would have hated it. But not having one, I wish I had.

"I can only tell you what I miss. Two years ago I was with a friend of mine when she got a call telling her that her brother's wife had their first child. She said, 'I'm an aunt!' A little while later I started crying. I realized I would never be an aunt. I hope I'm a grandmother."

Maybe you share some of these feelings. What would you add?

If you're an only child and are sad because you want a brother or sister badly and know you probably won't ever have one, all you can do is tell your parents how you feel and hope they'll seriously consider what you say.

Adding children to your family is up to your parents. If they've decided not to, there must be a reason. You might feel better if you asked them to explain their decision.

It might help to remember that just because you have a brother or sister around, doesn't mean you will definitely feel good and be less lonely. There are no guarantees.

In John's case, being alone forced him to become creative. He was always able to figure out something to do. Just because you're an only child and you're alone, doesn't mean you have to be lonely. They're two different things. If you find yourself lonely, you can decide to do something about it. Invite a friend over, curl up with a good book, write a story, ask if you can stay overnight with your cousins, listen to music, watch a movie, bake something yummy. Try asking your parents if they can get you a pet.

Being your parents' only child makes you a most precious gift to them. If you don't already feel special, it's time you start.

## Feelings About Being Adopted

Kevin, age nineteen, shared:

I was adopted before I was a year old. You know how kids have birthday parties? Well, the first thing I remember was that I always had two birthday parties. One on my birthday and one the day they got me.

My first blanket was the one I had in the orphan home. My first squeeze toy was also from before I was adopted. They brought those things home with me and always told me, "Oh, yeah, you brought those home with you when we got you." They made me feel special. It didn't make me feel weird. It wasn't like, wow, I'm so different from the other kids. It was more that I was special.

They read me all the children's books they could find for kids who were adopted. That made me feel special when I was a little kid. I have a younger brother who was also adopted. My mother is Irish Catholic and his parents were probably Eastern European. When people look at my brother and me they often say, "You don't look alike. Are you really brothers?"

I wanted to know what my real mom called me. Was it Baby X or Fido or what? But my new parents told me they kept the name my mother gave me because they were so grateful to whoever she was.

I didn't really think about being adopted until I was a teenager. I didn't know how kids are born until I was older. I didn't know what sex was. Then I'd think about it and wonder, who was my mother, who was my father? Didn't they like me? I tried to explain it to myself and make excuses because there were so many unanswered questions.

I don't ever want to look for them. My parents really love me. . . .

John, age thirty-three, shared:

My parents first told me I was adopted when I was about three years old. Their way of dealing with it was telling me that I was specially chosen, and that they went to a place where there were so many babies all over the place. But they wanted a special baby. And that was me. Throughout my life I really haven't given it a second thought.

I guess if you're getting a lot of love and support, it really doesn't make a whole lot of difference as to who your parents were and why they didn't keep you. I feel it would be no more different for a child to be adopted than to take a puppy away from its mother and raise it and love it in someone else's home.

I'm very happy with the way I've been raised and the way I was taken in and welcomed by everyone. They were my family. They were my relatives from the start. Nothing was ever said or hinted at that it was otherwise.

I can't even remember anyone making a crack about my being adopted when I was in elementary school. If someone said to me, "If you could have lived with your real parents, would you have wanted to," I could never say yes to that. What's real is the family that I have always known—my now family.

Maybe the reason why so many adopted children search for their real parents is that they want to find their roots. They're searching for their identity, where they came from. They're curious. They may get information that they've always been searching for and one day go knocking on their true parents' door. I imagine that would come as a great shock for the parent(s). I would guess there might be an overflowing of emotions for the moment. Maybe a great sigh of relief from the child who's been searching. There's no telling where the relationship would go from there. There's no telling if the parent(s) really will even want a relationship with their child. There's no telling if the child will feel good with his or her parent(s).

Some children want to know about their real parents. Others, like John and Kevin, never want to know. But perhaps the most important, wonderful thing is that children can be adopted in the first place. Adopted children can have special, warm, close family feelings the same as children brought into that family by actual birth. In fact, many babies are brought to their new homes shortly after birth. Others are adopted much later.

But no matter when a child is adopted, adoption is a blessing. It gives a boy or girl a home and a family that they may never have had otherwise.

## Grandparents and Other Relatives

An uncle who you feel is wonderful may be an old fogey to your brother or sister. Your elderly aunt may have a twinkle in her eyes when she looks at you that gives you the message that you're special. You may think your mother's sister understands you even better than your mother.

Your cousins may be a real treat to be with one day and real pains another. Sometimes comparisons made between you and your cousins may be worse than those made between your brothers and sisters or your friends. You may think your aunt cooks meat like shoe leather, or that your uncle's cigar smells gross.

You may live near your relatives, far away, or anywhere in between. You may think you see your relatives too often or not enough. It just depends. It depends upon so many things.

As you read through the many feelings about relatives that were shared with me, think about your own feelings for your own relatives:

Jennifer, age twelve, said, "The only aunt who I really ever see is my Aunt Dorothy. She's really great! She takes me places, and I always feel like she's spending too much on me. I really love her."

Marlene, age eighteen, said, "I love visiting my Aunt Sylvia and am sorry I only get to see her about three times a year. The last time I saw her, she took me shopping for my college clothes. We had so much fun. We ran around from one place to another and got so much done in such a little time. I wish my mother had that kind of energy. I feel cheated. Sometimes I wish my aunt was my mother."

Michael, age eleven, told me that he loves to visit his cousins. Since he only has younger sisters, it's great when he can spend time with a boy cousin who's almost his age.

Will, age twelve, told me, "For a while lately we thought my aunt and uncle would get divorced. They've been having a lot of problems. He's the laid-back macho kind of man who doesn't want to be seen at a counselor or anything like that. My aunt saw a counselor and took her children. They had to do it in secret because my uncle was against their going. But then they got him to go. I think it helped a little."

Hank, age twenty-two, said, "My father's brother, Ed, has been more like a father to me than an uncle. I have always felt I could talk with him about personal things, and he always made time for me. When it came time to decide if I could go to college, since no one in my family ever did, Uncle Ed was the one who encouraged me to try."

Leslie, age ten, told me that she loves to go shopping with her grandmother but she hates when her grandmother buys her cousin the same clothes that she buys for Leslie.

Elaine, now thirty-five, remembers her favorite uncle with love and sadness. She said, "I always called him Unk. He gave me my first tennis racket when I was eight and spent hours teaching me how to play. He taught me about music, took long walks with me, and called me funny nicknames. I loved him so much and we were very close. The sad part is that he moved far away after his divorce. He hasn't contacted our family or written me in years. I can't understand where all that love could have gone."

Nicole, age nine, said, "I love visiting my cousins. They live in a big house in the country, and I get to ride horses."

Peter, age fifteen, said, "I hate it when my relatives come. My father has never liked my Aunt Betty, and every time we have another holiday to plan, my parents fight for hours about how much my mother wants to see her family and how much my father hates them."

Jeanne, age ten, said, "It's not fair that I always have to invite my cousin to my birthday parties with my friends."

Martin, age fourteen, said, "I love to have dinners at my aunt's house. She's such a super cook and my mom's cooking is a disaster. My mom is great at heating up frozen dinners. That's about all. I love her, but I can't stand her food. At least at my aunt's we can have a feast."

So many different feelings for so many different relatives. This is probably a good time for you to grab a piece of paper (if you haven't already) and make your own list of favorites. Think about who's at the top of your list and who you'd like to scratch off if you could.

Also think about all the things that might make you feel the way you do. Now that you are so much wiser and, I hope, more accepting, are there any relatives who you have disliked for things that you realize are not their fault? Are you making unfair judgments or comparisons?

(For example, do you think your cousin is a wimp because he or she can't play ball the way you do? So they're no fun to visit? Do they embarrass you every time they come to your home and you have to include them in games with your friends? Maybe it's time to accept that they're just not athletic and perhaps you can play not expecting them to be better than they are, or perhaps you should think of something else to do while you're together.)

If you're lucky enough to have grandparents, you probably already know how special they can be. Grandparents just seem to understand even when parents don't. Grandparents will often have time to listen, when parents don't. Grandparents just love to go fishing, to ball games, and to the zoo.

Sometimes, even when parents are old-fashioned, grandparents can be with it. When you least expect it, your grandparent may slip you a dollar or two. Grandparents have been known to lend or just plain give large sums of money so their grandchild can go to school or start a business or follow any other dream.

Most grandparents are wonderful, but there are always a few that are grouchy, nosey, or just not interested. Some are overprotective and don't let their grandchildren do things for themselves, even when they can, and even when their parents let them.

Some live close by and can see you often; others live farther away and may come for a week or two for a visit several times each year. Still others may live with you all the time. (That can be tough on privacy, since they're always around. As much as you may love them, every once in a while you may wish you could be alone with your parents and brothers or sisters. That's a natural wish.)

Grandparents come in all different ages, shapes, and sizes. Some are fit, some frail, some ill. Some grandparents are forgetful. But most, if not all, are lovable and to be treasured.

Here are some ways you can get to know your grandmother or grandfather even better. If your grandparents are no longer alive, you can still ask these questions about them, so when you look at their picture, your smile can be a little wider and you can feel you know them better.

Ask them to tell you about when they were growing up:

> Where did they grow up?
> What were their parents and family like when they were young?
> What about their family feelings?
> What was it like living where they did?
> If they went to school, what was it like?

What subjects did they like? Dislike?

What was the world like then? Was there peace? What about the wars?

What did they dream about? Did they have any secret wishes?

Did they play any sport?

What things were invented when they were younger?

How did these inventions change their life?

Were they ever lonely?

Do they remember their first girl friend or boyfriend?

What was dating like?

What are their feelings about the way they have lived their life?

What would they change?

What makes them happy? What are their fears?

What's their favorite flavor ice cream?

What's their favorite food?

What's their favorite book? Now and when they were little?

Have them tell you stories about your mother or father when they were growing up.

Share your own experiences with them.

Tell them about school.

Let them in on a few secrets.

Tell them about your friends.

Talk about what bugs you, what scares you, and what you love.

Talk about your family feelings.

Share your dreams.

(This list can also be used for parents, aunts, uncles, friends' parents, teachers, and other adults.)

Have your grandmother (or your grandfather) write down some of her favorite recipes for you. Take pictures of your grandparents every so often and make sure to have someone take several of you and your grandparent together.

Remember to tell them, "I love you." No matter how many times they hear it, they'll love to hear it again.

As I told you at the end of Chapter 19, Your Parents, the greatest, most wonderful way to feel good about yourself and the people you love is to try to share your life with them as much as you can and make an extra effort to show them you care.

This is not a have-to list. Just because you're together doesn't mean you'll want to have long conversations every time. Maybe on some visits you'll get to speak for hours. On others you might only have time for one or two questions. And sometimes, you may just feel like sitting together silently, feeling the closeness you have in a nonverbal way.

Lots of people mistakenly think they're supposed to talk every minute they're together. Sometimes it's just nice to be together in silence. But, at least if you wish to talk, you now have lots of things to talk about.

Since it's not always so easy to get private time, this is wonderful table conversation for the whole family. You and any brother or sister would probably be fascinated to listen to the story of your grandparent's life. Your parents would too. (Remember, you can ask your parents to tell you about their life story too.)

As you continue to grow up and all through your life, I hope you'll be blessed with the chance to share family feelings that feel good to you. If they don't feel good, perhaps now you'll be better able to talk about what doesn't feel good and realize if both people care enough you can try to work together to make the feelings better.

But if the feelings are bad and only you want them to improve, I also hope you'll find the strength to accept that you cannot change or force anyone to care about you if the feeling is not within them or they don't want to. Even if the bad feelings are from parents, grandparents, brothers, sisters, aunts, uncles, or cousins.

When there's nothing there—no matter how deeply you dig—then as painful as it may be to walk away, you can and must try to create new family feelings elsewhere.

# 22
# Dealing with Death

Maybe you're wondering if you should read this chapter or not. After all death is not something that's very pleasant. It may make you sad or scared to even think about it. Those feelings are very natural.

So why should you even choose to read about death? Well, the fact is, death is a part of each person's life. Yours, mine, and everyone's. Maybe you've already had an experience with death and have felt the feelings that are part of losing someone you love very much. Or maybe a dog, cat, bird, hamster, goldfish, calf or horse of yours had died.

Maybe you've never talked about death with anyone. Lots of people keep feelings about death to themselves (grown-ups as well as children). That's why they may not have had the chance to learn how to deal with it better and may not realize that other people have similar feelings.

Lots of children have talked with me about not knowing what to say or how to act with a close relative or friend who is very seriously ill and is expected to die very soon. They want to know what they might say to comfort a friend when a person in their friend's family has died. They want to know how to deal with their feelings if this loss happens to them.

They're not sure how to make themselves or anyone else feel better when their pet has to be put to sleep (when a veterinarian, or animal doctor, has to inject an animal with medicine that causes them to die) or has been hit by a car.

This chapter will help you deal with death in a kind, comforting, honest way. You'll find that here, too, you can turn your feelings into words. I hope it will help you to understand how death is another thing all of us must try hard to accept, since we haven't the power to change it.

## Death Is Forever

This is one of the things that's so hard to accept and understand, no matter how old you are. Some parents think that their kids will be too sad to know this truth, so they tell them grandma has "gone to sleep" or that Uncle Ned has "gone away." But these well-meaning parents somehow can't bring themselves to say that these relatives and friends are never coming back.

If your parent told you that about someone you loved, you may have spent many years watching out the window, checking the mail, and running to answer the telephone, hoping and expecting your Uncle Ned would return. Each time the doorbell rang at holiday time, you might have imagined it was your Uncle Ned finally coming back to surprise you. Or you may have been afraid to go to sleep at night, thinking that if grandma went to sleep and never came back, you didn't want the same thing to happen to you.

Cartoons on television sometimes show steamrollers flattening out funny characters so they can't move, only to have them spring back to life the next minute. Cartoon animals and cartoon people that get pushed off cliffs always seem to appear moments later, fine as can be, ready for their next adventure. Cartoon people that get shot dead seem magically able to recover. They always come back.

But those are cartoons not real life. Real life death is forever. It's not sleeping, even though a dead person's eyes may be closed. Death is more like a peaceful stillness, a quieting.

When people die, their hearts stop beating, their brains stop working, and all the organs of their bodies stop functioning (working). They no longer have the supply of blood and oxygen needed to stay alive.

But when people sleep, their hearts still beat, their brains still work, and all their organs are getting the food, blood, and oxygen needed to remain healthy. That's a very big difference. So during sleep you are resting and giving your body a rest, but your body never stops working. In death you and your body stop working forever. There's no returning.

## Death Knows No Age

One of my students just told me that his sister was killed a few weeks ago. She was seven years old and was hit by a car when she ran out into the street in front of their house so she could get ice cream. She never ran back.

Robin, age eleven, told me, "My friend's mother died when she was five. Now she has another mother and acts like nothing ever happened. When we had parents visit school, she just said, 'Well, my mother's coming too.' I don't think I would be able to adjust the way she did."

Ben, age eighteen, talked about his brother's death two years ago. He was twenty-eight years old when he became ill and died. He left his wife and his two-year-old son. Ben said, "It just doesn't seem fair."

Sharon, age twelve, shared how good she felt that she was able to know her great-grandma for so long. Said Sharon, "When she died in the beginning of this year, she was ninety-three years old. I was very sad but I knew I was lucky to even be able to know her at all."

Fred, age thirty-one, shared, "I think one of the most difficult times while I was growing up was when my friend died. We were in tenth grade and it was during the summer. A lot of us spent hours each day practicing our diving in a nearby swimming pool. One afternoon my friend cut his dive a little close and hit his head on the side of the pool. The emergency squad took care of him really fast, but he had damaged his brain and died three days later. We were all in shock. He was only sixteen years old."

Lots of people probably still think that death is only for those who are old. But death knows no age. Death will take infants, children, teenagers, parents, grandparents, and all others. Death will take friends. Death will take the rich as well as the poor, the popular and famous as well as the lonely. Death will take one person, two, whole families, or entire cities of people all at once. Death is not choosey.

## Though We Can't Prevent Death, We at Least Can Try to Live Longer

Though it's not within our power to prevent death, we can try not to put ourselves in risky situations that play games with death. Unfortunately, too many people die long before they would have because they were careless, took chances, or had poor health habits and didn't get proper health care.

Paying more attention to what you're doing would help. You can be careful crossing the street, not run out in between two parked cars, not drive home with someone who has been drinking, not swing a baseball bat too close to someone's head, not mix alcohol and drugs, not run down the stairs holding a scissors, not go swimming alone, not point a gun at someone even if you think it's a toy. Being careful might add years to your life as well as to the lives of those you love and even those you don't even know.

Making sure you're healthy is also very important now and all through your life. Try to have breakfast each morning, eat foods that are good for you, and get enough rest and exercise. Be sure to get regular checkups with your family doctor or nearby clinic. Don't forget to have your teeth and eyes examined too. If there's anything at all that doesn't feel right to you, even if you think it's silly and will probably go away by itself, say something about it. It may be nothing. But if it's something, usually, the earlier you check a concern out and get the right medicine or treatment, the better off you are. You deserve to give yourself the proper care.

## Death Teaches Us a Lot

As much as you may be saying to yourself "Why do I even have to think of these things? It doesn't make me feel very good." Knowing about death is as important as knowing about life. Death is a part of life. In fact, death is probably the only thing in life that you can be sure of.

Knowing about death teaches us that we shouldn't waste time. Death teaches us to appreciate the little things as well as the big and not take the people we love for granted.

A fourteen-year-old boy shared, "I've been thinking about one person dying. I don't know if I could go on living without him—my grandfather. I've been seeing that he's getting older, a little more forgetful. I love him so much. He just went away on a trip. I've been thinking, what if he never comes back? When he does come back, I want to spend as much time as possible with him."

Death challenges us to live, to share, and to love as fully as we can each day. That way, when death comes knocking on our doorstep, we need never say we didn't live in the time that we had. That's all any of us can hope to do.

## If Someone Is Very Sick
## and You Know They Will Probably Die Soon

Dealing with this may not be very easy. It can be painful and sad. You might feel cheated that you didn't have more time with that person. You may be very angry. You might say to yourself, "Why him?" or "Why does she have to suffer so much? It's just not fair."

No, it's probably not! But, as I've said before, life isn't fair all the time. This is one of the times it isn't. So, since you don't have the power to change the illness, the only thing to try to figure out is what you can do.

If the ill person is at home (sometimes they may even be at your home), you don't have to be concerned with visiting rules, such as at a hospital. You can see him or her as much as you wish, remembering that they might be tired. So, you may want to make more short visits rather than fewer long visits.

You can make the ill person pictures, write him or her poems, play music, read aloud, or just sit quietly together, feeling close. You can go back to the list at the end of the chapter titled Family Feelings and ask them about their childhood and how they feel about different times of their life. You can also talk about yourself, your family, your friends, school, what your hope to do in the summer, and so many more things.

You can also talk about your feelings about their illness. If you're very sad, you can say, "I'm very sad you're so sick." If you're thinking you're going to miss them, you might want to ask your mom, dad, or someone else close if it's okay to say that. (Sometimes, people who are very sick aren't told how sick they are. So you need to find out how much they know.) If it's okay to tell them, you can say, "I'm really going to miss you."

Ronnie, age thirty, shared, "I had a very close friend who was sick for several years. Last year her illness became worse and she reached a point where the doctors said she only had a few weeks to live. I was having a lot of trouble with my feelings, mainly because I kept them inside. I realized that I hadn't told her how much I loved her, and I didn't know if I should say anything because I knew if I started talking, I would probably start crying and never stop. I spoke with another friend who suggested that I write my feelings down and give them to her. Finally, I did. In my letter I told her I loved her and would always be grateful that I did. She died two weeks later. I think if I never told her, I would have felt bad for the rest of my life."

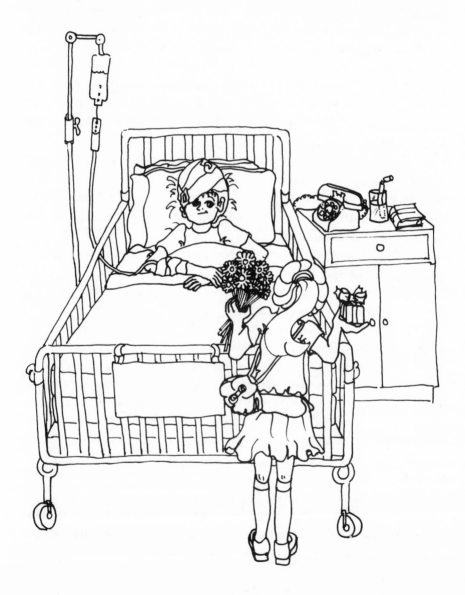

Ronnie's sharing of what she felt caused her not to look back and feel guilty or sorry. She was at peace with herself for taking the chance to share her feelings, as hard as that might have been.

If the person is in the hospital, you can ask if your parents or other relatives will take you to visit. If you don't like the smell of hospitals or the look of the tubes and things like that, tell your family your feelings. You might have to try harder to overlook the tubes (if you can) so you can realize that behind the tubes is a person who you love very much who would feel so good if they could see you.

Even if that person only opens his or her eyes every once in a while, if you are there at that moment, it will mean so much. (You might even notice smile wrinkles around the corners of the person's eyes. You also might notice a few tears because they're so happy you're with them.)

Sometimes when a person is too sick to open his or her eyes, you can just sit close by and maybe touch an arm or hold a hand.

It may be hard seeing someone who you always remember as being so healthy looking lying in bed with hardly any energy or strength. The sick person may not even be able to sit up, seeming to waste away because he or she lost so many pounds from the illness. It's hard seeing someone you love suffer.*

If you really don't like to go to hospitals and think you'll be too upset to go, then write a letter, card, poem, or story and have your mom, dad, or someone else read it to the sick person.

## If Your Friend Is Sad Because
## Someone He or She Loves Is Very Ill or Dies

Eleven-year-old Danielle asked, "My friend's mother is very sick and is going to die. I don't know what to say. When I say something, it's always the wrong thing. How should I act around her, because I can't forget that her mother's dying?"

---

*In fact, that's why there are so many cases in the newspaper of families who want to pull the plug on the instruments that are keeping their relatives alive. They often feel they would rather allow their relative to die sooner, but with dignity and a sense of respect, than to be kept alive by being attached to so many tubes and machines. There are lots of feelings about this, both for and against a person's right to decide to pull the plug.

First of all you can suggest some of the ideas I just gave you. Maybe that will give your friend a better idea of how she can share her feelings with her mother. As a good friend you might also tell her how sorry you are that she's so sad and upset. If you're not sure what to say, tell her, "I just never know if I'm saying the right thing." Or, "I wish I could say things that would make you feel better."

Your friend may feel comforted if you let her know it's okay to come to you if she feels like talking. Also tell her it's fine if she just wants to be together with you—silently. She doesn't have to worry about talking.

(Although I wrote this section as a personal answer to Danielle, the suggestions are for all friends.)

Neal, age thirteen, shared, "Just recently my friend's father died. He's had a couple of other experiences with death. A dog and a couple of birds of his died. His father was in the hospital for about four months and then he died. So it wasn't a great surprise or anything. He died two weeks later than they thought he would. I think his relatives give him support. They talk to him a lot and are really open. Many of the friends he feels open with have gone through or are going through things like divorces or deaths.

"I think it's becoming a little more common to see these topics on TV and in real life. We're kind of introduced to them earlier, so we're more prepared and can accept it more easily. But for some people, if they're very dependent upon the person who died, it can really take a toll on them."

## If Someone You Love Dies

When someone you love dies, you may have many different emotions, including surprise, shock, disbelief, anger, and sadness, until you are able to reach the point where you can really accept that this person is no longer with you.

Even when you know the illness has gotten worse and there's little time left to share, it's so hard to be prepared for such a loss. That's probably because you can't anticipate the feelings of loss until the person dies. Until then you only can imagine how losing someone feels. Only after the death will the loss seem final.

In the weeks or months after the death it may take a while before you stop dialing the person's phone number, stop saving reports to show them, and stop crying yourself to sleep at night because just thinking about the person makes you miss him or her so much. Holiday time may make you especially sad because of relatives who have died and can't be with you.

Each person will react to news of death in his or her own way. Some will cry. Some might scream. Some will just get very quiet and go off by themselves. Some people may not cry until weeks later, when the death begins to become real to them. But crying, whether right away or later, is not to be considered a measure of love. It's simply a very good way to get out your emotions.

In 1936 my mother wrote down her reaction to her grandfather's death in her diary. It reads as follows:

> October 22: While doing my homework about ten thirty, Daddy walked in and said that Grandpa died. I can't believe it yet. He was sick for nine weeks, poor thing. We stayed over at my aunt's, and everyone cried terribly. Dear Grandpa. Tomorrow is the funeral. I can't see him buried.
>
> October 23: We didn't sleep all night because mother was coming home from upstate with the undertaker. [They brought her grandfather home to be buried.] Grandma and all the family came to my house. We all carried on terribly. Then we went to the chapel. I couldn't help but cry because I couldn't believe that Grandpa died. We then went to the cemetery, and they put Grandpa in the ground. I'll never see him again. I still can't believe it.

## Death Can Be a Blessing

As much as we might wish that the people we love could live forever, those dreams of forever can fade when serious illness strikes. Especially if there's a lot of suffering, those who are watching it from the sidelines might begin to feel that death would be a blessing. In fact, the person who is ill might think that too.

In such instances, as hard as it is to say death's final goodbye, the people who live on are almost relieved, because they know in their hearts that death has taken him or her out of their suffering and finally put them at peace.

The other side of this is death also allows the healthy family members to be more at peace. Illness always takes its toll. The longer the illness, the more likely it is to drain the emotions of other family members who have to sit by and watch the suffering. Illness often requires a lot of attention, discussions with doctors, painful decisions, visits back and forth. Sometimes relatives live close by, other times, they're thousands of miles—even continents—away. The knowledge that someone close is ill is always on your mind. Beside everything else medical care over long periods of time can cost a lot of money. That's a different kind of drain.

So, if someone close is only breathing because he or she is attached to a machine, or is in a coma, or seems to have become "half of themselves" because of all the lost weight, or hasn't the strength to do anything but lie in bed and be cared for by others, or has trouble eating, or is in pain most of the time, try not to be too hard on yourself if you find yourself feeling that death would be a blessing. The person who is ill may just be feeling the same thing.

## Funerals

When a person dies, the family usually arranges for a funeral service. Each religion has its own customs, laws, and beliefs about when to schedule the service and how soon after death the person must be buried (lowered into a grave, usually at a cemetery) or cremated (turned into ashes).*

The funeral service can be a source of great comfort as well as a beautiful chance to talk about how much that person meant to his or her family and friends. It's like saying good-bye in public (in front of relatives, friends, and all others who wish to attend so they can pay their respects).

If someone close died in your family, did your parents allow you to attend the funeral service? Some parents think their children won't be able to handle the service, so they don't even let them come. Other parents may think it's fine for you to attend the service but not the burial

---

*This is usually done only if the person leaves written instructions saying he or she prefers to be cremated or if the relatives feel very strongly about doing it.

(at the cemetery). Still others give their children a choice. They also may tell them if they have chosen to go to the service and the burial, they can walk out of the room or walk away from the grave site if it gets too upsetting to stay there.

As you can see, my mother was allowed to attend the service and the burial. Once again her feelings were saved all these years in her diary. This time it's from 1937.

Grandmother died. And on Wednesday, May 5, my mother's diary read:

> Early in the morning we prepared for the funeral. I went with the family to the chapel. We cried so much, because it was so awful—just losing Grandpa six months ago. I saw her in the casket and she looked lovely, as if she was just sleeping. My friend and her mother were so nice, they watched over me and couldn't refrain from crying too. They felt the same way I did.
>
> We went to the cemetery. It was a horrible sight as Grandma was lowered. It didn't take long and we went home never to see her again. I'll always remember her, she was so sweet to me.

As my mother shared, it can be very difficult to watch a loved one be lowered into a grave. Perhaps that's the part that parents try to protect their children from, by telling them they can't go to the cemetery. That's a very personal decision, and, of course, parents need to know their own child to help them make the decision that will be best for him or her at the time.

But just because it's sad and you may cry and cry doesn't mean you should stay away. You need to learn how to deal with sadness as well as be able to enjoy all the happy things. Just because the experience might upset you doesn't mean it was the wrong decision. As long as you understand what the experience will be like, what you can expect to see, and what you can do if you don't feel like staying to watch, you should be able to handle it.

Death teaches you to appreciate life. My own son had never gone to a cemetery until last year, when he went to his closest friend's grandmother's funeral. At the gravesite in the cemetery, my son watched as the casket was lowered into the ground. The men began to shovel dirt over the casket. And as the casket was almost covered, my son started crying hysterically. I held him close as he continued to watch through his tears. Soon he stopped and just stood there watching in disbelief. He said, "She's gone!"

He was fine after that and said it had never been so clear to him before that when a person dies, he or she is never coming back. Though it was a painful lesson, no book or talk could have given him the understanding he felt from being there. He told me afterward that he wanted to start seeing his own grandparents a little more.

If you want to be a part of the funeral and your parents won't let you, it is important to let them know. You can say, "I know you don't think I'm old enough, but I really want to be there." Or, "Maybe you think I can't handle it, but please don't keep me away. It means a lot to me. If I get upset, I'll walk away or get back into the car. I want to try."

Remind your parents that a funeral is an experience that only happens once for each person. There's no second chance to go if they keep you away. Especially if you're very close with that relative or friend who died, keeping away would be hard and you might not ever forget that you couldn't go. If you're old enough to be reading this right now, you're old enough to talk with your parents about your right to choose.

If you don't want to go, you need to talk about that too.

## A Time for Grief

Usually after someone dies family and friends gather together so they can give each other support and strength, and offer comfort to each other. Neighbors and relatives often bring cookies, cakes, and even whole dinners to help out during this difficult time. This is considered a period of grief or mourning or sorrow.

It's very hard to get used to the idea that someone with whom you have always shared your life is suddenly just not there. Getting used to living without that person will take time.

A close friend of mine whom I have known since elementary school wrote the following to me in a letter after the death of her mother last year: "I'm trying to live and do things as usual, but they really aren't the same. Yes, time does help, and I am slowly coming to grips with the reality. But the hardest part is when something happens and I can't share it with my Mom. There are so many small things that occur that only she would really enjoy, appreciate, and want to hear all the details about.

We kept her very well informed on what was happening in our lives, and now there's no one else to share it with in the same way, no one else's life centered about our family. But, certainly, she had to make the same adjustment in her life, and I will too."

Each person's grief is felt differently. Some may cry for long hours; others may cry only a little; still others may not cry at all. Some people who don't appear to be crying save their tears for when they're alone.

One person might feel up to returning to school or work earlier than another. Someone else may need more time before feeling ready for regular activities.

But the amount of tears is not a sure measure of how much someone cares. And how quickly someone starts doing things that seem quite normal doesn't mean that the hurt isn't inside or that they loved the person any less.

While many people think they should be careful during the mourning period and not mention the name of the person who died, his or her relatives might feel very good thinking back to old memories. Such talk might even make them laugh. They would probably appreciate hearing how much the person they mourn for meant to you.

Don't be surprised if it takes many, many months before things even begin to get back to normal. If you find yourself saying "I should feel better by now," or "I shouldn't feel so sad!" remind yourself that "shoulds" have no place in your thoughts when you're dealing with your feelings. The fact is you do feel sad; you don't feel better. You'll have to get stronger on your own time schedule, no one else's.

Death takes time to get used to. And you never *completely* forget.

## When People Take Their Own Life—or Try

You might be sitting at your lunch table in school one day and hear someone say, "I just feel like killing myself!" If a boyfriend or girl friend has broken up with the person, or the person thinks that he or she is going to get a failing grade in a subject, or there are family troubles at home, it may seem like a natural thing to say. You probably would think nothing of that remark. Most people would let it pass right by.

The problem is some people really mean it. They may want to kill themselves or at least may be thinking about it. Those remarks are really their cry for help, but all too often no one takes them seriously.

When someone takes his or her own life, it's called committing *suicide* (soo-i-side). If a person tries to kill him or herself and fails, then he or she tried to commit suicide or made a suicide attempt. Thousands of young people do this each year (also older people). These are the people who might purposely leave the gas on in their kitchen; or they'll sit in their car, turn it on, and close the garage door, letting the carbon monoxide fumes kill them; or maybe they'll jump off a bridge or out of a window; or maybe they'll swim too far out in rough water. I hope that no one who did this was close to you. The sad thing is that they were close to someone. But he or she may never have known they were so badly in need of help.

Sometimes, people don't really want to end up dead when they attempt suicide, so they may only make a slight cut on their wrists instead of a deep one. Or they may only take some pills in the medicine bottle instead of all of them. Just two weeks ago a girl in the eighth grade in my town was found unconscious in the girls' bathroom at school. The teacher felt she had been out of class too long and sent someone out to look for her. It turned out she had taken several pills from a medicine bottls but not enough to kill her. Just enough to make her blackout and get the message across. Everything about what she did said, "Help me! I'm troubled!"

Some people who only plan to make an attempt at suicide, hoping that someone will find them, accidentally end up dead. For example, if the knife slips and they accidentally cut their wrists too deeply, or if they didn't realize how strong even the few pills would be, or if no one showed up in time to help them, as they had planned.

If you ever hear someone say that they would rather be dead, perk up your ears. It doesn't matter if they are the most popular person in school, the one who makes the most money in business, or the one who is the best looking. It just may be that they're crying out for help. Remember not to be fooled by what looks like confidence on the outside. You never know what they're really feeling on the inside. Any remark that even hints of a death threat is to be taken seriously.

Other perk-up signals might be if they start staying to themselves a lot, if they start to look very sloppy (like they're really not grooming themselves), if they don't care about their school work anymore, or if they're just not hungry each day at lunch.

What might you do? You can pay more attention to the other things they say and do. You can make them feel that you're interested in them. Ask if there's anything they'd like to talk about and tell them you care enough to listen. You might tell them they seem troubled and suggest that they speak to their parents, school counselor, or another trusted adult. There are also crisis hot lines or suicide prevention centers at many places throughout the United States. Looking in your phone directory might help you find services that will guide you to help. (Look under youth, children, mental health, health, social services and so on.)

If you're the one who feels that life isn't worth living, I hope you've learned that you can make a decision to help yourself, even if you think nothing will change. You can decide you're worth it. You can realize if your boyfriend or girl friend doesn't care about you anymore, you have no choice but to go on and find someone else. If your parents are splitting, it's not your fault. If your grades aren't in the high 90s, maybe they never will be. Maybe they don't have to be.

Even if it seems like there's nobody else in the world who cares about you, even if there's no one whom you know you can ask for help, even if you don't think you're worth it, remind yourself that somewhere inside of you is what makes you so special. Your specialness may be so protected and so locked away from years of being too scared to let anyone see it (including yourself), that it may have to be uncovered slowly and carefully, layer by layer, until it's no longer hidden and you can see who you are.

If you're confused, if you don't think you're special enough to be worth saving, then maybe at least you can get yourself angry enough to say, "Why me. That's not fair. I deserve a chance just like anyone else does."

Yes, you do! So, you can go right to your trusty old list of helpers (parents, counselor, youth services, etc.). This time you can also look up local crisis or hot-line phone numbers or even see if there's a suicide prevention center in or near your town.

Remember that going for any kind of help takes strength. You can at least feel good if you decide to try to do something good for yourself. If you think that committing suicide takes strength, just remember that the people who commit suicide might well think death is their answer, their blessing, even if they're not sick. It's much harder to stay around and prove to yourself that it's worth it for you to live. Committing suicide is the chicken way out!

## What About Losing Your Pet?

Neal, age thirteen, shared his feelings about when his dog had to be put to sleep last year.

> I was talking to my mom on the back porch. I don't exactly remember what we were talking about. But I had a funny feeling, and I said to her, "You're not putting the dog to sleep, are you?"
>
> She wasn't really saying anything like that, but I just had feelings about it. She went in to talk with my dad and when she came out, she said they were thinking about it, that the dog was very old, and they thought it was time. I started crying.
>
> My mom said we were going to do it in a week. So I spent a lot of time with my dog that week. I let her do anything she wanted. When we had to take the dog to the vet to be put to sleep, that was dramatic.
>
> When we had gone to the vet before, she never liked it. So as soon as we brought her there, she didn't want to go in. It was like she didn't want to die. The vet told us she would probably be gone by the time we got home.
>
> It took me a while to accept it. I think probably I was kind of like in shock for a while, like I didn't have any feelings about it. I'd say that after three or four months, I kind of started to accept it. But a year from the day she died, I was still crying about it. Not every day. But maybe once a month or something. I think the last time I felt so bad and felt like crying was about two months ago.
>
> I used to come home and expect to have to walk her. Then I realized she wasn't there any more. My parents didn't really say too much. They were basically just there for me. I had a friend who had just gone through the same thing, so that helped a lot.

Pets are almost like people in so many homes. They're loved, cared for, and often spend more time with kids than real people do (especially

368 • GROWING UP FEELING GOOD

parents!). Pets can fill the gap of loneliness; pets won't tell your secrets; pets can be best friends. No matter what kind of pet you have, the feelings of closeness, the attachment, and the love, can be very special.

Even a year after Neal's dog was put to sleep, he had tears from the memories of sharing all those hours together and the sadness of knowing that now his dog can only be a special memory. Even if he gets another dog, it will never be the same as that one.

In the same house with the same pet each person has his or her own feelings. Jeremy, age twelve, told me,

> We had a little cat. She was just a kitten, and she was run over by a car. We were on a trip. And when we got home, my mother and sister just sat on the couch and cried. I just couldn't really figure out why they were doing that. Sure you can be sad, but . . . Now I understand, but it just didn't seem like they needed to cry. They cried for about an hour. It was weird. So I sat at the other end of the couch and just watched them and thought, "What are they doing?"
>
> I don't think I was as close to the cat as my mom. My mom let me pet her every once in a while. But unless we sneaked and quickly petted her, she was really shy and ran away. It was hard to get near her because my mom fed her. They had our neighbors bury her. I asked if I could go down and ask them where they buried her, and they wouldn't let me go down. I couldn't see why. They said they just didn't want to know . . . . They probably threw her in the trash or something!

Just like with people each pet is different, and each relationship is different. One pet may prefer to sit on your lap than on your brother's. Another will run to your sister before anyone else. It often depends upon who spends the time, who feeds, and who really goes out of his or her way to show the pet love. It's not so different with people, is it?

If Neal ever gets a new dog, his parents will be replacing a pet but never the actual dog. No one can exactly replace someone else, they can only take the position they were in. They have to be themselves and create their own place.

That's why when parents think they can just switch one new goldfish for the dead one that they had to flush down the toilet while their child was at school, many little kids will be smart enough to notice that they swoosh their tails a little differently or the spot that was on the fin is no longer there.

Even though parents may be trying to protect their child from sad, hurt feelings, I question whether they're really doing their child a favor. Some parents don't want to deal with it themselves, because they don't know how to handle the feelings with their child.

Maybe besides buying a new goldfish, which can be fun to shop for together, parents could give their children a far greater gift if they allowed them, starting from an early age, to learn to deal with all the kinds of feelings that are so much a part of life, even if it meant that they'd be sad for a while. And that includes dealing honestly with death.

Kids have told me about special canary burials in shoe boxes with candle ceremonies and speeches. They've talked about the funeral service they held before flushing their last goldfish into fish heaven. (Fish rise after flushing, don't they?)

Somehow, when you're included and are even allowed to plan for the funeral, it not only gives you the chance to be at peace with your loss, it gives you practice for when people you care about die too.

## Yet, Life Goes On

Robert, age twenty-nine, said:

No matter how close the person is, ultimately life goes on. You're shattered for a period of time, but life goes on. Death is a life experience. It's kind of strange.

Every once in a while, we'll stop and remember, but there's no time while living to stop for the dead. We mourn for a period and it hurts. And we can't believe someone so close to us has died—or someone our age, a peer, has died. When I was younger and my friend died in the ninth grade, I was totally blown away.

I got a letter from the mother of a girl whom I had dated, telling me that she died. My mouth dropped. Now it's two months later and I passed her name in my phone book the other day. I stopped for a second and I thought about it. But I moved on.

No matter what goes away, what is lost, or how much pain is involved at the time, we have to move on.

Even my mother was amazed to look back in her diary and find that after the death of her grandmother, whom she loved so dearly, she went right on with what she had to do.

On Friday, May 7, 1937, the day after her grandmother's funeral, she wrote: "The family is sitting together again today. Went to school and rehearsed my speech all afternoon. It's going to be a hard fight."

On Saturday, May 8, 1937, she wrote: "Stayed up at Grandma's house and then went to Sonia's store. At night Martin, Lenny, Shirley, Harvey, Marvin, and I made posters for my campaign."

Life has to go on.

# 23
# Being Disabled

> PEOPLE MUST REALIZE THAT
> DISABLED PERSONS HAVE
> THE SAME HUMAN QUALITIES
> AS EVERYONE ELSE, THEY
> SHOULD NOT BE TAKEN
> BY SURPRISED,

"People must realize that disabled persons
have the same human qualities as
everyone else."

Anonymous, age nineteen,
Born with cerebral palsy,
confined to a wheelchair
since birth

## People Come in Many Packages

I like to think of our bodies as being packages. Each package is like a wrapper for the person who's inside. Just like people compare clothes, grades, labels on their jeans, they also compare body packages.

It's amazing to me how much people depend upon someone's package to judge whether or not they even want to say hello. Think about the body packages that you see every day. Imagine your class at school. Can you think of anyone (be honest) who you have never approached simply because you didn't like their package? What did their package look like? What turned you off? Who have you gone up to just because you liked their package, knowing nothing else about them? Did you end up liking the person who was in the package?

Packages come in so many different sizes and shapes. Some people prefer taller packages; others like packages that are short and cute. Some like packages with long, slender legs; others prefer packages with arms that are muscular.

But, what about packages with legs that are slightly bent out of shape and crooked? What about the packages that no longer have any legs? What about packages with hands that are twisted into an odd shape that never changes? What about the packages that can't move by themselves and must sit in a wheelchair each day? What about packages with eyes that don't see, ears that don't hear, nerves that don't feel? What about packages with heads that jerk around out of control? Or, how about the packages that cause the person inside to see certain letters and numbers backward? All of these packages wear the disabled label.

Different disability labels create different feelings, both for the person in the package and for those around them. Disabled labels are the kind nobody runs home to ask their parents to buy. Disabled labels are often lonely labels to wear.

At times disabled packages have a lot of power. Imagine a package having the ability to make people cross the street when they never even planned to go that way. Imagine a package having the ability to make people laugh and tease. Imagine a package having the power to fool people into thinking the person inside doesn't have the ability to love and be a good friend or feel the need to be loved.

All packages, disabled or not, seem to have the power to allow people to feel good or bad about themselves. Too many people don't realize it's

up to them (the person inside the package) to keep reminding themselves that no matter what their outside looks like, no matter how badly
their package is "damaged," they are whole people inside. They can
decide to feel good if they want to. Feeling good comes from each
person's mind and heart, not from their package.

It would also help if people would remind themselves that they are
not their package. They are not their arm; they are not their leg; they are
not their crutch, they are who they are inside. As I said in Chapter 17,
what makes a person beautiful is something you can't see! How sad that
people spend lifetimes feeling so bad about parts of themselves that have
nothing to do with who they are.

Your disabled package is not your fault. While it colors your appearance on the outside, it doesn't have to affect your personality on the
inside. The inside part is up to you.

## Feelings About Being Disabled

Lisa, age seventeen shared:

> I have a mild case of cerebral palsy. When I was born, there was
> not enough oxygen being supplied to my brain, so part of the
> brain cells are not functioning, they kind of died. I have it on my
> right side mostly. My left side is pretty good. [Lisa gets around in
> a wheelchair.]
>
> I have my ups and downs. Sometimes I get depressed be-
> cause of my disability. I used to feel like I was totally different,
> like I was really weird. Though I know there are other people
> worse off than me, sometimes I do get the feelings, Why me?
> Why am I like this? Why can't I be like anybody else?
>
> But then I think there's a reason for me being like this.
> Maybe God saw me as an individual who was strong, that I could
> handle what he was going to put me through. Sometimes I feel
> privileged, because I can now understand what other people feel
> and what they're going through. So I'll never make fun.
>
> There are still times when I don't feel able to accept my
> disability. Sometimes I feel like I could dig a little hole and could
> hide in there. I especially get upset with guys. I really get
> annoyed when they just look at my wheelchair and then they

don't say anything to me. I feel really bad because I want to be like anybody else. I go home and I look in the mirror and wonder, what was he looking at? My face? My chair?

I still have a hard time. Some days are worse than others. But isn't it that way with people who are not disabled, too?

When Lawrence was growing up, he didn't do well in school. His parents kept having him tested, but the tests didn't prove anything. So, the more he tried, the more frustrated he got. His mother told me, "Nobody discovered he had a learning disability. I kept being told that he didn't want to do school work and he was a troublemaker. We were told he should have been doing better.

"As his friends passed him in their learning and as the years kept passing by, everyone got smarter and he felt dumber and dumber and dumber. My son felt he was stupid. 'I can't read,' turned into, 'I don't want to read.' This was then taken as not obeying or a mental attitude rather than a physical problem."

Lawrence was later found to have *dyslexia* (dis-lex-ee-a), a learning disability that caused him to read certain letters and numbers backward. Nobody noticed he was doing that.

Is it any wonder why he had so much trouble reading and doing his work? How sad that he felt so frustrated and bad about himself all those years, when it was really a physical problem that prevented him from learning. It wasn't his fault that his package was pulling switches!

After his disability was discovered, specially trained teachers helped Lawrence catch up in his reading and learning in a way that he could finally understand. His mom told me that he began to feel much more confident about himself and became happier in school.

Michael, age thirty-one, is paralyzed from the waist down. That is called being a *paraplegic* (para-plee-jik). Before the car accident that left him in a wheelchair, his nickname was Shorty. He felt that he wanted to keep on being called Shorty, figuring that anyone who meets someone called Shorty in a wheelchair will never forget him. He shared:

I can't speak for people who have been handicapped since birth. I know that when I first got hurt, I was seventeen. I was Mr. Popularity and was into sports and everything.

At first I didn't want to go out in public, didn't want to go to restaurants, or even back to school. I felt like kind of a freak. People would stare at me, especially little kids. But they were just being honest. It took me a while before I realized it was just human nature for them to be curious and I might have stared, too.

I might have stayed by myself a little longer if I didn't have to go back to school. Being in school forced me to be with a lot of people. I got a lot of support from my family and friends, which helped.

I felt like I was the only one when I was first hurt. All I saw was this long, long road ahead of me. But it's like if someone just throws you in the desert. Do you just lay down and die and let it happen to you? A person has no choice but to try to live.

I started getting over my injury when I went to the rehabilitation center and met other people who were handicapped. As soon as I met someone who had a more severe disability than I had, I realized I have a lot to be thankful for. That's when I started to quit feeling sorry for myself.

After I learned that important lesson and was starting to appreciate what I had instead of being upset about what I didn't have, that's when my life changed and I became valuable to society. My personality also changed back to my normal, fun-loving self. I still seemed to be fairly popular, even though I had a different deck of cards to deal with. It just took more effort on my part to get someone to realize that they might want to be my friend.

A woman who worked with physically disabled children shared, "There was a very attractive fourteen-year-old girl with cerebral palsy. Her legs were a problem more than her arms. She was mainstreamed [that means that she attended regular academic classes with the other kids who were not disabled] in our junior high. There was an eighth grade dance and she really wanted to go. We talked to her about it for a long time. Finally, she decided that she wanted to go in her wheelchair. So she went.

"At the dance she stood up from her wheelchair and moved in place to the music, holding onto somebody who had come over to her, who was one of the chaperones or people in charge. She told me later that he was gorgeous. She was in her glory."

(I'll bet you didn't think that a person in a wheelchair would even care if someone was gorgeous or not.)

Shirley, age sixty-two, shared, "I was a year old when I became ill and lost my sight in one eye. I have learned to live with it. My uncles used to call me the cockeyed kid.

"This really has been a hidden disability. Nobody really knew about it but me. Because I had a popular childhood, it never was a problem for me, except when I wanted to go swimming at camp. If I took off my glasses, my eyes crossed. I was upset that anyone would see them.

"Also, when I was fifteen, I went out with a boy who complained about my glasses, because our glasses clacked when he tried to get close to me. I think I wore them on purpose just so he wouldn't kiss me.

"The only scary thing is getting older. My glasses are getting stronger and stronger. I have heavier and stronger lenses. And if anything happens to my other eye, then I'll be blind. I've been fortunate so far, and have always had an active life. So, I'm only going to think positively about it. So I cope."

Bobby, who was paralyzed from the waist down because of a bullet that wounded him in the Vietnam War, shared: "I've stopped thinking of myself as disabled. It's been so long since I've thought about my disability. . . ."

Bobby, maybe that's the whole point. To have stopped thinking of your disability, you can't be allowing the injustice, the anger, and the resentment of what the war did to you get in the way of continuing with the rest of your life. It means that you've come to accept yourself as you are even though you had a package change.

The bullet may have injured your spine, but it couldn't get deep enough to scar who you are unless you let it. You are still the special person that you always were when you were able to run around without your wheelchair.

I guess the main difference is that you have to do what you normally did in a different way. So, instead of walking, you move in your chair. But you still drive a car; you still get out and go where you want to go. Even if you go a little slower (which I understand, you don't!), you still get there with your wheelchair. You still have your same needs, and you still have your dreams. If your old dreams are no longer possible, you've got the power to create new ones. And you can love and relate to people as you always did.

Shorty, too, was able to accept his car accident and resulting disability as something that can't be changed. Since he doesn't have the power to put the feeling back into his legs, he concentrates on putting all the feeling he can into life: not only for himself, his wife, and other family members, but also for many children and adults who are also disabled one way or another. He's teaching them how they can go on camping trips, travel down river, or even climb mountains if they allow themselves to.

Ann, who used to be a marathon jogger before her car accident and who is now paralyzed from the middle of her back down, works in the physical education department of a college. She plays racketball in her chair, mountain climbs in her chair, goes disco dancing in her chair (and even banged her nose a few weeks ago while dancing because she fell out of her chair), and doesn't see her disability as an obstacle to anything she wants to do.

Lisa never knew herself as anything but disabled (she has had cerebral palsy since birth). She, too, has had to work at accepting herself and has tried to do as much as she can to live each day fully. She's in student council, home economics club, and on the hockey team at her school. She'd like to be an actress, a model, or a lawyer.

More and more people who have a physical disability are doing physical activities that they themselves and their families and friends might never have thought possible. When they get *disabled* out of their heads, so many things are possible.

And, you try not to be bitter about how unfair life can be. The amazing thing is that what you believe is unfair (like if you suddenly have a package change and can't do things the way you used to), you never know until it happens whether it may be just the thing that will push you to accomplish what you never would before. Even if you can't walk.

Once you accept yourself and your package, the only disability left to deal with is in your mind!

## Accepting Yourself and Your Package

Whether disabled since birth or disabled because of an accident or illness when you're younger or older, the key seems to be the ability to accept yourself and your package. Lisa, Shorty, Bobby, and Ann have clearly come to accept their packaging, each in their own way. Their personal strength continues to prove that no matter what, you go on.

According to Bobby:

> Not everybody adjusts to disability well. Some people find it a devastating [de-va-stay-ting: disastrous, awful, horrible] blow from which they really don't fully recover. Others find it the kind of a blow that consistently hampers [continues to get in the way of] their pursuit of a happy and rewarding life. And others basically take it as just one of the many different kinds of problems that you encounter in life.
>
> I don't know what the trick is in trying to figure out who will or who will not be able to adjust well to various types of disabilities. I've seen some of my friends who I would have thought would be the strongest become disabled and commit suicide because they couldn't handle it. I've seen people who seemed like they'd never get it together become the best adjusted of all. Even with those who adjusted very well, it's important to realize that this doesn't happen overnight.
>
> In my case [Bobby is paralyzed from the waist down because of a bullet that wounded him in the Vietnam War], it took years of getting to know myself, and getting to know my body, to really come to terms with what had happened. For the first couple of years that I was disabled, my main concern was regaining as much of the use of my body as I could in as normal a functioning way as possible.

Support, lots of love, understanding and acceptance from family and friends is very important in helping a person overcome his or her disability. Michael shared, "It's really important to force yourself to be with other people."

Said Bobby, "Family support needs to balanced. You need a family that's there to assist you when you need help, but you also need a family that's there to give you a little kick in the pants when you need that, too. The most damaging factor can sometimes be those that are overly protective and those that respond with pity and sympathy. They're well meaning but they can kill you with their kindness."

It's important for family and friends to realize that the person who must adjust to disability (or any kind of life change) needs an outlet for feelings. They need to be able to talk openly with people who care enough to listen. And, if he or she screams and yells more than usual, it would help for others to realize that may be their way to get anger and frustration out. As Shorty told me, "It's like a tea kettle that you can't hold in. You've got to let off the steam. It's good to cry sometimes."

Bobby shared, "I think in the end, what helps an awful lot is just to realize what you are, what you're capable of, stop dwelling on what's beyond your reach and to relieve some of the frustration in life by making goals that you can obtain."

## Feelings About Being Disabled Shared by Those Who Are Not

Jen, age twelve, said, "There was a girl with a disability in my second- and third-grade class. I don't remember her too well, but when other people made fun of her, sometimes I'd try to be friends. And then people would make fun of me because I was being her friend. Then I'd try to avoid her and I'd always feel guilty about this."

Isn't it interesting that having a friendship with someone who is disabled can create the same type of peer pressure situation as being friendly with someone unpopular and not disabled? The difference is that the disabled person doesn't even have to do anything to become unpopular. All they have to do is appear.

Fran, age ten, said, "I saw a guy with one leg using one crutch who was dancing with this girl right in the middle of the dance floor. I thought it was great that he could dance and everything. It was kind of gross to look at his pants hanging, but . . ."

Christina, age eighteen, shared, "Because my sister is handicapped, my mother always used to take her side when we were having a fight."

Timmy, age twelve, said, "Well, the people with artificial arms, like plastic arms, at least they could use it like their fake arm was a regular one. As long as you're alive, that's what's important."

Pamela, age eleven, said, "I'd rather be deaf than blind. Because, what if I never saw my parents? There's more to see in this world than there is to hear. Don't you think so? Wouldn't you rather see someone than hear someone?"

(Do you agree or disagree with Pamela?)

Barry, age fourteen, told me, "I can't stand looking at retarded people. It gets me sick."

Sean, age twelve, said, "My sister has cerebral palsy. I help take care of her when my parents aren't home. I have to watch out for her when she's sitting in her wheelchair in front of our house because sometimes the kids are mean.

"She says some very funny things, but it's hard to listen to her because the words sound like she's speaking in a space tunnel. It takes so long for her to say something, but I can understand her. The only thing that bothers me is when saliva runs down the side of her mouth."

Andrea, age eleven, shared:

When I was in the fourth grade, a girl in my class had a learning disability. My teacher favored her. She wasn't crippled or anything. She was a normal person but she needed help in talking. She just talked and slurred. So she was normal except for that.

On the playground, she would kick people and call them names and then run to the teacher and tell and lie and get the other kids in trouble.

When I was at a pancake restaurant with another friend and her family, we saw D there. We didn't look at her because we hated her. So on Monday in school she told the teacher that we weren't talking to her over the weekend, and we got in trouble.

Then five girls asked to talk to the teacher. We told her about this girl and how she acts. The teacher said, "Well, she has a problem. And we just have to help her and try to ignore it." And it was really annoying because D would stand there smiling.

I think she used her handicap to get whatever she wanted.

David, age nine, talked about a boy who has a speech problem. He said, "Everybody knows this boy is very smart. Sometimes we talk about how smart he is. People don't like him because he always acts funny in class and laughs at everything. And he talks out loud when he's not supposed to. But everyone knows he's very smart.

"Whenever he slurs or stutters and someone laughs, everyone tells them to shut up and that he can't help it. Everyone knows how he acts and tries not to let the other kids make fun of him, because he can't help it. One time no one made fun of him. But it took him about twenty minutes to read one or two pages."

Neal, age thirteen, said, "There are certain people who are physically disabled. Some of them have become friends with kids who aren't disabled, and they're recognized as being nice. They're just normal and accepted.

"There are other people with physical disabilities who are discriminated [separated or set apart] against and singled out. The other people seem to be more popular and happy. The ones who are singled out seem to be shy.

"I kind of got to know the person and I felt, not having anything to do with their disability, that I didn't want to be friends with them. They're attitude toward life was a little different than mine."

Neal continued, "In terms of mental disability there's a boy at our school who is really treated like dirt. He's very close to his family, I feel, because he doesn't have too many friends. When you don't have too many friends, you turn to your family. He has a very understanding, nice family.

"Many people ridicule [make fun of] him. Because of this he isn't athletic; he's not in any sports, and he's really not recognized as a nice person, even though he is really kind."

Maybe you or someone you know has had many of these feelings. It may be more or less comfortable for you to look at and be near a person's package, depending upon his or her disability. But perhaps a change of approach would help. Maybe, instead of looking at what they're not, you can try looking at what they are. Look for the good in each package.

For example, instead of dwelling on the leg that's not there, or the pant leg that's swaying empty in the air, why not concentrate on all the rest of the person's package that's filled in. Instead of being turned away by saliva, look past that part of the package to the expression in their eyes. Try to reach in and touch the person inside.

I don't pretend that changing your approach will always be easy. But just keep reminding yourself there's a person inside each package. Their package isn't who they are.

So often someone who first appears unattractive or even ugly can grow to be more and more beautiful as you get to know the person. And, of course, someone who might make you swoon from his or her outside beauty can turn out to be yucky, rotten, and very unattractive once you take a closer look inside.

George, age thirty-four, said, "Last year I met someone who was a paraplegic (paralyzed from his waist down). It was the first time I had any real contact with someone who had to stay in a wheelchair. It was very strange for me because I love to jog. I had to catch myself from saying, 'Last night when I was running,' or 'After I leave here, I'm going to run,' or making any mention at all about what I took for granted. As it turned out, the hang-up was mine and not his. And as we got more friendly, I found out it was okay to talk about anything I wanted, and now he's a very valued friend."

A word about guilt: maybe sometimes we feel so guilty that we're okay and they're not that we hold ourselves back from talking about things that we normally would. We especially hold back talking about activities that we think the person who is disabled can't or might have difficulty doing. We think they might feel upset, hurt, pity for themselves, or even rejected.

Our problem is that when we don't say what we feel, because it's real for us (like our love for jogging or our achievements in physical activities, such as the way we beat out the other person playing tennis in four sets), what we end up doing is giving the person with the disability the message that they can't possibly relate to our experience.

If you don't tell the person the truth about your feelings, they can sense (nonverbal communication) that you're not telling them the truth, that you're holding back. That's when they feel hurt, rejection, and pity.

So this is a long-winded way of telling you not to censor your conversation. Say what you would say anyway. You'll be a lot closer for it.

One more thing: some people have more than one disability in the same package. But just because they appear to not be able to control their muscles, it doesn't mean they can't hear or answer a question, even if you'll have to be patient as the sounds very slowly, sometimes with great difficulty, form words.

As Lisa said, "I hate it when people ask 'How's Nancy?' and she'll be sitting right there." Henry said, "When people see my crutches, they yell in my ear and think I'm deaf!"

## Disabled Doesn't Have To Mean Mentally Retarded

Though a body package may appear twisted, shaky, have to remain in a wheelchair, and lets out grunts instead of words, the person hidden inside may be beautiful and bright. The problem is too many people think that such a package means the person inside is mentally retarded. Very often that's just not true.

A person who is mentally retarded also needs love and friendship, is able to share love with others, and can be very special. My point is simply to make sure you understand that you can't make judgments about people because of what they look like.

One of the most meaningful movies I have shown my college classes for many years is one about a young man and woman who have cerebral palsy. Both must move around in wheelchairs. Both enjoy a very special, loving relationship with each other. I never got the feeling that they felt sorry for themselves. They didn't want pity from anyone else either. All they wanted was to be accepted and treated as equals, instead of being stared at and thought of as being so different.

Her speech was pretty easy to understand, but he had trouble getting sounds out. In fact, he could barely count to five. Because he's in a wheelchair, his speech is so garbled, and he jerks his head around a lot, someone looking at him might think he's retarded. But in one of the scenes when he sat in front of his typewriter and slowly tapped each key with the only finger that wasn't in a permanent fist, he typed beautiful, sensitive poetry that brought tears to my eyes.

It wasn't his fault that he was a prisoner of his package. Yet, people are so quick to judge. And they're quick to stay away. And they're quick to decide that their normal package means they're better. And they can't imagine that such a package has any feelings or need for love. And they can't imagine that someone so crippled could possibly give love and even enjoy sex. They imagine wrong.

What did you do and how did you feel the last time you saw someone wearing a disabled label? If you wear one yourself, what feelings do you get from people when they're with you?

## Disability Isn't Catching—Feelings and Attitudes Are

Said Henry, an actor and comedian, who contracted polio when he was four (he walks with leg braces and uses crutches): "Attitudes are the real disability. Nobody wants to be around a disabled person. Society will take care of us, but they don't want us. They need to understand that disability isn't a disease. It's not catching. People who are disabled are not considered sick."

Where do these attitudes and feelings come from? They come from parents, the media (television, movies, newspapers, radio), friends, school. We also get messages from the person who is disabled. Depending upon how withdrawn, angry, accepting, or full of life the disabled person is, his or her message may be negative or positive, weak or strong, or somewhere in between.

Starting when children are very young, they seem to learn to stay away from disabled people. They're taught that the disabled person is different, or not our kind.

When you were little, do you ever remember when you saw someone in a wheelchair, or on crutches, with one arm, or with only part of an arm? If you said to your parents, "Oh, look, Mommy or Daddy, that woman has only half an arm!" did they say, "Yes, she must have been sick or had an accident. Or maybe she was just born that way. But even though her arm looks a little different, it doesn't mean that she's different. She might be very nice. But you'd have to get to know her to find out."

Or did they say, "Come along, we don't want to get too close. You'd better not talk to her. Leave her alone." Message: she's different. If your parents are uncomfortable with any disability, they might have passed that discomfort on to you. If they have negative feelings, they might have passed their feelings on to you.

And so the attitude begins. It can grow stronger as a child gets older. And it's fed by so many different things. The media so often present the disabled as being weak and very helpless. That makes many people feel

sorry for them and feel that they're doing their part if they pat a few disabled heads!

Said Henry, "People are so aware of what we can't do. They should look at what we can do! People with disabilities can adapt; they can adjust. They must adapt if they want to live." Henry plays baseball, flies airplanes, goes bowling, and swims a mile every day. He does all this, and more, even with his leg in braces and crutches. He's comfortable with himself. He's stopped wishing that he'll get better every time he blows out his birthday candles. He accepts himself and is very independent. How absurd that some people can look at him and only think of him as a cripple.

Shorty, too, feels, "Most people are unaware of what people with handicaps can do. They have a conception [image, idea] that people who are handicapped need help with every curb, help with every door."

The problem is too many disabled people actually believe the weak image that's presented by the media. The helpless attitude is very strong. It can trick disabled people into thinking that they're supposed to be weak. So a person who must walk with crutches or move in a wheelchair might say, "I'm crippled, I can't do anything."

An eight-year-old girl who walks with crutches went up to Henry and said, "Do you feel handicapped? I don't!" How wonderful that she can realize at an early age that just because she has a disability doesn't mean she has to feel different. Disabled people need to understand that weakness is a choice—so is strength. Isn't that true for everybody?

If you're disabled (or know someone who is) and are not feeling very good about yourself and your life, you can check my usual list of helpers (parents, counselors, teachers, youth services) and add to it local chapters of organizations that deal specially with different kinds of disabilities.

If you can't find a chapter near you, have someone help you write a letter to or call a chapter in the nearest large city. You can also try to find out the national address or telephone number. (Sometimes those national numbers are toll-free 800 numbers and can be found by asking a telephone operator for 800 information).

It's normal to be scared or confused or angry or resentful. It's also normal to feel that you might not be so useful to yourself, your family, and society in general. But you don't have to stay with those feelings. And you don't have to handle them alone. There are things you can do and many people you can talk with who can help you if you just push yourself to find them. You can choose not to let your disability limit you more than you must. Sometimes it's hard to find the "right" someone to help you (this goes for any kind of help for problems). If one person can't help you, keep trying to find another. If it doesn't feel good to speak to one person, go on to the next, or, if you can, let them know what you're feeling, so they can learn to be more sensitive to your needs.

If you're calling for help, try not to be frustrated if you're told to call several different telephone numbers. One phone call can often lead to another and another until you get the right person in the right place.

Push yourself not to give up. You're worth it!

## Another Attitude to Clear Up

Many people feel that because someone is disabled, he or she does not have the ability to enjoy and share sexual feelings. That's not true. Some even believe that having a disability prevents you from being able to have a child. Though certain people cannot, there are many disabled people who can, even if they're paralyzed. Also, many disabled boys and men are able to have erections or partial erections. Many disabled girls and women can feel genital sensations on the vulva and in the vaginal canal, and many can reach orgasm.

As you already know, there are many different ways to share sexual feelings. A couple may choose to kiss, hold hands, touch, hug, and even make love (have sex) if they feel they are ready.

Whether disabled or not each touch, each feel, each kiss, is going to be different for each person. There is no one way to do any of these things. And there's certainly no right way. It's up to each person to decide if what they share seems right and feels good to them. And if what's shared doesn't feel so wonderful one time, people can teach each other what might feel better the next time. It is important to talk about those feelings.

I think the attitude that disabled people don't need or want such closeness might come from the false package messages that so many people believe. To look at certain packages one might wonder not only if that person has such feelings, but also how could they possibly share them even if they wanted to? Fair question.

It would take too long for me to start listing each disability and how sharing can be accomplished. But I feel it will be enough for you to understand that people who are disabled can learn new ways to feel good with each other. They can find new tingly spots if the other ones no longer have feeling.

Since the ability to feel love and closeness (also called intimacy) is always able to be felt inside, all people who are disabled need to work on is how their packages can share these feelings with each other.

No matter how many parts of a person's package have no feeling, the inside feelings, needs, and wants can be very sensitive. A person never stops feeling inside, no matter how they're born or what accident or illness strikes. Inside needs are the same for everybody, no matter what the outside package.

I'll never forget a program I saw when I was a child. A man had been in an accident and could not move any part of his body. He was completely paralyzed. As a close relative of his was sitting next to his bed, crying and feeling very pained by what had happened to him, the camera zoomed close to his face and showed that a tear had dropped out of his eye! He couldn't speak, he couldn't move, he couldn't communicate in any way, his package couldn't feel, but he could feel inside. And he cried.

So how can that inside feeling be expressed when someone is paralyzed, has lost a limb, has hands that are always in a fist, or cannot see? If people can't move one limb, they'll move another. If they can't touch with their hands, they'll feel with their feet, their arms, or just their elbows. If they can't see with their eyes, they'll "see" with their hands. If there's no hand to touch, they'll touch whatever part of the package is there to touch. If they can't have sex with their sexual organs, they'll have sex with their hands or whatever.

Sex is not just "penis meets vagina." Sex can be the most special, close sharing of feelings between people. Just to be able to crawl out of a wheelchair or take off your braces, hug someone very close, touch them with any part that feels, and have your lips meet can be a sexual sharing. Sexual desires stir from inside.

Be careful how you judge people who are disabled. Even though their outside "package" may be different than yours, their inside feelings and needs can be the same.

## When a Child Is Disabled, Parents Often Overprotect

According to Ruth, mother of two disabled children, "There's a human part of the breast that reaches out for the ones who can't do things for themselves." She talked about the frustrations, the pain, the over-whelming burdens, tremendous needs, and always the affection and love for her children.

So often parents of a child who is disabled have the tendency to be overprotective. Ruth talked with me about this and was very aware of not being that way. But she agreed that too many parents are. It's almost a natural tendency because, as parents, the concern is to take care of your child no matter what. If a parent sees a child's disability as a weakness, then it's possible they'll smother the child with care. And as much as the smothering might feel safe for the moment, eventually children who are disabled become grown-ups. If they've never had practice being inde-pendent then what?

Sometimes parents are overprotective because they feel so guilty. They may think the disability was their fault. But also a parent might be truly afraid that his or her child will get lost, just not know how to get on a bus, or be taken advantage of or abused.

According to Jane, who teaches children with learning disabilities, "Parents also deny. They'll do as much denying as the children some-times. For whatever reason they'll often say, 'My child doesn't really have a problem. They're just lazy.' That puts a great burden on the child who is trying very, very hard but finds it difficult to do better."

Jane also feels that parents need to allow children to make mistakes, even if they fall on their faces, to prove to themselves that they can get back up again. Ruth agrees. She shared, "Only if children are permitted to make the errors, can they begin to learn the skills that will make them independent, eventually . . . at least to the extent that they can be."

Parents, too, must work harder at accepting what they know they cannot change. In all my conversations with people who have many different types of disabilities, the one thing that all of them agree about is the need for parents to balance giving their child the room to grow and attempt to be as independent as is possible while still providing the security that is so important.

If your parents are being overprotective (whether you are disabled or not), it is very important for you to: first, recognize that they are being overprotective; second, understand it's out of love, or perhaps guilt or the fear that you can't do it for yourself; third, find some private time so that you can talk with them about all these feelings and the need for you to try, however slowly, to learn to rely on yourself as much as possible.

Shared Henry: "Love, affection, strength. . . . A child needs that. And a child can sense that parents are comfortable with them, or whether they feel guilty.

"Parents have to give a disabled child more so that child will be able to compete. If the child can't use his or her legs, they should be encouraged to develop their arms.

"When I was sixteen, I traveled by plane to Mexico by myself. I went to school for the summer. I wouldn't be as independent as I am today without my parents being the way they are."

Shared Lisa: "When I come home, it's just me and my mom. If it wasn't for her, I wouldn't be physically where I am now. She's the one who said, 'You got to do this, You got to do that.' "

Shared Michael:

Overprotection from parents is the worst. It's the reason that many handicapped kids grow up immature and unaware. It's easy for parents to protect them to such an extent that they never leave their mother's apron.

One of the best things that can happen is that parents get tired of dealing with their child's attitude [being spoiled or expecting the world to treat you like family] and allow them to grow and learn on their own. There's just too much love, too much protectiveness. You have to get in the street and have to learn how to live.

You have to learn who to trust and who not to trust, what is real, what is phony, what is the truth, what is false, what is love, and what is pity. There are a lot of lessons to be learned in the street. And it's too easy to retreat back to your mother or father's open arms.

## Being Disabled, Being Challenged

As I said in the beginning of this chapter, after a person accepts him or herself and package, then the only disability left to deal with is their mind. I meant it!

It all boils down to attitude, beliefs, self-confidence, not allowing your disability to beat you, and accepting that you cannot change. It's realizing that if you can't paint by holding a brush in your hands, you can hold it in your teeth or in your toes. If you can't learn to be a brain surgeon, you can be a heck of a good auto mechanic. And it doesn't matter what your sisters, brothers, and friends are capable of doing. They're not you!

If you can't learn as you'd wish, then you can go as far as you can go, understanding and accepting your own limits and not hating yourself for something you can't control. You can learn to make lists and get things ready the night before school to help you organize your thoughts and remember what you have to do. You can learn to communicate how you feel when your parents, teachers, or friends compare you to anyone but yourself.

If you can't walk on your feet, you can walk on your crutches or "walk" on your wheelchair. If you can't express yourself in words, you can press one key at a time on a typewriter or learn sign language.

People who are disabled can do so many of the same things as others who are not; they just have to do them differently. Henry doesn't even like referring to himself as disabled. He'd rather say he's "differently able!" You, too, can still enjoy activities that fit your ability. You can probably do more than you think you can do, perhaps even more than anyone has told you would be possible. And you can still dream.

It will help to understand that your parents, friends, and teachers may try to prevent you from following your dreams. Think carefully about what they advise, talk with them about any concerns, and begin to separate their imagined fears from what could be real.

Lisa (she wants to be an actress, model, or lawyer) told me: "What gets me the most is when people will tell me, 'Oh, you can't do that; you're in a wheelchair. What actress do you know who's in a wheelchair? What model do you know?'

"A guy who talked at our school was from a place where they give jobs to the handicapped. He said, 'You just got to make people see the way

you are.' I was asking him about being a lawyer because he went to law school at one point. He told me not to be surprised if people tell me I can't even reach the books! He said not to get hung up on those people who don't feel you can do it.

"When people tell me I can't do it, that makes me want to do it ten times as hard."

Shorty shared:

I'm trying to change the attitudes of the public and also the attitudes of those people who are handicapped. This is no small job. I like challenges. I like to do activities in the outdoors, like camping, scuba diving, and boating. To me, it's a real adventure.

That's why I'm putting all my efforts into sharing these adventures with other people who have physical disabilities. The outdoors opens up a whole new world for the handicapped.

I have told other people, "What's a city curb when you've crawled through the swamp?" If you've been through the woods crawling on your butt trying to get over a creek, the city curbs are not that frustrating anymore.

On the other hand it's confusing to me why city curbs and other barriers were ever built by man in the first place. There are moments when I think the nondisabled are plotting against us!

But the laws are slowly changing. As days go by, more bathrooms are being built that are easier for the disabled to get to, more buildings have ramps for our wheelchairs and crutches, and more parking lots have wider spaces. There are all sorts of changes taking place in the buildings of our country, so that we can be part of society instead of outside society.

# 24
# School

School can mean friendship, rushing to your locker in between classes, "Yo, what's up?" in the halls, learning about worlds you didn't even know existed, football games, homework, meeting in the bathroom seventh period, lunch lines, after-school sports, sitting next to your best friend in English, and checking to see who gets breasts first.

School can mean bake sales, class trips, detention, locker rooms, new math examples, passing notes, pom-poms, concerts, having a crush on the new art teacher, late passes, election campaigns, exams, track meets, and going down to the nurse.

But it can also mean being teased every time you get on the school bus, standing alone at recess, being yelled at for something you really didn't do, cutting classes, loneliness, being sent to the principal's office, hearing a rumor spread about you in the halls, being suspended, being put down for how you dress, being told "me and my friends will be waiting to kick your butt after school," being picked on by your teacher, failing. It just depends. . . .

School is a blending of so many things. Besides learning facts, school teaches you about responsibility, about your ability to achieve, how you relate to teachers (adults) and make friendships. School also has a lot to do with how you feel about yourself. Like whether you feel confident, shy, afraid to try, smart, or dumb.

This chapter will give you a chance to think about the feelings that you have about you, your teachers, and the many different parts of your life at school.

Just like your family feelings weren't from today, neither are your school feelings. Looking back to your earliest school days will give you a clue as to why you may feel so good, so awful, or so-so about going to school now.

You might want to grab a piece of paper so that you can write down past school experiences that you remember made you feel good as well as those you wish you could forget. After taking a good look at your list you can begin to see more clearly how you school history might have influenced the attitudes and feelings you have today. Here are some questions that will help you remember some of your feelings:

Did you like school? Dislike school? Not care one way or another?
Were you praised a lot? Punished a lot? Teased?
Did you like your school work?
Did you find you could learn easily or was learning a struggle?
Did your teachers think you were smart, average, or maybe a little
     below the rest of the class?
Did you ever read from the blue book while everyone else was on the
     red?
Did you feel your teachers liked you?
Did you have a lot of friends at school?
Did your teachers put gold stars and "Good Try!" on your work?
Did they crumple up your papers a lot and say you should do them
     over?
Did any teacher ever hug you?
What were your feelings?
How do you feel about school now?

If you still have your family feelings list (if not, you might want to make a new one), see whether your feelings at home were similar to your school feelings during the same years.

Before we talk about teachers and classes and all the other school-type things, I'd like you to understand why we really can't talk about school feelings without mentioning family feelings. I'd also like to make sure you realize that if your family feelings aren't good, you can still have good school feelings.

## Family Feelings Can Influence School Feelings

There are many ways in which your school feelings might be influenced by your family feelings. For example:

> If your parents always expect you to get high grades, you might always be pressured in school.

> If your parents and grandparents have never gone to school, and you're the first one in your family to be able to attend, you might feel a lot of pressure because you want them to be proud and may feel like you'd be letting them down if you don't do well.

> If your family is having troubles, it can be hard to concentrate in school.

> If there's a lot of competition within your family about how well you do and how well your sister or brother has done, you may end up working harder, or you may resent all the pressure and just decide to stop trying.

> If you have to take on a lot of responsibilities at home, as much as you care about school, it may be very hard to spend time on your work.

> If you have no (or very little) privacy at home, it may be very hard to concentrate on your work.

> If. . .

You can add your own experiences and feelings to this list. The main thing is that you get the idea that there is a connection.

When your family feelings are good, and you know your family accepts you for who you are, and you know they'll help you when you need it and will give you support and encouragement and love you, even if you screw up on your report card, then you have much more freedom to try.

If your family puts pressure on you, doesn't feel what you're trying to do is important, or is just not there, then it's harder.

But, no matter what, you are the one who will walk through those school doors in the morning. You are the one who will sit in your classes. You are the one who has the chance to speak with teachers, or nurses, guidance counselors, or school social workers or school psychologists, if need be, in order to go forward in a way that feels good to you. You need not be held back by a family who's insensitive to how much school can mean or how important it is to be free to achieve at your own level.

I'm not saying that any of this is easy. I'm only suggesting that you have more control than perhaps you think you have. You have more choices. You don't have to sit back and be miserable and say, "Look what everyone is doing to me. I can't help it! How can I work? How can you expect me to try?"

I'm suggesting that you can help it. There are enough people at your school who will help you help it. But first you have to make the decision that you care enough about yourself to want to take the first step and let the people who can help you know you want to try.

## All Different Kinds of Teachers

One of the most important parts of school is being able to get along with all kinds of teachers. You never know who you're going to get and how they'll act with you, no matter what kind of stories you've heard.

I will never forget how scared I was on the first day of school in the eighth grade. Everyone had told me what a horrible, scary person my homeroom teacher was. So I walked in expecting to see a monster! Well, she wasn't warm and wonderful, but she wasn't a monster. She was at least fair and didn't really bother me. She just wasn't the kind of teacher who you felt like hugging. But she also wasn't as awful as everyone told me she would be.

It really boils down to how *you* relate to your teacher. The person who tells you how rotten he or she is might have really misbehaved in class, been fresh, not worked very hard. Or the teacher might really be rotten, but you're better off deciding that for yourself.

Throughout your years in school you'll have so many different teachers, each with their own personalities, their own styles of teaching, their own rules, their own ways of getting you to work harder. Some will be exciting, some will be okay, some will be booor-ing. It would be unfair to expect every single teacher to be terrific.

However, teachers are hired to teach, not to entertain or love you. Some have warmth and some don't. Though it can be wonderful to be fond of your teacher, it's more important to realize that you are in class to learn. As long as a teacher is fair and teaches the subject he or she is supposed to teach, that's all you can hope for. The smiles and affection are gravy!

But, no matter how little control you have over who your teacher is or what he or she is like, you *do* have control over your behavior and work effort in each of your classes. It will help you a lot if you can try to do the best you can, even if you are not as happy as you might be with a particular teacher. It will help if you try to deal with each teacher as he or she *is* rather than waste your time and energy expecting them to be who they are not.

Remember: If you feel that a teacher is not treating you fairly, speak up! Share your feelings with that teacher as he or she may not even realize how their actions are affecting you.

If your teacher won't listen or continues to treat you in a way that doesn't feel good and may even cause you to have bad feelings about coming to school, it's important to talk about this with your parents. They can try to discuss these feelings with your teacher (with or without you present). If there is still no change, they can approach the guidance counselor or the principal of your school in the hopes that changes will be made for the better.

## Teacher Power

Teachers have an incredible amount of power. Imagine a teacher being able to stare at a child and make that child go to the bathroom in his or her pants. Imagine a teacher having the power to keep a child from opening his or her mouth for a whole school year. Imagine a teacher having the power to make a child have stomachaches and vomit almost every morning. Imagine a teacher having the power to rob a child of his or her confidence and self-respect.

But some teachers have the power to make a child believe in him or herself for the first time. Some teachers have the power to make a child trust that somebody really cares. Some teachers have the power to make a child feel warm and safe. Some teachers have the power to stimulate, to challenge, to encourage a child to learn and achieve in a most exciting way.

It just depends. Perhaps you'll understand even better what I mean by teacher power after reading through the following experiences.

Because Samantha was editor of her junior-high-school year book, she had the freedom to wander the halls and collect interesting stories and tidbits about the students and teachers. She could also take pictures when she wanted to. Because much of her wandering took place during class time, many hall moniters came to know who she was, and she never needed a pass.

One day when a teacher asked her for a pass, Samantha answered, "Don't you know who I am?" And he said, "No, and you're going to the office!"

Mrs. L., the guidance counselor, scolded Samantha and told her that she would continue to get a U in behavior. (Even though she was a fine student academically and got good grades, she talked too much.) She also said that if Samantha continued her conduct, she wouldn't amount to much in life. On any day that Samantha was sick from school, the guidance counselor would call her home to check to see if she was really sick.

Said Samantha, "She made me feel stupid, unworthy, incapable of doing a good job in junior-high school and high school, because she made me wonder if I was really a bad person because I had a big mouth. Sometimes teachers and guidance counselors really don't know you at all. And they can really hurt."

Teachers have the power to make false judgments, confuse, reduce confidence, and question ability.

Diane works part time in a fast-food restaurant so that she can help pay for college. She and one of the guys were preparing food and singing. She turned to him and said, "Hey, you have a nice voice! Do you want to come Christmas caroling with a group of us after work?" He told her, "No, thanks. I never sing in public or with groups, ever since my third grade teacher told me that my voice was too loud when the class sang."

Teachers have the power to silence.

Hal, age fifteen, shared, "We have this one teacher who is really great. Any time we have a problem, we know he'll listen. We can go to him after school and talk for hours. A few weeks ago my girl friend's group of friends had a huge fight. Everyone decided that they should go to this teacher so he could help them settle it. They stayed talking for about three hours after school and everyone felt better."

Teachers have the power to listen, offer guidance, and to be there and show they care.

George, age thirty-four, told me about a language teacher he had in high school. Said George, "He would totally try to intimidate [threaten, scare] people. He made me scared to even ask a question because he'd yell at anybody who didn't know the answer and would make that person feel stupid.

"He had profound impact [big influence] on my learning ability for foreign languages. He was such a bad teacher. He was more like a clown in a show. Instead of encouraging me to learn, he instilled fear. He definitely turned me off foreign languages."

Teachers have the power to turn-off. (So often it's the teacher who turns a student off, not the topic. It's just too bad that the student doesn't always realize this difference at the time.)

Robert, age twenty-eight, shared: "I had an English teacher in high school who was an absolute tyrant. He led the class by totally scaring the death out of the students and embarrassing them. He was very bright, but he was really sick! He loved to embarrass people in front of everybody. He would stand a girl with a large chest up on one of the desks and ask the class, 'How does this girl remind you of a merchant ship [a ship that carries cargo and goods to people]?' He failed me. He hated me. If he hated you, there was no way to get around it. It was almost impossible to do well."

Teachers have the power to embarrass, to scare, to take all the joy out of learning, to make someone not even try for fear of failing.

Lisa, age thirteen, told me; "I have this teacher who goes out of his way to bust on you [make jokes on you]. He usually chooses one person every year who he picks on the most. This year it's me and one other girl.

"There are some people who don't have to work hard to get good grades. I work my butt off. I spent the whole weekend at the library, was up working until one o'clock one night, and when I turned in my paper, he said, 'I'm surprised you had time to do it because you're always so busy shopping.' "

Teachers have the power to frustrate.

Paul, age twenty-three, said, "My English teacher in college really cared so much. She gave so much of herself, was so patient. I really struggled and stretched myself to do as well as I could. It was a real positive experience. She was the first teacher who took that kind of time to teach me. She was very happy when I did well."

Teachers have the power to encourage, to strengthen confidence, to motivate (stimulate you to want to learn).

A seventeen-year-old girl shared:
This is something that's not easy for me to say. I quit school. I had a lot of problems in high school. Teachers were always trying to tell me something was wrong with me. I never was interested in what they were teaching.

The teachers sat up there like they were kings and queens and would treat me like I was dirt. The kids that were interested in school and were looked at as smart, were treated better. But the kids that were not as school oriented [not as inclined toward school, didn't like it as much, weren't interested] were shunned and shut off. I felt I was treated so badly during high school. That's why I quit.

The school was trying to tell my father that I need psychiatric help. Anything I did, even the slightest thing, they would kick me out and suspend me. They didn't handle me right. They said all these things about me that weren't true.

The best thing I did was drop out. I recently got my high school equivalency diploma [diploma that's equal to a high school diploma, but earned at home, not by going to school] and I'm doing well now. I'm going to start going to college soon.

I like doing things slowly. The slower I do it, the more I realize everything can be better. Even my friends are saying, "Why don't you go to college now? Why aren't you going?"

What they're going for now is something I may decide to do in ten or twenty years from now. I'm going to take my own time.

Teachers have the power to shun, to turn away, to misunderstand.

One mother shared: "My daughter's teacher constantly embarrasses her in front of the class. She's quick to point out what she's done wrong but never pats her on the back when she's done well. Now my daughter hates the teacher and school. She can't even eat in the morning because her stomach is upset. I've spoken to the teacher but nothing seems to help."

Teachers have the power to destroy.

The story of Mrs. H., as remembered by V:

Mrs. H. was an old woman with graying hair and sagging jowls [cheeks that are sort of like a bulldog's]. When she looked at you, you thought you heard her growling. We were always afraid of her. In the sixth grade I was very talkative and verbal—I had a big mouth!

Mrs. H. would stick her head out of the window to see whether her 6-2 class was quietly and obediently lined up. One day, when she had her head out of the window, I was standing on the back of the line—I was the tallest girl in the class—and talking animatedly [in a lively way].

When the 6-2 line came in, all the students went to their desks and she put up her arm to prevent me from entering the classroom. She growled, "Why were you talking on line?" I told her I had found my mother's appointment book in the schoolyard and couldn't possibly imagine what it was doing there.

At this point she said, "I'm not interested in your mother's appointments, I'm only interested in your behavior, young lady.

For that I'm ripping off two gold stars on your chart!" I looked at her and said, "Mrs. H., I only have one gold star." She said, "Then you won't get the next one."

Having no gold stars meant that I was the last one to be able to choose what class project I wanted to do. This left me devastated and angry and at the point of tears.

Mrs. H. was so loud, everyone in the class heard. I walked in humiliated, anxious, and only wishing that the desk would open up and swallow me.

I never got to do my report on the Audubon Society because Charlie P. got to select before me. Everyone hated her. At least that's what I thought in order to make myself feel better.

Teachers have the power to anger to the point of tears, to humiliate (dishonor, outrage, take away dignity), to take away gold stars.

Said V., now a teacher and counselor: "No one really took the time for me. If I had a few teachers who adored me, loved me, nurtured me, watered me, and took the time for me, they would have gotten everything from me and more. All you need is that one special teacher who helps you see the world differently.

"So I decided to become a teacher myself. . . . so that I could give to students what I never got."

I'd like to believe that somewhere inside all teachers is the power to love. How incredibly sad that so many students never have the chance to feel it.

How special those teachers are who do reach out and give.

## Talking with Your Teachers

Have you ever been bursting to say something but just were too afraid, too embarrassed, or too concerned that your teacher or classmates would think you were dumb?

Lots of kids would love to say much more to their teachers, both in class and privately. But somehow that's often not so easy to do. Sometimes your teacher just might not seem like the type who would listen.

Don't be fooled by what your teacher looks like. Even if he or she is six feet tall, has a gruff voice, doesn't like ice cream, and works as a part-time troll that eats billy goats, you owe it to yourself to say what you need to say to your teacher. Speak softly, respectfully, honestly, but speak—even if you're scared, even if you think they'll think you're dumb.

I tell my own students and the kids at my programs that the only dumb thing would be not to ask their questions. How else would they learn? How else would I know what they don't know? It's possible your teacher feels the same way. The only way to find out is to talk with him or her, no matter what the person looks or sounds like. It's usually best to talk privately.

You deserve the right to speak freely and say what you need to say. You deserve to get answers and explanations if you don't understand something. That's what teachers owe you, just because teaching you is their job.

Sometimes your teacher may be too busy to make him or herself available for you. If they seem hard to find or won't give you time, tell them you need to speak with them very badly and perhaps the two of you could meet before or after school. Sometimes it's a good idea to ask them if they have a free period during the day. If so, perhaps you can get a special pass to see them at that time, or see them during lunch or study periods.

Maybe it would help to go back to all our talk about guts, taking charge of your own feelings, and the fact that the only way someone will be sure to know what you're feeling is if you tell them.

## Finding the Right Words

It might be very helpful to turn to the beginning of Chapter 19, Your Parents, where I have suggested many different ways you can turn your feelings into words.

The same sentences you can say to a parent can also be said to teachers. For example:

If you think the kid who sits next to you cheats off your paper, you can privately say "This is hard for me to say, but I think [so and so] is cheating off my paper. Could you watch him or her or change my seat?" (Or, just cover your own paper.)

If you think you're being blamed unfairly, say so.

If you'd rather sit next to someone different on the bus ride for the school trip, say so.

If you didn't cheat and you're being blamed for cheating, talk about it.

If you weren't the one who was really talking, you can say, "I just want you to know that it really wasn't me who was talking."

If you find something hard to understand, say, "I'm finding this hard to understand."

If you don't know the answer, you can say, "I'm sorry, I don't know the answer."

If you're sorry you talked out of turn, say so.

If you think your teachers are expecting too much of you, tell them in exactly that way.

If you think they're pressuring you, tell them that you don't know if they realize it, but they're pressuring you.

If you did something wrong, all you can do is apologize, say you're sorry, say you didn't mean to break the rules (or whatever), and say you won't do it again in the future.

If you think they're comparing you unfairly with an older sister or brother, say so.

If you can just remember to turn your feelings into words, you'll never have to wonder what to say to your teachers, your parents, your friends, or anyone.

Remember, too, that you won't always be comfortable speaking to your teacher. But that doesn't mean you shouldn't talk. Sometimes you'll just have to push yourself. After that each time will get easier and easier.

And remember that you don't have to have all the answers. If you're honest, that will usually count. Instead of making up something absurd, just tell it like it is! Say, "I don't know"; "I'm not sure"; or "I'm sorry. I'm just not prepared. Can I speak with you later?"

Nonverbal messages from teachers can be quite loud. You can get a good idea about whether they're relaxed, are in a good mood, are kind of grouchy, or whatever. Be aware of their facial expressions and other clues, such as whether or not the veins in the neck are bulging. (Bulging veins might mean they're tense. You can tell them you need to talk with them, but it might be wiser to set up your meeting for the next day. Unless, of course, their veins always bulge!)

There are many ways to communicate. Try one.

One more thing: there's usually a favorite teacher or two in every school, the kind of teacher who everybody talks to when they have a problem. Don't take it personally and think they care about everyone else and not you if they don't talk with you on the spot and take care of your problem immediately.

Sometimes, because everyone wants their time and they like giving their time, it's hard to be there for everybody.

## Teachers' Pets

Jennifer, age twelve, told me, "Sometimes the teachers of my cluster seem to pay more attention to one girl. She's always going down to get messages, and she gets special privileges. She's pretty intelligent. I can't really think of any other reason. I don't really care. I just notice."

Probably each teacher has a few favorites. I guess that's natural. But very often you won't even know who the favorites are because the teacher treats each student fairly, with the same care.

Other times one or two boys or girls may be singled out as special. As Jennifer said, they're the ones who are asked to do the errands and have other privileges. Unless you have a person in your class who's a big flirt and he or she wins the teacher over, it's often not the student's fault that the teacher is playing favorites. Yet, other students become resentful of their classmate and even jealous.

Kevin, age fourteen, said, "I feel I get along with teachers well, no matter who the teacher is. I think they like my attitude because they seem to show it with their comments on my report card. I don't try to be a favorite. If they like me, that's their choice. But I don't try to be the teacher's pet."

One teacher said that many of the teachers he knows end up calling on the kids who raise their hands the most. If you feel your teacher is overlooking your raised hand, let them know you'd like to be called on more.

You can also try to be more friendly with your teachers. Say hello to them in the halls, smile, ask them how they are when you walk into class. You might be pleasantly surprised that they'll pay more attention to you too. Not as a pet, but as a person.

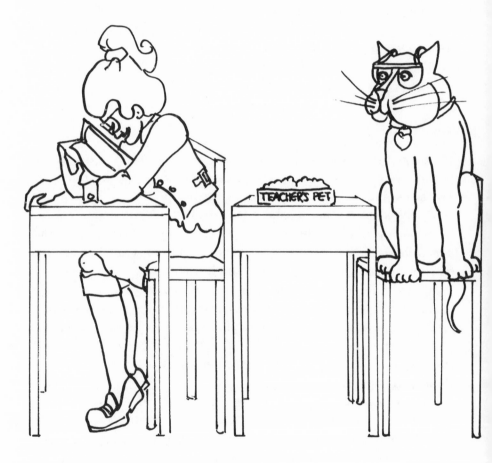

## Homework

Do it:

When it's assigned, complete it on time.

In an organized way. Keep a little notebook for your assignments. Check off your work for each day before closing your locker at the end of the day. That way you can be sure to bring the books home that you need.

Try to be up to date. Hand work in on time.

If you know in advance that you have a book to read or paper to write, then try to pace yourself, doing a little each day, so you won't be faced with doing it all at the last minute.

Sit at a comfortable desk or table, with enough light.

If you're confused, you can contact a friend. But it is better to try to see your teacher before school or before class the next day. That way you can show you're interested and get an explanation at the same time.

If you have tons of work and it seems like you'll never finish and it's all just too much, try taking one assignment at a time, one paper, one book. And as soon as you finish one, go on to the next. You'll be surprised how you can just keep crossing things off your assignment list.

If you are overwhelmed by the burden of doing everything, then you may sit back and say, "It's just too much, how can my teachers do that to me? Don't they know I have other subjects too?" Since you don't have the power to change the assignments, you can concentrate on being able to choose to get on with one assignment, then the next, and the next, instead of complaining and talking about what you can't possibly do.

Don't Do:

Last minute work (if you can help it). If you rush your assignment, you won't have the full chance of testing out what you know and what you don't.

Try not to leave your homework to do on the bus (don't leave it on the bus either), in homeroom, while the teacher is going over it in class.

While lunch offers extra time to study or do work, it is not a good idea to make a habit of saving all your work until then. You're likely to be more rushed, as you'll only have a limited amount of time. And wouldn't it be nice to relax and take a break from the day's schedule? Doing your homework at lunch may even cause you indigestion!

Don't do your homework all over your home. Try, if possible, to keep your books and papers in one area. That way you can find things as you need them and won't have to go around searching.

## Taking Tests

Many people hate to take tests. But, like them or not, they're a fact of life. Think about how you feel about tests. Are you one of those people who does very well in class and then bombs (does poorly) on each test? Lots of people seem to have difficulty taking tests. Beside the preparation the amount of pressure you feel is an important thing to consider.

Pressure is not always negative (bad). It can challenge you and push you to do better and better. But if the pressure is too strong, you may have a great deal of trouble concentrating.

If we talk about the different things that you can do to feel better taking a test (besides put down the right answers), then maybe you'll approach your next test a little differently—with more confidence.

Once you have your pencils, erasers, tissues, and any other essentials, you're set to begin. Be sure you either have a watch, can see a clock, or can ask the teacher to keep you aware of how much time you have left.

Reading test instructions is very important. Right at the beginning, check if you have all the pages of the test, see how many questions there are, and read the instructions carefully. Ask questions, if you're not sure what to do. (Yes, even if no one else has a question.)

Work carefully and steadily. Don't be concerned about what anyone else is writing. Everybody is different. Everybody works at his or her own pace. If some people seem to whiz through the exam and finish before you've even gone on to the third question, just remember that speed doesn't always mean accuracy. They could finish very quickly and get everything wrong! And just because someone else is writing a lot, doesn't mean what he or she is saying is correct.

So, rather than concerning yourself with everyone else's pace, you need to set your own. Make sure to check that you've answered every question before turning in your paper.

Also know that some teachers will think you've cheated if you even look a tiny bit away from your paper, stretch, drop your pencil, drop your paper, or suddenly have a great need to tie your shoe. Know who is watching you and play by that person's rules!

Sandy, age fourteen, said, "I do well in class, but I never seem to do well on tests. I panic!"

Gail, age fifty-eight, shared, "I was always slow taking tests because I was a slow reader. My grades were very good, but it just took me longer than most of the other students to finish. Even though I knew what my problem was, I remember being embarrassed that I was still sitting there when just about everyone else was ready to leave."

Marilyn, age forty-two, told me, "I always hated taking essay tests. There was nothing worse than sitting down to take an exam and having your mind go blank while everyone around you was scribbling their answers."

Allen, age thirteen, said, "I love taking tests! They usually take up the whole period. Tests are easy for me."

Just like with everything else, there are so many feelings about tests, so many different kinds of pressures. If a boy or girl comes into a test thinking that his or her parent(s) will "kill" them if they don't do well, or that this grade will make them pass or fail for the whole year or even just the marking period, how well do you think they'll be able to concentrate?

My guess is that the panic, worry, and tremendous need to do well might not only interfere with their thinking, but it can also force them to feel they have to cheat!

## Cheating

Jennifer, age twelve, said, "Sometimes when kids don't get an assignment done, they ask someone else if they can copy theirs. I don't think I'd give them my assignment to copy. But I wouldn't report them or anything. I'd just let them do what they want. But not with my paper. I don't think it would be hard to say no, even to a friend."

Kevin, age fourteen, told me, "There's a lot of cheating in the classes. If the teacher walks out for one second, the kids start asking for answers. Or if we're doing classwork some of the kids will just wait for me to finish so they can get the answers. I won't give answers to them. I can't stand that! Just that they would even think that I would give them the answer because they neglected to do their work and I didn't."

Bob, age twenty-eight, said, "I was great at cheating! I was a master cheater! I think probably the worst part about it was that I really studied hard. But still I made sure to sit next to a kid who was smart, because I couldn't take a chance that I would fail. Even after staying up sometimes until two in the morning studying, I couldn't allow myself to try to do the work on my own. I couldn't take a chance on myself. Because of the way I was brought up, I was never allowed to make mistakes. So even though I really studied, I was too scared not to cheat."

Neal, age thirteen, said, "I think some teachers are very strict and make it hard to cheat. But in certain classes cheating on tests is very easy. You'll never get caught. Personally, I don't really cheat. But I don't like to have a teacher watching over me when I look up at the clock.

"I would say that the majority of students don't cheat. But those that do cheat, cheat a lot. I don't think it's really fair. It's the person's responsibility to do their own work and not take it from other people."

Kim, age eleven, said, "It's not cheating when someone asks you a question on a test. . . . It's just asking."

According to one teacher, "Kids don't like it when another kid gets away with cheating. Someone who has gotten a 90 and hasn't cheated would probably feel their 90 is worth more if someone else gets it and doesn't deserve it."

As a teacher I am always amazed at how many students think I can't see their eyeballs looking sideways, while their bodies seem perfectly straight in their chairs. As you have seen, the need to cheat is a little different for each person. Some people just aren't prepared; some, like Robert, are too afraid to be wrong, too afraid to allow themselves to be truly tested; others are lazy.

There are several concerns about cheating. One, of course, is how your fellow students are going to think of you, knowing that you cheated to get your grade, and they didn't. Another is what might the conse-quences be if you get caught? At some schools you get kicked out, and that's that! Will your teacher tear up your paper if he or she sees you? Will your teacher also tear up the paper of the person from whom you are cheating, even if that person doesn't know you are?

Sometimes, though a teacher may not tear up a paper, he or she will let everyone know that you cheated and that you just ruined your relationship with him or her (the teacher) and the class. That kind of embarrassment can often be much worse than one low grade.

As much as your parents might be pressuring you to get good grades, how would they feel if you got them by cheating? If you haven't ever asked them that question, maybe it's time!

Still another concern is just how long you intend to keep up your cheating. If, for example, you are able to get into college because of the high grades that you got from cheating, how are you going to be able to stay in that college unless you keep cheating? How much pressure do you think you'd feel then? When do you call it quits to keep trying to be someone you're not?

If you allow yourself to do as well as you can do, then you might even find that learning is more enjoyable. You don't have to pretend, and you won't set yourself up for unfair expectations from parents, teachers, and friends around you.

## Passing Notes

How could I write a chapter on school without including note passing? All I am thinking of right now is the time in the sixth grade when my teacher caught me writing down all her sayings so that I could imitate her with my friends after school. I nearly died when she came over and picked up those pages! I thought she was going to read them aloud to the class, but she didn't. It was enough that she knew I was doing that to her. I think I still have my composition somewhere, promising to be a better person and never do that again.

According to Hilary, age eleven, "Passing notes is a part of school. Classes would be so boring without notes! They're a new way of talking."

I suppose, without notes, some girls and boys wouldn't be able to find out who likes who, who just got her period, who smells, who's cute, who's coming to the party on Friday night, where everyone is going to meet after school, who's finally wearing a bra, who's parents are getting a divorce, or who's bored.

Just be aware that whatever you write down might be intercepted! If you're comfortable with what you say in your note, then you have little to be concerned about, even if you're caught. But notes (like mine) can sometimes be very embarrassing. If you're telling secrets, you'd be wise to remember that some kids who you think you can trust might just open up your note and pass it around the school instead of to the person in the blue sweater.

Some teachers have very creative ways of dealing with notes. I was told about one teacher who takes every note he captures, makes copies, and hands one out to each person in the class!

A note about notes: If you're spending much of your class time writing notes, as much as you might love to pass notes, it would help for you to think about how distracting those notes can be to other classmates, your teacher, and, believe it or not, yourself.

If you're concentrating on notes, you're probably not concentrating on the lesson. If the reason is that you're bored and notes are the best way to pass the time, then I suggest you speak with your teacher about your feelings.

Several of you might want to get together with your teacher and share ideas as to how the class can be more interesting and challenging such as creative projects, debates, interesting research papers, challenging assignments, or role playing (that's when classmates act out a certain situation).

Although I can't speak for all teachers, I could say that many would appreciate such honesty, as long as the feelings were presented in a respectful way. Teachers can't be sure how their students feel unless they're told.

On that note I think we'll go on to the locker room.

## The Locker Room

While lots of kids can't wait to get into the locker room to talk about who they're going out with, how their date was, what they just did in class, or the cute boy or girl who just moved in, there are other kids who wish the locker room was never invented. This is often because they hate the idea of having to change clothes in front of everyone else, especially if they're more or less developed than everyone else.

Since we've talked about this many times before, here's a quick reminder:

> If you find yourself changing alone in the bathroom or away from most of the other kids, the first thing you need to do is realize that's what you're doing.
>
> You don't have to come out of the bathroom if that's what makes you comfortable.
>
> You don't have to move your locker just to be near everyone else.
>
> It would help you to begin thinking about what's making you hide. Is it something you can't help? Something about your development that is not within your control? Can you begin to try to accept you and your body and realize that you are not your body (it's just a package, remember?). You're the personality inside.
>
> If comparing yourself to everyone else makes you believe they're normal, and you're not, don't be fooled.
>
> Growing at different rates is just part of being a kid and growing up.
>
> It's time you stop judging yourself unfairly.
>
> Locker rooms can be a lot more fun when you realize you no longer have to hide in the lockers.
>
> All you have to do is come out and be you.
>
> If you don't know where to begin, perhaps you can start looking for girls or boys in your gym class while walking in the halls. If you enter together and start talking, you can continue talking while you change. If you're concentrating on what each other is saying, you'll be amazed at how quickly you'll change.

## Moving To a New School

Moving to a new school in a new town can be exciting. You get to meet new friends, do things in a slightly different way, maybe even see what life is like in a different part of your country. But it can also be a little scary and a little lonely, until you get to meet some people you feel comfortable with who'll take you around and show you everything.

You might meet one person who you click with immediately who will show you around, or you might want to observe and watch the different groups at school and see which kids appeal to you the most, or you might want to wait and see who extends themselves to you and says, "Hey, come and join our group!" You also might want to join a club. This way you'll meet friends through enjoying a common activity. Anyone of these choices or any combination of choices is fine.

Keith, age fourteen, said, "When I was younger, I used to say hello and act nice to a new person. I tried to show them around and tried to make friends with them. There was a new kid who came into school this year. I said hello and tried to be nice to him, but other people influenced him away from me. They said something to the new kid behind my back so he wouldn't associate with me."

Debby, age twelve, said, "I was really nervous the first day I went to my new school. I didn't know if the kids would like me. I missed my friends. I didn't know what the teachers were like and how hard the work was going to be."

L., age thirteen, talked about her friend that moved to a nearby town. Said L., "When I first talked with her, she said all the kids were drinking and she would never do anything like that. Then I saw her a few weeks ago, and she talked about how she went drinking with her new boyfriend. She changed so much. If you don't smoke or don't drink in that town, you're a priss. She used to be a really good student, really smart. Now she doesn't even care about her grades anymore."

Sometimes in order to be accepted people will do things they never expected to do. All the more reason to always be aware of your feelings and choices.

Jeff, age fourteen, said, "When I moved in the third grade, there was one boy who came up to me and said hi and that made it all okay. He took me around and introduced me to the other kids. We're still really good friends."

H. moved into her new neighborhood when she was eleven. A girl came over very quickly and acted very nice. She started introducing her to people but then would take them off to the side and tell them she was faggy because of what she wore. Said H., "She did this each time she introduced me, and while everyone would laugh, I would stand there like an idiot. I trusted her, that's what hurt so much."

If your grade is going on to a new school, at least you know you've got company. Most of the time you'll be moving with your friends. So if you're scared and think you'll get lost, at least you know you can all be lost together. But sometimes, because a school district is quite large, your group of friends might be split up. In that case moving to a new school might seem like it's also moving into a new town.

Be patient. Understand that your scary feelings are normal. Just go slowly, learning as much as you can about the people, the rules, and kinds of choices that are there for you to make your move feel as good as possible.

New schools probably will seem humongous for the first days. But after a week or so you most likely won't be able to imagine that you went to that small elementary school. Your high school will probably be larger than your middle school or junior high, and if you go to college, that will be larger still with a lot of different buildings instead of just one (unless your high school had a campus).

Each new step takes adjusting. But once you adjust, you'll know for sure that you were ready to arrive and wouldn't want to go back.

If you're having trouble getting used to your new situation, you can check your school list of adult helpers and speak with someone who can make helpful suggestions to you.

## Fast Learners, Slow Learners, and Special Education

Often times students are put into what is known as *tracks* (a term that teachers use to group students together by their learning ability).

There's usually a group of students who are placed in either an accelerated or an advanced class.

Those placed in an accelerated class are the students who may complete a program in two years instead of three or in one year instead of two. For example, they may complete two years of math in one.

Those students placed in an advanced class will usually be offered more difficult or enriched subject matter.

While many of these accelerated or advanced students are happy at the chance to work at higher levels, some feel quite pressured.

John was placed in the advanced class in seventh grade. All his friends were in the advanced class, and he had a difficult time keeping up with the work. His teacher wanted to place him in the regular class for the eighth grade. But John insisted that he would do everything in his power to keep up with the work. He was really concerned that people would say he wasn't good enough for the fast class.

He went into the regular class anyway and felt he needed to make all sorts of adjustments to this new group. He still has not quite gotten over it.

Other students are grouped together in regular classes. Because all the students in these classes are usually able to do the work at that level, there is less competition among the students in the class, but as a group, they may feel they're not quite as good as the advanced class. Some kids were relieved not to be in the advanced level because they don't want the pressure.

Some kids get placed in special education classes for all or some of their subjects. Many kids really work well in these classes and find that the teachers' attention to their homework and school work is exactly what they need to be able to understand the subject.

Other kids find that the label of a special education class is less desirable. Being in this class may make them feel badly about themselves and inferior to the students in the regular and advanced classes. I feel that's very sad. Isn't it fair for each person to be able to learn at their own rate (and be able to feel good about it)?

Remember all that I've said about doing as best as you can, no matter what your grade level happens to be? Your grade placement says little about who you are. It only reflects the level at which you are able to learn. Some kids need more time than others to learn the same lessons. Several students on the special education class may have a learning disability, several may not.

Very often, being placed in a special education class is just the experience that can cause you to have more confidence and feel better about yourself. The next story is a good example of how that can happen.

When F. was in junior high, she could never ever learn math. She had a social studies teacher teaching her algebra, and as a consequence got off to a wrong math start. As a result of having a rotten math experience in the ninth grade, all math classes became a nightmare.

She barely passed tenth grade math and then was asked to take a special education class for eleventh grade math. Instead of doing eleventh grade math in a year, she now had to complete it in a year and one half.

At first she was embarrassed and ashamed for being placed in what the kids called dummy math, but the class was slow enough to give her the opportunity to finally learn math the way she should have in the ninth grade. She got 95s in math on all her report cards and felt great.

> You have a right to be accepted for who you are
> without being judged, without being labeled.
> You have a right to be given the freedom to learn,
> but first you've got to believe that yourself.

# 25
# When People Are Different

## More Packages, More Judgments, More Comparisons

This time, instead of being concerned with the shape of the package, we're going to talk about the color of the package, what kind of beliefs and how much money the person inside the package has.

Just like a person who is disabled is not his or her package or any part of the package, so, too, are we not to be fooled by a person's color, religion, country of birth, or whether they're rich or poor.

Maybe we all need to learn that there's a basic human person underneath any package, no matter what the size, shape, color, or what religious beliefs are inside. Maybe if we weren't so quick to judge, we wouldn't hear statements like, "She's Mexican. Why are you so surprised?" "He's white. He should have known better." "She's black. What do you expect?" or statements like these about anyone from any place of any color.

Maybe we all need to work harder at understanding and accepting that packages are only an outside covering, only a wrapping. The shape or color of the wrapping or even the belief of the wrapping doesn't tell you anything about the person inside.

I'm writing this chapter in the hope that you, as a boy or girl, will be able to see what your parents and other adults are perhaps no longer able to see. Perhaps you, by the end of these pages, will be more able to look at new people and ask them such things as their names, whether or not they like chocolate, if they've ever tried asparagus, who they think will win the World Series, what hurts them, what makes them feel good, what they like to do, what kinds of music they prefer, what their family is like, whether or not they like the outdoors, what their dreams are. . . .

Maybe you will be able to allow yourself to meet a *person* instead of a package, learn his or her name, and say, for example, "Mom, Dad, this is Ted, he's a human being!"

If you introduce them to Ted as Ted, maybe all of you may have a real chance to get to know each other. If you introduce him by saying, "This is Ted, he's Catholic, or Jewish, or Moslem, or Mexican, or black, or Hispanic, or Oriental, or whatever," then you may not have a full chance to let them know who he really is.

First let's talk about color differences. A person's package color is something he or she is born with and keeps forever. It has the ability to affect the feelings of everyone who's close enough to see. When you look at a person's package, you can know right away whether you're seeing a red, yellowish, tan, black, white, or whatever package.

The color of a person's package has an amazing amount of power. Imagine a package color having the power to make someone afraid. Imagine a package color having the power to make someone feel they would never want the person inside that package in their home. Imagine a package color having the power to make one or more people become violent and want to kill the person inside without ever having spoken to them. Imagine.

Kids who've gone to school all their lives with people who have different package colors, usually don't see the packages as having colors. They just see their friends who they've always gone to school with. They see the person inside.

However, when kids are forced into situations with kids who's package colors are different, it may be very clear to them that there are racial (color) differences. If their parents are comfortable with color differences, they'll probably be comfortable too. If their parents are not comfortable with color differences, it may take a lot of work for kids to see that color is only a wrapper.

Depending upon where you grew up, what your experiences have been so far, and especially what your parents have taught you, you will either have friends with packages of many colors, or you might prefer to stick with friends who have the same package color as you do.

## Feelings About Color Differences

Neal, age thirteen, said, "I don't feel there's a racial problem at our school. I'm kind of glad it's integrated [mixed colors]. I basically judge people on the way they feel about things, not where they're from."

Frances, a woman who devotes herself to spreading understanding among all people, has worked for years with black youth and is a leader among black people. She shared:

> Usually, for the small children, there is little concept [idea] of hatred, except that which might be influenced by their parents.
>
> A mother or father might say, "You don't want to be like those people. You can't play with them. They're dirty." If left alone, black and white kids can play together. If they're strong enough, they can overcome the differences.
>
> I can always tell the attitude of a parent. I love children. And when I'm in an airport and see a mother with a baby, I very often smile at and say something to the child. I don't care whether the mother is black, white, or a purple-people eater, I'll look long enough to try to see if I can get the child's attention. I'll say "Hello, what's your name?"
>
> I can pretty much tell they're antiblack if they pull the child away. Or, if it's okay, they'll often say, "Tell the lady your name; talk to the lady," and so forth. Where the parents don't show negative vibes [feelings], the kids don't show any.

Patricia, age eleven, said about kids of different colors: "At parties, I don't like to kiss them."

Jonathon, age seventeen, said, "I don't understand why my parents are so upset. Just because my girl friend is part Cherokee Indian and part Mexican, I don't know what all the fuss is about.

"She's still my girl friend; she understands how I feel; she's pretty, and she means a lot to me. Is it ever possible that I could have a relationship with someone out of my race where I could feel comfortable and not get hassled?"

Natalie, age fifteen, told me, "Three other girls and I were really close. We went to Girl Scouts together; we were a real foursome. You couldn't see one without the other. The only problem was that one of the girl's parents was really prejudiced.

"All four of us had our birthdays four months in a row. Mine was the last month. The first two girls had parties, and we all went. Then came time for my other friend's party. Her parents objected to letting her invite me because I'm black. It really hurt because we were such good friends.

"I have never set foot into her house. Her mom has calmed down a little. But her dad, forget it! I'm really happy that at least my friend is not prejudiced."

T., age fourteen, said, "The majority of my friends are white. All the other black kids used to look down upon me. They used to call me names and make fun of me. I knew they just envied me because I could get along with just about anybody.

"You can be turned on even by your own color. It doesn't have to be that you're talking with someone of a different color."

Donna, age seventeen, said, "When I was fourteen, I had to leave my house because my father was getting sexual with me. I lived on the subways for a year with no one to talk to and no one to turn to, and a police officer took me into his home.

"My new family was black. They adored me, fed me, clothed me and gave me a new life. My new sisters come to visit me from time to time. And people give us strange looks when I introduce them as my sisters. We get very amused at their reaction."

Lisa, age seventeen, said, "I have friends that are normal and friends that are handicapped. It doesn't matter to me. I have friends of all different religions and all different colors. It doesn't matter to me, and it doesn't matter to my mother. One good friend of mine—she's black and I'm white—and I go up to the people and we say we're sisters. People say, 'What?' Then I just tell them that I fell in a bucket of bleach!"

A clergyman, who lives in a small town in the Midwest and is one of the only Philippine families in the town, shared his feelings with me about color. He told me that his daughter, who is now in kindergarten, has begun to notice that she's different from everyone else. He explained to her that many people spend hours in the sun during the summer, trying to get their skin to look as beautiful as hers does all year round. She seemed happy with that answer. His only fear is that she will grow up hating her color.

I've decided not to share all the different comments that were told to me. Some of them are too painful and nasty to mention. Probably, you can make your list of kinds of things that people who don't respect each other might say to each other. Too often, the words aren't pretty; the feelings aren't good.

Some of the common situations in which these feelings arise are:

When a girl of one color and a boy of another color go out with each other.

When one person of one race is teased or pushed or bothered in any way by someone of a different race, friends of the one race will be quick to get back at the other.

When a boy or girl of one color and boy or girl of another color are close friends, and the parents don't approve of the friendship.

Feelings about color, as Frances agreed, seem to be the most influenced by parents. Natalie found that out in a very painful way when her good friend couldn't even let her come into her house (which she still hasn't been in).

I'd be guessing if I tried to figure out all the different reasons why one color can't get along with another. It may go back to all those years of struggling, the riots, the fighting, the unfair laws. But for right now, maybe we have to just ask ourselves to look again at whoever it may be. Maybe there would be better feelings if more people started giving each other a chance.

It is very important for you to discuss the feelings you have about differences with your parents. It's their right to teach you what values they feel are correct. But if those values include hatred, at least be sure you understand what the hatred is all about. Maybe it's time for you to be free to make up your own mind.

## What About Differences in Religion

Differences in religious beliefs can be found among all types of packages, all colors, all shapes, and all sizes. You can't look at a package and tell what religion a person is, unless that person is wearing special clothes that are a symbol (represent, are a sign) of his or her religion.

You might say that a person's religious package is worn inside out. Only the person inside can see it. They have to choose to tell you what their belief is. Otherwise you can't be sure.

Differences in religions seem to center around how each religion sees and worships God. Everybody see God in his or her own way. Everybody worships in his or her own way.

Some people feel they have a very close relationship with God. Some people are not so close, and others have no relationship at all. Some people worship at home, attend religious services, and live a religious life according to their beliefs. Other people attend religious services and go through the motions of doing religious things but really don't feel it inside, for instance, if they just worship because their parents tell them to. Still others have religious feelings but worship only in a very private way. They never go to religious services, but they believe there is a God. There are also people who have no belief in God.

Sometimes people from other cultures worship in a way that may seem interesting and exciting. It might be fun to take some books out of your school or public library so you can learn more about them. If you've ever traveled to a foreign land or if you live in a big city, you might already have had a chance to learn about other religious differences.

There are some people who believe in God only when it seems absolutely necessary to believe in God.

Samantha has blessed us with her pink-bathing-suit story. When she was twelve years old, Samantha lost her pink bathing suit. She searched and searched to find it, but it was nowhere. Her mother spent a tremendous amount of money on this pink suit and didn't let Samantha forget it.

Samantha kneeled in the bathroom, put her elbows and her clasped hands on the bathtub, and prayed to God like she had never prayed before. She promised God that she would go to temple on Saturdays.

She promised God that she would help him any way he wanted. She promised God that she wouldn't throw her sister into a shark pool. (Now do you remember Samantha?). She promised that she would be the best girl possible if only he would make her pink bathing suit appear. Her pink bathing suit never appeared. Samantha decided that God wasn't home when she was praying.

Kim, age seventeen, said that she once had a conversation about God with a woman for whom she worked. Kim said that she hoped she would go to heaven and the woman answered by saying that Kim's religion didn't believe in heaven or hell. The woman then told Kim that she had stopped believing in God a long time ago.

A few months later the woman found out she was losing her baby. Kim heard her say she prayed to God that she wouldn't lose the baby.

Said Kim, "She prayed to God. I don't understand. She said she didn't believe."

## When Religious Differences Get in the Way

While some people are able to see past any differences and find the person inside, there are too many who play upon the differences in a way that doesn't feel very good.

They taunt, tease, name call, and even paint disrespectful symbols on houses of worship. It's too bad that we can't learn to live with each other, allowing each person to worship as he or she pleases, but at the same time realizing that each of us is human and can learn to share our love.

When people strike out at different religions, it's usually because they have tremendous anger at not being able to feel good about themselves and good about their lives. And they blame certain religious groups for their problems.

This type of behavior is called *scapegoating*. Some people scapegoat races; some people scapegoat religions. Scapegoating is a very unhealthy, unnatural way of dealing with your feelings.

If you sometimes feel the urge to lash out at different religious or racial groups, it is important for you to stop, think, and ask yourself that very private question, "Who and what am I really angry at?"

If you can't seem to get to the answer or don't want to get to the answer, I urge you to sit and talk with someone about your feelings. Perhaps your own religious leader would be a good place to start.

## Here Too

Here too, the religious part of a person's package is very powerful. Strong enough to break close friendships, strong enough to burn buildings, strong enough to burn people, strong enough to separate nations.

Maybe you, your friends, and all the other children in this world can begin, however slowly, to try to accept people for who they are instead of what they believe, what they look like, or what color they happen to be.

Maybe through the children we'll learn to share more love.

## Rich or Poor, Where You Live

Seventeen-year-old Meghan said,

> There are some rich people that you'd never know are rich. Other rich people make it a point to talk about their boat and their big cars. They'll make it a point to say you're poor and I'm rich. When they throw it in your face, that's the worst!
>
> I just let them tell me all about their stuff. I don't say, "I have this," or "I have that too." I just let them talk. I know I'm comfortable and I'm happy.
>
> I have a friend whose grandmother paid for everything so she could travel and go to college. She would dig that into me. She knew that every penny that I worked for goes into the bank so I could save up for going some place.
>
> She would tell me that she toured Europe and all the other places where she's been, and I'd just say to her, "That's great. I'll have fun too."

Sometimes the comparisons don't have to be that dramatic. It can simply be an excuse that you feel you have to make if your friends come home with you. "Oh, don't mind the empty room, my parents are fixing it up." "Oh, I hate my room."

Those statements are telling enough. Whether it be clothes, homes, cars, jewelry, what vacations you're going on, or which part of town your house is located, the labels are the same (even though the comparisons seem to be about bigger and bigger things).

The big-house, far-away-vacation, large-boat, beautiful-clothes labels are supposedly better. The smaller-house, hardly-any-vacations, no-boat, few-changes-of-clothes or maybe some-or-all-hand-me-downs are supposedly not as good.

## Where You Live Is Not Your Fault

First of all do you feel it fair for any boy or girl to be blamed for what his or her parent(s) have or doesn't have? What kind of control do you think any child has over the house they live in, the vacations they take, or what clothes they can buy?

How about the children who live in big mansions who would do anything to be able to live in a tiny apartment or anywhere else as long as the family feelings could be there. Big houses can be warm and wonderful but they can also be lonely. And poor houses can be warm, joyful, and very rich.

It's not the money, it's the love.
All the money in the world can't buy love
if it's not there.

# The Road
# to Independence

I feel like we've been on a very special journey together. Even though I may not know you personally, I feel, somehow, we've touched.

But your journey is just beginning. And the road to becoming an independent adult will be filled with cracks and gravel, rocks and detours. It may even be blocked up by a boulder or two. This is why they call the growing-up years the time of confusing choices.

I hope now you realize that you can decide to avoid the cracks, walk on tippy toes over the gravel, and step carefully around or over any medium-sized rocks. If you come to a detour, you now have the tools which will help you decide what your other choices might be.

You also know that you don't have to panic if you move onto a turn in the path that leads you to a field of weeds instead of a rainbow. You need only realize your mistake, forgive yourself for not being perfect, and make the decision to turn around so you can try again in another direction. You've even got the strength to build your own road when there seems to be no other way out.

There may be many people and situations that will try to influence you to stray from the path that will lead you to independence. They may tell you that you're making all your decisions and choices the wrong way. Because of this, you may feel insecure, lonely, afraid to take a chance, confused, and easily influenced by anyone who offers promises and solutions (which are usually false) to your problems.

431

If you're too afraid to make decisions because you think that you'll make a mistake, just remember that your decisions could also result in giving you great happiness and fun. You'll be able to tell when you've made a wrong decision because you'll feel "oooooouch!" Nobody wants to feel that way purposely.

Wouldn't it be wonderful to have a decison-making genie who could stay with you for your whole life and help you make decisions and choices, especially the ones that make you really feel uncomfortable?

Well, nice as that would be, you now know that you must take the responsibility for making your own genie, for finding your own answers. The more decisions you make, the more you'll be able to build confidence and learn to trust your senses.

As you pave your own road to independence, I hope you will keep *Growing Up Feeling Good* as a special friend that will always be there to help you understand your choices, answer questions, and give you ideas about how to better handle the many different experiences that you will have while growing up.